INTO A DESERT PLACE

INTO A DESERT PLACE

A 3000 mile walk around the coast of Baja California

GRAHAM MACKINTOSH

W. W. Norton & Company
New York • London

First published in Great Britain by the Trade Division of Unwin Hyman Limited, 1988

First published as a Norton paperback 1995
by arrangement with the author

Manufacturing by the Haddon Craftsmen, Inc.

British Library Cataloging in Publication Data
Baja California: the true story of one man's 3,000 mile walk
around the inhospitable coast of the Baja Peninsula.
1. Baja California (Mexico)—Description
and travel I. Title
917.2′204834 F1246

ISBN 0-393-31289-5
Library of Congress Catalog Card Number 90-91690

W. W. Norton & Company, Inc., 500 Fifth Avenue, New York, N.Y. 10110
W. W. Norton & Company Ltd., 10 Coptic Street, London WC1A 1PU

Printed in the United States of America

1 2 3 4 5 6 7 8 9 0

Contents

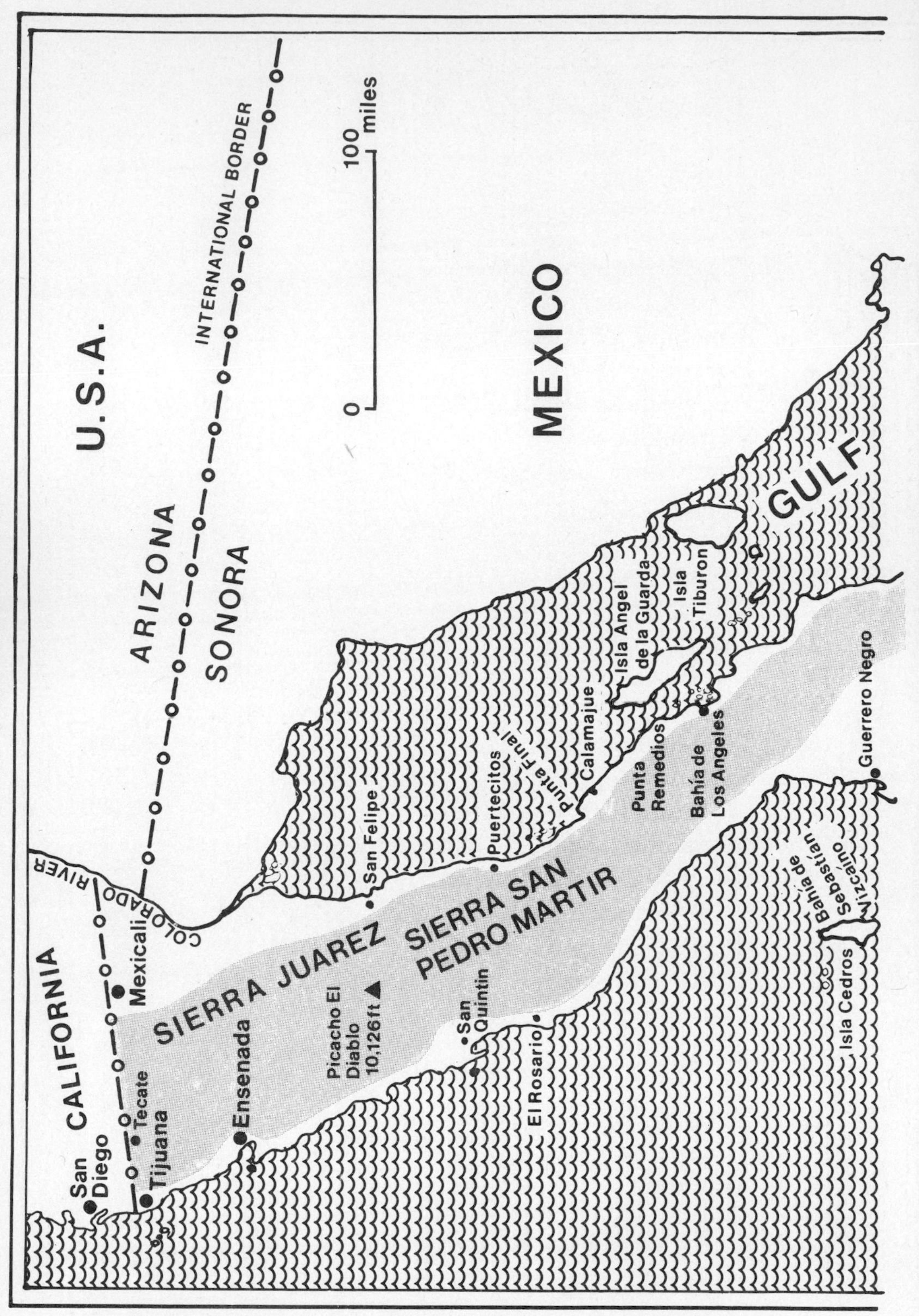

The 800-mile long Mexican peninsula of Baja California around which the author walked. (Stage 1: San Felipe to Bahía de los Angeles.

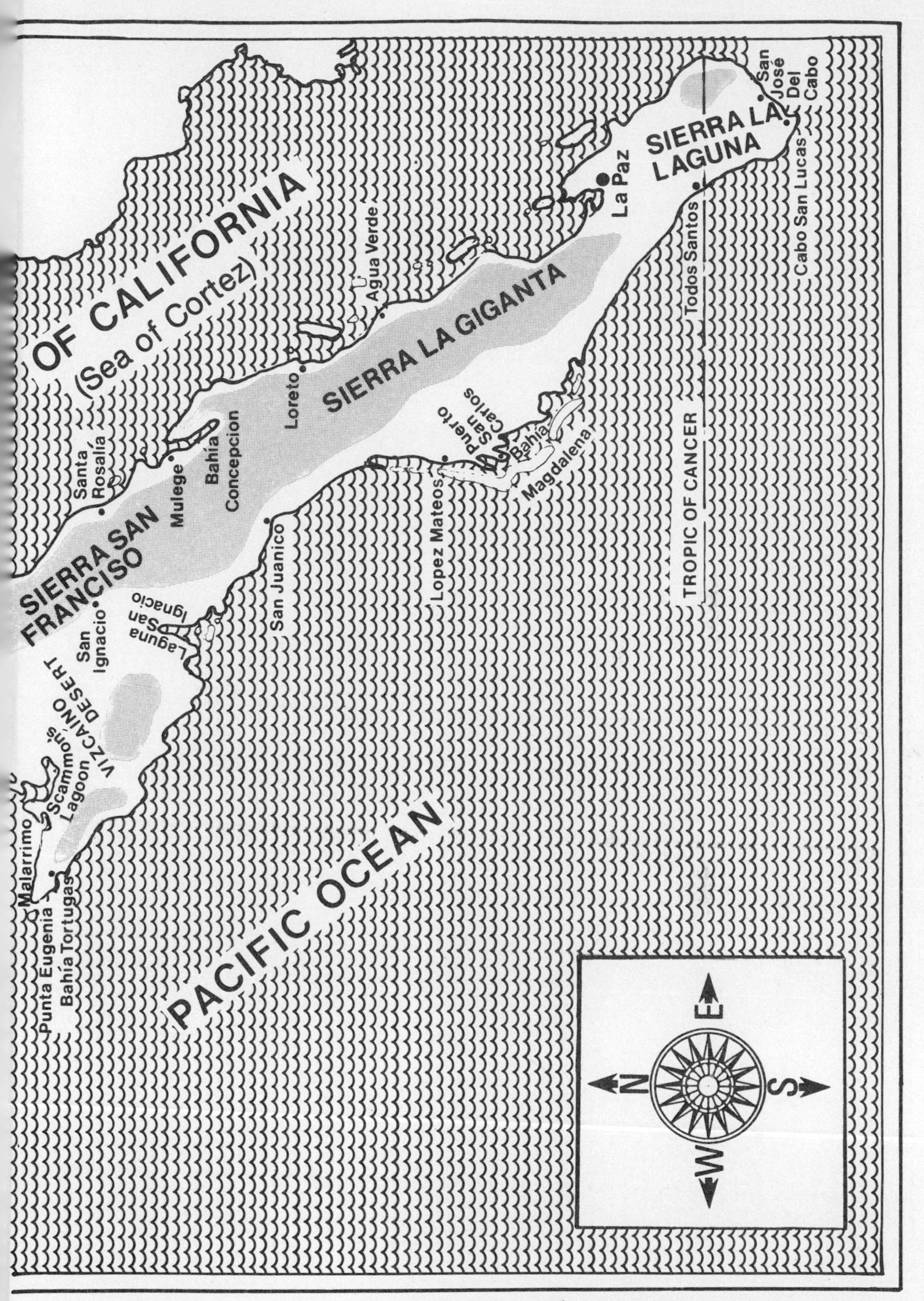

Stage 2: Ensenada to Laguna San Ignacio. Stage 3: Bahía de los Angeles to Cabo San Lucas. Stage 4: Laguna San Ignacio to Cabo San Lucas.)

TO MY PARENTS
AND
THE PEOPLE OF BAJA CALIFORNIA

Chapter 1

The Adventurers' Club

I had never been particularly good at anything except catering to my own comfort and safety. Yet there I was – not so long ago the most unadventurous person in the world – about to address the prestigious Los Angeles Adventurers' Club.

That evening in April 1985 really brought home to me what I'd done. The president was introducing me to the no-nonsense audience of seasoned adventurers. I listened as if he was talking about someone else.

'Graham Mackintosh, interesting chap, grew up in London, England, even though he is of Scottish descent [cheers and applause]. In England he went to Leeds University to study sociology but he has been utilizing his talents a heck of a lot better trekking 3,000 miles around Mexico's Baja California peninsula . . . travelling light, living off the land, eating rattlesnake and cactus, distilling seawater to survive . . . 500 days and nights in the desert and on lonely beaches. I know we're in for some fabulous adventure. He's going to tell you more about it.'

Rising to the applause of an audience not too dissimilar from the original band of soldiers and sailors, trappers and travellers, journalists, writers and scientists who had inaugurated the first Adventurers' Club in New York in 1912, I approached the rostrum. Trophies enough to dignify any museum glared down at me. My mind went a total blank!

Was it four, five, six hundred days I'd been walking? I hadn't even counted. A hundred more or less didn't seem to matter. To others it was just a figure. To me every day had been a breath-taking experience, an adventure, an unforgettable mixture of ecstasy and agony, and some days were even a struggle to stay alive. What sense could I make of it? Where did it begin? And what about the two or three hundred days I had spent preparing back in England? How could I pull all that together and talk for an hour?

I was nervous, but having lived with fear for so long I'd learned not to panic. While I was walking, fear became a near constant companion, a friend bringing out my best and honing my mind to razor sharpness. It was the icy grip of fear that had enabled me to take a thousand or even ten thousand steps when, in my weakness, I swore I couldn't take another one. And what fear couldn't do, faith did. As I put the microphone around my neck, the applause died and the audience waited. A video camera began to roll. I had a second or two to stop my mind vacillating between nothingness and an indecipherable overload. I said a little prayer: 'Thank you for smoothing my way over some pretty rough mountains. If you could just walk beside me a little more to get me over this one I'd be ever so grateful.' I hadn't a clue who I was talking to, but raised my eyes in the general direction of up.

I thanked the president for his introduction. Above me were the enormous heads of a bison and a water buffalo. I joked that they were no doubt there to symbolize the bullshit I was about to deliver. Promising to keep it to a minimum, I carried on as relaxed as I could have wished, once again wondering if there wasn't someone way up beyond the bison and the water buffalo keeping a friendly eye on me.

Without notes I must have looked a model of composure as I explained: 'Basically what I've done over the last two years is walk around the entire coastline of Baja California. But before leaping into the rattlesnakes and scorpions, I'd briefly like to mention why I did the trip. I am a self-confessed non-adventurer. Never in my life had I done anything adventurous before I went to Baja. I was the kind of guy who was happiest feet up in front of the television or drinking beer in an English pub. So why I went to Baja is an interesting question for me, and I'm still trying to figure it out. Perhaps the nearest I came to the truth was the answer I gave in a tiny fishcamp five hundred miles south of Ensenada. After being asked why I'd walked all the way down from Ensenada, I could think of no better reply than pointing to my head and saying "loco".

'Assuming there is more to be said, and as society makes us masters at rationalizing our own weird and wonderful behaviour, you must make of the following account what you will.'

Be careful what you read, books have a lot to answer for! Never having been a great reader I surprised myself by developing a taste for true-life adventure stories. Starting with tales of maritime survival and endurance my fascination evolved from the sea on to the land. So there I was, at twenty-eight, rapidly becoming the ultimate armchair-adventurer, and I hadn't even ventured beyond the shores of the British Isles.

Reading as if my life depended upon it, I found that my voracious appetite soon led to a shortage of suitable material. Like an addict desperately banging his empty pill bottle I searched the library shelves in vain. The extent of my addiction was painfully revealed in those awful times between finishing one book and finding another.

It got so bad that I even thought of doing something crazy and adventurous myself, like getting married. With so few good books to take to bed it seemed like a good idea at the time: one of those lightning romances, all roses and optimism, real head-over-heels stuff.

With my new love tied up in exams, I decided to take off for a last, and first, fling in order to get any lingering dissatisfaction out of my system.

As it happened, some good friends of mine, Dave and Denise Bowyer, had recently settled in Los Angeles, and invited me over. It was a city which had always fascinated me. Even as a child, walking to school on a cold blustery morning, I'd longingly pictured myself walking between rows of palm trees under a Californian sun. It would be fun to visit my friends, make a dream come true and maybe have a little adventure.

A short while later it was with a strong sense of 'déjà vu' that I found myself walking beneath the palms imbibing the heady, if somewhat smoggy air of the city of my dreams.

What happened next can be blamed on John Fairfax and Sylvia Cook. In 1971 this English couple thought it would be a good idea to row from San Francisco to Australia. Not surprisingly, they had one or two problems on the way. In their book *Oars Across the Pacific* they describe being forced into the little Mexican port of Ensenada for repairs. Their description of that town on the other side of the world gripped my imagination.

Realizing in Los Angeles that Ensenada was just a few hours away, I felt compelled to do the most irrational thing of my life. I jumped on a bus determined to spend the following day, my birthday, in Ensenada. Although unable to speak a word of Spanish I, nevertheless, paced that town as moved as a Moslem in Mecca.

I had planned to go no further than Ensenada but, adventurism running amuck, I hitched my way 1,000 miles south to explore the rest of the Baja California Peninsula. I had no tent or sleeping bag, just an old borrowed backpack and $150.

The Baja, as the Americans call it, was like nowhere I had ever seen before. I couldn't believe that such a desolate, unspoilt wilderness of mountain and cactus could exist so close to the urban wonderland of Southern California. It well deserved the epithet of 'the Forgotten Peninsula' attached to it by the essayist and naturalist Joseph Wood Krutch.

There was so much space and so few people. Turn your back on one of the scattering of small settlements and the scene was primeval. My first glimpse of Bahía de los Angeles, a fisherman's paradise on the shores of the Sea of Cortez, was unforgettable. I thought it was a land-locked lake studded with deserted islands. The sea was warm and beautifully calm, the bluest of blue. Monster stingrays shuffled around in the shallows. Huge fish chased smaller fish almost on to the beach. Dolphins skipped around the bay. Friendly fishermen invited me out to try my luck. With each fish I hauled aboard, I became more hooked on Baja.

What's over those mountains, I would ask. 'Nothing,' was the usual reply. For hours I stared at those beautiful mountains and pictured myself on the other side. Crazy thoughts invaded my mind; images of challenge, adventure, destiny and belonging. I found myself wrestling with an overwhelming feeling that I was going to write a book about Baja, even though I knew practically nothing about the place, and I'd certainly never felt able or inclined to write about anything before.

I continued travelling. Dead snakes lay in the road, a scorpion found its way into my swimming trunks, I was able to hitch a ride in an aeroplane from Loreto to La Paz, and while swimming in the Sea of Cortez the water erupted beside me as a large sailfish leapt clear shaking its speared victim.

Hospitality followed my every move. When it all seemed too incredible, I took refuge in an old Jesuit mission and marvelled at the depth of my feelings.

By the time the money ran out and I reluctantly headed back to the border, I had forgotten the girl back in England and fallen madly in love with Baja. I couldn't understand why it moved me so much. Maybe Erle Stanley Gardner, one of Baja's greatest explorers, publicists and devotees, as well as the creator of 'Perry Mason', was right when he claimed:

> It is impossible to account for the charm of this country or its fascination but those who are familiar with the land of Baja California are either afraid of it or they love it, and if they love it they are brought back by an irresistible fascination time and again.

I knew I'd be back. I knew it in a way and with a certainty that I had never known before.

Chapter 2

To walk alone around Baja

As I stepped off the plane at Heathrow I wondered if it had all been infatuation. But as the months went by, the peninsula was still far from forgotten: even the sheep seemed to be saying Baja. Although romance and marriage were in the air again, I had to return. Recalling what happened before, I persuaded my new love to chuck in her job and come with me.

For six weeks we travelled the length and breadth of the 800-mile long peninsula. To me it seemed as sacred as ever. I still had my visions of the 'nothingness' beyond the mountains, and if I stopped to think for too long I'd be thinking about that book again. Dearly wanting to share my vision, I tentatively suggested to my girlfriend that we should stay in Baja a year or two and write a book. Sensing that my sanity was coming into question I dropped the subject and let it simmer away in silence.

Even though we went from one exhilarating experience to another, such as finding a black widow in our bed, my companion didn't seem to share my enthusiasm for the place. And not working left her with feelings of guilt and lack of identity. A bad case of the Protestant work ethic! I had no such scruples. Baja, for me, wasn't a vacation, it was a vocation.

A crack was beginning to appear in our relationship. The strain of living rough for six weeks widened it to a chasm. We returned to England and made a half-hearted attempt to get back together but as sure as the Baja California peninsula is slowly splitting away from the rest of Mexico, we drifted apart.

Work reared its ugly head again. I found myself teaching a course for unemployed youngsters, and was amazed at their assumption that work and the street corner were the only alternatives. Every time I suggested they could take advantage of being unemployed, get a backpack and see Europe or Africa I would hear a dozen reasons why they couldn't.

Having been such a stick-in-the-mud myself, I tried to convince them that life could be a great adventure. I showed them my slides of Baja and hoped some of my enthusiasm would rub off. However, what I was suggesting was clearly beyond their comprehension. Whatever else the British class and educational systems had given those kids, it had poisoned them with negativism and stifled their imaginations.

To so many, unemployment was just a reaffirmation of your own worthlessness, one more reason to give up and take comfort from the fact that the world was against you. Perceiving such demoralization in the eyes of even the strong and healthy students before me, I wanted to cry out: 'No, no, no, maybe it's a golden opportunity. Let your imagination run riot, dare to dream, have faith.'

I was surprised by my own thoughts. Was this really me coming out with all this? Maybe I should never have read all those adventure books.

In the midst of my frustrations, an expedition to circumnavigate the globe from pole to pole was making the news in England. It was called 'Transglobe' and the patron was Prince Charles. Although hailed as a great British adventure and a challenge to the human spirit, I couldn't relate to it. Certainly, in terms of inspiring the average man in the street, it seemed totally irrelevant: too much organization, too much money, and too much equipment being shifted around in boats, ships and planes. It had lost something on the way.

I turned to *Quest for Adventure*, a book edited by Chris Bonington. But even that had me wringing my hands in despair. The book was a compilation of great adventures. The tales were as diverse as you could wish – from land, sea, air, and even space. Bonington posed the question, what did all these adventurers have in common? Apparently, one physical trait he noted was the size of their hands – 'strong capable hands, very often large in proportion to their size'. As an aspiring adventurer with small hands I felt peeved at the suggestion that one has to look like Rambo to be an adventurer.

I decided an example was needed. Amazing myself, and all my friends and colleagues, I boldly declared that I was going to walk around Baja (where?) and live on what I could scrounge from the desert and the sea. I could think immediately of a hundred reasons for not going but I'd had enough of that kind of self-defeating nonsense. I was going to do it or die trying. All the passions of my life seemed to be coming together. I was going back to Baja, I would see what was beyond those mountains and I was going to write that book and make my point on a grand scale. If I was to die, at least I'd be doing it in Baja, doing what I wanted to do.

I had no intention of dying, however. I was going to walk alone around Baja, and all that remained was to prepare myself properly. There were many problems to solve. Five came immediately to mind. I wrote them down and somewhat tersely wrote the solutions beside them.

	Problem	*Solution*
(1)	No Spanish	Learn Spanish
(2)	Not fit	Get fit
(3)	No knowledge desert survival	Research
(4)	No money	Sponsorship
(5)	Fair skin/Intense sunlight	Sunscreen

The more problems I listed, the more I realized I was the last person in the world who should be doing this. I was so ill-suited for what I was trying to undertake, it became clear that I was, in fact, ideally suited. If I could do it, anyone could.

Thus encouraged, I joined a Spanish class at the nearest college. It wouldn't be easy. I had no talent for languages. Looking back on my mis-spent childhood, I'd had enough trouble trying to learn English.

To solve the fitness problem, I joined a badminton club, started weight training, and signed on for the village soccer team. At first I was hopeless, the worst player in the side, but over the months I derived considerable satisfaction from becoming the team's leading scorer.

I began reading everything I could on desert survival and the problems I'd likely encounter on the walk. As General Douglas MacArthur once said, 'preparedness is the key to victory'. I was going to Baja prepared and, hopefully, equipped for anything. I drew up a hierarchy of fears and dangers. My main concerns included sharks, snakes, scorpions, illness, injury, and loneliness. Dying of thirst was at the top of the list. I had to be confident that I could, if necessary, make my own drinking water and survive for weeks anywhere on the coast. I opened a file on each conceivable hazard. Most evenings, after fulfilling my teaching duties, I'd be found working out, or filling my files with more facts and figures.

I revelled in the sense of purpose. Before, when I'd been concentrating on a dozen different things at once, I never really got anywhere. Now everything fitted into a plan. I knew what was necessary and I tackled each project as part of a meaningful whole.

Now I knew what that book was going to be about, I realized it would be more than just a personal vanity. Alone in the desert, it would be an indispensable prop for my morale. I sent an inquiry letter to over sixty British publishers. The letter began:

This is an initial approach to see if you would consider publishing a 'travel' book about a 3,000-mile walk around Mexico's Baja California peninsula, a book I wish to dedicate to all adventurous souls with little money but lots of time.

I went on to write about 'the challenge of Baja' including the following quote from W. W. Johnson, the author of the Time-Life book on Baja California:

> Baja California, in pictures taken from 110 miles up, is almost always sharply and minutely recorded – a region of tumbled mountains, yawning chasms, desert plains, lonely shores, barren islands. It appears to be wholly unmarked by man, untouched by man's busyness . . . That Baja California should be so plainly seen from afar presents a certain irony. Except for a few towns at the extremities, north and south, and a handful of oases in between, comparatively little of the peninsula is seen by the earthbound, and this in an age when not much of the world is left unseen or uncrowded.

I added something about myself, and then went on to state what I was trying to achieve:

> As well as completing a hazardous 3,000-mile walk, I intend doing four things.
>
> (1) Demonstrate what can be done with a weekly budget roughly equivalent to what an unemployed youngster might receive on unemployment benefit or on a government financed 'youth opportunities programme' . . . and prove that an expedition mounted on a shoestring can be equally as exhilarating and captivating as one requiring large sums of money.
>
> (2) Write a book not just for armchair adventurers but one that readers might finish and say 'If he can do it then so can I.' Through stressing my ordinariness (5 feet 6½ inches, contact lenses, avoided sport at school, never ventured abroad until 28, happiest beer in hand, feet up before the television), I hope my adventures will help others reconsider their own potential.
>
> (3) Carry my readers with me as I leave the complexities of modern life and voluntarily enter the great simplicity of a survival situation. The constant struggle to obtain food and water whilst avoiding the dangers of sea and desert should make compelling reading.
>
> (4) Describe the people encountered as well as any interesting facets of local history or culture, and also unearth and record the stories of fellow Britons who have found themselves in this strange land. Even in this most unlikely corner of the world, they have lent their names to rivers, excavated mines, bombarded towns and plundered Spanish galleons.

It was fun waiting for all the replies. I opened each with eager anticipation. To the sixty letters sent, I received about fifty replies. Forty-five were outright rejections of the 'not for us' type, and five were of the 'let's see something when you return, if you return' variety. Even if most replies were negative, I refused to be disappointed. It was a long shot and I was going to write the book anyway. I didn't expect anyone to share my vision – yet!

Most of my friends and colleagues thought I'd flipped. I was told that what I was doing was futile and irrelevant, that I was biting off more than I could chew. One drinking partner said in all seriousness, 'What are you going to do about sex, I couldn't wander around the desert for nine months without a woman.' I felt like saying 'fuck sex', but settled for, 'I'd rather miss out on sex for nine months than spend the rest of my sex-sated life wondering what might have been. I know what I'd miss by not going.'

I was offered a new contract at the college, which I refused. I stepped down from running the course to the role of assistant. With my preparations getting into top gear, I couldn't give as much of myself, and I had to be free to leave when the moment arrived.

A new year came, 1983. Winter was the best time to walk Baja. Ideally I should have started in September or October and walked till April or May. (At that stage I was assuming I could do it in 6–9 months.) However, impatient to return to Baja, I wanted to start this side of the oncoming summer, leaving no later than February or March. That meant I had to step up my preparations and start collecting the equipment I was going to need.

Chapter 3

Something for nothing

First of all I needed a pair of walking boots, a backpack, and a few other items of camping equipment. As I couldn't afford to buy them, I plucked up courage and walked into a camping store, asking to speak to the manager. I was brought into the presence of a large stone-faced gentleman who seemed to know I was up to no good. Feeling it would be a blessing if the earth opened up and swallowed me, I did my faltering best to explain what I was doing and why. I then somehow managed to blurt out something about his sponsoring me, and would he like to give me some boots and things. I made such a hash of it, I would have dropped dead if he'd said yes. Luckily, he curtly dismissed me, mumbling that he was not in the habit of paying for other people's vacations.

It was time to get back to the drawing board and analyse what went wrong. Two points came immediately to mind. First, I had no credibility; second, I didn't expect anyone in their right mind to give me anything and it showed. My attitude was all wrong.

To tackle the credibility problem, I wandered down to the local newspaper office and asked to speak to a reporter. He found my intentions extremely interesting, a photographer snapped some pictures, and a few days later, on 14 January 1983, I was reading about myself on the front page of the *Kent and Sussex Courier*. Under the headline, 'A 3000 MILE TREK IN SEARCH OF ADVENTURE', the story ran:

> College lecturer Graham Mackintosh believes unemployed people should 'get off the street corners' and go abroad in search of adventure. He intends to practise what he preaches. In March, he is to

leave his job and set off on a 3000-mile trek among the rattlesnakes and scorpions in some of the most hostile terrain in South America (sic). 'I want to prove, particularly to the unemployed, that you can have an adventure on the cheap – and to show what an ordinary man can do if he wants,' said Graham, 31, who lives at Station View, Wadhurst. Graham is to walk through the Baja California peninsula in Mexico – alone, and often utterly cut off from civilization.

'I am going to spend a maximum of £25 a week which is about the figure you get on the dole. I am going to prove that you don't need a yacht to have an adventure,' he said.

Graham has already spent some months in preparation for the trek, including exhaustive research and physical training.

He is accumulating exotic equipment including a speargun for use in the shark infested coastal waters, and a solar still, a device for making seawater fit for consumption. He is seeking sponsorship from companies for the trip.

'There are 16 species of rattlesnake in the desert and many other dangers, and it is obviously going to be hazardous,' he said. 'But I have prepared as completely as I can and I am rather looking forward to it.

'I think the spirit of adventure is in everyone. My advice to unemployed people would be to get a rucksack and work your way around France. It is better than hanging around on street corners.'

Bachelor Graham is a lecturer at West Kent College, Tonbridge, and he gives courses for unemployed people. He expects his adventure to last 6 months – and then he intends to describe it in a book.

I felt sure this would do wonders for my credibility. It helped convince some of the doubters who thinly veiled their opinion that my plans were a lot of hogwash.

Getting to grips with my attitude problem, I inquired about the local newspapers advertising rates. As expected, an 'ad' of any consequence was likely to cost many hundreds of pounds. What was I asking for? Just a couple of hundred pounds worth of equipment. I whipped myself into a frenzy of enthusiasm and self-confidence. The article was a beginning, there'd be more. There was the book. I'd soon be on the radio and television. Thinking of all the other ways I could repay my backers, I realized they weren't giving me anything. I was giving them a great promotional opportunity. I was doing them a favour.

Thinking in such terms I breezed into another camping store armed with a copy of the newspaper story. I left having got what I wanted – boots, backpack and tent. All I needed to do was put my request formally in writing:

Dear Mr Eate,

Thank you for your interest in my Mexico expedition. If Kestral Leisure Ltd would be willing to donate the agreed items, I should be able to offer the following in return:

(1) Prominent display of Kestral insignia on tent, rucksack, T-shirt, cap, etc.
(2) *Courier* coverage of presentation of equipment.
(3) Local radio mention.
(4) Possible television coverage immediately before departing and on return to Tunbridge Wells.
(5) Incidental advertising in the book and magazine articles.
(6) Photographs and testimonials for promotional use.
(7) Potential continuous advertising from sending back accounts, pictures and tapes to my agent who will forward them to local newspapers and radio stations, and seek the widest possible media coverage.

I am sure you will agree that for a relatively small layout, the publicity and promotional payout is potentially enormous. . . .

I vowed to myself that Kestral would get back much more than they gave. I wasn't sure I could come up with everything I'd promised but it was no good being timid about it. If I didn't have faith in myself and my purpose, I could hardly expect anyone else to.

Events have a way of following in the footsteps of faith. I managed to get the equipment presentation covered by another local newspaper. I gave several local radio interviews and made sure Kestral got a mention. Whenever I was photographed I was proudly wearing my navy-blue Kestral sweatshirt. Inside the store we set up an exhibition/display which would include maps, photographs, newspaper cuttings and literature on some of the equipment I'd be carrying. I agreed to send back postcards and information to enable my progress to be followed.

Getting one sponsor made it a lot easier to attract others. More sponsorship meant more publicity which meant more sponsorship, and one by one I was able to cross the items off my list of outstanding needs – sunscreen, sun glasses, slingshot, fishing tackle, footwear, knives, machete, medicines, first-aid kit, etc., etc.

Sometimes, with the shimmery spectre of summer rushing up, I was wishing I could just buy everything I needed. However, as well as equipment, I was given confidence and an increasing faith in my purpose. That incidental encouragement was probably just as vital.

One item I could not safely do without was the solar still I mentioned to the reporter. I had seen it in a survival catalogue:

SOLAR STILL. Specialized inflatable unit designed to supply the occupants of a liferaft with 0.5 to 1.5 litres of fresh water a day through solar evaporation of seawater. Can also be used on land... Weight 2 lbs.

It seemed ideal. I contacted the manufacturers, Airborne Industries of Leigh-on-Sea, Essex, and was grateful to add this vital piece of equipment to my list of acquisitions.

Another interesting item listed in the catalogue was:

LOCAT LDT 25 Radio Distress Beacon. The Locat is a modern lightweight, low-cost radio beacon which operates on 121.5 or 243 Mhz to alert either military or civilian search and rescue services. The signal can be pin-pointed exactly and the device is a proven lifesaver. Output power of 500 mW and endurance of 36 hours at 20°C. Size only 5 × 2.5 × 1.75 inches. Weight 11.5 oz.

I wrote to the manufacturers, EMTRAD Ltd of Hull, and received the following reply from the chairman, A. D. Marshall:

I can confirm that our company is prepared to supply, on loan, one Locat 25 for the journey plus a dummy unit as part of the exhibition display.

Arrangements have been made to dispatch a 'live' unit immediately to ensure that it arrives in good time. I trust that you never need to use the unit, but it will afford some security for you on the journey. I enclose a sample of some press cuttings that we are steadily acquiring; also, as you are well in range of satellite coverage, details of the SARSAT which will pick up the Locat.

I would genuinely appreciate any publicity... a device such as Locat 25 is ideal for such ventures and to be carried by parties of walkers in remote areas. Keep in touch, the very best of luck...

Carrying that extra 11.5 ozs would take a great load off my mind. If in trouble, I need only 'pull the pin' and the signal should be picked up by satellite, my precise location and the fact of my distress should be known and, hopefully, someone should come and rescue me, should...

Everything seemed to be falling into place. Given time, I felt confident I would have everything I needed; but, of course, time was pressing. I was still trying to do a dozen things at once. I managed to get a couple of magazine editors interested in stories on my return; and I also wrote to Buckingham Palace inviting Prince Charles to be my patron. I wasn't exactly sure what that entailed but he was patron for 'Transglobe', so why not for 'Circumbaja'?

I received a prompt and extremely tactful reply from his assistant private secretary:

> The Prince of Wales has asked me to thank you for your letter and kind words about the Transglobe Expedition of which he was patron.
>
> Sadly his Royal Highness is unable to accept your kind invitation to become patron of 'Circumbaja'. This is certainly not through lack of interest in the project. The problem is that his Royal Highness only takes on positions of this nature if he feels that he will be able to give at least some time to the organization concerned. He is so heavily committed at the moment that he is having to turn down many excellent suggestions of which yours is sadly one.
>
> I am sorry to have to send you a disappointing reply. Nevertheless, his Royal Highness wishes you good luck with the project.

I was touched that HRH Prince Charles would take the trouble to wish me 'good luck'. Making that known to potential sponsors helped me claw my way even further up the cliffs of credibility.

Even so, the big prize still eluded me – the flight across the Atlantic. I threw everything into an attempt to get some kind of deal over this, my one major expense, but not even mention of HRH's interest and expressions of 'good luck' could save me from disappointment.

I was always hoping to find a major backer to work with me and wring out the publicity potential of my scheme. I needed so little, yet I could see so much I could offer in return. I was amazed not many others could see it.

Still needing a camera, I kept calling and writing to every camera manufacturer I could think of. For example to Pentax I wrote:

> I need a light, reliable model that can prove itself against sun, salt and sand. Naturally the name of Pentax comes to mind when one thinks of this level of quality and durability. Would you be willing to donate or loan a suitable camera?

Looking for a camera really tested my enthusiasm. I got the run around. With all the money I spent on phone calls I could have bought a decent one. I wondered if the manufacturers were too pessimistic about their products under such testing conditions.

Olympus promised to help me, then later retracted the offer – so and so 'wasn't authorized to do that'. After hearing that, I slumped in my chair at home. The frustration and disappointment hit me. I half mumbled a prayer, 'Thanks for everything, I'll go with what I've got.'

Suddenly the phone rang, a sound I loved to hear. It was usually good news, but I couldn't believe it when the caller said, 'I was reading about you in the local paper, I think what you're doing is admirable, and why I'm calling – I read that you were still looking for equipment. Have you got a camera yet? I have a nice little model that would be ideal, you're welcome to it if you want.'

The poor man must have wondered why I was so excited. I arranged to pick it up, then replaced the phone unsure whether to leap up and down or quietly marvel at the coincidence. By turns I did both.

A few days later I had another camera. Giving up on the manufacturers, I walked into a camera store in Tunbridge Wells and walked out with a beautiful little semi-automatic, regular battery-using, idiot-proof Konica which came complete with self-timer and built-in flash. Looking through the viewfinder I saw again how important was faith in fending off frustration and despair.

National Panasonic agreed to give me a walkman-type radio/cassette recorder. The headphones radio was going to be important on those dark coyote-howling nights, and the tape recorder would enable me to make the 'live-action' tapes I had promised to the local radio stations.

I was planning to leave for Los Angeles on 28 March. That date was racing up all too fast. I had most of the equipment I was going to need. Realizing weight was becoming critical, I decided to do without the speargun and other such 'exotic' items.

My finances were also critical. It would be no good landing in the United States with $100 in my pocket and telling the Immigration and Naturalization Service that I'd be living off cactus and rattlesnake for a year. I'd be sent back on the next plane before I could say 'jet lag'.

A couple of cheques arrived out of the blue, donations from people who barely knew me and certainly knew nothing of my financial plight. It was an enormous encouragement, but it wasn't enough. I paid a visit to my bank manager. Would he extend a line of credit to someone about to disappear on some hare-brained scheme, possibly never to be heard from again? Almost to my surprise he did. Those were heady and exciting days. Vowing to battle to the last moment for support and sponsorship I made my plans to leave on schedule.

Then something turned up that had me cancelling everything. BBC Television invited me to their Lime Grove studios in London to take part in a 'Nationwide' programme on 28 March. Who knows what might come from this? Dare I defy the oncoming summer and hang around long enough to see?

With the help of BBC technicians, I erected my tent for the first time; and, standing beside the equipment laid around the tent, I explained to an audience of millions where I was going and what it was all about. Many of them must have heard the name Baja California for the first time. I wore my Kestral sweater and felt pleased that so many of my backers were having their products aired on television.

Driving away from the studios through the rush-hour traffic, I found myself laughing. Tension release? No, I suspect it was from just looking back over what I'd done: newspapers, radio, television. I had accumulated a mountain of equipment, been given money. I'd got all that and I hadn't done a thing. It seemed so incredibly funny. I had not taken one step on my journey, yet I was 'famous'. All because of what I said I was going to do.

Still, there was no question of going back on my word – an Englishman's word is his bond, even if he is half-Scottish and half-Irish! In spite of my fears I'd rather have died than feebly allow my vision to fizzle out. I had deliberately manoeuvred myself into a no-way-back situation. When Cortés landed in Mexico in 1519, he burned his ships to ensure no retreat for the faint-hearted. His little army of 600 men was going to conquer the Aztec empire or perish in the attempt. I was going to meet my destiny in Baja, be it good or bad.

Instead of flying over Greenland, I spent the evening of 28 March watching myself on television for the first time. My only regret was when the commentator erroneously declared that I was leaving 'tomorrow'! That put paid to all hopes for last minute sponsorship miracles. With no further point delaying, I rescheduled my departure for 3 April and made my final, fruitless, attempts to persuade an airline to ferry me across the Atlantic.

Chapter 4
Hazards

Starting the sponsorship ball rolling had taken up so much time, that I'd largely neglected my hazard files. Realizing that, in just a few short days, I'd be alone struggling to stay alive in a baking hot wilderness, I made a last review of the dangers before me. Perusing page after page of notes and comments, I did my best to sort out the contradictions and exaggerations and fix in my mind whatever seemed important.

Rattlesnakes
Western diamondback, aggressive and dangerous, babies can kill, up to 8 feet long. Red diamondback, vicious, deadly, common in northern part of Baja, up to 6 feet. Venom attacks blood vessels, violent pain, vomiting, thirst, severe swelling, tissue death, possibly gangrene, amputate . . . consider chopping off envenomated fingers or toes if no medical aid!

Carry snakebite kit with razor blade, suction cup and tourniquet. Place constricting band between bite and the heart, make cross cuts across the bite, suck or squeeze out the venom . . . rattlesnakes bite downwards, venom deposited below fang marks, cut below fang marks, shallow cuts half-inch long, avoid cross cuts, no alcohol, sedatives or aspirin. Keep calm and still.

Most active at night, can't stand the heat of the day. Rattlesnakes have sensory depressions between the eyes, sensitive to infra-red heat, can strike at warm-blooded prey in complete darkness. Watch your step, where you place hands when climbing, wear leather boots, several pairs of socks and loose trousers.

Scorpions
Kill ten times as many people as rattlesnakes in Mexico. Common in

Baja, up to 6 inches, usually smaller, hide in the day, come out at night. Found in dead wood or dry cactus. Check clothing, boots and bedding.

Really dangerous species normally yellow. Stings delivered in self-defence contain the most poison. Some venoms are local in effect and relatively harmless. Others are neurotoxic, similar to snake venom causing partial paralysis, fever, destruction of red blood cells, etc. Local pain followed by tightness in the throat, swollen tongue, difficulty in speaking, involuntary twitching, continuous flow of fluid from the nose and mouth, convulsions, then the victim turns blue and dies in 1–12 hours.

Spiders

The bite of the black widow can be fatal. There will be swelling at the site of the bite with pain spreading throughout the body, followed by nausea, dizziness and difficulty in breathing. Black widows found under rocks, in rodent holes and other shaded areas. They have a shiny black bulb of a body with a distinctive red hourglass mark on the underside. The webs are filmy grey.

Stingrays

Flat, often several feet long, found in warm shallow coastal waters. The poisonous spine is in the tail. Tread on one and you trigger a reflex that brings the tail up in a powerful whiplike motion capable of causing extensive tissue injury. The barbed spine may break off and remain inside the wound. Pain almost unbearable. The sting of a large ray may be fatal. Waders should shuffle their feet or clear a path with a stick.

Sharks

Large shark population around the coast of Baja. Shark fishing a brisk industry. Blood and body fluids, and splashing are likely to attract them and spark off a feeding frenzy.

Barracuda

Common. Attacks indiscriminately. In some areas considered more dangerous than sharks. Young barracuda are schooling fish and not generally aggressive. It is the lone predator that is likely to attack.

Toxic fish

Do not eat the viscera, liver, gonads or intestines of tropical fish. Avoid eating large reef fishes such as snapper, barracuda, grouper and jack. The puffer fish, common around Baja, is possibly the most poisonous fish in the world. The flesh contains a powerful nerve poison called tetrodoxin, produces the disease 'ciguatera' where the nervous tissue of the stomach is attacked giving rise to violent spasms which spread throughout the body. The victim 'expires in a paroxysm of extreme suffering'. No known antidote. Most victims die within 24 hours.

Cactus and desert vegetation
The cholla cactus has been described as the scourge of the desert traveller. Expect to spend hours removing spines from clothes, boots and skin. The agave has needle-like tips and fierce curved prickles. Some bushes poisonous, touch them then rub your eyes, severe irritation and even blindness follows.

Climatic and geographical problems
Temperatures up to 120°F., agonizing glare, baffling mirages. Tropical storms, winds over 100 mph, flash floods, lightning and thunderstorms of great violence. San Felipe wiped out . . . Loreto almost destroyed. Earthquakes, dust devils, sandstorms, pounding surf, huge tides in the northern Gulf.

Dehydration
With the body pouring out perspiration an almost constant intake of fluids is necessary, a gallon a day minimum. At temperatures over 100°F. your life expectancy without water is about 24 hours (assuming complete rest).

Dehydration causes sleepiness, loss of appetite, rise in temperature, loss of speech, tingling, dizziness, headache and breathing problems. Never eat if short of water; food especially protein, has a damaging effect, hastening dehydration. Drinking seawater worsens dehydration. 'Never under any circumstances drink seawater.' Dr Alain Bombard, who used himself as a guinea-pig by setting himself adrift in the Atlantic, proved that the intake of seawater was possible under certain closely defined conditions: don't wait until you're thirsty before drinking it, match your intake to the body's need for salt (800 ml a day), take it in small doses, and for no more than 6 to 7 days. As Bombard declared – 'I drank seawater for 14 days . . . and fish juice for 43 days, I had conquered the menace of thirst at sea.'

Fish juice can be squeezed from the cut up muscles of fish. The cerebro-spinal fluid and eyes contain water. The eyes can be sucked or munched. Seaweed can be chewed for water. The big barrel cactus is a good water source.

Rabies
An infectious disease of mammals always fatal to man if it takes hold. Exposure to the saliva of an infected animal (usually through its bite)

results in a horrible death. Restlessness and depression followed by increasing anxiety, fear becomes terror, violent rage alternates with listless calm, brain tissues are first irritated then irreversibly damaged, the victim turns into a raging maniac at the sight of water, death from cardiac or respiratory failure comes 3–5 days after the onset of symptoms. Symptoms may appear anywhere from 10 days to 2 years after the bite, 50 to 60 days being normal. A person who has been bitten by a suspected carrier must receive repeated doses of vaccine before the symptoms appear.

Avoid mammals that appear to be sick or dying or acting strange, especially bats, foxes and skunks. Attacks on humans by species not normally prone to attack may be due to rabies. 'A rabid animal, however small, is the most dangerous creature alive. Unlike snakes, scorpions, spiders and all other venomous forms, untreated bites of a rabid animal are 100% fatal.'

Psychological dangers

Injury, pain, hunger and thirst tax your will to live. Prolonged isolation in a hostile environment can lead to despair and suicide. As sure as thirst kills quicker than hunger, despair is the greatest killer of all. Constant preoccupation of body and mind helps, as do religious feelings and the inspiration derived from others who have endured similar or worse predicaments. Thorough knowledge of your survival equipment and the confidence which this brings are essential, as is preparation and conditioning for the possibility of life under survival conditions.

Almost instinctively, I had been preparing myself for 'life under survival conditions'. I knew that in the end, the battle was going to be first and foremost on the level of spirit and morale. I had done my best. Not only would I be setting off appropriately equipped and with a fair grounding in the techniques of desert survival, but my morale was excellent. Even the prospect of death had lost some of its terror. That's not to say I'd lost my love of life. Far from it, I never felt happier or more fulfilled. Doing what I really wanted to do, the sense of self-discovery and self-potential were exhilarating.

Perhaps Alain Bombard was struggling with a similar contradiction between love of life and acceptance of death when he wrote:

> Life is the object of man's presence on earth. From the day he is born he must be taught two basic principles – to love life and to prepare for death. Living and dying are the only two things we can be absolutely sure of; but if every child should be prepared for death and every man face it calmly as the one inescapable certainty, love of life and a fierce resolve to preserve it as long as possible must also guide man's thoughts.

The day of departure came. With my suitcase ready, and still bubbling from the excitement of it all, I hugged my father and kissed my mother goodbye. 'I'll be home by Christmas,' I said cheerfully.

'I don't pretend to understand why you're doing this,' my mother replied with tear-filled eyes, 'and I know nothing I say is going to stop you, but just because you're in the limelight and you've made all those promises and public proclamations, please don't do anything stupid. If it's too much for you, don't be ashamed to admit it and come home. You don't owe them anything. They'll forget you in a moment, but we will never forget you. We love you very much. Come home for us.'

Chapter 5

'The greatest killer of all'

I felt more than the usual tension and excitement as the Los Angeles-bound 747 roared down the runway at Heathrow. My dream was getting off the ground at last.

After climbing for a minute or two, the huge jet turned from a westerly to a more northerly course. Getting a right-side window seat was a stroke of luck. The right wing dipped giving me a final glimpse of my home town and the Berkshire countryside I knew so well. The turn seemed to be hinged on my parents' house. Like a ghostly echo I heard again my mother's words, 'Come home for us.' The wing rose again. The salute was complete.

As the jet followed the westward advance of the sun high above Iceland, Greenland and Canada, I was leaning against the plastic inner-window wondering what it would be like to be down there alone, feeling the cold, listening to the wind or the silence and looking up to see a tiny silver speck trailing across the sky.

'What will be the best and worst moments of the trip?' Possibilities flashed before me. My mood turned sombre. There would be so much anxiety and pain, I couldn't imagine any pleasure compensating for it all. I just knew I had to do it, wherever it led, whatever the consequences.

Having touched down at Los Angeles, my first problem was getting past the US Immigration and Naturalization Service. With no return ticket, not much money and an implausible story about living on $10 a week, I was an obvious candidate for suspicion and interrogation. What an ignominious start to the great trek to be sent back on the next flight!

Presenting my passport, I took comfort from my bank manager's letter testifying to my upright moral character, and another from Dave and Denise Bowyer saying they would house and take responsibility for me while I was in the United States.

I needn't have worried. No questions were asked. A six-month entry permit was stapled to my passport and Dave Bowyer was there to whisk me away to my home from home ten miles from downtown Los Angeles. Relieved, I was able to laugh, joke, drink and take pleasure in the company of old friends. We had been next-door neighbours in Sheffield for several years, and were like family.

The following day, trying to shake off the combined effects of jet lag, culture shock and a hangover, I limited my preparations to sun-conditioning my winter-pale body. Coating myself in a high protection sunscreen, I stretched out in the April sunshine. The blistering Baja sun would have no mercy on my fair skin, and how I would react was a major anxiety. I had noticed that a combination of sun and sunscreen had often irritated my skin and sometimes produced a rash.

Aspro-Nicholas Ltd, a company based in my home town, had given me a supply of ALMAY 'hypo-allergenic' sunscreen of factor 8, 10 and 15 strength. It was specifically designed not to induce irritation. I could only hope it worked.

As recovery allowed I threw myself into more demanding preparations. For several weeks I had hardly removed my new boots, and I continued breaking them in around the streets of Los Angeles. No longer did my feet feel as if they were encased in concrete.

With dying of thirst my most probable fate, I carefully examined and experimented with my stills. The uninflated solar still looked something like a large stranded jellyfish. I studied the diagram on the package and followed the step-by-step instructions. The buoyancy ring inflated like an inner-tube. That was relatively easy. But blowing up the main cone-shaped chamber above the ring took several minutes of hard work. Then I filled the still with a gallon of water and placed it in the sun. Would it work? I had to see it to believe it. Within an hour water vapour was condensing on the inside of the cone and running down into a collecting gutter. It was unpleasantly warm and had a strong plastic taste, but I would hardly worry about that in the desert.

I drained, dried and repacked the precious device. The one thing I could not afford to do was puncture the vulnerable plastic.

The second still consisted of a kettle, a length of tubing and a simple idea. Boiling seawater produces steam; condense the steam and you have drinking water. Again, I had to see it to believe it. Half filling the aluminium kettle with water, I added a couple of ounces of salt, screwed on the hard plastic cap, inserted a length of plastic tubing into a hole drilled in the cap, put it on to boil and was relieved to find that the water dripping from the end of the tube was salt free and drinkable. Like a mad professor I skipped around the kitchen bubbling almost as much as the kettle. 'It works, it works,' I chuckled. It certainly did work but the question was, for how long? Not wanting to buy more tubing I, somewhat foolishly, left that question unanswered.

The third still was even simpler. It consisted of a plastic sheet to be spread over a freshly dug hole in the ground. Supposedly the heat of the sun would draw water from the soil which would condense on the underside of the plastic. If a stone were placed in the centre, the droplets would run down to the stone and drip into a collecting vessel placed underneath.

I had no intention of digging a hole to test this out. I would have to take the plastic sheet on faith and figure it out if and when I needed it. But it was comforting to know that I had a back-up solar still, just in case.

When I spread all my equipment out on a large table it was immediately apparent that I couldn't take everything. I began stuffing into my backpack all the things I regarded as essential. The stills went in first, then the radio distress beacon, first-aid kit, passport, machete, Swiss army knife, filleting knife, frying pan, fork, spoon, mug, sun glasses, sunscreen, torch, slingshot, snake-bite kit, maps, mirror, matches, sewing kit, clothes, hat, towel, batteries, contact lenses, glasses, toothbrush, toothpaste, dental floss, toilet roll, multivitamins, water-purifying tablets, sponge, film, tapes, sharpening stone, cord and straps, Spanish book, journal, desert survival booklet, wire saw, pen, and most important of all for my morale – my furry fork-tongued rattlesnake mascot, 'Seth'.

When I could squeeze no more in, I attached my tent, sleeping bag, spare boots, tennis shoes and foam pad to the outside of the pack. Trying to pick it up I got a shock. Without food and water it weighed 80 lbs. So out came a pair of jeans, a jacket, two shirts, several tubes of sunscreen, some batteries, the towel and off came the boots.

It still wasn't enough. Looking again at the heavier items I was forced to make more drastic decisions. I discarded most of my Spanish book ripping out and taking just a few key pages, and I could do without a journal by writing my log between the lines and along the margins of the survival booklet. The 9lb-tent was too heavy. Most of the weight was in the waterproof flysheet, and as it probably wouldn't rain for months, I decided to leave it behind.

Still not convinced that the load was manageable, I reminded myself that I'd grow increasingly accustomed to it and, as I used up batteries and sunscreen, etc, the pack would also get lighter. In more ways than one the toughest part would be the start!

The next day, with equipment checked, knives sharpened, maps perused and last minute letters in the post – I was ready to go. Ready in every way except one – I was in no great hurry to leave the security of my 'base' and throw myself into the unknown. When Dave Bowyer said he was going backpacking with a couple of his American friends I allowed myself to be talked into joining them.

For three days we wandered around the Cuyamaca State Park close to the Mexican border. It turned out to be an excellent training hike although I got little chance to adjust to the heat and the sun. The days were cool and the nights were bitterly cold. One night it snowed and our water bottles froze. As there was a park regulation against campfires, the four of us huddled guiltily around our discreet little fire.

A deathly hush seemed to settle on the world as the snow muffled every sound except for the crackle of the fire and our own subdued voices. Mexico and my plans became the subject of conversation. In case I wasn't miserable enough with the cold, the two Californians left me in no doubt that they thought my idea was crazy and if I went ahead with it, I'd never be seen again. They told me that I was bound to fall ill from the food and water, how violence was a way of life down there, how gringos were detested and considered fair game for police and official corruption, and how friends of friends had been locked up, ill-treated and had lost expensive equipment confiscated on the slightest pretence.

Back in Los Angeles I found it harder than ever to make a move from my base. It helped having other friends to visit, such as a lovely family I'd met on my first trip to Baja. After bidding farewell to Dave and Denise, I bussed and hitched my way down to their Orange County ranch, fifty miles south of L.A.

I arrived at the ranch almost certain that I would start my walk at San Felipe on the Gulf Coast. Although it would be hotter, the lure of the Gulf with its rugged shores, excellent fishing and lake-like calmness (it can also be wild and dangerous) was irresistible. South from San Felipe I could expect to run into fishcamps and tourists and, after fifty miles, the small town of Puertecitos. A dirt road would be close by for a hundred miles.

If I needed anything else to finalize my decision, my ranch friends introduced me to Larry, a neighbour and fellow Baja enthusiast who had a secluded beach home ninety miles south of San Felipe. He offered me a wealth of advice and information and even the use of his house. I accepted gladly. It would be good to have somewhere to head towards on those first difficult days.

Before I attempted the coast below the ominously named Punta Final, Larry strongly recommended I consult with Ed Wills, an American, who had a place ten miles below his. 'He has lived there for years and knows everything there is to know about the area.'

Larry was convinced I'd find little except trouble after rounding Punta Final. There was one isolated fishcamp, but he warned that the fishermen, many of whom come from the Mexican mainland, might not be friendly. 'If they get drunk,' he said, 'they may turn nasty. It might be best to get out of there before dark. You would be a tempting target alone and at their mercy.'

The morning of 23 April 1983 found me saying goodbye to my Orange County friends. With less than $200 at my disposal, I decided to hitch to Mexico. It was a beautiful blue-sky California morning. The cars joining Interstate 5 looked as if they had been driven fresh off the assembly line. The houses and commercial buildings all seemed flawless amidst the rolling green hills. More than one flag proudly waved its colourful stars and stripes. Even the people seemed driven to perfection. This was Mission Viejo, a bastion of middle-class affluence fifty miles south of Los Angeles. Standing there thumb out by the freeway entrance, I fitted into the picture about as much as an old battered car or a house with graffiti and flaking paint.

Nevertheless, I didn't have to wait long. The first ride took me fifty miles. A series of short rides then took me on to San Diego where I had my first real wait overlooking the airport. Although there was little traffic joining the freeway, the aerial traffic was fascinating. And beyond the runway, the carriers and other ships of the Pacific fleet lay at anchor in San Diego Bay. Mexico was just fifteen miles away.

There were several places to cross the border. The likeliest was Interstate 5 to Tijuana. However, the first person to stop was going east on Interstate 8. It was only a short lift but I had waited too long to turn it down. My new goal was to cross at Mexicali. The driver, who was half-Mexican, was fascinated by my plans and invited me to have lunch with his family. I was touched and encouraged but too full of thoughts of Baja to accept. Later I would take a more relaxed approach to goals and timetables.

I got my next lift from a retired, disillusioned Easterner. He hated Californians and swore that everyone in the state was trying to rip him off. With such an attitude, I was surprised he'd stopped. To help my confidence, he gave me a chronicle of his Mexican experiences, all bad of course. It sounded depressingly familiar. He dropped me in the middle of nowhere.

After a long wait, a car slowed down to let out another hitch-hiker. He pulled his pack from the trunk and kissed the lady driver goodbye. Blond, early twenties, serious, not easy to communicate with, he did manage to relate that his last lift was the young lady who had driven him to a 'shady valley' and, 'It was love, man, it was great.' Doubting we'd see another car that day, I walked off to find a place to camp.

Next morning, I once again had the freeway entrance to myself. An old VW car came down the 'off-ramp' and to my amazement it crossed straight over to the 'on-ramp'. I shot out my thumb. Seeing an attractive blonde girl behind the wheel my arm involuntarily dropped through eighty degrees. To my surprise she stopped and, in the sweetest, friendliest voice imaginable, asked where I was going. Images of shady valleys flashed before my mind!

As we headed east Sharon explained that she was from San Diego and just felt the urge to go for a drive. She wasn't going anywhere in particular so she thought she'd give me a ride. My imagination was in overdrive.

She was very likeable and sincere, the kind of person I felt immediately close to. However, all thoughts of shady valleys quickly disappeared. Sharon was given to Christ, and my mind turned to more serious and appropriate thoughts about walking through the valley of the shadow of death.

She told me about her life, her wandering urge, her finding 'the Lord' and what that meant to her. Soon we were reading her Bible together, finding meaning and inspiration in passages on thirst and the desert. When she offered to take me all the way to Mexicali – nearly 100 miles – I wondered if she was indeed heavensent.

We dropped down from the mountains to the hot, flat expanse of the desert giving me my first glimpse of what lay ahead. Ocotillo shrubs dominated the plain. I recalled that their bright red flowers were edible and nutritious. As we sped across the desert Sharon's presence helped keep the lid on the myriad anxieties welling up within me. I felt as if I'd known her for years.

I arrived at the border with mixed feelings. I wasn't looking forward to saying goodbye to my amiable and reassuring companion. She insisted on buying me a beer and a taco as a final gesture. I reluctantly accepted, promising to return the favour next time we met.

I walked to the crossing point. Recalling all the comments I'd heard about Mexican water I decided to fill a canteen on the US side. A border patrol officer was leaning back against the wall, apparently asleep. I asked if he'd watch my pack while I got some water from the washroom. At first he didn't condescend to answer but seeing I was going to leave it there anyway, he grunted something unintelligible. I felt like kicking the chair out from under him. In contrast the Mexican officials were polite and friendly. I asked for and got a six-month visa. My passport was returned with courteous good wishes.

Calexico – the Californian town on the border with Mexico – prepares you for its neighbour Mexicali – the Mexican town on the California border. It prepares you in the sense of being so Mexicanized that it is easy to forget you're still in the US. However, it does not prepare you for the size and bustle of Mexicali. Mexicali is the capital of the state of

Baja California Norte and the centre of a large and prosperous agricultural region. Its population is well over 500,000.

Shortly after crossing the border I found myself walking down one of its more crowded shopping streets carrying my backpack with tent and sleeping bag emerging almost a foot on either side. I made good use of the words 'lo siento' – 'I'm sorry' – as I made my way along the busy sidewalk. A sense of paranoia came easy, as cars, buses and faces flashed by. The pack and my bright red hair did a fine job of calling attention to me.

I inquired about a bus, but the uncertainties of which bus, where, the cost, and would it show, had me thinking about hitching again. Just beyond the city centre I made a half-hearted attempt before realizing that no one had the time or the inclination to stop.

A glance at my map convinced me that I should walk on about four miles to the junction where Highway 5 took off for San Felipe. It would be a good training hike. I shouldered my pack and headed in what seemed to be the right direction.

Those city miles were never-ending. The day grew hotter and I wasn't sure if the tingling in my face was due to the sun or to embarrassment. My arms and neck felt tight and burned. The pack cut into my shoulders, sweat stung my eyes, my head began to ache and no matter how much I drank I was continually thirsty. The water in my canteen turned warm and sickly. I began to feel dizzy.

Anxious about throwing up or even collapsing on the sidewalk, I took refuge in a dingy alley. Huddled there in my misery I feared I had taken on something I was physically incapable of finishing. Pulling out my mirror I looked beyond the swimming dots to see if my face was beetroot red or deathly pale. It seemed to be both. All I wanted to do was sit there on the ground. All I could think of saying was 'shit'.

A family of Mexicans appeared from the back of one of the houses forming the alley. They had no idea what to make of me. After a few awkward moments, I picked up my pack, mumbled something about it being hot, and walked out into the stifling heat.

Somehow I made it to the junction. There I got talking to a young Mexican fruit seller. He asked in English where I was going. I told him I wanted a ride to San Felipe. He replied encouragingly that I wouldn't have to wait long. I hoped he was right. It was late afternoon and I didn't want to walk any further looking for a place to sleep. Taking up station one hundred yards from the boy's fruit stall I held out a thumb but the car that crawled towards me was painfully overloaded. Yet to my surprise it stopped.

'I hear you're going to San Felipe,' said the driver. 'Right. How did you know?' I replied. 'Oh, that Mexican kid said you were a fellow countryman needing a lift to San Felipe.' 'Actually I'm British. Does that make a difference?'

It apparently didn't. The two good samaritans from San Francisco had to repack the whole car to get me in. As we drove off I caught the eye of the Mexican boy and sent him a thank-you wave.

What a joy to just sit down and be chauffeured. I was offered a cold beer and couldn't believe how good it tasted. After a burst of friendly conversation the beer and heat seemed to catch up on us. We drifted off into our own worlds.

My mood turned sombre as we crossed the flat expanse of the so-called 'Desert of the Chinamen', forty-three of whom had set out to walk from San Felipe to Mexicali in search of work. Only seven made it. The rest died of thirst. The sun-baked mountains of Baja rose before us red and seemingly devoid of life. My self-doubt intensified. What have I done? This land does not tolerate fools.

The sun was setting as we arrived in San Felipe. It was a beautiful evening, calm and warm. The dramatically blue sea was still dotted with swimmers and boaters. My companions invited me to camp with them on the beach just south of town. Thankful to have someone to watch my irreplaceable equipment, I walked into the town trying to adjust to the fact that I'd arrived. The hitching adventure was over. The real ordeal was about to begin.

I still felt somewhat delicate as I wandered around the darkening, dusty streets of the town. I felt as if I walked in another world from the trickle of people flowing past the brightly lit shop windows. Loud aggressive American laughter drifted in and out of my consciousness, as did indecipherable snatches of Spanish. The sound and smell of frying pervaded the air, and Mexican music wafted from a dozen bars and alleyways sweeping me along into a whirlpool of sadness.

Buying a beer in one little store was quite an ordeal. The Mexicans waiting in line appeared inscrutable behind their language barrier. I couldn't understand what they were laughing at. Was it me? Beer in hand, I was in too much of a hurry to get out to bother counting the change. Only outside, curious about the unfamiliar money, did I discover that I had been short-changed. The amount wasn't much – about 20 cents – but feeling cheated was the last thing I needed as I tried to convince myself that the accusations levelled against the Mexicans, in particular the good people of Baja, were so much slander. I was angry at myself for not going back, but I did not feel up to airing my grievance in a foreign language. Besides, what's 20 cents? Just then, it represented my faith in mankind. The costly beer did little to wash away the wave of misery crashing through me.

Although hungry, I could not be tempted by the sidewalk sellers of tacos and tamales. To my revolted stomach, they might have been leering corpses purveying pufferfish complete with toxins reputed to be hundreds of times deadlier than cyanide! The warnings I had been given about Mexican food had not gone unheeded. I satisfied my hunger with crisps and peanuts.

My paranoia intensified. The whole universe was mocking me and my crazy idea. The strength and bravado that had brought me that far had totally deserted me. The prospect of weeks and months alone in the desert terrified me.

Tall, bronzed, athletic Americans sauntered by confidently and aggressively. It was one of them who should have been attempting the walk, not me. They seemed strong in every way that I felt weak.

As I trudged back to my tent, even the normally well-cowed Mexican dogs sensed I didn't belong. Three of them emerged from the dust and the darkness barking and snapping at my heels. Amused Mexicans watched the sport as we engaged in a running battle down the length of that lonely street. Finally satisfied that they had chased the misfit out of town they returned to their various holes to scratch and suck out other bothersome vermin.

Safe inside my tent I listened to the waves and stared at the fabric-softened image of the moon. I didn't want to think. Every chain of thought had a depressing conclusion. It was easier to lie on my back and just stare.

However, there was no escaping the question. Why did I feel so miserable and inadequate? I was tired, the pack seemed unbearably heavy, I was sunburned, and the heat was murderous – hardly surprising since I'd just come from a long English winter. I was apprehensive about what lay ahead. My Spanish was still basic and there were a dozen other worries, but so what? None of that accounted for the depth of my feelings.

More likely, the psychological onslaught had begun. This is what I'd read about and prepared for. As well as understanding it intellectually, I now understood it in all its emotional reality. Lying there in my tent I could feel why 'despair was the greatest killer of them all'. I had to break its hold. I didn't need the burden of a troubled mind to add to my over-heavy pack.

I needed a friend. Yet there was no one. All the old assumptions, securities and props had been stripped from me. Tomorrow it would be just me, my word, my few possessions and my bruised morale against a terrifying uncertainty.

Forcing myself to accept that I must just soldier on through the crisis I found myself mumbling the words of some half-remembered hymn:

Abide with me, fast falls the eventide.
The darkness deepens, Lord with me abide.
When other helpers fail and comforts flee,
Help of the helpless, O, abide with me.

Tears ran down my cheeks. I promised myself that tomorrow or the next day or the next, all this madness would seem ridiculous. Although I would gladly have called the whole thing off I forced myself to say, 'No major decisions when you're down; just keep going for one week.' I knew that if I could get that first week behind me, I would see it through to the end. 'Maybe there are millions of Americans better qualified than me to walk around Baja, but it's me that's trying, and with God's help it will be me that succeeds.'

Someone once said, 'There are no atheists in the trenches.' Feeling a bit like a soldier about to go over the top to certain death, I knew exactly what he meant.

Next morning, 25 April 1983, I wrote postcards, walked back into town, bought a floppy wide-brimmed leather hat – my face, neck and ears had suffered enough from the sun – rearranged my pack and prevaricated in a dozen other ways. I was still looking for an excuse not to leave. There wasn't one. The moment had arrived. Like a machete crashing down, I made up my mind, took down the tent, stuffed everything into my backpack, filled my water containers, said my goodbyes, then made my way south along the beach. It was that easy. I had begun.

Chapter 6
That sinking feeling

Looking and feeling like something from another planet, I walked past a group of bemused tourists. One asked where I was going. With bravado bouncing back, I replied, 'Oh, I'm just walking down the coast to Cabo San Lucas.' The idea was so absurd that it seemed superfluous to mention the Pacific coast as well. Between San Felipe and Cabo San Lucas was 1,000 miles of some of the most rugged and isolated coastline in the world. The looks on their faces as they wished me good luck did a lot to lift my morale.

I walked on head high and dignified even though the pack and the burden of my anxieties were doing their best to crush me. My arms ached from carrying the bulk of my three gallons of water by hand. Walking on sand, especially dry sand, is less easy than it looks. After two hundred yards every step was agony, but I was determined not to stop before putting a respectable distance between myself and my well-wishers. Fear and insecurity were soon mercifully dissolved in a flood of physical pain.

I carried my water in three separate containers: a three-gallon plastic bag, a half-gallon canteen, and a smaller belt water bottle. The two larger containers I carried by hand, switching them around as the more burdened arm grew tired. After all the dire warnings about Mexican water, I drank only from my belt bottle which contained water treated with chlorine purifying tablets. When it needed filling, I added another couple of tablets and waited the prescribed twenty minutes before drinking.

I was no more than a speck in the distance when I thankfully put down the water containers and eased the pack from my shoulders. With only myself to impress, I carried on at a more relaxed pace. Having taken the all-important first step how far I got that day no longer mattered. Every fifty yards, I bent over to rest my hands on my knees and relieve the weight cutting into my shoulders. Every two hundred yards or so, I would 'pack-down', sit on the sand and feel the ache dissolve from my arms as I admired the fascinating interface of sea and desert.

But any thoughts of an early halt for the day were soon abandoned. Finding myself sandwiched between an unbroken line of sand cliffs and the sea, I felt as if I were in a long tunnel. Mindful of the enormous tides there in the upper gulf, I couldn't relax till I'd emerged from the other end.

At one point I caught the unmistakable smell of putrefaction. Slipping off my pack, I sought out the source of the offensive stench. Behind a block of fallen cliff was the carcass of a large bull sea lion. There were no obvious wounds. Wondering how he died, I took my first photograph, then gladly retreated to the fresh air. My head filled with morbid thoughts. I worried about being found putrefying and fermenting inside my closed tent. It seemed awfully undignified! If I knew I was about to die, I hoped I would have the presence of mind to crawl out of the tent and allow my bones to be picked clean by the army of scavengers always willing to oblige. Then I had second thoughts. I saw a hungry gull pecking the eyes from a still living fish stranded by the tide.

The miles fell behind me. I would have settled for walking two that first day, three the second and so on till I'd built up my strength and found my level. However, by the time I stopped to make camp, I had the satisfaction of knowing that I had walked almost ten miles.

Just before dark I erected my brown and beige tent on the narrow haven of dry sand between the high-tide mark and the cliffs. The pack and water containers were dusted off and placed on one side of my new home; after spreading out my foam pad and sleeping bag I placed myself on the other. I made a pillow from a pair of jeans and a couple of clean shirts. The only things left outside were my boots. I would just have to bang and shake them in the morning to ensure no scorpions were inside.

So this was my mansion for the forseeable future and quite adequate it felt too! Whatever transpired outside no longer mattered. The creatures of the night could do as they pleased. The thin fabric represented my line of defence and my security. I stretched my exhausted frame knowing I had earned a guiltless hour just lying there listening to the distant sea and the sounds of the night.

Digging into the pack, I found Seth. In spite of his long ordeal stuffed deep down with the radio distress beacon and the solar still, he was his usual big-headed smiling self. I laid him on top of the backpack and apologetically patted his head, laughing at my sentimental attachment to this idiotic looking rattlesnake. I laughed again as I thought of our TV appearance back in England. As the camera moved in for a close-up of

Seth precariously wrapped around the top of a tent pole, I vowed to the nation that we were going to see it through together. He was the one possession I would never discard. Glowing pale blue in the moonlight, his smile seemed to broaden as I reminded him of my promise. I pictured myself as the cowboy hero staggering thirst-crazed across the desert dropping one piece of equipment after another until crawling, rattle-snake in hand, there was nothing left but the final agony and the promise of eternity. Seth, of course, would be found held lovingly to my bleached breastbone!

One of the problems of being alone is having no one there to tell you when you are about to do something stupid. You have to think of everything yourself. Imagination helps, allowing the possible consequences of your actions to flow through your mind, but a too vivid imagination combined with a negative outlook and all too quickly you can be washed away in a flood of terror.

With the sound of the waves sloshing closer as the tide came in, I pictured myself being swept out to sea struggling inside my zipped-up tent or being battered senseless against the base of the cliff. Needless to say I didn't sleep too well that night. I lost count of the times I poked my weary head from the tent willing the water to go back again.

Glad to be still high and dry next morning, I watched a beautiful sunrise over the sea. The orange ball hung cool in a cloudless sky as I crunched my way through a breakfast of cornflakes. It was a shock to see someone walking towards me along the beach. A young bull-built Mexican had spotted me on his morning stroll. I relaxed as we got talking. He became extremely interested in my plan to live off the sea and the desert, offering all kinds of useful advice. Apparently there was something good to be had beneath the rocks at low tide. 'Pulpo, pulpo,' he kept repeating.

The strange creature he described was clearly some kind of monster to be hacked to pieces and beaten to a pulp. Eat them before they eat you seemed to be the recommended approach. Thanking him for his advice, I hurriedly broke camp and began my second day's walk terrified lest I bump into a wild 'pulpo'.

The day warmed up and I sweated through an agonizing morning learning that there was no easy walking along the coast. Beaches of sand, boulder and pebble all conspired to make me suffer. It was a welcome relief to take a swim. After ensuring that there were no people or pulpo about, I waded naked into the sea. However, it was fear of sharks and drowning that kept me to the shallows.

My first attempt at fishing almost proved disastrous. I was still getting used to the new telescopic rod and spinning reel when a large fish hit the flashing silver lure. The thrill turned to pain as the freely spinning handle crashed into my finger. I thought it was broken or dislocated. The fish got away and I was lucky to escape with a bruised and swollen finger. It was a timely reminder that there was no room for stupidity or unnecessary risks. I couldn't afford to be injured or incapacitated.

The telescopic rod was ideal. It could be collapsed and carried by hand, with reel and lure attached. By extending it again I could be fishing in seconds. Only the absence of shade dampened my enthusiasm for fishing the prolific waters of the Sea of Cortez. In the mid-day heat, when I was less inclined to walk, I was also less inclined to fish, except standing chest deep in the sea wearing my wide-brimmed hat.

The afternoon seemed to drag on forever. Grunting and wheezing, with water slopping and kettle banging, I walked head down not seeing much beyond my boots. The glare was intense. With sweat running into my eyes, I crested a sand ridge and found myself almost stepping on a shapely young lady sunbathing topless. Executing a shocked side-step, I blurted out an embarrassed 'hello' and received an understandably cool reception from her and her mostly male companions. Wanting nothing more than to give them back their privacy, I hurried on.

Unfortunately, after fifty yards, I came up against the mouth of a large lagoon. The channel was too deep to cross. All I could do was drop the pack and wait for the tide to fall. I might as well have been on a different planet from the people behind me. My presence was ignored and resented. I sensed it through every overworked sweat pore in my none too thick skin. That awful sense of loneliness and self-doubt descended again. I hadn't fully shaken it off since San Felipe. Paradoxically, it is so often people who make you feel lonely.

The shock image of that curvaceous, half-naked bronzed body kept flashing in my mind. Six or nine months seemed a long time to be alone. The more I thought about it the more depressed I became. Giving up the pleasures of the world is never easy.

When the tide at last allowed, I got under way again. 'Just one week,' I reminded myself, 'day by day for just one week.'

An hour later I met a young San Diego couple camped near the beach. It was a joy to talk to them. I asked if I could buy some food. They wouldn't sell anything but insisted on giving me bread, carrots, apples and an avocado. I was touched and grateful that I didn't have to spend the evening looking for and pounding pulpo. Apparently they had paid a young Mexican boy $2 for the privilege of camping there. I couldn't afford $2 a night so I went off in search of a place where I wouldn't be disturbed.

Just before dark, not far from what looked like a fishcamp, I secreted myself in the dunes feeling sure no one would find me. With the dying breeze, a tangible peace seemed to descend on the twilight world. Sitting in my tent munching on a delicious avocado sandwich, I watched flights of pelicans executing their clumsy but effective dives. After each splash they would pop up, throw their heads back and swallow the catch. Swallowing a piece of sandwich, I felt a twinge of sympathy for the poor sardines on which the pelican dined so well. One second swimming freely with their buddies, the next . . . gulp! . . . The sea drains away, then they go sliding down a dark tunnel into a vat of digestive acid. Gasping for oxygen, with eyes stinging in the blackness, they wriggle out their final frantic minutes. As they do so, the pelican is already taking off looking for another victim.

By such thoughts I was probably building up a pelican prejudice in case I had to eat one. Judging by the amount of chewed pelican bones and feathers on the beach, the coyotes found them palatable enough.

Next morning a heavy dew had soaked the inside of the tent. I began day three mopping it up with the small sponge brought for the purpose. This added another cup of water to my supply.

A little further down the coast there was another lagoon. This one looked huge, a vast depression of marsh and salt flat, stretching away to a distant border of dry desert. I ventured down to inspect the channel separating me from a line of dunes on the other side. It was low tide and the water still too deep to cross. Most of the lagoon had drained, leaving courses of black mud between blocks of salt-covered solidity. It seemed a good idea to follow the main channel into the lagoon until I was able to cross over to the dunes and continue down the beach.

That crossing point always seemed to be just ahead. Yards became miles, minutes became hours and my boots became caked with mud. Several times I played with the idea of retracing my steps, then making my way around the edge of the lagoon, but the thought of repeating the morning's suffering only to end up back where I started was too much. I had to go on.

The tide was rising fast behind me, and the torrid air was pregnant with the sensation of a trap about to spring. A million-strong army of fiddler crabs intensified my fears. They were everywhere, crossing the mud at leisure, comical kings of the morass, continually beckoning me on with their enlarged pincer arms. Yet always around me there was a ten-foot clearing. As I moved towards those in front, they would back away. The ones behind would then close the gap. I was getting quite affectionate towards them till I realized that these lovely little crabs might be beckoning me to my doom. They would certainly make short work of my carcass if I perished in that slimy morass.

At last I came to a place where the channel of water was no more than a foot wide, and the black mud a band of only thirty feet. Running across were a few islands of tufty vegetation. The almost palpable proximity of the dry sand of the dunes on the other side perhaps made it more tempting than it should have been. Carrying pack and water, I ran on to the mud with visions of island-hopping to safety but instead sank as if stepping into the shallow end of a swimming pool. Quicksand! I was up to my waist. I dropped the water containers, threw my pack back towards the solid ground, sinking even more as I did so, then tried to swivel round to climb out over it. Falling backwards instead, my arms shot deep into the mud. I thought I was going under. Panic and horror took over. Somehow I twisted round to embrace the pack. I pulled with all my might to extricate the leg less trapped, but it refused to move. With pounding heart, clenched teeth and locked muscles, I clung desperately to the sinking pack. Just as I thought I was losing the trial of strength, one leg slurped free of the mud, then the other. Scrambling over the pack, I rolled exhausted, shaking and nauseated on to the relative solidity of the salt flat.

The pack! The water! I sprang back to life. Trapped there without water and survival equipment . . . the danger was far from over. Digging my fingers deep into the clay beneath the sheen of salt on the bank, I sent my reluctant body sliding over the mud till I managed to slip a foot beneath one of the straps of the backpack. I pulled for all I was worth. My fingers slipped, leaving deep brown 'claw' marks on the ground, but the pack was also moving. Caked in mud I lifted it gratefully out then used my fishing rod to retrieve the water bag and canteen. The canteen came in easily but I had to be extremely careful not to puncture the heavy plastic bag. Getting a hook under the wooden handle, I half-lifted, half-dragged it in to reach.

With everything safely gathered, my first instinct was headlong flight from the lagoon, but I forced myself to sit down and think as I scraped the mud from myself and my equipment. The deep holes in the ooze before me were slowly filling with water. To go all the way back through a rapidly filling swamp was probably inviting disaster. I had to try crossing again.

Scouting ahead, I found a place where the black mud barrier was narrower and the tufts of vegetation more numerous. Inside I was screaming, 'Are you bloody crazy?' as I tentatively tested the mud. It felt a little firmer. I made up my mind to go over fast and light. The pack might have saved me, but it had also dragged me down.

Taking a little run up, I dashed on to the mire. The sinking sensation was sickening, but I managed to reach the first patch of grass, then the second. Two more and I was over. My feet were firmly planted on warm golden sand. Scaling the dunes, it was good to feel a cool sea breeze caress my face as I surveyed a beach stretching as far as I could see.

I went back for my equipment. Opting to take the water first and the pack second, I had to cross the quagmire four more times. The final time I turned and called back to the crabs, 'better luck next time!' They were still beckoning me to return as I stood on top of the dunes and surveyed everything around. My jubilation passed. The swamp also stretched to the distant horizon. If this was just an 'island' separating the sea from the swamp, I'd be trapped with no way forward or back. The lagoon would be my only option. Perhaps the crabs knew something I didn't.

Although badly wanting to rest, swim and wash the muck from my body and clothes, I had to find out what was ahead. After a mile, the dunes dropped to a sandbank and what was left of the island tapered to a distant point. Before me was a channel into the lagoon much larger than the one behind; it was wide and deep and the current was vicious. I was indeed trapped on a desert island. The tide was still rising and visibly spreading along the sandbar.

Realizing there wasn't much I could do till the tide fell, I retreated a hundred yards to enjoy a good splash around in the surf. I kept my clothes on to wash them as well, then used my wet shirt to remove the grey-black mud from my backpack which was already looking old and abused.

The midday sun was intense. There was no shade. After putting on clean clothes, I covered all exposed parts of my body with factor 10 sunscreen. Over my hands, face and knees, freckles appeared as islands of protection in a fiery red sea. But the hypo-allergenic sunscreen was living up to its promise; in spite of the fierce ultra-violet assault, I'd experienced no real sensitivity or irritation.

My food stock was down to cornflakes and there wasn't much to forage on my little island, yet there was plenty of wood and kindling for a fire. So, as the high tide was supposedly the time to fish, I cast a lure into the wind and slowly retrieved each cast until – bang! After a thrilling little fight I dragged a 4lb corbina on to the beach.

Wanting to make my first fish meal of the trip one to remember, I built a fire on the sand, filled my frying pan with seawater, dropped in two sizeable fillets of fresh fish and allowed my mouth to water at the prospect of a wholesome meal. A few minutes later I removed the cooked fish, put the kettle on to boil, picked up my fork and swivelled around to get at the tasty looking layers of protein. Like a golf club in a bunker my foot sent a shower of sand over my lunch reducing a good meal to a few gritty mouthfuls. I had learned one of the great lessons of beach cooking – keep your feet still.

I made a better job of preparing my cup of tea, and had to chuckle as I pictured an Englishman clutching his cuppa on a rapidly disappearing desert island. The tide was still rising. I was sandwiched between the shark-filled Sea of Cortez and a treacherous lagoon. Facing the prospect of being totally submerged, I finished the tea, gathered together all my belongings and retreated even further towards the dunes. Horrified, I discovered that the sea had broken in behind me. Powerful waves were surging over unwadably deep water into the lagoon. There was no choice. The sandbar would have to be my home till the tide fell or I was washed away. I placed my equipment in the centre of the fifteen-yard wide strip of sand and looked around for something to do apart from worry.

A hundred birds had taken up residence at the other end of my island. Wondering how close they would let me come, I edged towards them, slingshot in hand. Hours of practice had left me confident I could down any bird less than thirty yards away.

With a handful of stones, I moved closer and closer. Nervous wings were spread, then relaxed, then spread again. All kind of unlikely birds had congregated together: pelicans, vultures, gulls and terns. A pelican took off and suddenly the air was full of birds. Some flew directly overhead. They were tempting targets. I raised the slingshot, pulled back the elastic and fired the empty pouch. I wasn't that hungry yet.

When at last the tide turned, it fell rapidly. The great body of lagoon water swept back into the ocean. I stood and watched, and willed it down. It needed to fall dramatically, and over the next couple of hours that's exactly what it did. The mighty river of water became a delta-like maze of sandbars and streams.

An hour from sunset I guessed the tide was as low as it would ever be. With my cameras, tape-recorder and passport wrapped inside plastic bags and buried deep inside the backpack, I made my move. Again I decided to split the load and make two journeys – one with the pack and one with the water and boots. Carrying the heavy pack my bare feet seemed to be sucked deep down into the sand. The water rose to my waist. Just when I needed to be steady, my legs started trembling. With tired arms and aching back I passed through the deepest point and edged up the other side. At last I was over. Dropping the pack a little harder than I intended, I fell to my knees laughing. The sense of euphoria continued as I dried my feet and replaced my socks and boots. The sunset and the blue Sea of Cortez looked stunningly beautiful. I felt as if I had crossed much more than just a barrier of water.

Chapter 7

Weathering the storm

As I looked for a campsite I noticed there were some nicely constructed tourist houses with people outside. Curious, needing water, and wanting to know about any more lagoons, I walked towards them, shouting hello in my finest English accent.

The warm reception given me by Carol and Dick Anderson, and their son Steve, turned my good mood into something even better. We were soon laughing, joking and rabbiting away. A cold beer helped. After relating my plans and adventures, they invited me to make camp and join them for dinner. As darkness descended, I erected the tent, put away my pack, tidied up a little, then rejoined my hospitable hosts.

In an hour I felt as if I'd known the Andersons all my life. Dick was the epitome of the armchair adventurer, totally fascinated by my project, but as he pulled the ring on another can of beer, he was quick to point out, 'Like most people I need my security and comfort. I couldn't do what you're doing.' Steve chipped in with a good-natured, 'You couldn't do without your beer.'

They invited me to hang out there for a few days, but I knew I had to push on. It wasn't playing around and drinking someone else's beer that had put me on such a high. It was the deeper and more lasting satisfaction of knowing I had pushed myself to the limit in attempting something extraordinary, and that I had survived the first onslaughts of fear, self-doubt and pain.

I thanked them sincerely, feeling that our evening together had been a turning point. Less afraid now of my feelings, I made my way out to the tent, managing to carpet the inside of it with sand as I fell in clumsily and surrendered to the sleep of the just, or more accurately the just pleasantly drunk.

Next morning, day four, we took up where we left off, sharing a protracted breakfast of pancakes, orange juice, hot chocolate, and beer. They took some photographs to send to my parents along with a letter I'd hastily put together. A week without hearing from me, and my mother would be seeing my bones bleaching in the sun.

It wasn't easy leaving that haven of kindness, especially weighed down with a full stomach, a full load of water and a pack full of beer, fruit juice, sweets, apples and oranges. Making my way along the edge of the lake-calm water, all I could think about was eating and drinking as much as possible to lighten the load. It must have weighed 80 lbs or 85 lbs.

I passed several deserted fishcamps, and the usual assortment of dead pelicans, dolphins and sea-lions, before taking my lunch break squeezed into a shady crevice along a low line of compacted sand cliffs. It wasn't comfortable, but better than being out in the sun.

Emerging after an hour of eating and drinking, it was good to feel a gentle on-shore breeze. The wind seemed to follow a pattern. Calm in the morning, it would pick up as the day warmed, then drop away in the evening. Progress that afternoon was slow and painful but I wasn't discouraged. A few casts into the afternoon's rising tide soon had me doing battle with a 10lb bass. He fought magnificently. As I had plenty of food, I gently removed the hook and returned him to the sea.

The desert beyond the beach was barren. Just a few tall cacti and thorny bushes broke the distant mountain skyline. The stark reds and yellows were still beautifully unreal to an eye accustomed to the greys and greens of England.

I spotted a Mexican fisherman attending to a boat ahead. Feeling aggressively sociable and determined to talk to a native, I quickened my pace. I walked up smiling and bade him 'Buenas tardes' and then asked if he spoke English. He didn't, so I felt better about my poor Spanish. We chatted for ten minutes, my first real Spanish conversation, and he was very helpful and friendly. I hoped all the fishermen would be like him.

Half a mile later, keeping an eye open for a place to camp, the calming waters by the beach erupted as a black shape torpedoed through the water sending fish scattering in all directions. Soon there was another, then another. A school of dolphins were leaping, chasing and playing as they went about their joyful slaughter. Pelicans and other birds arrived to watch the show. I stood mesmerized, camera clicking, trying to resist the absurd urge to swim out and join in. It was a moment to savour, and only the necessity of finding a campsite forced me to leave.

As the day drew to a close a wave of satisfaction washed through me. 'Almost finished,' I told myself. My consciousness had accepted its one day at a time command. Why worry about tomorrow? Soon I will be making camp, content to rest, eat and imbibe the sights of the Sea of Cortez.

Once again, I could see houses ahead. For the second evening I surprised a group of tourists on the beach, and again I was enthusiastically outlining my plans and adventures to a fascinating audience which this time consisted of a couple from New Zealand and two lovely ladies from California. I was beginning to realize that if you want to be the centre of attention think big! Who cares if you're hiking thirty miles? If you're hiking 3,000 miles eyes light up. Yet what is 3,000 but 30 times 100? The trick is to channel all your time and energy into one direction. That is what gets results and makes you interesting.

The party were all staying at the little beach house of Judy McAdam from Los Angeles. She invited me to pitch my tent, grab a shower and stay for dinner. My mouth watered at the prospect of barbecued chicken, salad and wine. The wine seemed superfluous. I was already drunk with the knowledge that I was growing physically and mentally stronger and beginning to love every minute of the journey. Judy proved to be a goldmine of information about Baja. I listened with admiration to some of her incredible adventures. The tales deserved a wider audience than our little gathering.

Wined and dined and warmed by the conviviality, I felt positively glowing as I took my leave to retire to the tent. Outside, the air was still and warm. The sea contentedly lapped the shore. The attenuated moon softened the explosion of stars across the desert sky. A sense of peace and belonging came over me as I stretched out inside the tent. I had good reason now to be optimistic. The pack would seem lighter as I got stronger. I was healthy. My feet were free of blisters. Already I was averaging ten miles a day. The sunscreen was doing its job. All the time I was learning and adapting. I half-unzipped the tent door to take a final look at the sky. I stared into eternity, not the vacuous stare of a few short nights ago, rather my mind was full of thoughts and questions I hadn't known since I was a child.

I guess I was seven or eight, sitting on a brick wall with my mates, taking a break from mischief, gazing up in wonder at an all-too-rare cloudless night. 'Where does it end?' we debated. Agreeing it must go on and on for ever, the thought disturbed me. How can it just go on and on? I desperately wanted it to end somewhere. Maybe it ends against a brick wall – everything in our neighbourhood ended in brick walls. Then the brick wall had to go on forever!

As adults we learn not to waste time with futile questions. There on that beach, staring at the stars, I was a child once more. Nothing was beyond question. Perhaps I'd been born again at San Felipe. If so, it wasn't an easy birth, and now I was growing up and wondering and seeing things anew with a child-like freshness. I certainly had a child-like trust and faith in what lay ahead. To the accompaniment of a distant band of coyotes irreverently breaking the silence, I found myself singing out one possible, and just then, very meaningful answer to the question of forever:

> Oh Lord my God, when I in awesome wonder
> Consider all the worlds thy hand has made.
> I see the stars. I hear the roaring thunder.
> Thy power throughout the universe displayed.
> Then sings my soul, my saviour God to thee.
> How great thou art, how great thou art.

Day five began with the sounds of enthusiastic early risers taking advantage of the low tide to search beneath the rocks. Fearful of pulpos, I declined to join in the fun, preferring to tackle a breakfast of coffee and banana sandwiches.

As I munched away, crabs, clams, disgusting looking slugs and other such creatures were placed on the table before me. No doubt hunger would make them appear more appetising. When Judy took the trouble to show me how to dispatch and prepare a crab, all I could think about was the poor thing struggling to get out of a pot of boiling water.

I picked up lots of useful advice and information that morning. 'Be careful when the wind blasts off the desert,' said Judy. 'It can blow so hard it will hurt. You'll literally get sand blasted.' As I had only experienced the pleasant and predictable afternoon sea breeze, I found it hard to imagine.

After another beautiful lukewarm shower, I exchanged addresses with Judy and once again took off into the unknown. The day was hot and still. The breeze was late. Sweat flowed freely.

The nature of the coastline changed, less sand and more pebbles and rocks. Springing from boulder to boulder, my foot slipped and I came crashing to the ground. After more falls, cuts and bruises, I started learning fast. Getting it right 99 times out of 100 wasn't good enough. One careless step could result in a broken arm or leg. Concentration was the key. Hour after hour, I studiously avoided wet, slimy and angled rocks.

Something else had changed. When the breeze at last picked up it came warm off the desert not cool off the sea. Huge black clouds towered above the mountains. Suddenly, with no more warning than a few fitful dust devils, I was struck by a storm blast of wind. The calm blue sea was almost immediately transformed into a grey-black frothy mass of agitation.

Sand flew in horizontal sheets. The particles stung my sunburned legs. So this is what Judy meant! I thought of putting on a pair of jeans but did not dare open my pack for fear of having everything torn from my grasp and blown out to sea. Checking that everything was secure, I carried on leaning sideways into the wind, squinting in case my contact lenses were ripped from my eyes.

Deafened by the wind, blinded by the sand and stunned by the shock of it all, I battled on for another hour until I saw just above the beach a small cliff-like ridge of rock. It looked dark and forbidding but shelter from the wind was my first consideration. The ground was hard and stony. The gale whipped and funnelled along the rock face. Not wanting to risk erecting my tent, I huddled over the pack praying it wouldn't rain.

As it grew dark, I became increasingly wary about rattlesnakes and scorpions. Wind or no wind, I had to get inside the tent. After a dozen unsuccessful attempts to peg it out, I just threw my pack inside, crawled in and zipped it up. The borders of my cold, shadowy world flapped vigorously around me. All I could do was wait.

As dramatically as it had started, the gale died. I crawled out to peg the tent up properly. In the hushed stillness my home appeared luxurious compared to the 'body-bag' I'd just vacated. With the comfort of a foam pad and a sleeping bag beneath me, I laid awake tense and thoughtful. Nothing interested me on the radio. Slipping the machete under my 'pillow' I drifted into an uneasy sleep, bringing that fifth day to a welcome end.

Next morning, it was a different world. The sky, the sea and even the rocks seemed friendly. With the prospect of company that night in Puertecitos, I wasted no time in packing and getting underway. After an hour I was exhausted. I had no energy to pick myself up, never mind the pack! Although as light as it had ever been it seemed unbearably heavy. Not sure if I was ill or just plain spent, I forced myself on. By mid-afternoon I was rounding every point and cresting every hill vainly asking, 'Where is Puertecitos?' Anger at the fact that it maliciously seemed to be further away than it should be was the only thing that kept me going.

At last, just when I wondered if I'd ever make it at all, I reached a string of fishcamps which I correctly surmised were outposts of the town. Then, a mile from Puertecitos, I came across a tiny beachside bar and restaurant. Reckoning I deserved a beer, I removed my pack and splashed out. A few moments later I was joined by an inquisitive American couple. They were so amazed that I'd walked from San Felipe they pulled out a bottle of tequila to help celebrate. Compared to what lay ahead, I hadn't put that many miles behind me – a mere fifty or so – but, always willing to celebrate, I picked up a shell from the beach, rinsed out the sand, poured myself a tot, toasted the spirit of adventure, and then unceremoniously proceeded to get blind, blotto drunk! (Which didn't take long on an empty stomach.)

I thought it wise, though, to maintain sufficient sobriety to wobble that last mile into town. I was too drunk and exhausted to take it all in. A small plane circled overhead, then landed on a runway surrounded by shacks. In between bidding passing Mexicans 'Buenas tardes', I found myself mumbling a somewhat mixed up version of the Star Spangled Banner, an expression of gratitude to those Americans who had befriended a fellow traveller in a strange land far from home. By the time I got to 'the land of the free and the home of the brave', I found myself on a beach in a bay looking south to the distant mountains and islands down the coast.

Somehow I got talking to a father and his two grown sons from El Centro, California. They invited me to camp in front of their house and join them later for dinner.

I lapsed into another 'Oh, say, can you see . . .' as I made a comical attempt to pitch the tent. With everything safely inside, I resisted the urge to crawl in and go to sleep. I'd be out for hours. Instead I went in search of the local store. Ironically, I had to eat something to sober up for dinner.

The only store in town was a modest little thing attached to a restaurant on the beach. Just the basics were on offer. The señorita behind the counter was a delight to talk to. She spoke excellent English. Being half pickled, I fell instantly in love with her. Incredulous at my plans, she asked, 'Are you not afraid?' 'Of what?' I boldly retorted. I wished I hadn't asked as she went through a list of horrors that added coyotes, centipedes, mountain lions and tarantulas to the list I had compiled back in England. She was convinced, and half-convinced me, that just south of Puertecitos a whole army of terrors was lying in ambush.

My hosts had spent the day fishing and gathering butter clams, and we were about to enjoy the fruits of their labour. The fried fish was delicious, much better than fish boiled in seawater and sprinkled with sand! I carefully noted the clam procedure: boil them, eat only those that open, fork them out, dip them in butter. I made a mental note to get some butter from the store tomorrow.

Their beach house was a real fishermen's den, decorated with rods and tackle and hundreds of photographs of friends and prizes. It was beautifully functional, a no-nonsense man's home from home. The photographs revealed how the father had watched his sons grow on a score of visits. From picture to picture, the boys got bigger and so did the fish proudly held for the camera.

The father and one of the sons seemed very jolly and talkative. The other was quieter and appeared uninterested. I had eaten well, perhaps too well in trying to combat the effects of the alcohol. Nursing my bulging belly, I watched the quiet son leave his seat, turn pale green, put a hand to his mouth and kick a couple of chairs aside in an effort to get outside. We all looked at each other. The father did his best to assure me that there was nothing wrong with the fish or the clams. His son had been unwell for several days.

The unfortunate young man came back smiling apologetically. After a respectable interval, I thanked my hosts for their excellent dinner and took off into the night fearful that I might also be sick. I felt better inside the tent. The following day would be number seven, the day of decision! It would also be Sunday and fittingly enough a day of rest.

It was a rest day of sorts, but already clothes needed washing and repairing, knives had to be sharpened, and boots cleaned and polished. There were letters to write and a journal to bring up to date. Otherwise it was good to rest in the shade and allow overworked nerves and muscles to relax.

After my chores I got talking to a young Mexican fisherman. He spoke excellent English, claiming that his grandfather came from England. From him I learned that the mysterious pulpo was just an octopus. I asked, would a rattlesnake bite necessarily kill you? 'Man, the pain would kill you,' was his encouraging reply. Everyone seemed so damned cheerful in that town. I returned to the store to pick up more dire warnings and a few provisions, including the butter.

After dark the El Centro trio invited me to join them on a drive over to the famous Puertecitos 'hot springs'. The falling tide leaves a series of rock pools which rapidly warm up. When one gets too hot you move to another.

It was the perfect way to dissolve the aches and pains of that first week. My companions tired of it long before I did. I was quite content to lie there alone counting the shooting stars and satellites. The gentle rush of the surf was pleasantly hypnotic.

The week I had promised to endure was up. Would I be going on? Of course. I had come a long way in seven days. My morale was up there with the stars. Self-doubt and anxiety seemed hard to imagine. If my spirits needed a bigger boost, a bunch of California firemen dropped in with their infectious laughter and sense of fun. Soon everything was a joke.

Reluctantly I climbed out of the warm water and walked back to the tent. On my bedroom wall in England there was an inspirational poster which showed a sailing ship on a wide ocean. The caption read: A SHIP IS SAFE IN HARBOUR BUT THAT IS NOT WHAT SHIPS ARE FOR. After too many years of bobbing timidly at anchor, I had at last set sail. The first storm had been weathered. Having come through, my confidence had grown accordingly. Assured that adventure, exhilaration and discovery lay ahead, I could hardly wait for tomorrow.

Chapter 8

Crusties

Putting in my contact lenses was the first task of the day. With sand carpeting the inside of the tent and clinging to every part of my body, I had to lick my fingers clean before handling the delicate hard plastic discs.

Unzipping the door facing south – just enough to get my head out – I stared beyond the beach and the bay to the uncertainty beyond. Through the settling blur, islands and mountains drifted into focus.

The points of the bay faced out defensively like the horns of a bull. There was something different and threatening about the land 'out there'. Everyone seemed to sense it. The girl in the store had warned me. So had Erle Stanley Gardner in his book *Hunting the Desert Whale*:

> South of Puertecitos civilization comes to an abrupt halt. You don't go below Puertecitos unless you have a four-wheel drive automobile, ample stores of petrol and drinking water, and know what you're doing – that is, you *may* go but you may not come back.

But I wasn't thinking in terms of automobiles, or ample stores. My thoughts revolved around self-sufficiency and being able to survive off the sea and the desert. I knew what I was doing, I hoped!

Gardner's book was one of only three I had found on Baja while preparing back in England. I came across it by chance while browsing in a second-hand bookshop. Through constant re-reading, whole passages had taken on an almost biblical familiarity.

There is a road running south from Puertecitos, an extremely bad road. It more or less follows the coast down to Punta Bufeo, where the comforts of Larry's house waited, and Alphonsinas resort, where I could count on the reliable advice of Ed Wills. Erle Stanley Gardner had given me some idea what it would be like:

> For a distance of twenty miles or so the road goes up and down in short pitches. These grades are not over a few hundred feet in height, but they *are* steep. And these steep pitches are very, very rough in places . . . Occasionally, one will see the ruins of a loaded truck down at the bottom of the canyon . . . and a wooden cross indicating that the road had taken its grim toll.

I finished breakfast, packed away my gear, took down the tent, shook it free of sand, slid my knife on to my belt, shouldered the pack, picked up three gallons of water and walked proudly out of Puertecitos.

In spite of the siren call of the coast, the road was an adventure in itself. I followed it with delight as Gardner's descriptions and anecdotes came to mind. I was like a pilgrim in the Holy Land marvelling at sights long dreamt about.

To my left the deep blue Gulf stretched to mainland Mexico. There was hardly a cloud in the sky. The desert was sunbaked brown desolation. The scanty vegetation seemed more dead than alive as if shrinking into itself and into the ground in an effort to avoid the fierce sun.

There was nowhere for me to shrink. What I wore – a long-sleeved white shirt, long white socks, faded blue denim shorts and the navy blue leather hat – was a compromise between keeping cool and keeping covered. The floppy hat was too heavy and the colour was wrong. Before long sweat was trickling down my face sending my sunglasses sliding annoyingly down my nose. With both hands carrying water it was tiresome and awkward constantly sliding them back up.

Away from town, less concerned about looking ridiculous, I pulled out the tape recorder and slung it around my neck. If I step on a rattlesnake, I thought, I may as well record my final utterances for posterity. And there were other things to record, impressions of space, stillness, freedom and excitement, the sight of inquisitive hummingbirds and graceful pelicans, the sound of my heavy breathing and the lonely crunch, crunch, crunch of boots on gravel.

The road ran down to an inviting patch of beach. Wriggling out from beneath the load, I removed my boots and socks to splash around in the water. Wading through rock pools, turning over boulders and digging beneath the sand and gravel, I kept a careful eye open for whatever looked edible. Only one thing spoilt my fun. There was no escaping the sun. The tops of my feet were soon burning. In spite of continuous applications of sunscreen, my hands, legs, face and neck felt tight and tender. I made a depressing calculation. At this rate of consumption, I had less than a month's supply left. What would happen then?

A piece of wood caught my eye. A sturdy six-foot long paddle had been washed up on to the rocks. A walking stick? I could cut off the blade and fashion a V-shaped groove where I did so – I'd then have a walking stick capable of pinning down rattlesnakes. So I carried on walking with the paddle in my left hand and a plastic bag with two and a half gallons of water in my right. The crunch, crunch of my boots became interspersed with the occasional tap of the 'walking stick'.

A mile down the road, I heard a motor. An aeroplane? No, too much stop and go. A rising cloud of dust raced towards me. A motorcyclist! I stood leaning on the paddle as he sped by. Even beneath helmet and visor I couldn't mistake the look of astonishment and the involuntary smile. Other equally amused motorcyclists flashed by in blurs of bold colour. It must have been a race.

Another surprise lay in store. I bumped into my firemen friends of the previous night. With both of their off-road vehicles having blown a tyre, they had made camp by a little beach and resolved not to venture any further from Puertecitos. Even so, they remained in infectiously good spirits. The sight of me and my paddle probably helped enormously.

The laughing and joking continued while I posed for photographs and did my feeble best to turn down an invitation to join them for lunch. Salami sandwiches and cans of cold beer were slapped into my hands as I protested that I should be eating sea slugs and seaweed. No sooner did I finish one thing than something else miraculously appeared. When I was too stuffed to eat more, my hosts proceeded to fill my backpack with all kinds of other goodies.

'Do you need any water?'

'Well, er . . . I'm not sure I can carry any more.'

'No matter, here's a couple of cans of beer. If it gets too heavy, drink it.'

This taste of the good life wasn't doing my pioneering spirit any good, so I deflected the conversation to what lay ahead. Out came the books and the maps. Spreading them over the bonnet of one of the cars, we pointed, debated and gesticulated like generals at the front. Battle plans confirmed, it was time to get into action. I thanked everyone for their generosity. As a parting gesture I was given a Stanton Fire Department cap.

As the good-natured banter gave way to the familiar sounds of the road, the day grew distinctly more torrid. At every halt I had to force myself to get up again. No longer the general, I was now the poor bloody footslogger and the cajoling and bullying sergeant. All I wanted to do was stop, make camp and take it easy, but the sergeant did his job well, keeping up spirits and not tolerating feeble excuses. To get into top shape I had to push myself hard. Only when the sun dropped behind the bare red mountains did I allow myself to look for a place to spend the night.

Steering my leaden steps towards the shore, I followed a sunken sandy wash across the boulder-strewn desert. It ended against a bank of stones behind which was the sea. The site was ideal – flat, soft and sheltered on three sides.

The descending silence accentuated the wilderness 'feel' of the place. My senses were on full alert as I snapped the poles together and pegged out the tent. The road, still visible behind, brought little comfort. It seemed safer not to advertise my presence. I opted to do without a fire.

Tent up and everything, except the paddle, stashed inside, I scrambled up the wall of stones to scan the coast ahead. It rose and fell so steeply that it was hard to imagine what course the road took. The eastern horizon was a beautiful blend of pastel pink, flesh and purple. The colours were even more subtle reflected in the gently rippling sea. In contrast, the broad beach had been thrown up into dark frozen waves of stone.

Feeling as spent as the fading light and breeze, I made my cautious way back over the pebbles and driftwood, then clambered down to my sheltered campsite.

Opening the tent, I noticed movement on the sand. Ants! Bloody big red ants! They were everywhere. I must have disturbed a nest. I quickly closed the tent again and backed away, not daring to stand still.

Should I move the tent? No, they would probably end up all over me and the equipment. No point trying to kill them all.

Unable to think of any better course of action, I untied my boot laces, half unzipped the tent door, plonked my rear end inside, kicked my boots together to remove ants and sand, then swivelled inside as I pulled off the boots and zipped up the door. The zip closed perfectly. Unless the ants ate their way in, I should be safe. A quick flashlight inspection revealed just one intruder who was summarily dealt with.

I had learned about desert ants on my first trip to Baja. Sleeping out one night. I fashioned a pillow of clothes around a small water bottle filled with Coca-Cola. Unfortunately the cap leaked. The sugary treat seeped out on to my clothes, hands and face. I woke spitting and snorting coke-crazed ants of every size and colour. After swatting and scratching furiously, I spent the rest of the night in extreme misery. The bites burned fiercely and it took most of the following day to shake all the ants from my clothes and possessions.

It was time to make myself as comfortable as I could. I laid out the foam pad and sleeping bag, slipped my machete beneath the bundle of clothes serving as my pillow, and placed the torch beside it. Thanks to the Stanton Fire Department I enjoyed a sumptuous and protracted dinner. I threw the cans and packages as far from the tent as possible. The ants were still there but paid no particular attention to me or the tent.

The night sky was as magical as ever. Every night it seemed blacker and the stars brighter. A shooting star flashed across the sky. There was an indefinable presence in the blackness, something one senses in those quiet moments when nothing stands between you and your God. In my vast desert cathedral my breathing seemed to resonate across eternity.

Suddenly, I was down to earth again. Something was coming straight towards me down the wash. I held my breath. My head locked still. My eyes were straining into the blackness, and my heart thumped audibly against my chest as I felt for the flashlight. A grey shadow drifted towards me, passing just a few feet from the tent. I didn't need the torch to see it was a coyote. He must have known I was there. Even when movement betrayed me he just shot me a disdainful glance, then dislodged a few pebbles as he trotted up to the beach. Like the shooting star, he was gone, but his image remained.

Disturbed by his boldness, I slipped back into the cocoon-like cosiness of my sleeping bag. How would I deal with a determined coyote attack, a pack of them assailing me in the open, or savagely ripping their way into the tent? More conceivably, I imagined having to fend off a crazed, possibly rabid individual.

I felt beneath my pillow for the machete. It had to be handy at all times. At night, inside the tent, inside my sleeping bag, machete in hand, I'd be far from easy canine fodder. During the day the machete was rolled up inside the sleeping bag, but in a way that made it instantly accessible. Thinking of my other means of defence, my insecurity worked itself into a frenzy of fear and hatred, as I kicked, chopped, stabbed, stoned and bludgeoned my way over a mountain of coyote flesh. All the while the instigator of such thoughts was no doubt getting on with the very practical business of stalking star-gazing pelicans.

I put on my headphones and spun the radio dial, picking up stations from California, Oklahoma and Texas. The news was the same depressing round of war, disaster and man's inhumanity to man.

Next morning, however, found me in adventurous mood. I had plenty of food and water and 'civilization' wasn't, as yet, too far away. It was a good time to explore the possibilities of my new world.

Instead of walking back up the sandy wash to the road, I left 'campo coyote' and struck out across the desert. Climbing up and down and leaping from boulder to boulder I did my best not to spill too much blood on the sharp and tearing vegetation. Every scrape of boot or pack pulled taut my strained nerves. My fear of snakes intensified. Shouting like a demented drover, I hoped to scare every rattlesnake from my path, but as snakes are 'deaf' to everything except ground vibrations, all my ya-hoos and wo-hos probably did little except make me feel better.

On top of a bare rocky hill I placed my pack against a large boulder and allowed the magnificent view to have its soothing effect. Not a cloud hung in the sky. A tentative breeze brought comfort and gently stirred little patches of ocean. From my map I read off the names of the islands ahead: El Huerfanito – the little orphan – stood alone and dramatically white; beyond it, the intriguingly named Dead Man's Island sat mysteriously on the horizon. It was one of the classic views of Baja.

Glad to be back on the road, I noted that things had changed little since Erle Stanley Gardner's visits. Battered relics of cars and trucks still littered the bottoms of the most precipitous descents. The road got progressively worse. In places it was no more than a broken path of naked rock. I wouldn't have driven a tank along it. On both sides, tall ocotillo bushes burst up like exploding shells. Spined, gnarled and seemingly leafless, they were little more than a collection of sticks, offering no protection from the sun or wind. An air of barren solitude hung over everything.

Ahead, a massive ridge ran down to the sea. Its truncated end fell steeply into the water. With no passage along the coast the road turned sharply inland and rose steeply. I didn't fancy the prospect of climbing fully laden in the worst of the afternoon heat. It was time to return to the water's edge.

The rewards were immediate – shade, breeze, exhilaration and uncertainty. Little challenges and triumphs punctuated my struggle. Could I round that point, scramble over those rocks, wade under that cliff? The need to know drove me on.

A mass of little armour-plated crustaceans was in full flight before me. Like huge woodlice or miniscule armadillos these alert and highly-strung creatures covered the seaweed on which they fed. On my approach they scattered in audible confusion. Falling over themselves in sheer panic they either flowed in a lemming-like mass into the sea or disappeared beneath rocks and rotting seaweed. The scene was so comical as each desperately sought his own salvation, I had to wonder if God sometimes looked down on us in the same pitying light.

There was something endearingly attractive about their antics. You couldn't help but like them. Up and down they went over the rocks like a comic Grand National. Nicknaming them 'crusties', I regarded them as my friends and went to great lengths not to tread on them.

When I stopped to rest they would come cautiously back. Hardly daring to breathe, I'd see a pair of waving antennae emerging from behind a rock. That would be followed by a very suspicious 'crusty'. He'd dash forward then stop, look around, then dash a little more. When he relaxed again he'd be back merrily munching on his seaweed. I could almost hear him humming, dum de dum, de dum, de dum. Then when I moved,

'Arrgh!' his eyes would pop from his little crusty head, and he'd be gone as fast as his dozens of little legs could carry him. Apart from the occasional slurp or glug where the sea lapped the rocks, only my laughter broke the silence.

Hiss! A new sound had me shooting to my feet. Dolphins! A school of them right off the rocks. They were closely huddled together making their unhurried way south. More than one black tail deliberately splashed down on to the surface. It was easy to believe that they had spotted me and were saying hello.

All afternoon I pushed my weary limbs to their limit. Sandwiched between the sea and the cliffs I had only two choices, to go forward or to go back. I dreaded the thought of having to retrace my steps. So, racing the tide and the approaching darkness, my whole being was charged with one task, to get out from under those cliffs.

Falls were becoming too frequent. After each potentially bone-snapping crash, I angrily turned on myself. 'Not good enough, concentrate, concentrate.' Then underway again, I'd be thinking, 'Don't tread on that seaweed; that rock is too angled; that one too smooth; not that little one, it'll roll; the gap's too wide, don't over-reach; land on the centre, not on the edge.' Crash! Fuck it! Once again I'd be pushing myself up, nursing a scraped shin, and carefully examining my water containers. The best of it was, I knew when I was putting a foot wrong. I could see it coming but given the feverish pace I could do nothing about it.

At last I rounded another headland to see the beginnings of a long stretch of relatively flat coast. One more crisis over, I carried my equipment down to the beach and made camp. Totally exhausted, it was all I could do to get the tent up and crawl inside.

As I lay on top of my sleeping bag redundant heat seemed to rise from my body. Feeling strangely detached I drifted into a world of my own. It was soon dark. The stars twinkling through the fine mesh of the tent fabric became a river of spots flowing before my eyes while my heart seemed to be pounding angrily inside my head. I had been pushing myself hard all day, perhaps too hard.

Later that night I noticed there were bumps on my hands. Mystified and a little alarmed I looked at them with my torch. They were covered in blisters. Despite the factor 10 sunscreen my hands were blistered! Again I had good reason to wonder if I was capable of finishing the walk before it finished me. Anxiety fed anxiety as my mind went off into a whirl of negativity.

Morale was slipping. It was time for the sergeant to step in again, 'You've got Punta Bufeo and Larry's house two or three days ahead,' he said encouragingly. 'You can recover there. You're getting fitter, stronger and more acclimatized every day. Think of all the kindness and hospitality you've received.' I only had to look at my Stanton Fire Service cap to feel better. The pep talk worked. I slept more soundly than I should have.

The following morning's struggle was largely over stone and boulder beaches. The air was heavy and still – no comforting sea breeze. By midday my blistered skin felt as if it were boiling and bubbling. All I could think about was finding shade, but there was none so I put up the tent, opened it at both ends and crawled inside. Dead Man's Island lay off the coast, a mile-long block of lifeless mountain. It was well named, looking like an enormous giant on his back, arms folded across his stomach. I was lying on my back in a pool of perspiration, gasping for breath. Without any breeze it was unbearable. I felt as if I'd crawled from a grill into an oven.

Wearing only hat and shorts I walked – if my footsore drunken gorilla movements could be called walking – across the baking hot stones and slid gratefully into the sea. Sitting neck deep beneath the shelter of my hat I soon lost all track of time.

The water was so calm it was hard to tell where the sea ended and the sky began. Even the fish and the pelicans appeared confused. Leaping out and crashing in, it was as if life had forgotten its appointed limits. An air of unreality hung over everything. The outline of Dead Man's Island seemed to pull me. I felt I could just let go and drift into the horizon. Like a burning Viking longboat with the body of a fallen warrior, I could see myself floating into eternity.

With my stomach rumbling for food, I scooted back to the tent and rummaged through the pack to see what was left. The butter bought in Puertecitos had turned into a nasty-smelling oily mess. So much for my dreams of butter clams: I threw the glass jar and its contents into the sea. Taking a long swig of water I had second thoughts about eating. In that heat it was probably only the continuous intake of liquid that was keeping my body from disaster. I looked at the amount of water I had left. I had drunk more than I had realized. My sweaty fingers almost subconsciously ran along my tacky lips. It was enough to relegate my appetite to its rightful place.

I prayed for a breeze but my prayers remained unanswered. Not wanting to die in the tent and go the way of the butter, I packed, smeared myself in sunscreen and crawled back out from the oven to the grill.

The first hint of a breeze coincided with the welcome afternoon descent of the sun. Gradually it blew stronger and cooler, but I hardly had time to enjoy it before it whipped itself into another wild howling frenzy. I felt like a rain dancer watching his parched land suddenly washed away in a flood.

Finding a campsite was now my main concern. At dusk, with nothing better in sight, I chose a gravel beach sheltered from the violent northwest wind.

As I struggled to get the tent up, the heaving sea beside me boiled with desperate fish. Big fish tore in and out of a densely packed shoal of small fish. There seemed to be as many fish in the air as in the water. Such scenes of carnage were common along the shores of the Sea of Cortez, but for once the birds missed out on the feast. The gale had grounded them. I thought about casting a line into the 'bait-ball' but it was almost dark and my tired body was fit only for weighing down the precariously pegged tent.

Not long after I'd made myself comfortable inside, the wind dramatically shifted. Suddenly my little world was exposed to the full force of a south-easterly gale. After a gallant resistance the inevitable happened, down went the tent. There was nothing to be done except endure a largely sleepless night dwelling on my fears. I must have looked a strange sight tossing and turning with the tent flapping around me.

Breakfast consisted of a mouthful of bread crumbs and a multivitamin. That was it. I was out of food. Time to worry about that later. With the sun low, the pack relatively light and the wind still strong, I was more concerned to eat up the miles.

As waves crashed against the cliffs I cut into the desert and snaked my way through an expanse of low hills. The sun and temperature rose. When the wind fell I went back to the water's edge. As long as there was the slightest breeze, I pushed myself furiously. By 11.00 a.m., with five hours near continuous walking behind me, I felt barely able to put one foot in front of the other.

To escape the midday sun I squeezed into a little cave at the base of some low sand cliffs. I was so tired I had to fight the urge to go to sleep. An earthquake now, I thought, and I'd be buried alive. Looking at the half a gallon of water I had left, I reluctantly stepped back into a world of pain.

With not enough time, energy or water to seek out a meal, I swallowed a second multivitamin, scooped out a handful of seawater and pressed on. Larry's house was ahead. It was the Valhalla towards which I drifted. I staggered on dreaming of a cold beer and a good meal. The coast was relatively flat. No mountains barred my way, only the mountain of my own weariness.

There was something moving on the beach . . . about a mile ahead. People! My spirits soared. But reaching them was painfully slow. Unable to walk more than fifty yards without a rest, I stopped maybe thirty-five times. Either sitting down or bent over hands on knees I looked up to see if I was any closer. I never seemed to be. A mile! It felt like a thousand.

The people on the beach had plenty of time to wonder who or what was coming towards them.

At last I could make them out. They were fishermen – two of them – repairing their nets. I closed the last fifty yards not daring to believe that this was Punta Bufeo. Maybe Larry's house was over the dunes. Maybe there were Americans here. The prospect brought a new surge of strength.

The two men might have been brothers. They were both thin, bearded, thirtyish, and deadly serious. They eyed me with suspicion.

'Buenas tardes,' I said. In unison they bade me good afternoon, but without a hint of a smile.

'Is this Punta Bufeo?' I inquired hopefully. The man nearest to me answered.

'No, not here. It is another ten kilometres.' He made a gesture as if inviting me to carry on.

Ten kilometres! That's six miles. 'Are you sure it's ten kilometres?' I asked.

'Yes,' he answered tersely.

'Maybe more,' said his mate.

My new found strength evaporated in the heat. I had to rest. 'Can I stop here for a minute?' I asked rather lamely.

There was an embarrassing silence. They looked at each other as if Count Dracula had just invited himself to stay a month. Beyond caring I put my pack down and sat beside it.

The fishermen carried on mending their nets. They clearly had no idea what to make of the mysterious gringo with the wild red hair. I stared at the bare feet of the man nearest to me. On top they were tanned almost black. I pictured my own feet, white with a tender blush of scarlet.

Attempting to break the ice, I volunteered some information about myself. They just nodded. Sensing they wanted nothing more than to see the back of me, I stood up, forced a smile and said goodbye. They wished me luck, then they smiled.

Steeling myself to the task I vowed to reach Bufeo, and immediately doubted my own sanity. A furious inner debate started with me shouting abuse at some obstinate irrational part of myself. 'Ask for water, you idiot.' The idiot part replied, 'You can't carry the extra weight. Besides, they'll say they haven't any to spare for crazy gringos.' 'You're paranoiac! They're probably great people. They have every reason to be suspicious. You come wandering up, carrying a paddle and full of "loco" nonsense about walking down to Cabo San Lucas. What if anything happens, what if you collapse? Go back and get some water before it's too late.'

When it was too late, I couldn't believe I hadn't asked for water. However, the anger I directed at myself helped fuel my resolve to reach Punta Bufeo.

Each of those six miles was worse than that interminable mile behind me. 'I'll never make it,' my dry mouth mumbled. Even when I saw houses two miles ahead I had to fight that insistant and awful thought 'I'm so tired, I'll never make it'. 'Don't say that,' roared the sergeant.

I had been pushing myself hard for almost twelve hours. Weak with hunger, and almost too thirsty to talk, I approached a mixed party of bronzed middle-aged tourists gathered around one of the beach houses. This had to be Punta Bufeo. About eight or ten houses ran along the sheltered east end of the beach, protected by a massive rocky point behind.

The Americans were nearly as bemused as the Mexicans, but it was good to be able to explain myself in English. No sooner had I begun relating my story than a can of cold beer and a tuna sandwich appeared. A dream come true! I removed my pack, and almost collapsed on to a chair. I had made it! The pain and anxiety were forgotten. I was soon laughing and joking again as euphoria trickled through my revitalized system.

Between them the Americans had a wealth of Baja off-road racing experience. I listened attentively. They heard my story with interest. More than most they could appreciate what my task involved.

Loaded down with fruit and a gallon of pure water, I stepped inside Larry's house and closed the door on the world. It was an eerie feeling to be alone inside a strange house. For several minutes I leant against a wall and imbibed the novelty of being indoors.

The house, well away from the others, was the last occupied one before the point. A lot of sand had blown in from somewhere and little dunes had formed on the floor, a quaint reminder of the more familiar outdoors.

'Thank you, Larry. Boy do I need this,' I said to break the silence. Then I forced myself to make a thorough inspection for snakes and scorpions before fully relaxing.

The construction and layout of the rectangular one-floored house was simple enough. The front, facing the beach, consisted of a spacious open-plan sitting room/kitchen area, while two bedrooms and a bathroom made up the rear.

Several cases of beer and soda were stacked on the kitchen floor. Orange juice, syrup, sugar, hot chocolate, cinnamon and other spices were in various cupboards. I noted a bookcase containing several books and leaflets on Baja.

As the day came to an end I rolled out my sleeping bag on the sofa and made ready a couple of kerosene lamps. I tried to peruse the Baja books but my eyes were too heavy.

Chapter 9

Punta Final

I slept well. The sun was up long before me. It was good to feel the security of a house, and to be able to look forward to shade and relaxation. I had stacks of relevant reading material and a bunch of Baja experts for neighbours.

For four days I made myself at home, largely avoiding the sun, carefully studying maps and books, writing letters, building up my strength, enjoying good food and hospitality, washing clothes and checking my equipment.

I had an uneasy feeling about the water containers. The caps on the canteen and belt-bottle were leaking while the large plastic bag was vulnerable both to puncture and the loss of its press-in plug. I had already learned the value of water. The loss of a mouthful could mean the difference between life and death. I should have given greater thought to the safest way of carrying my water. As it was, I had to make the best of a bad job. The sensible thing was always to distribute the load between as many containers as possible.

The double front doors opened on to a small covered porch and a fifty-yard wide beach of soft yellow sand. A mushroom-shaped, palm-thatched sun-shade stood just above the water line. I could fish and swim at leisure.

After borrowing a mask and snorkel from the house I waded carefully into the sea. It was now second nature for me to do the 'stingray shuffle', dragging my feet through the sandy bottom. Touch a stingray and he'll probably swim off; tread on one and you'll know about it.

As I slipped underwater and glided around I soon saw the wisdom of such precautions. A stingray darted from under my nose, his barbed and venomous spine whipping uncomfortably close to my face. A cloud of sand settled around the hole he'd just vacated. There were several stingrays in the shallows. Buried and well camouflaged, some would refuse to budge, others would wait till the last moment before exploding into a cloud covered tail-waving retreat. The more I swam around the more I got the hang of seeing them. Usually they were betrayed by two wary eyes protruding from a just visible oval outline.

Apart from stingrays, I didn't see too many fish near the beach. On the whole, the fishing at Punta Bufeo was disappointing. But one day I joined three of the Americans on a boat trip.

It was late afternoon. The sun had lost most of its power as the four of us waded waist deep out to the large powerful-looking motor boat. Our skipper was Sue, a gutsy little lady who had made a name for herself as an off-road motorcyclist. She opened up the throttle sending us surging around the point sheltering Bufeo from the east. The hazardous rocky bottom was clearly visible as we eased steadily in under the cliffs, lowered our baited hooks and began pulling up a continuous supply of fish. In the brief intervals between bites I glanced at the rocks and narrow stone beaches over which I'd have to walk.

A curious sea lion appeared and swam excitedly around the boat investigating us from above and below. He seemed peeved that we were so freely pilfering from his larder.

We returned to the beach with enough fish to feed a colony of seals. Most of the fish were still alive as we dumped them on to a table. We all did our share of the dirty work. I always felt a twinge of guilt when holding down the victim. Invariably big lidless eyes would be looking up at me accusingly. Slicing the knife through head and backbone, I'd have to grip harder as the victim made its final struggle.

Sue, though, thought nothing of filleting her fish alive. Matter-of-factly chatting as if she were washing dishes, she slipped the knife along the backbone and removed the slabs of flesh on each side. The still wriggling fish was thrown into a box of refuse. I gazed in horror but said nothing, and to my eternal discredit I eagerly accepted the invitation to join everyone for fish dinner that night. It was to be my last night in Bufeo and possibly my last good meal for a while. I returned 'home' to dig out my cleanest dirty clothes and wash the smell of fish from everything but my conscience.

It was an evening of great merriment. I was treated to as much fish, steak, salad and fruit as I could eat. Then, like a camel filling his hump, I washed it all down with a fine mix of booze. For my journey the good people of Bufeo, who'd looked after me for four days, gave me three gallons of water and a couple of large bags of dried fruit.

I outlined my plans to leave early and work my way around the rocky shoreline down to Papa Fernandez resort. That raised some eyebrows. They all doubted that I could get by under the cliffs. To a chorus of insistence that I take the road, I boldly declared with all the certainty of alcoholic enthusiasm, 'No, I must stick to the coast and see for myself.' There was no point arguing with me. The resistance died and melted into the easy flow of goodbyes.

I walked along the shore back to Larry's house and managed to keep upright long enough to stagger through the door. Somehow I got into the sleeping bag where I uttered a few inane chuckles before disappearing into a whirling black vortex of Kahlua, beer and rum.

Next morning, after closing up the house, I left Punta Bufeo with a heavy load, a heavy head, and the paddle cut down to a walking stick.

It wasn't easy psyching myself up to face the agony and uncertainty again. In a fit of bad temper I threw away the 'paddle'. I didn't have enough hands to carry water, grab rocks and hold a walking stick. I was glad to untie the canteen from the pack and get that weight off my back.

The pressure of the rising tide had me racing again, but when I was forced to stop by a massive wall of rock sliding deep into the sea, I was tempted to go back and take the road. But what happens where there is no road? The only other option was to climb up a rugged little gulley in the hope of finding a way down behind the obstruction.

Jagged rocks, stunted trees and tearing bushes spitefully conspired to thwart my ascent. I hated to see seagulls flying below me. The sea looked a long way down. After pausing to catch my breath and admire the view, I began the descent, and was soon sliding and scrambling down a narrow gulley of chute-like steepness. Brittle rocks came away in my hands and crumbled underfoot. Avalanche-like slides threatened to send me tumbling to my doom.

I am no mountaineer. I have no head for heights, least of all on that kind of precarious terrain with both hands clutching water containers.

I decided to tie the canteen to the pack. That did nothing for my balance but I desperately needed a free hand. My right hand clung tightly to the precious water bag which had become an extension of my body. I recoiled from every knock and scrape it received. At any moment I expected it to be ripped wide open. If my own adrenalin soaked frame was immune to hurt, the heavy water bag was like a sensitive abscess, a gathering of pain just waiting to explode.

When at last I made it safely down I realized there was no way I could climb back up again. I was effectively trapped beneath the cliffs. And what was I to do with the full canteen on my back? It was too heavy to carry like that. If I insisted on having a free hand then I'd have to go against the principle of dividing the water between all the containers.

A little apprehensively I emptied the canteen, a good portion of it down my throat, the rest divided between the belt bottle and the bag.

No need to worry, I reasoned, if disaster struck the water bag, I had enough water in the aluminium belt bottle to give me time to get the stills operating.

Switching the bag from hand to hand I continued my race with the tide. Another tight spot forced me to crawl along dragging the pack and water behind me. Huffing and puffing I was almost through when a sea lion stuck his head from the sea and looked at me incredulously. I sent him a wave and shouted a friendly hello. As I did so the heavy water bag slipped from my grasp and rolled down towards the sea. Wallop! It lodged itself in a crevice with such force that the cap shot off and the precious liquid glugged into the sea. As horrified as if watching my own blood spill, I let go of the pack and scrambled head-first down to retrieve the bag. As I stretched to reach it, my belt water-bottle slid from its pouch and went rattling down over the coarse granite. I watched in disbelief as it plopped into the sea and sank. A wave brought it back into reach. At full stretch I just managed to grab it by the cap. As the wave fell I found myself cap in hand but no water bottle. It had dropped back into the sea!

Salt water flooded in. Another wave. Another desperate lunge. This time I had it. I reached over for the water bag and what was left inside. With the sea lion still looking on in bug-eyed bewilderment, I stood up holding a capless water bag with maybe three pints of water and a small aluminium bottle mostly full of seawater.

In a moment of clumsiness, a comfortable situation had become a crisis. I had lost nearly two and a half gallons of water from the water bag. There was no easy way back to Bufeo and possibly no way ahead. I was literally up against a wall, a wall of cliffs running in both directions as far as the eye could see.

Trapped there on the rocks there was no wood for a fire to boil seawater; I couldn't dig a hole to rig up a solar still by covering it with the plastic sheet. There was only my inflatable solar still. What would that give me? Two or three pints a day. In that kind of heat I'd be dead in a few days. Such was my concern, I preferred to keep the contaminated water. The water in the bag I poured very carefully into the more sturdy canteen.

My race with the tide now took on even greater urgency. I prepared myself for the worst, and it wasn't long before more sheer cliffs dropped into unwadably deep water. No way up, no way around. Possibly the tide would fall enough to let me pass. I gambled and waited.

As if sensing my sombre mood, the Sea of Cortez tried to enliven my spirits with one of its interesting little shows.

Over the water and along the cliffs, pelicans and other sea birds performed their graceful acrobatics. Dolphins appeared as black dots bouncing on the horizon. Closer in, all kinds of fish were splashing free from the slick water, and right off the rocks their big fat cousins were contentedly gliding through the sun dappled underwater canyons.

Fishing seemed a better pastime than fretting. Seeking only diversion – with water concerns the last thing I needed was fish protein – I pulled open my telescopic rod, attached the reel, threaded the line, tied on a lure and cast it thirty yards from shore.

There was no need to cast. It was enough to dangle the lure in the water. Events followed predictably – tug, the strike, the run, the struggle and, more often than not, frantic tails slapping air, as I hauled in fish after fish. Fishing the Sea of Cortez, you never know what you're going to pull out next. I studied them all, familiar and exotic – blue eyes, golden stripes, purple dots – before gently returning them to their watery homes. It was the best hour's fishing of my life. My only regret was losing my best two lightweight lures.

Still trapped I resolved to keep active. There was plenty to do. Allowing the whole of my body to take a controlled amount of sun, I cooled my feet in the ocean, playfully tried stalking the crabs and the crusties (without success), prised some shellfish from the rocks and found time to write a letter to my family, record some of my experiences on tape and catch up with my journal.

The tide began to fall. Submerged rocks slowly rose above the water and dried in the warm air. At last, a walkable path appeared. Jubilantly I was underway again, almost relishing the return to my sweaty, stumbling, back-breaking ordeal.

My jubilation was short-lived, however. Another sheer wall dropped deep into the sea. This time, the tide wasn't going to help. The water was much too deep.

Before lapsing into my wailing wall routine, I climbed up to see if I could get around. By sheer chance right where my path had been unequivocally blocked, there was a natural rock stairway leading up and over into the desert.

The flat open landscape rose through a succession of low hills to a small range of mountains. Every few steps found me collapsing ankle deep (and once even knee deep) into a labyrinth of animal tunnels. The desert had been totally undermined, and I grew increasingly anxious about dropping in on a rattler.

Even so, taking comfort from being close to the coast on one side and a road somewhere on the other, I rather enjoyed meandering my way through the desert. Dry yellow grass, scrawny bushes and lonely ocotillos made up its tentative covering. There were still very few cacti to be seen. I ascended arroyos that probably hadn't heard the sound of boots for years, if at all.

The higher I climbed, the more I lost the heady sense of freedom of the open desert. The options were fewer. Only the ridges and valley bottoms were tenable pathways. When a valley divided, the advantage of choice was nullified by anxiety about which way to go.

Keeping half an eye on the dropping sun, another on my water level, and a whole eye wide open for rattlers, I made my increasingly uncertain way through a maze of ridges and valleys.

Becoming unsure about my bearings I went out of my way to climb the highest ridge around; but all I could see were more ridges, no coast, no road, nothing to aim for. My increasing thirst forcefully reminded me that I didn't have enough water to play games.

I climbed another ridge to see yet more ridges. What was going on? How could I be this far inland? I had a moment of panic as I began to doubt my senses. There I was close to the sea and a well-travelled road (by Baja standards), and I was near terrified. How would I cope fifty miles from help?

Apart from brief golden moments of peace and confidence this adventure was going to be incessant anxiety with no certainty, no guarantees, no trails, no decent maps, no road to follow, no guide to lead. I was a complete novice staking my life on my decisions. I had good reason to be worried!

Exhaustion threatening to overwhelm me, I leant on my good friend fear and climbed from disappointment to disappointment until at last – a glorious sight – framed by the black gunsight sides of the sharp valley, I could see my target in the distance. The familiar beaches and islands of Papa Fernandez and Alphonsinas resorts were still bathed in soft warm sunlight. The time spent back in Punta Bufeo perusing navigational charts and aerial photographs had not been wasted.

Picturing the joys of cold beer, warm company and the hopefully reassuring advice of Larry's friend Ed Wills, I purposefully made my way down. The descent seemed easy enough. 'Please, please, no surprises,' I implored. 'Just a nice easy stroll down to the sea.'

The sun sank behind the far peaks. The welcome shade all too quickly became a worrying forerunner of blackness. And the arroyo did have a nasty surprise for me. Instead of starting difficult and getting easier and easier – like the model river course of my high-school geography days – the deceptively gentle descent gave way to a series of steep drops. I found myself clambering over boulders and sliding down near-vertical rock walls. I came to the point of no return. 'Go down there and you'll never get up again.' But I had no choice. Down I went, trapped in an ever-deepening V-shaped valley. My radio distress beacon will be a fat lot of good down here, I thought. Every scrape had me doing my rattlesnake jig. Occasional piles of bones on the valley floor did much to keep my exhausted muscles in top gear. Like a missile locked on target I burned myself up in single-mindedness.

What untapped reserves of strength we all have. My legs threatened to buckle but always found that little extra to stay upright and keep going. Pain and exhaustion seemed irrelevant. I had to know if I could get down.

At last, the valley eased into a broad sandy wash and then disgorged me on to a vast ocotillo covered plain. Once again freedom and options. With terribly un-English enthusiasm, and looking more like an excited contestant on one of those ghastly American game shows, I danced out my delight shouting 'Made it, made it, made it.' I was as happy as an exhausted boxer who'd just flattened his opponent. Suddenly, spontaneously I had all the energy in the world to skip childishly around the ring.

The adrenalin was still pumping, No point stopping and wasting it all. I struggled on determined to make 'civilization' before dark. Spinning round and walking backwards I took time to admire the red and gold sunset above the black hills from which I'd gratefully emerged. Taking a deep breath, perhaps a sigh of relief, I spun back to the front to weave my way through the ocotillos until I picked up the road running into Papa Fernandez resort.

'God, life is beautiful, Baja is beautiful,' I chuckled to myself, feeling sorry for all the safe, bored and aimless people wasting their lives back at home. Who needs drugs? This is the greatest 'high' in the world. These were the highs we were made for; they enable us to see further, do better and stand taller.

And there it was, Papa Fernandez resort – a landing strip, a beach, a protected bay, an island joined to the coast by a capricious corridor of sand, a scattering of beach houses and a tiny unremarkable cantina which also served as radio shack, restaurant and store.

In the cantina I met Chi Chi, a short, well-rounded young man.

'Hello, friend, we have been expecting you,' he said.

'Expecting me?' I replied, baffled.

'Yes. I listen to the radio. They talk about you in Puertecitos and in Punta Bufeo. You're the Englishman walking to Cabo San Lucas?' he asked, smiling.

I hadn't realized my comings and goings had sparked so much interest on the local airwaves. Short-wave radio was clearly of great importance to these isolated settlements. I wondered, could I get a message back to Dave and Denise in Los Angeles?

First things first. In Mexico it's bad form to rush into 'business matters'. I ordered a beer and found myself staring at a cold can of Tecate. The familiar red and gold can looked every bit as beautiful as the sunset. My dry mouth watered as I clutched its cool promise. With foreplay relish, my fingers slipped along the can wiping off the condensation. There was a little gasp as I opened it up. Oh, the first sip of cold beer when you're thirsty! I could have drunk the lot in one go, but like one or two of life's pleasures, it needed to be savoured, experienced and definitely not rushed.

Chi Chi was a jovial, kind-hearted man, one of the many sons of Papa Fernandez who had given his name to the resort. Propping up the bar, I settled down to an enjoyable evening drinking, talking and laughing with my hospitable and informative host. After the work, the reward. The $2 I paid for the beer was well spent.

As euphoria gave way to exhaustion I ventured out into the night and spread out my tent on the concrete porch of what I hoped was an unoccupied house. Throwing my equipment in on one side of the tent, I crawled in on the other. Huddled in my security I allowed myself to ponder what might have happened had I spent the night in that steep, darkening 'valley of the shadow of death'.

Next morning, I was woken by a cold wind flapping the tent. For once I welcomed the sun's warmth. In the cantina, Chi Chi plied me with coffee as we discussed the possibilities of getting a radio-phone link to the US. It seemed I had to wait for conditions to be right. While waiting, I got talking to two American couples. They insisted on giving me several cans and packages of food and one of them disappeared into his workshop and emerged with a couple of much needed lures and a selection of corks to replace the cap lost from the water bag.

Equally encouraging, Chi Chi charged me a mere $1.50 for countless cups of coffee, seven lemons, an orange, a bag of tortillas and a cold beer. The only disappointment was failing to get the radio link. Whatever we were waiting for hadn't happened! However, it was a marvellous morning. Waiting in Baja doesn't have the same connotation it has in more 'civilized' parts. It can be more fun than what you're waiting for.

In excellent spirits I made my way the short distance to Alphonsinas resort where a young Mexican directed me to Ed Wills' house. It commanded an excellent view back to Papa Fernandez resort and over the bay to Punta Final.

Obviously Ed Wills was greatly respected. I found him, like a king holding court, surrounded by a circle of friends and admirers. Others came seeking advice and judgement. He must have been about sixty, a portly gentleman of benign, if somewhat serious, disposition. In the best 'frontier' tradition he was unshaven and unkempt and, judging by his confidently expressed opinions, quite well versed in things mechanical and practical.

My turn came. Standing before his little coterie I explained my plans. Walking down the coast to the Bay of L.A.! Walking around Baja! He clearly thought he had a suicide on his hands. Shaking his head he left me in no doubt about his opinion.

'I've been up and down the coast by boat, plane and burro. As for walking from Punta Final to the Bay of L.A., you can just forget it. Apart from the tiny fishcamp of Calamajué, there's a hundred miles of nothing, probably no one, no trail, no help. If anything happens, you're dead!'

As if that were the end of the matter, he unfolded a map, and pointed out a dirt road that ran well inland. As respectfully as I could I re-emphasized my intention to try walking the coastline.

'Look,' he said, obviously losing patience. 'There's nothing but sheer cliffs and rugged, treacherous mountains. There's no water. Get bitten by a rattlesnake and you're a goner. Believe me, it's impossible.'

For good measure he threw in two other 'impossible' stretches of the Gulf coast. Banging his hand on the appropriate section of the map he declared, 'North of Santa Rosalia, forget it. Loreto to La Paz, forget it.'

While I was still recovering from hearing him declare most of the Gulf coast impossible, he turned his gaze to the Pacific coast and with a dismissive gesture added, 'And there's no way you're going to walk down all of this coast. Why do you think there's no road? Because there's no way through. If anyone could get by, there'd be a road or trail. There isn't because it's so damned rugged. The Mexicans know. That's why there's nothing there.'

I was given a beer. I needed it. Looking towards the ominously sounding Punta Final I wondered what to do. No way could I lightly dismiss the opinions of Ed Wills. Should I venture behind the mountains, down the beautiful valley of Calamajué, past the old mission site? There would be much to see, but I would be in the middle of the peninsula, not on the coast, not doing what I'd planned. It would be a betrayal.

Trudging wearily along the beach, I made my lonely way to Punta Final. For two days, I wallowed in indecision. A fierce storm whipped the sea into a wild Pacific-style surf. I had never seen the Sea of Cortez so rough but the dolphins loved it, riding the waves and leaping through the foam, they were just having a bloody good time.

My spirits lifted. I climbed high into the hills above Punta Final, a dangerous climb on the loose rock. I studied the coast carefully and looked inland to see the dusty road that worked its way to Calamajué. In the sea a huge manta ray glided by.

I made up my mind. I wasn't going to defeat myself without even trying. I'd aim to get to the fishcamp first and take it from there. As Napoleon once said, 'The key to victory is to throw yourself in and see what happens.'

Chapter 10
Shark fishermen

I left early to catch the low tide. Thanks to the generosity of a friendly group of fly-in tourists, I left loaded with food, water, and advice. They assured me that I didn't need to follow every twist and turn of the rugged shoreline around the point. I could cut off the worst by taking an old Indian trail over the hills between two inroads from the sea.

Struggling along the shore, leaping from rock to rock and edging my way around some of the trickier spots, I quickly became convinced that cutting inland was the way to go. Indeed, it was only the extreme low tide that enabled me to make any kind of progress. The enormous tidal variation of the northern Gulf was being accentuated by the new moon. For a while the lows were going to be very low and the highs very high.

The storm had passed. The sky was blue. The air was still, and the sea had fallen back to its customary morning flatness. Another huge manta ray drifted eerily just beneath the surface. Only the tail slapping, torpedo lunging, hissing exhalations of excited dolphins rippled the smooth water and ripped into the silence.

With sweat soaked face and shirt, I at last reached the long ramp-like beach that led up to the trail. Finding some shade, I ate a quick meal, then with apprehension rising as fast as the tide behind me, I threaded my way up the steep overgrown valley. It was a long time since the tramping of Indian feet had kept the pathway clear. Ocotillos clawed at me like wizened beggars. Gingerly I lifted the fiercely spined stems and watched them whip back viciously. Painfully aware that my life was in my hands, I cradled the water bag like an anxious mother.

The air was filled with insects and the pungent smell of bloated-trunk elephant trees. The insects buzzed me with such purpose, I was sure they were after my blood.

One wasp-like creature might have had other intentions. Big and black, with bright orange wings, it dragged behind it what appeared to be an inch-long stinger. Thinking it might be a device for laying eggs deep in the body of some living victim, and not wanting to find my flesh erupting with maggots, I watched it with great concern.

When something suddenly dropped from out of the blue and hung blurred and buzzing inches from my nose, I instinctively covered my face and backed away. The startled creature made a more graceful retreat. It was a beautiful iridescent purple-and-green hummingbird. Having satisfied his curiosity, he was gone.

At last I reached the watershed. Before going down the other side, I looked behind me. Above and beyond the grey valley and bushes through which I had climbed, I could see the beach-fringed calm of Gonzaga Bay. Above and beyond the bay a grey and smoky-green plain rose gently to a distant range of flat-topped, vaguely pink mountains. Above them, of course, was the eternal Baja blue, interrupted only by a trio of circling vultures and the lonely wisp of a vapour trail.

I remembered when I had sat in that passenger-packed plane, staring at the frozen wilderness beneath. Then I'd imagined what it must have been like to be on the ground, looking up at the mighty, distant symbol of another world. Suddenly, it was real. There I was below, alone, marvelling at the silence, looking up and picturing the scene aboard as I was about to leap into the unknown.

Before me a valley dropped sharply to meet an arm of the sea punching inland. Turning my back on the sound advice of Ed Wills, I climbed down to the edge of what turned out to be a lagoon. The deep water looked lifeless and stagnant, totally different from the self-refreshing sea. Something about the lagoon disturbed me. It was an irrational feeling, yet my mind tried to give form to my fears. I half-expected something hideous to burst from the foul water and tear me limb from limb.

Even back beside the sea, I continued to race ahead, wanting to put as much distance as possible between myself and the lagoon. The feeling was so absurd, I began to wonder if my mind was playing tricks, concocting a threat to hurry me on and make sure I didn't think seriously about going back.

Now that I had rounded Punta Final and taken up the challenge of the 'impossible', the rugged coastline began exacting its toll. I fell many times. Both my ankles were sprained and tender. With the midday sun high in a still breathless sky, I decided enough was enough. From noon till three, I rested in the shade of a huge overhanging granite boulder.

The fishing was good. It usually was, off the rocks. I caught, and carefully returned, several trigger fish. Tiring of that, I worked on my Spanish. The fishcamp of Çalamajué (pronounced Car-lar-mar-way) couldn't be more than two days ahead. Almost certainly, there'd be no tourists there, just rustic Mexicans with little or no English.

I thought of Larry's warning about getting out of there before dark. Get out to what? The dangerous desert, mountains and cliffs which Ed Wills had warned me about? I looked back towards Punta Final. It was a final backwards glance to all that was familiar and safe. Ahead there was only uncertainty.

The same sombre, brooding, self-doubt descended as I experienced at the start of the walk. At least here, I thought, I was unlikely to be confronted by a half-naked young lady shaking up my morale. Unless, that is, I found a mermaid on the rocks! Encouraged by the possibility I stripped off and went for a swim, taking care not to deflate my excited imagination on a wickedly spined sea urchin or venomous scorpion fish. In no hurry to leave the refreshing water, I eased myself on to an underwater rock platform and sat neck deep in the sea.

It would have been nice to have had a mermaid sitting on the rock above, fanning me beneath the shade of her dripping tail. But with no such decadence to enjoy, I returned to my shady boulder and dug out a packet of sweets, a present from California. To sooth my insecurity I chain-sucked and crunched them till just a pile of empty wrappers testified to the vast pit of anxiety I'd vainly tried to fill.

The cliffs ahead beckoned. With only a hint of a breeze, I continued my way over the gold and black speckled, coarse, white granite. An hour from sunset, I came to a little beach between an otherwise unbroken line of cliffs, and made camp on the sand just above the high tide mark. Ten yards away, the skeleton of a dolphin offered his dubious company.

Tent up and everything stashed inside, I went exploring along the narrow valley that wound into the mountains. Turning over rocks and logs and carefully examining the various plants, trails and tracks, I took stock of nature's resources and tried to reassert my confidence in my capacity to survive 'out here'.

Back at the tent I was perturbed to see that my dolphin friend had changed dramatically. In the bright sunlight he had seemed innocuous enough, but in the semi-darkness, his white bones and toothy grin took on such a sinister appearance that I half-expected to hear some doom-laden pronouncement issue from his sand-choked beak: 'Be warned. Go back while you can. There is only death ahead.'

With my vivid imagination, I had avoided watching horror films before embarking on my trip. On the other hand, almost instinctively I developed a taste for the 'religious'. It wasn't planned. I was simply more receptive.

As I paced beside the gently lapping water I confided my half-baked thoughts to the tape-recorder:

'Perhaps one of the greatest lessons I've already learned is that the most practical activity of all – staying alive – is very much influenced by feelings of faith and religion. In the concentration camps, assuming you weren't exterminated on the spot, spiritual attachment to a deeply held belief system was a powerful factor in survival. The ordinary, practical men and women with nothing solid to cling to were the first to despair and die.

'And the springs of action are often spiritual. It would be interesting to examine the philosophies of all the people who have shaken up the world (for better or worse). I'll bet most were moved by a sense of tapping some unknown power, some feeling of communion with God, fate, or what have you.

'It's a reality we can't ignore. I certainly can't out here. Maybe everyone should do their forty days and nights alone in the desert.'

There was plenty of wood on the beach, but I still didn't want to advertise my presence with a fire. Keeping a low profile was one of my basic instincts. It was a survival lesson I had quickly learned in the rough neighbourhood in which I grew up. Call attention to yourself and trouble invariably followed.

Zipping myself inside the tent, I had some cause for satisfaction. I was slowly adapting to my new circumstances. All my fears and woes – though real enough – were much more in perspective.

It was Friday the thirteenth. There were many opportunities for disaster as I engaged in another early morning race with the tide. Only my tightly laced boots seemed to be supporting my weakened ankles.

I was happy to sit out the worst of the midday heat inside a large cave-like overhang. It commanded an excellent view of the sea and of a narrow valley running down to it.

I clambered back down to the water's edge, fishing rod in hand. Within minutes, I was battling with a three-pound triggerfish. He must have known I was fishing in earnest. He fought for all he was worth. Getting him up on the rocks wasn't the end of the matter. He flipped and flopped. Even his tough chain-mail skin refused to yield to my knife. I gave up trying to remove his head. It was too risky. I'd more likely end up cutting off a finger or slicing myself open.

That fish wanted desperately to live, and he deserved to live. I would have let him go but he'd dashed himself so heavily against the rocks that he would probably have died anyway. Unable to watch his final struggle, I walked slowly down to the little valley to gather together some firewood. When I returned, the fish was still alive, but his eyes had turned opaque and wrinkled. Each feeble opening of his gills brought him closer to death. Small consolation as it was, I saluted him for his struggle. No doubt about it, he was a believer filled with the spirit of the great fish god.

Once he was dead, I cut carefully into his tough hide and removed the fillets from both sides. Boiled in seawater and well sprinkled with lemon juice, they tasted delicious.

Taking advantage of the falling sun and tide, I left to tackle yet more imposing cliffs. I had just a gallon of water, a packet of sunflower seeds and a couple of lemons. Could I reach Calamajué? What kind of reception would I get?

The rocks and cliffs changed dramatically from coarse granite to slippery sharp black slate. I edged cautiously forward adjusting to the new surface. Rounding one tricky point, I stepped on to a ten-foot wide pebble beach, and found myself staring into the eyes of something as lovely as the mermaid of my dreams.

The golden-yellow apparition stretched head to tail across my path and stared back at me with lion-like defiance. 'Are you real?' I whispered. The answer was most certainly yes! I glanced quickly behind me in case a hasty retreat was necessary.

'I've got to get a photo of you,' I said, gently easing off my pack and fumbling in the top pocket for my camera. Before I could get it out and ready, the creature did a quick U-turn and dragged its bulk back into the sea.

It was a sea lion, a big golden sea lion. Back in the water he watched me from a safe distance before disappearing beneath the waves. He was as different from his more familiar shiny black cousins as I was from the Mexicans. Right now he's probably somewhere beneath the Sea of Cortez telling his laughing comrades of the time he met a brown-speckled, pink-skinned human with orange hair. Sure pull the other flipper – it's got shells on!

It was getting close to sundown. I had almost given up the idea of reaching the fishcamp. Then, peering around another wall of black rock, I saw a little white fishing boat bobbing at anchor in the gentle evening light. No shadows reached out from the shore. The cliffs must have ended.

I peered around further. There were other boats in a wide bay and houses on the beach. This had to be Calamajué, and getting dark or not, I had to venture in. I needed food and water.

With a mixture of prayers and Spanish phrases on my lips, I approached a rough-looking bunch of young men sitting together on the grey pebble beach. Clearly, I was the last thing they had expected to see on this very ordinary Mexican evening. None of them spoke English but, thanks to my recent efforts at Spanish (and some imaginative gesticulating), I managed to make myself understood.

They were amazed that I had come from San Felipe and, judging by their laughter, even more amazed that I intended walking to Bahía de los Angeles. The laughing grew louder when I explained that I was walking all the way around Baja.

Although I couldn't make out everything being said, there was plenty of joking and liberal use of the word 'loco'. The mood seemed positive enough. I put down my pack and sat beside them. It seemed necessary to stress again that I really did intend walking all the way down the coast. They were laughing so hard I began to wonder if they'd all been smoking pot.

Watching the big sun sinking down the valley, I inquired, perhaps a little desperately, 'Please, I need food and water. Can I buy any here?'

The laughing petered out. Heads shook and dropped. One fisherman, rubbing his unshaven face and looking at everyone except me, declared, 'No, there's no food here. No, no water.' The rest nodded in agreement.

I was as baffled as they were seemingly embarrassed. Of course they had food and water. Had they something against Americans, I wondered. 'Yo no gringo, soy Inglés,' I said. 'I'm not American, I'm English.'

'Inglés!' Eyes lit up. They rattled on excitedly about something I failed to understand. Then, as one, they all stood up and walked off, beckoning me to follow.

Wondering if I'd said the wrong thing, I was taken to a house that was little more than a plywood and cardboard shack knocked together on a floor of compacted sand and dirt. A dozen fishermen escorted me inside and sat down on chairs, boxes and a battered old bed. A chair was pulled out for me. I was strategically positioned so everyone could get a good look. Larry's warning came back with even greater force. Powerless, I put on my sweetest smile. If I was about to be murdered, I could at least try to make them feel guilty about it.

'Would you like coffee?' someone asked. They all waited for my reply. So far I had kept myself in my own sterile little world at arm's length from the Mexicans, their homes, their food and their water. But eventually I would have to cast off my ridiculous inhibitions and prejudices.

Hiding my squeamishness, I beamed an even broader smile across my sunburned face and said, 'Yes, please.' A dirty cup was quickly rinsed and filled with warm, thick, black coffee. Then a young fisherman, with clothes generously covered with holes and fish scales, picked up a spoon from a table buzzing with flies and scooped in two spoonfuls of coffee-speckled sugar.

'Do you want milk?' I was asked.

'Yes, many thanks,' I said out loud. 'Why not?' I said to myself. 'This is it – you're going native. Good luck.'

I took the fateful sip. It tasted awful, almost salty. It wasn't easy to keep smiling. Somehow, I managed, and everyone seemed pleased by my gratitude.

'Are you hungry?' was the next question.

I laughed saying, 'Yes, yes, I'm always hungry.' Inside I was begging, please don't offer me anything to eat.

'Good, amigo. We have much food. Look . . .' I was invited to peer inside a large blue pot. A fish head stared back.

'Hmmm . . . very nice,' I said. 'What is it?'

'Fish soup,' he said, triumphantly. 'Would you like some?'

I'm sure it was someone else who answered, 'Yes, please. Thank you very much.' The fisherman dusted off a plate and covered it with a couple of good scoops of his fish soup. Another young man warmed some tortillas on the gas stove.

Ignoring my churning stomach, I forced down the meal and feigned a show of sheer delight. That had a pay-off in more friendliness.

It occurred to me that what they meant by there being no food or water, was none that any normal American would touch. They were probably surprised I had accepted.

Suddenly, a young fisherman leapt to his feet and cried, 'Hey, English, you be at lays?' Everyone laughed.

I had no idea what he was talking about, but getting into the spirit of things I replied. 'Si, si. Ha, ha, ha.' Saying yes to everything seemed to be the thing to do.

'Good,' he said, enthusiastically. 'Un momento.' Then he disappeared outside. The rest of his colleagues moved forward on their seats in anticipation.

'Be at lays,' I wondered. 'What the hell have I said?'

Kerosene lamps were lit and turned up. The stage was being set for something interesting. Not too interesting, I hoped. Half-expecting the excited Mexican to return with a gun, I was pleasantly surprised when he walked in with a guitar!

The guitar was thrust into my hands. There were smiles all around. 'We love be at lays. Very good,' someone said.

Then it dawned. Beatles! They were saying I was English, therefore a fan of the Beatles, therefore a phenomenal guitar player, therefore I had a guitar in my hands! Oh God!

With everyone waiting, I declared, 'But I'm not much good, I can't really play.' What I meant was, I can't play a note, but I didn't want to let them down too hard.

They assumed I was just being modest; and in the face of their insistence, I didn't have the words to argue my way out of it. I had to prove how hopeless I was.

Much embarrassed and vowing to be more exact in my use of language, I made the most appalling racket. It was my idea of a joke, but instead of laughing, they all listened in respectful silence. Perhaps they thought it was the new wave of English music ready to shake up the world. With my stomach still shaken from its culinary ordeal, I did my best not to end my performance by throwing up.

I handed the guitar back. No one offered it to me again. Instead a kind of fiesta started. My fears subsided. These were fine hospitable people. Their virtuosos played some beautiful songs. Asked if I had a request, I replied, 'Guantanamera'. I'm no judge of music but it was played beautifully and the fishermen almost brought tears to my eyes with their singing. Lonely, unsure, and so far from home, the words were full of meaning: 'I am like a wounded deer seeking refuge in the forest . . . it is with the poor people of the world that I wish to share my fate . . .'

They were shark fishermen. It was fascinating to hear their adventures. Having shown my interest, a warm and dignified young man in his twenties, Victor Manuel, invited me to join him on a fishing trip. Shark fishing! Having seen *Jaws* about six times, I jumped at the chance. I would have to get up very early. The boats would be leaving at first light.

The party over, the men trickled back to their homes and families. Offering to pay for the food, I learned that I was in the house of Victor Manuel's father, Victor. He was in his sixties, equally warm and dignified. With kindness shining through his brown, weather-beaten face, he refused to take a peso.

It was time to find a quiet patch of beach. I picked up my equipment and stepped out into the blackness. A hand touched my arm and a tough-looking wiry, little fisherman said, 'Come with me. You can sleep in my house.'

I would have preferred the security of the tent, but I decided to go with him. We walked along the beach weaving past nets, boats, and boxes, while dogs barked loudly into the night.

'My name is Tortillas,' he announced in English.

What a strange name, I thought. It was like being called pancakes or chapattis.

The inside of his shack was dark and shadowy. A single kerosene lamp burned dimly. There were two beds. Pushing down on one, he said, 'You sleep here, okay?' I unrolled my sleeping bag, laid it out on the bed, and, still wearing shorts and shirt, slipped into it. After saying goodnight, I laid awake wondering if the tearing feeling in my stomach was more psychological than physical. Could I get up in time to go fishing? Being ready at first light seemed a tall order.

I wasn't sure how long I'd been asleep when I felt a hand clutching my shoulder and shaking me. A ghostly voice poured forth something unintelligible. I opened my eyes. For a moment I wondered where I was. By the light of the dim lamp I saw a very irate Mexican standing over me, gesticulating and none too pleased about something. 'Who the hell are you?' was written all over his face.

Recovering my senses, I sat up on the bed searching for enough Spanish to throw more light on my presence. Luckily Tortillas woke up and came to my rescue. His explanation didn't seem to satisfy his disgruntled colleague, but Tortillas had a solution. 'It's okay. You come sleep with me,' he said.

I returned the bed to its rightful owner, gathered up the sleeping bag and stepped nervously across the shadowy floor.

The light went out. I found myself staring into the blackness, sharing a narrow bed with Tortillas. After a while, he had, judging by his snoring, fallen into a deep sleep. I pretended to be asleep, but I'd never been more awake.

Still snoring, he put his arm around me and muttered something tender. I gently placed it back on his side of the bed. Eventually, I relaxed enough to drift once more into welcome slumber.

Chapter 11

'Mi casa es su casa'

I failed to get up for the crack of dawn. By the time I was ready to greet the world the boats were long gone, but Tortillas greeted me with all the warmth of the rising sun. With genuine concern he said the words that were to become so familiar in the months ahead, 'Mi casa es su casa.' My house is your house. And he meant it. He seemed to understand what I was feeling and bottling up behind all my smiles and thank yous.

With the sound and smell of frying filling the house, I was offered breakfast. Not really hungry I accepted anyway. The sergeant bellowed, 'Right you horrible little man, there will be more shacks and fishcamps ahead, and you're going to force yourself to lower your dainty little standards. You're going to eat what they eat and drink what they drink.'

Yes sir, no sir, three bags full, sir.

I sat dutifully down at the table while Tortillas cracked eggs into a fat filled frying pan. Before me there was a jar of coffee, a tin of dried milk and an open bowl of sugar spotted black with flies. Above me a line ran most of the length of the kitchen. On it were suspended a drying rattlesnake tail and a couple of Mexican sausages (chorizos). One was open and bursting with fat and meat, but for some reason no fly lingered there for long.

All the food, cups, plates, pots and pans, were openly displayed on a dusty cobwebby shelf running along one of the flimsy plywood walls. The windows had no glass, and there was nothing on the floor except black sand and eggshells. The kitchen was open at both ends. The front entrance faced the beach; the rear looked down the valley. On one side of the rear door there was a sink full of dirty dishes, on the other a stove hooked up to a cylinder of gas.

Tortillas plucked a plate from the shelf, dropped on a couple of real tortillas, a hunk of fried brown fish and two eggs. Normally I would have wolfed the lot down and looked around for more. That morning I ate as if I'd just eaten a six-course meal. Having difficulty in swallowing I washed down each greasy mouthful with a sip of brackish coffee.

Suddenly a suggestion of nausea came over me. Asking where the toilet was, I steadied myself at the back door and took a deep breath before hurrying past several huge plastic drums of water.

The outside toilet was just a square enclosure of cut and tied ocotillo branches. There was no roof. It was little more than a hole in the ground covered with an open box luxuriously crowned with a toilet seat. Mexican comics and magazines were thoughtfully strewn around the floor.

Convinced that I was about to part company with my breakfast, I positioned my head above the toilet. The rising stench struck me as if I'd stuck my head in the exhaust blast of a jet. Opening my eyes I was horrified to find myself looking down at a heaving mass of maggots. After swallowing hard my mouth stretched wide and emitted a kind of involuntary retching grunt. That was enough to send up a swarm of flies. They couldn't miss my wide open mouth. I leapt back spitting them out and swiping them from my face.

By some miracle of self-control I managed to avoid supplying the maggots with their mid-morning snack. For ten minutes I sat outside breathing deeply until I'd gained sufficient colour and composure to venture back into the house.

Tortillas told me he'd lived for a while in the United States, but he didn't like it. 'Too much violence, too much crazy,' he said. Nearly everything he said in English began with the phrase 'too much'.

I asked him why he wasn't fishing. 'I work in the freezer.' he replied. Grabbing my arm he led me on to the beach. 'You see the white building? We store fish . . . Too much ice.'

Walking back into the shade of the porch he pointed up to a board with dozens of gaff-sized hooks. 'Sometimes we use for sharks. But for me, no more hooks, no more nets, no more boats. For three weeks I no fish, too much remember,' he said intriguingly.

I inquired further and tried to make sense of what he was saying.

'We go for the net. Long way out. We head back. Motor no good, no start, nothing. Then big storm, too much wind, we blow a long way. No water, no food. One day, two days, three days, no help, nothing. Too much thirst. Too much sun. No shade, I drink sea water. Very sick, want to die. Twelve days . . .' Staring vacantly at the blue sea he added, 'Too much thirst, too much . . . no good to remember. I don't want to think. Too much pain.'

With that he made a dramatic exit and walked off towards the cold store. He was lucky to be alive. I felt guilty that I had a radio distress beacon and a solar still, either one of which might have saved him from the worst of his agony. These fishermen went out with little except their courage and their faith.

A few minutes later a tall young Mexican came walking towards me. Dressed in a stylish grey and white tracksuit he didn't seem as rough and ready as his companions. Using a mixture of about one quarter English and three quarters Spanish he introduced himself as Guillermo, the teacher, and invited me to accompany him to his house for coffee. I learned that he was nineteen and just out of teaching college. He pointed out his little 'school' along the valley and the rarely used landing strip beside it.

All the shacks seemed to be much the same inside; a dirt floor, a bed, a table, a couple of chairs, a cooker and one or more shelves for the food and pots and pans.

Guillermo filled his kettle from a five-gallon glass bottle – the kind normally seen on top of drinking water dispensers in the United States. 'This is good water from Ensenada,' he said. And in case I hadn't already found out, he added, 'The water here is not very good. Too much salt.' By lifting one leg, blowing a raspberry and pulling down an imaginary toilet chain he left me in no doubt that drinking too much of it was likely to produce the runs. If it could do that to a Mexican I dreaded to think what effect it would have on my poor stomach.

He gave me a heavenly cup of salt-free coffee and motioned for me to sit down on the bed. 'Once a week the truck takes all the fish to Ensenada and then brings back the supplies,' he said.

'Supplies! Can I buy supplies here? I'd like to buy food and water to take with me when I go.'

'Now no one has any food,' he replied. 'I have almost no water left. The men who go to town will get whatever you want. They will leave soon, maybe tomorrow.'

Letting that idea sink in, I explained my plans to Guillermo. I was still not convinced that the fishermen knew or believed what I had in mind. Guillermo didn't know too much about the coast or my prospects for success but at least we could more or less communicate.

I wondered how he felt about his appointment and the twenty or so children he had to teach. He seemed dignified, cheerful and contented enough. How many British teachers would remain so, sent to live in little scorpion infested huts, side by side with their charges, low pay, no privacy?

Guillermo gave me a guided tour of the camp. We stopped at several houses. The women and children seemed happy and friendly. I was shown the well supplying the village with its dubious water and the tiny trailer hauled in to serve as the office and radio shack, then taken over to see a much more cheerful Tortillas shovelling ice in the cold storage building, while his companion, Margy, leant on his shovel, grinned like a Cheshire cat and said over and over, 'How do you do?' He was very proud of his one English phrase.

Eighteen year old, square-jawed, chain-smoking Margy wasn't a fisherman. He was down from Ensenada paying a visit to his cousin, Tortillas, before embarking on a new life as an illegal immigrant in the United States – what those north of the border disparagingly call 'wet backs' in honour of the many Mexicans picked up after swimming across the Rio Grande or the Tijuana river. Poor Margy had only a naive idea of what life in America would be like. I could just see him being picked up by a couple of burly border guards. 'How do you do?'

The humming approach of the little open boats was the signal for the fishcamp to spring into life. Women and children, and the men who had stayed behind, walked down to the water's edge and stood sharpening knives and stacking boxes. An army of vultures and sea birds filled the air with their cries and expectation.

As the boats raced in, the engines were cut and lifted from the water, leaving the boats to run up on to the pebble beach. They were pulled and tied broadside before the fish were thrown out and piled on the grey stones.

Small sharks, mostly three to four feet long, made up the bulk of the catch; though there was one big mean-looking hammerhead. It took three men to lift him onto the beach. With a few snapping exceptions all the sharks were dead, lying with their grotesquely open mouths black against their creamy white bellies.

Children as young as six or seven were skilfully handling razor-sharp knives, cutting off heads and tearing out innards. The fins were sliced off and piled separately. Thanks to a certain type of soup they fetched a higher price than the rest of the meat. The whole operation went on with precision and efficiency. A dozen boats chafed gently against the shore. A dozen mounds of red and white shark meat lay beside them. Half a dozen people worked and chatted around each pile.

The nets were taken from the boats and any remaining fish extracted. The insides of the boats were then washed down with seawater, gasoline tanks were refilled and everything made ready again.

Victor Manuel and his father Victor came up and laughed about my over-sleeping. Other familiar faces said hello, and once more I found myself being escorted up to Victor's house. Everyone was being very kind. They took me seriously and did their best to answer my questions. When I said that I'd like to leave as soon as possible, several restated

Guillermo's point about waiting for the truck and fresh provisions. Otherwise they could only offer me dried fish and brackish water. Considering what lay ahead that hardly seemed the ideal fare.

Echoing the opinions of Ed Wills, Victor Manuel declared, 'I'm not sure you can make it to Bahía de los Angeles. No one has ever walked it. There are many cliffs, probably no people. It is dangerous.'

'I must try,' I said trying to convince myself as well as my audience.

Quite a debate started. Some thought there were other fishcamps en route to the Bay of L.A., others were sure there weren't. I was told there was a well with good drinking water in an oasis of palm trees but almost before my imagination had time to summon up the appropriate image it was gone. Palms! What palms? Water? There's no water.

It reminded me of the survival literature. Every opinion seemed to generate an equally fervent counter-opinion. The only thing I knew for certain was that I'd have to find out for myself.

As the fishermen drifted away, still debating and possibly betting on whether I'd make it, Victor Manuel said, 'We are going fishing again this afternoon. Come with us. We'll show you the coast.'

In spite of my queasy stomach I jumped at the chance and hurried over to Tortillas' house to get my camera and water canteen. I asked Tortillas why I hadn't seen Victor's wife. Tortillas explained, 'She died recently. It was very sad. Everyone liked her.'

Apart from a few dents, some flaking paint and one or two deep gashes in the fibre glass hull, the *Crazy Pirate* looked sturdy enough. Like all the boats it was white on the outside and a white-speckled pale blue inside.

The twenty-foot 'panga', as they called it, had a dark blue Yamaha motor hung on the stern. The centre was filled by what appeared to be a hopeless tangle of green net, yellow rope and red floats. A pair of oars was stashed along one side. In the back there were two portable red 'gas' tanks, a tool box, a baling jug, a pair of crude anchors and not much else. Certainly there was no radio, no lifejacket and no flares.

Victor Manuel waved me aboard and directed me to the front of the boat. 'You won't need that,' he said, pointing to the canteen. Holding up a full half gallon jug he added, 'We'll be back in two or three hours; we have plenty of water.' I pretended to feel foolish but Tortillas' dramatic story had made quite an impression.

Victor jumped aboard while his son and another helper pushed the boat out and likewise leapt in. The outboard coughed into life and Victor Manuel, looking every inch the captain, steered us out from the bay. His father stared into the blue, seeming to see something we couldn't. I felt a little rush of sadness. He looked so dignified. It was a warm unaffected dignity which made me trust him implicitly. And he seemed very happy to leave everything in the hands of his son.

We headed out around the point and paralleled the coast south. Victor Manuel shouted, 'I'll take you close in to show you what you must walk.'

It was a depressing sight. Mile after mile of cliffs. No valleys sliced through them. It was hard to see any way up or down. I found myself saying, 'God, it's impossible, I can't walk that.'

About ten miles from the fishcamp we left the coast and headed out into the Gulf. I remained transfixed as those awesome cliffs slowly shrank into the wake-roughed, sun-sparkled sea. When the motor was cut, silence came flooding back like the tranquil waters smothering the agitation behind us.

The fishermen fed out the net with smoothness and efficiency. Far from being a tangle these experts had it flowing swiftly into the water. It was several hundred yards long. Each end was marked by a large white float supporting a flag. Lead weights were strung along the bottom, and red floats along the top, yet the entire net sagged down to the depths. The opposition of float and weight was to keep it spread out. The sharks were, I was glad to hear, mostly prowling on the bottom.

All had gone well. The net was to be left overnight. The motor roared back into life and we were on our way 'home'. Or so I thought . . .

The engine suddenly spluttered and died. It was restarted. A few seconds later it conked out again. No amount of tinkering or cussing or tugging on the starter cord could change its mind.

Once again all was silence and gently slapping water. In spite of Tortillas' story I wasn't unduly worried. The slick sea seemed warm and friendly, and I had every confidence in my companions.

The troublesome Yamaha was brought aboard for dismantling. As they searched the tool box for the appropriate spanners and wrenches my knowledge of colourful Spanish improved greatly. Obviously they didn't have the right tool to open a critical part of the motor. No problem; the Mexicans are and have to be adept at improvisation. Little bits of the engine casing were broken off in an attempt to get a tool to fit. I offered my Swiss army knife which they put to good effect until its most useful blade snapped in half.

It was time to take to the oars. I offered to help but, hospitable to the end, they wouldn't hear of it. We reached the coast but, rather than landing, continued rowing a stone's throw from the shore. I was getting an even better view of what I was going to have to walk. Oddly, it didn't look quite as 'impossible' as it had from a distance.

As we rowed slowly north, I peered into the crystal clear depths, watching the rocks, fish and seaweed drifting by. The sunset was magnificent above the cliffs. Sea lions swam alongside us. The occasional bird swooped down, and the occasional fish leapt out.

As it got darker we sensibly pulled further out from the rocky shore. Even in total darkness the black mass of the coast stood out solidly against the starry blackness above.

For once it wasn't the glittering heavens that seized my imagination. The dipping oars and the boat left an eerie green trail. The sea was alive with luminescence. Little specks of light rushed across the surface of the water. They seemed to be attracted to one another, coming together and fusing. Fish darted beneath the boat leaving tell-tale trails of glowing green. It was the stuff of dreams or nightmares, made all the more incredible because it was real.

As the night drew on the wind picked up. Wearing only a thin shirt I began feeling too cool for comfort, and insisted on doing my share of the work. A brisk row warmed me up nicely. Every dip of the oars in the water sent galaxy-like whirlpools of ghostly green spinning back into the night.

The wind was our worst enemy. While the sea remained calm we made good headway, but the more the wind blew from the north the less sure I was that we were going anywhere. It was virtually impossible to measure our progress against the black mass of the coast. A blaster from the north-west could have made it impossible for us to land and put us in real Tortillas-type trouble.

The hours slipped by. The four of us alternated between periods of animated conversation and solemn silence. During one quiet spell something made me look out to sea. It wasn't just me; as one we were all staring into the blackness. Through the wind we could hear the distant hum of a motor. A boat! The fishermen knew immediately it was another panga, a search party.

Of course, we didn't even have a torch on board. Victor pulled out a box of matches and stood up. In spite of his cupped hands every match struck was immediately blown out. There had to be something we could do to call attention to ourselves?

I had a bright idea. The flash! The built-in flash on my idiot-proof Konica. Not wanting to waste film and with no time to explain, I positioned a bemused fisherman between me and the searching boat. The flash popped up. There was a little zing as the power was drawn from the batteries. The 'ready' light shone amber. Click! The flash lit up the night.

A light shone back. They had seen us! Five minutes later I took another flash picture. Again a torch beam shot back in acknowledgement. But by then we could see the luminescence about their boat. 'The vessel drove before her bows two billows of liquid phosphorus, and in her wake was a milky train,' as Charles Darwin wrote in *The Voyage of The Beagle*.

There was jubilation and laughter as the other boat pulled alongside. Everyone was relieved. We could all go home. I carefully stepped over into the rescue boat and was given a warm jacket. I needed it. With the crippled boat in tow we raced back to camp.

From our glowing wake ribs of green shot out from either side as schools of fish took to panic flight.

Although it was the middle of the night when we arrived back in Calamajué, almost the whole village turned out to greet us. The lost sons of the sea were home. Everyone was laughing about the camera flash and cracking jokes about my unexpected ordeal.

The party atmosphere continued in Victor's house. Having shared in the drama of their lives I felt closer to these lovely people and, at their insistence, satisfied my hunger with several tortillas stuffed with fish, beans, tomatoes and chili. Even the sweet and vaguely saline coffee went down without too many qualms.

Warm to the point of sweating I walked out to pay a final visit to the toilet before hitting the sack. Any cosy thoughts I had about adapting and belonging were about to be rudely shattered.

I expected to see the maggots. I was even prepared for a scorpion or a rattlesnake, but . . . I was shocked when I shone the light down into the toilet. It was alive with big, black, ugly looking cockroaches, a hideous nightshift spilling out on to the seat and the floor.

In size and appearance they weren't too dissimilar from 'crusties'; but if crusties were likeable and clean, free and fun-loving, cockroaches were horrible and filthy and very much at home crawling around in their maggot pit. I have no doubt heaven has its well-managed quota of crusties, while cockroaches make their invaluable contribution to the hellishness of hell.

Chapter 12

Failure of communication

Next morning, I woke eager to go out again, and dashed to the front of the house. Great! They hadn't gone. Father and son were still working on the sick engine. I hurried over. They were all smiles and confidence, saying they would soon be ready to retrieve the net.

Nothing was said about my bringing a full canteen of water. The *Crazy Pirate* was ready. We were off again. It was a beautiful morning and no one seemed unduly worried . . . until the motor started coughing and conked out again!

This time they had the right tools. A few minutes tinkering and thumping brought the purr back to the motor and the smiles back to four anxious faces.

We approached the flag marking the landward end of the net. The flag and float were hauled aboard. The attached rope was tied to the boat, and by a protracted business of circling and heaving the net came slowly up. The team work was excellent. The three Mexicans worked together calmly, quietly and efficiently. An air of good-humoured dignity hung over the boat.

The entangled fish appeared ghostly white as they were hauled towards the surface. The first one was pulled from the net and thrown back into the sea. The same fate met the second and third. When the fourth fish was cast back, I asked Victor Manuel why. He explained that it was only the sharks they wanted. They were the most valuable part of the catch. It simply wasn't worth freezing the rest and transporting them back to Ensenada.

The weakened and wasted victims of fish economics continued to smack the sea. Some floated and gasped feebly, others spiralled and flashed back down to the depths. But nothing is really wasted in the prodigious Gulf. Hungry, quarrelsome gulls appeared, filling the air with raucous cries while a pair of sea lions cruised cautiously around barking out their delight.

At last the first shark was hauled aboard and dumped into the centre of the boat. Sharks in fact made up more than half the catch. Most were small, in the three-foot to four-foot range. There were several larger specimens but nothing in the man-eater category. I was both relieved and disappointed.

Nearly all the sharks were dead. They have to keep swimming day and night to pass oxygen over their gills. To stop swimming is to stop breathing. Trapped in the net they soon suffocate and die. The few that came up alive were probably the last to be caught, and they weren't exactly full of fight.

As the boat sliced its way back to Calamajué my stomach seemed to be growling as much as the motor. But the day's work was only half done. There was a pile of fish to be sliced through.

After watching the young girls and boys going about their butchery with consummate ease, I borrowed a knife and asked one of the girls to instruct me in how to cut up a shark. I made my contribution to a background of good-natured giggles.

Another Mexican meal was my reward. I finished it, hoping it wouldn't finish me first. Then I discovered that the truck was about to leave. I gave the driver $20 and a shopping list that included a small bottle of tequila and a six-pack of beer.

'Spend the change on some beer and tequila for the village,' I said.

'Gracias. We'll be back in three or four days,' he replied.

Three or four days! As the implications of hanging around that long sank in, I realized how much I wanted to be alone. There was something awfully lonely about being unable to express the fears and feelings that I was bottling up inside. Ironically, the loneliness of being alone bothered me far less.

So, did I have to wait in the camp?, I wondered. Why not leave and ask one of the fishermen to meet me down the coast? Victor Manuel was the obvious person to ask. He agreed to bring me the supplies, but pointed out he couldn't make any promises with his present motor. He had, however, ordered a new one. It might arrive on the truck, then again it might not. So he cautioned against leaving until the truck had returned from Enseneda with the supplies and hopefully with the new engine. I allowed myself to be persuaded.

I spent the rest of the day sharpening my Spanish and playing dominoes with Margy, Guillermo, Tortillas and Victor Manuel. God knows where they got their rules from. I had no chance. It cost me nearly a dollar.

I developed a craving to communicate with someone who could speak half-way decent English – an American would do! I looked at the radio set. Guillermo must have read my mind. He suggested I try contacting someone in the United States to put a reverse charge phone call through to my friends in Los Angeles. I wanted to let Dave and Denise know that all was well in case my mother had been calling them. But I knew nothing about radios and the thought of using one to talk to a stranger hundreds of miles away almost had me in a panic. Even so, that evening I decided to give it a go. Guillermo switched it on and spun the dial, bringing the world into our tiny fishcamp.

At last we found a conversation in English. They sounded like a couple of aging Americans. It was fascinating to eavesdrop on their chat about cattle, fences, and cowgirls in Wyoming. Satisfied that it was only small talk, I looked at Guillermo and asked, 'What do I do? What do I say?'

'Press this button and say, "Breaking! Breaking!" then give your message.'

'Are you sure this is O.K.?'

'Si, Si. No problema. Es normal.'

Feeling a little embarrassed, I cut in saying, 'Breaking! Breaking! Sorry to interrupt your talk in Wyoming. My name is Graham Mackintosh. I'm an Englishman travelling in Mexico. It's very important that I get a message to someone in the United States. Over.'

I released the button and listened not really believing that anyone had heard me.

'John, John,' said the excited voice, 'I'll get back to you. It sounds like we've got an emergency. Over.'

'Breaker, Breaker, please give your call sign and the nature of your emergency. Over.'

Not wanting to be responsible for a heart attack I leapt in to reassure him, 'Actually it's not an emergency; but I'm down in a remote part of Mexico; I've been out of touch for a while and it would save a lot of people worrying if I could get a message to a friend in Los Angeles. Could you make a collect call to Mr or Mrs Bowyer at the following number and let them know I'm O. K., and that I'll be in touch as soon as I can. Over.'

'Breaker,' the voice said sharply. 'What is your call sign? Repeat, what is your call sign? Over.'

I turned to Guillermo and asked, 'What is my call sign?'

He didn't understand, and I couldn't understand his quick fire Spanish. But, full of faith in common sense and human nature, I replied, 'I'm sorry Wyoming, I don't know what the call sign is. I'm in a remote Mexican village. No one here speaks English. They've let me use the radio. I'm sorry if I'm doing this wrong. I know nothing about radio procedures. Over.'

Rather hoping for a helping hand I was amazed to hear, 'Breaker, I am not making that call. Negative, repeat negative to your request. Over and out.'

I was shattered. I couldn't believe anyone could be so rude and inconsiderate. Resisting the urge to tell the unhelpful bastard what I thought of him, I replied with a tame, 'Thank you very much. Over and out.' On the air or not, I should have vented my anger. Having said nothing, I suffered, and developed a deep and dreadful hate for people from Wyoming.

The waiting wasn't easy. The Mexicans did their best to entertain me, and I was invited out on as many fishing trips as I wanted. Unfortunately, each morning, I kept oversleeping and found myself waiting with the women and children for the boats to return.

Guillermo invited me over to see the children at school. Apart from the cold store the school was the best built structure in camp. The walls were hung with colourful posters celebrating the great events and personalities of Mexican history. Suitably inspired I asked the class of sixteen youngsters to sing their national anthem. At first they reacted with shy smiles and giggles but with just a little prompting from Guillermo they were happy to oblige. I taped the performance. There was something about these children that was totally different from their British and American counterparts. They displayed a healthy and relaxed respect for themselves and for others that was quite refreshing. I wondered whether this was partly because they hadn't been subjected to the insidious daily dose of media violence, rebellion, anxiety and neurosis so prevalent in the privileged countries of the West.

Unfortunately I had probably received an overdose. With too much time to think I grew increasingly troubled. Like a net-held shark, I found myself twisting and writhing in a vain attempt to escape something unknown that was slowly suffocating me.

When solitude seemed the answer I'd brave the heat and wander back along the coast with my fishing rod. One such venture proved disastrous.

Perched on a comfortable boulder beneath the shade of the cliffs, I stuck a hook through a piece of dried shark meat and, with the aid of an old spark plug, cast it into deep water. The fish were lining up to be caught and I wasn't really concentrating on what I was doing. The tip of the rod quivered. Another bite. I struck hard and up. This time there was a tremendous tug. I thought I'd hooked 'Jaws'. The rod arched and I was almost pulled into the sea. The drag on the reel was too tight. Something had to give. Zing! Crack! The line parted and the rod broke.

After gazing dumbly at the sea, I snapped out of it and made my first attempt to swear in Spanish. Still cursing my stupidity I turned around to pick up my shirt. The little Minox camera was in the pocket. It seemed a good idea to get a picture of the battle-scarred knight holding his broken lance. The shirt was strangely heavy. It was soaking! This time I swore in English. The weight of the camera had dragged part of the shirt down into an unseen sliver of a rock pool. The camera must have been submerged.

As fast as I could I tried to rewind the film. The lever snapped in my hand!

Racing back to camp, I opened the camera in the blackness beneath some blankets. Too late! The inside of the camera was filled with seawater and the film was soggy wet. The open camera dried quickly enough in the sun but it was visibly salt encrusted and corroded. After much deliberation I decided to throw it away. I was down to just one roll of film and my little red 'idiot-proof' Konica. I had a feeling that I was going to give it plenty of opportunity to prove itself.

Luckily I had more success with the rod. The telescopic design enabled me to tie the broken section inside another. Apart from being shorter, the rod was fine.

I wish the same could have been said about myself. When solitude brought no release, I'd writhe back into the easy-going sociability of the fishcamp. For a while the fun and games did the trick; but my insincerity and the aimlessness of it all caught up with me. I had to find the courage to face my pride, prejudice and disgust. Inside me something had to come down. Whatever the barrier was, I felt awfully lonely behind it. I needed to bare my soul and be myself in all my weakness and foolishness. There in Calamajué, I didn't know how.

Ever since I'd arrived in camp, I'd been waiting to fall ill; and I wasn't feeling too well the day I went exploring down the coast. Finding an impassable wall of rock on the southern point of the bay didn't make me feel any better. The cliffs fell sheer into ten-feet deep water. There was no way around except by cutting inland.

I followed a steep-sided little valley separated from the coast by a bare knife edge of rock. Trying to climb up one likely looking spot I found myself staring at a 200-foot vertical drop. I explored the length of the valley looking for another way over. There wasn't one. I recalled the unbroken line of cliffs I saw from the boat. Leaving Calamajué wasn't going to be easy.

With that realization, the will-power that had kept me exploring suddenly vanished. As much as I wanted to get back to camp and escape the heat and sun, I couldn't find the energy to take another step. Frightened, I sat down on a flat table-like rock, my head dropped to my knees and stayed there till my back ached and my brain threatened to explode. Convinced I was becoming seriously ill, I lowered myself on to the rock and remained there spreadeagled. The rock's heat burned into my back while the sun burned me from above. Staring at the expanse of blue I felt like an Aztec victim stretched out ready to have his beating heart ripped from his chest. Beads of sweat formed all over my body.

The food and water appeared to have finally caught up with me. 'Montezuma's Revenge' they call it; the debilitating sickness and diarrhoea that almost inevitably hits gringo travellers in Mexico. The languor and the lassitude had already struck. No doubt, the runs would follow. Here we go, maggots by day, cockroaches by night; if it's not coming out one end it'll be the other, and in this heat you'll be lucky if you don't disappear in the middle.

Beneath that pale blue sky I lost track of time and saw how sweet it could be to just surrender and die. Surrender and die... the thought echoed seductively inside my skull.

Fear forced me to snap out of it and summon what was left of my willpower. I had to stand up. I had to walk. I had to get back to camp. Forming my futile moans into encouraging curses I staggered as if drunk back towards the safety of the fishcamp.

As I entered Calamajué, it seemed immensely important to appear normal and cheerful; stiff upper lip and all that; the British strength and weakness. But behind the smiles I was suppressing the urge to vomit.

I found Tortillas, Guillermo and Victor Manuel playing the inevitable game of dominoes. They had acquired beer from somewhere. I was offered one. Hoping it would help, I took a good long thirst-quenching swig. However, the sickly warm taste almost had me rushing to bury the maggots.

I had to get away. With the excuse that I was hot and tired I headed off to Tortillas' house. He came after me. I couldn't fool him.

'Remember,' he said. 'My house is your house. Whatever you need is yours.' His sensitive eyes were full of caring concern.

Struggling to express myself in terms other than tears of gratitude, I replied, 'But I have no money to pay you back.'

'Money? What do I want with money? I have what I need and what is mine is yours.'

As Tortillas walked back to his amigos, I stepped inside his house wondering how I could be so squeamish and stupid.

I was a total stranger, at times a nuisance and quite obviously 'loco'. I had nothing to give, yet I had received nothing but kindness and hospitality. How ironic that those people, who had so little and worked so hard for what they had, would have given me the shirt off their backs. No wonder Christ chose so many simple fishermen for his disciples.

And what do I do? React like a delicate sickly schoolgirl. Disgust! I was disgusted with myself.

I thought of how Tortillas was treating me as the honoured guest in his country and his home, and how he would have fared in the United States. To most he would have been a mere Mexican, a wetback, an uneducated peasant, a 'loser' to be treated with suspicion and derision. No wonder he couldn't stand it.

The bed was a more comfortable place to lie than the rock, but otherwise I felt the same. Sleep would have been a merciful release but it didn't come. Semi-delirium was as close as I got. As best I could I made preparations for the night ahead, gathering together a bucket, a toilet roll, my torch and a pair of shoes. With Tortillas' kindly words echoing inside my head I waited . . . waited to be sick, to get the runs or, if I was really lucky, to fall asleep.

After drifting in and out of oblivion I was thoroughly confused when Margy breezed in with his 'How do you do?' Oh God! I wasn't in the mood for Margy. Standing there with his kerosene lamp he looked a cruelly comical caricature of Florence Nightingale.

'Can I borrow your torch?' he asked.

Oh fuck! I don't believe it! Suppose I have to dash to the toilet in the dark? The idea was too horrible to contemplate. Yet I couldn't say no.

'O.K. Margy,' I said resignedly, 'but please leave the lamp. I may need it.'

'Si, si, gracias, amigo.' He left as I mumbled confused nonsense about wetbacks, imbeciles and God bless America!

Hardly recovered from his visit I found myself woken by Tortillas. He was drunk and kept muttering, 'Too much, too much beer, too much pot, you forget, forget everything, forget tonight.'

I would gladly have forgotten that whole day. It was like a bad dream. Wondering what he might do, I pretended to be asleep – I'm sure I was a possum in my previous life – and prayed he'd hit the sack or go away.

He left with the lamp and spent the remainder of the night elsewhere. Mercifully, after he'd gone I slept uninterrupted.

Much to my surprise I woke feeling fine and in the best of health. Was all that sickness in my head, I wondered. Can our minds really do that to us?

The more I thought about it the more determined I was not to give in to my fears. I made up my mind to stop moaning about the lack of hygiene and actually do something about it.

I started tidying Tortillas' house, cleaning the shelves, washing the dishes and covering the food. Then I picked up the eggshells and other litter strewn around the floor. Reaching into one dark corner my hand touched a web. Thinking nothing of it I continued to fumble for a piece of shell; then something made me recoil sharply.

Shining the torch in the corner I saw that the web belonged to a black widow. The red hourglass on the underside of the black shiny abdomen was unmistakable. I ground the spider into the dirt before carrying on slightly more cautiously with my spring cleaning.

Margy came in to fry some eggs for his breakfast. 'What are you doing?' he asked.

'Tidying the house,' I replied.

That obviously made as much sense to him as walking 3,000 miles.

He cracked his eggs and threw the shells on the tidied floor. I politely pointed out the absurdity of my picking up eggshells at one end of the kitchen while he was dropping them at the other. He looked at me as if I'd totally flipped.

I just laughed. I even laughed every time I banged my head on that sausage on the line. Let it hang there; let Margy do what he likes. I'll do what I think is right. My attitude had changed dramatically. I felt good and cheerful and quite beyond the petty little frustrations of life.

Snatching a well-earned break, I relaxed outside in the morning sun. The gentle rhythm of the waves seemed to be telling the world to . . . hush . . . hush. Flicking through a Spanish Bible, Psalm 23 caught my eye. I wrote it out, then translated it.

'He leads me beside still waters, he restores my soul . . . Even though I walk through the valley of the shadow of death . . .'

The words were full of meaning. I closed my eyes. Momentarily Sharon's loveliness came to mind. It was quite a let-down to open them again to see Margy standing over me with his angelic smile.

Once too often he said, 'How do you do?' For the sake of my sanity it was time to teach him a little more English. It was a bit like banging my head against a brick wall but he did pick up a few more useful words and phrases. His new favourite seemed to be, 'I would like to buy some beer, thank you very much.'

Perhaps I was being too hard on Margy. He was likeable in his own way; just a little lazy and slow. The only thing he did quickly was disappear like a startled 'crustie' when I suggested we go back inside and finish tidying the house.

19 May arrived – my birthday. It was steamy and hot. Those who could languished inside. I spent most of the day talking, playing dominoes and, for want of something better, drinking chocomilk. I had intended to explore further along the coast, but the debilitating heat precluded anything so adventurous.

Even so, there was an air of hope. Along with everyone else I was hoping the truck would return. We were all in the mood for a little celebration. When the truck hadn't appeared by dusk, the hope disappeared. So much for my birthday fiesta.

I must have looked a lonely figure walking slowly along the beach. Victor called me up to his house and presented me with a can of beer: 'I was keeping this for a special occasion and I heard it was your birthday.' I protested that I couldn't possibly take it, but he insisted. I was deeply touched.

As I made my way back to the shore the last trace of colour was sucked from the sky. I sat on a rock still warm from the sun and listened again to the gentle hush of the sea. The beer was as warm as the rock but it tasted beautiful. A crescent moon hung half-way down the heavens. I thought of my family and friends on the other side of the world and wondered if they were thinking of me.

I had no fear of rattlesnakes or scorpions, nor any anxieties about what lay ahead. The peaceful feeling in my soul was in total contrast to the turmoil that had seized me just two days before. I was as healthy as I'd ever been. I didn't even have a cold.

It seemed like another barrier had been surmounted. I felt relaxed and very much at home. Future fishcamps would hold no terror.

It was getting late. I strolled back to the house and threw myself on the bed. Picking up my headphones I listened to a distant American radio station putting out country music and providing useful information about conditions on Oklahoma's freeways.

I was more asleep than awake when Tortillas came rushing in. The truck! The truck was coming. Its sweeping beams lit up the night. I put on my boots and followed Tortillas outside.

We rushed up to find the driver relating his adventures to the gathering crowd of fishermen. Six-packs of deliciously cold beer were pulled from the ice-filled rear of the truck and passed around. Soon everyone was laughing and happy. The truck was back. Now there was plenty again. Guillermo had his Ensenada water. Victor Manuel's new motor was aboard. I was given the change for my $20 in the form of a litre of tequila and a dozen cans of beer. 'This is for you all,' I shouted, 'to say thank you for your hospitality.'

I was getting into the swing of it and what a marvellous birthday present it turned out to be. Four cans of beer later I sang my way back to bed, dispatched by merry rounds of 'Happy birthday'.

Everything was set. The waiting was over. I had one last chance to go fishing. 'Loco Diez' had offered to take me the following morning – if I got up on time! I liked Loco Diez. He was one of the characters of the camp, a big jolly sumo-wrestler type who liked to bang his knee and slap my back every time I said something amusing. In his eyes almost everything I said was amusing.

Ever since I arrived in camp he'd worn the same T-shirt sporting a big number ten. His pals introduced him as 'loco', so I called him Loco Diez (Crazy Ten). He liked the name and thought it very original.

Unfortunately, I overslept again. Instead of fishing, I spent my last morning in Calamajué watching the unloading of the truck and the division of the spoils. There was a marvellous spirit of giving and sharing.

Guillermo had bought a great slab of mouth-watering steak. He fried it up and dished it out to anyone who came by, myself included. Suddenly it was all gone. It must have been heart-breaking for him.

Meat was a precious commodity in the fisherman's paradise of Baja California. Clavigero, a Jesuit missionary writing in the eighteenth century, described how the natives had learned to string out their enjoyment of the all too rare treat:

> They . . . tie a mouthful of meat . . . securely with a string; they put it in their mouths, and having chewed it a little, they swallow it, allowing the string to hang from the mouth; they keep it in their stomachs two or three minutes, and then they bring it back to the mouth by pulling it up by means of the string . . . When many individuals eat together in this manner they sit down on the ground forming a circle. One of them takes the morsel and swallows it, and after pulling it out he gives it to another and the latter to still another; and thus they proceed through all the circle with the greatest pleasure until the morsel is consumed.

As soon as I finished the steak Guillermo gave me a mango. Before I finished slobbering on that, others came in and presented me with more bits and pieces for the journey. The spirit of giving was almost like Christmas. I soon caught on. I divided a large bag of sweets between the children, and gave away an orange here and an apple there. These lovely people were teaching me one of the greatest lessons of my life.

Thanks to all the interchange my supplies had taken on a much more Mexican flavour. I had tortillas, flour, oil, coffee, sugar, chili, 'Tres-Minutos' (the local version of Quaker Oats), and enough tiny limes to make a passable model of Mount Everest. Apart from holding scurvy at bay, I was assured they were excellent for combating thirst.

I divided the food into two stacks. One I put aside ready to load into the backpack, the other I sealed in a cardboard box to be left with Victor Manuel. To ensure there would be no misunderstanding, I wrote out and attached a little message in Spanish.

'Please bring this food and three gallons of water to me three days after I leave. Many thanks.'

The boats returned. In spite of the heat I felt honour bound to be down on the beach gutting the catch and carrying the stacked boxes of shark fillets up to be weighed and stored. The carrying was heavy, exhausting work. Three of us would take two crates up at a time. More often than not I found myself in the middle with a crate and an over-eager fisherman on either side. Everything was being done at a feverish, very un-Mexican pace. I felt sure they were testing me but I did my share without complaint. Towards the end I was ready to drop but I wasn't going to show it. At last, with some satisfaction, I noticed the pace slackening. I had survived their playful onslaught and earned their respect.

Whatever else these fishermen were, they were 'macho' – men and proud of it. Like fishermen everywhere they held in high regard the manly values of strength, courage and uncomplaining forbearance. To them I was an enigma, 'el gringo loco', the little redhead with the big ideas. They wanted to know what I was made of.

Some of them were also drinkers. The litre of tequila I'd left for the village hadn't lasted long – largely, I suspect, due to Tortillas and Margy. I wasn't altogether surprised to see the empty bottle in Tortillas' house.

Dreaming of tequila-sipping nights by my campfire, I was finding a place for my little bottle in a side-pocket of the backpack when Tortillas walked in. He spotted the bottle and his eyes lit up. He didn't say a word but I knew . . .

He was too fond of drinking. Not wanting to encourage it, I held up the quarter bottle of tequila and a solitary can of beer, 'These are for my trip; a little campfire comfort.'

Again he didn't say a word but his eyes said it all. I had a crisis of conscience. I thought of all he'd done for me . . . Sod it! It wasn't my job to moralize, and anyway I'd be better off keeping my wits in the wilderness. I poured him a glass and thanked him for his hospitality. Then I gave him the rest of the bottle and said, 'I'll be back in five minutes, save a glass for me.'

Picking up the can of beer, I stepped outside and walked over to Victor's house. It wasn't the easiest thing I ever did but it was the right thing. I offered it to him and thanked him again for his thoughtfulness. He seemed as touched and grateful as I had been on my birthday.

The sun was setting on my last evening in camp. I found Margy still at work in the cold store. He was a great guy. I wished him well in the United States, reflecting that he was unlikely to find the same hospitality north of the border as I had received in Calamajué.

I returned to Tortillas' shack to find another empty bottle of tequila on the table. He was nowhere to be seen. I would trust Tortillas with my life but not with a bottle of tequila.

I went to bed that night with just one care. I had to get up on time. Victor Manuel had agreed to take me in his boat beyond that impassable spot at the southern end of the bay. That short ride would save me having to venture inland and make a dangerous climb back down to the coast.

My final thoughts were on Calamajué, the camp I was supposed to get out of before dark, but in the end I'd stayed over a week. I was still in one piece and as healthy as I'd ever been; psychologically perhaps even more healthy.

The good people of that little fishcamp had taught me a lot. My respect for them had grown day by day. In a way it was a wrench to be saying goodbye; but in another way I wanted very much to be off. Aimlessly sitting around doesn't bring out my best.

I was determined not to miss that boat.

Chapter 13

Difficulties and dangers

I stepped into the boat just as the sun was peeking over the horizon. Its warmth was immediate. Before long it would be glaring down in red-hot anger. I looked at the three gallons of water Guillermo had given me and felt reassured.

The new motor burst into life and whisked us beyond the awkward point. My mind was a whirl of excitement, apprehension and uncertainty as the boat weaved between the rocks guarding the narrow stone beach on the other side. I advised caution, not wanting to be responsible for damaging the new engine. It sounded beautiful compared to its predecessor, a purring kitten in place of a growling old tom cat.

Looking and feeling a bit like a spy landing on a hostile shore, I leapt out of the boat and on to the beach. Victor handed me my equipment and one final piece of advice. 'Remember, in twenty or thirty kilometres you will find the palms and possibly water.'

'I won't forget! Adios, amigos. Good luck! I'll see you in two or three days; perhaps at the palms. Thanks for everything.'

Their panga disappeared into the rising fireball, leaving me alone and insignificant beneath the cliffs. Full of adrenalin, I had to force myself to keep still long enough to swallow an orange, get in my contact lenses, cover myself in sunscreen, and repack my equipment. Then there was no holding me. To the crash, bash of boots on pebbles I was underway again.

In spite of the weight of the pack and the awkwardness of the water containers, I was flying along over the narrowest of pathways between the sea and the cliffs. Ribbon-like stony beaches were interspersed with steep tumbled piles of fallen boulders and great spurs of smooth rock cutting into deep water like the bows of a ship.

There was no obvious way around one such point which loomed up sheer before me. In no mood to stop and think, I turned to my right and scrambled up a dam-like slope of loose debris. I was hoping I could climb high enough to traverse the ridge and make it down the other side.

Near the top, an outcrop of solid rock defied me to pass. The only way was an inches-wide, downward-angled ledge of crumbling granite. I stared at it for several minutes. If I fell, I'd have a ten-foot sheer drop before hitting the hundred foot face of the 'dam'. At its base was the sea and an assortment of skull-cracking rocks.

With my feet slowly sinking into the loose material of the slope, I tied the canteen to the pack, tightened up all the straps, then, holding the water bag in my left hand, I shuffled nervously on to the ledge.

Half-way across I stepped on a loose slab of stone. Without warning it crumbled from the ledge taking me with it. I found myself kicking and grasping air before my boots crashed into the rubble below. The water bag went flying as I flipped into a rocket-like, head first, belly-dragging descent. Riding on a sliding mass of debris I accelerated like a toboggan out of control. A large rounded rock raced towards me. My arms shot forward to protect my head; somehow they took the blow without fracture and I skidded off into a spin before sliding to a halt a few feet from the sea. Cradling my head I waited for the noise to die and the dust to settle.

I was lying awkwardly, head down and half buried. Although I couldn't feel any pain, I knew I'd been hurt; the question was how badly.

When I tried to get up, nothing happened. I couldn't move. The shock sent me wriggling furiously till I'd overcome the weight of the pack and thrown off the rocks that had come down on top of me. I scrambled to my feet to inspect the damage.

Predictably my hands, chin, knees and elbows had suffered most. Blood flowed freely from a dozen cuts and scrapes. Having satisfied myself that they were all superficial, I turned my attention to that equally important liquid – water!

The aluminium belt bottle had been bashed in on one side, but otherwise it was still intact and full. The water canteen had remained tied to the pack and had suffered nothing worse than the loss of some of its felt covering. But where was the water bag? After several anxious minutes searching I found it wedged under a boulder halfway down the slope. Miraculously, it was still full and apparently undamaged.

I had been incredibly lucky. Water aside, I could have easily broken my back in the initial fall or fractured my skull at the bottom of the slope. As it was, I felt perky enough not to want to waste a good photographic opportunity. I pulled out the camera and set it up for a self-timer shot of me washing off the blood and writhing in agony. My posing was to no avail. The camera was dead! Suddenly the pained expression was deep and genuine.

Camera or no camera, I still had to find a way out of my predicament. Reconsidering the possibility of getting by in the sea, I strangely became optimistic and enthusiastic about what was, to any sane person, a very dubious prospect. Not wanting to start a shark-feeding frenzy, I washed off most of the blood in a rock pool before wading into the sea with the pack balanced above my head. Keeping on a thick pair of socks for protection against the submerged rocks and stones, I waded as far out as I dared but couldn't see any way of climbing up the smooth wet rock. Standing shoulder deep and slipping, I came to my senses and struggled out of the water before I dropped the pack.

My first instinct had been sounder. There was only one way I was going to get both myself and my pack out of there – and that was up the slope, along the ledge and over the ridge.

Mindful of another fall, I put on a pair of jeans instead of shorts. My legs began trembling, no doubt due to the combined effects of injury, delayed shock, and fear. Feeling a bit like Sisyphus, I struggled back to the top of the steep wall of rubble. The trembling grew worse as I stood by the ledge and tied both the water bag and the canteen to the pack. Having both hands free will make a big difference, I reasoned. A pity they were shaking so much. I needed those big, strong adventurers' hands noted by Chris Bonington.

For several minutes I alternated between gazing hopefully ahead and looking despondently down. Then, knowing I had no option, I shuffled across again. My toes were digging instinctively into the soles of my boots. Twice I slipped and hung on desperately while bits of rock cracked their way down to the sea. It was real B-movie stuff.

Overcoming the panic urge to run the last few feet, I kept whatever cool I possessed to make it safely to the ridge. But I should have guessed what was on the other side; another dam-like descent of loose rock. If anything, it was steeper!

Well, I certainly wasn't going back. So, I took the water bag in my hand again, went through my customary hesitation, then stepped from more or less solid rock on to loose scree. Straightaway I found myself sliding alarmingly fast with half the slope avalanching down with me. I made a vain effort to keep feet first. The weight of the pack threw me into an uncontrollable tumble. The water bag, once again, went its own way as I concentrated on avoiding breaking my neck. When the sliding and the racket had stopped, I'd added a few more superficial injuries to my collection and virtually ruined a good shirt and an irreplaceable pair of jeans. Otherwise my luck had held once again.

With adrenalin to burn, I picked up everything and pushed on. There were more ups and downs, thrills and spills. Having been cooped up in the fishcamp for so long all I could think of was . . . go . . . go . . . go! It was crazy. Just like those flat-out, rat-race mornings driving to work – usually late – when every red light was a disaster. Then, all I could do was rant and rave. Now the energy had somewhere to go, pent up muscles had something to do.

However, Erle Stanley Gardner had wisely said, 'It is almost axiomatic in Baja California that haste not only makes waste, but completes destruction.' He was talking about driving conditions, but it wasn't just a lesson for Baja's roads. It was one I learned just in time along that rugged stretch of coast. I forced myself to stop and think; to try difficult moves first without the equipment; to split the load and make two or three journeys if necessary.

In spite of the low tide, one point was only passable up to my chest in the sea. After trying it unburdened, I took the pack forty yards over and then waded forty yards back for the boots and water. In total, I had to make five bare-footed, chest deep journeys over the same rough rocks. After that I sat out the day's high tide in a hollow beneath the cliffs. The two miles I'd put behind me had been horrendous. I hoped the next eighty would be better.

After tending to my wounds and repairing the damaged clothing, I pulled out the camera. What a disaster! I could see no alternative but to return to the United States and somehow procure another one. It would be just my luck to get bitten by a rattler and have my leg balloon up purple, green and gangrenous, and be unable to get a photo. More as a gesture than anything else, I tried changing the batteries, and that did the trick. The camera hadn't been damaged at all!

Overjoyed, I packed everything away, laced up my boots and bounced over the rocks as pleased as a porpoise.

On the beach I came across a large shark, one of the biggest I had ever seen. It was tempting to knock out some of his wicked looking teeth for souvenirs, but he was going off a bit, so I pushed on with my usual escort of seals and dolphins. It was a great afternoon's work. I kept going as long as I could. Just before sunset, the rising tide forced me to halt and make camp on a narrow little stony beach under a high cliff. I wrote in my diary:

> Probably finished the day with ten miles under my belt. Couldn't pass deep water so camped under cliff on stone. Not very comfy but slept well. Beautiful calm evening, sea flat, almost tangible silence. Red, pink and orange sunset. Pelicans active, coasting wingtips on water,

diving for fish, splashing clearly heard over remarkable distance. I slept in optimum position above rising tide and away from rockfall danger. Heard some rubble falling as I entered tent (never erected, just crawled in). Before sleeping sat with head out listening to country music and watching stars and moon shadows above. INJURY REPORT: Palms cut and skin removed (lemon juice and sea water sting). Left palm, base of thumb swollen and bruised, problem when rock climbing. Other cuts and scrapes, no problem. Soles of feet bruised and tender from wading and all day pounding on rocks.

Next morning, I got by with the low tide and raced as fast as I dare. I was surprised and delighted to see a panga ahead. Whatever the two fishermen were doing they weren't shark fishing. They were in relatively shallow water only fifty yards from shore.

I shouted out, excitedly stringing together a whole bunch of fairly basic, comically ungrammatical, mispronounced Spanish. One of the fishermen could stand it no longer. He called back in perfect English.

'Say what you want to say in English, I can speak it as well as you.'

A little embarrassed, I asked, 'Where are you from?'

'Alphonsinas,' he replied. 'We know all about you.'

'What's the coast like ahead?'

'Terrible. There's nothing ahead. You won't make it. Come back with us.'

'Thanks for the offer, but I've got to try.'

'There's no water.'

'Some of the fishermen from Calamajué will be bringing me water in a couple of days.'

'Don't depend on anyone out here. Anything could happen. Are you sure you won't come back with us?'

'No thanks. I must try.'

'You won't make it,' he repeated. 'If your friends show, go back with them.'

'Perhaps I will. How far ahead are the palms?'

'About eighty kilometres!'

'I was told they were just a few kilometres from here and I might find water there.'

'They're eighty kilometres – maybe fifty miles – and you won't find any water.'

He gave a dismissive wave as if to say, be it on your own head, then started his motor and speeded back to Alphonsinas.

I was forced to climb high over huge rounded boulders to get by one headland the size of a football stadium. Approaching the point I heard what at first appeared to be mocking laughter. I had become used to the apparent laughter of the gulls but this was different.

My suspicions were confirmed. Looking down, I saw a sea lion colony. About thirty of them lolled on top of a little rocky island while another twenty rested on their backs in the water with flippers up as if about to clap: 'Well done, gringo, you've made it this far, only another 2,800 miles to go . . . ar, ar, ar.'

The smug looking sea lions floating on the surface looked totally vulnerable, but from my vantage point I could see other sea lions swimming beneath their colleagues, perhaps on watch for sharks.

I thought of an incident that the ex-Royal Navy officer Lieutenant Robert Hardy had witnessed while exploring the Gulf on behalf of The General Pearl and Coral Fishery Association of London between the years 1825–8:

> My attention was suddenly diverted . . . by a splashing in the water below . . . It was a combat between a seal and two monstrously large sharks . . . Never did I witness anything half so terrific . . . the long tails of the sharks were four or five feet out of the water . . . and flouncing with ferocious energy to keep the seal from rising to the surface. Presently their tails entirely disappeared, and in an instant more, the ruffled surface of the water . . . was discoloured with blood, bubbling up from below!

The scene below looked so peaceful I had no wish to witness a sea lion being bitten in two amidst a billowing cloud of crimson.

A very big, bull seal lion – he looked capable of biting a shark in two – spotted me on the rocks, leapt into the sea and swam beside me, head up and barking furiously. I had the feeling I was being escorted off the premises.

The coast ahead seemed to be a succession of 'impossible' looking stretches; but one by one I got by them. The sun was sinking, yet there was no sign of a suitable campsite. I pushed on, hopeful to the end, telling myself that just ahead, just around the next point, there'd be a beach, or a fishcamp, or the elusive palms.

I took off my shirt and stuffed it under the shoulder straps of the backpack for added comfort as I leapt from boulder to boulder along the water's edge. Suddenly . . . Shisssh! I froze in my tracks. A yard to my right a rattlesnake was coiled, hissing and rattling. What a racket! It was a four-foot long, perfectly camouflaged, greyish coloured diamondback. If he hadn't drawn attention to himself, I would have walked right by him. He looked and sounded like the incarnation of evil.

So much for all the photographs and sleepy zoo specimens I'd seen, this guy was real, viciously alive, and determined to stay that way.

Like a cat caught between caution and curiosity I remained frozen, unsure what to do. When the snake was convinced that I wasn't going to back away, he slowly uncoiled and slid into a crevice.

Emboldened by his retreat, and realizing that all I had to eat were limes and cornflakes, I found myself reaching down for a rock. The snake spotted me and struck out so quickly, I dropped the rock and got away as fast as I could. Suddenly, marinated cornflakes sounded very appetising.

I dashed on with a fresh burst of energy. The rustle of scattering 'crusties' and the crunch of boots on crisp, dry seaweed had me hearing rattlers everywhere.

Just before dark I reached a broad valley, and made camp on a cracked, sun-baked river bed. Several cacti rose from the valley floor. They were more in evidence as I travelled south.

Inside the tent I was content to rest on top of the sleeping bag and listen to the silence. The moon was big and bright. I was reflecting on the fact that I was probably days from the nearest road or person when a nearby coyote sent his chilling yelp rising into the still night air.

On a ridge above the valley a lone coyote stood dramatically silhouetted against the moon-lit sky. He looked down on me long and hard before baying the moon again in fine Hammer film style. That started off a whole chorus of his unseen comrades.

I slid the machete beneath my pillow and, to help drown out the disturbing cacophony, slipped on the earphones. I heard that Texas was being battered by storms and tornadoes. In my little corner of the Mexican desert, all was quiet and peaceful, coyotes apart.

I woke with water on the brain. I had just two pints left, barely enough to get me through the morning. Beyond that, only my stills or the boat from Calamajué could save me from death by dehydration. So breakfast was just a symbolic mouthful of cornflakes and a couple of tiny limes. The terrors of thirst were putting my hunger in perspective.

Before long my way was decisively blocked by a little steep-sided salient of rock. It probably wasn't more than thirty yards from beach to point, or much higher than a truck, but it was too smooth to climb and wading around was no easy option. Sliding off my pack, I stripped and slowly edged into the sea. There wasn't a ripple or a wave. The bottom dropped away alarmingly fast but, thanks to an underwater ledge, I managed to claw my way out to the point and pull myself up to stand lord of all I surveyed. The northern tip of the forty-mile long Guardian Angel Island floated between the blues of the sea and the sky. The island would be my constant companion all the way to the Bay of L.A. (assuming I got that far). The coast immediately ahead was invitingly flat. If I could just get my pack past that awkward little spur, I'd have a comparatively easy run.

The climb down the other side wasn't easy. I had to lower myself off the rock into waist deep water and wade up to the beach. Well, it was certainly possible, if a bit risky. I swam back around formulating my plan. My main fear was dropping the pack.

The tide was rising. I had to act fast. I slipped the camera, tape-recorder and suchlike inside a slightly torn black plastic bag, and buried it deep inside the rucksack.

Balancing the pack on my head, I sidled out to the point without too much trouble. The problem was to lift it high enough to wedge it on the rocks. My arms were aching and there wasn't much of a foothold. I gritted my teeth and gambled. Like a snatching weight-lifter, I pushed up hard with both hands. As I did so, my feet slipped and the weight of the pack bowled me over backwards. The water crashing over my head cut short my curses.

I was underwater, hanging on desperately to the pack. I daren't open my eyes for fear of losing my contact lenses. All I could do was push up from the bottom to take a breath and my bearings, and then half-swim and half-claw my way back to the shallows.

As soon as I reached a sunny spot I pulled everything out as fast as I could. It was nearly all wet – the diary, first-aid kit, passport, cornflakes, tent, and sleeping bag. My main worry was the camera and tape-recorder, but luckily the water hadn't penetrated.

Thirty minutes later, with almost everything dry, I heard a motor, looked up and saw a panga cruising down the coast. Guessing it was from Calamajué, I picked up my mirror and flashed it towards them. Sure enough, it was Victor, Victor Manuel and Loco Diez, three of the most beautiful, weather-beaten faces in the world. They had brought the food and water, and, thoughtful to the end, a breakfast of three hard-boiled eggs.

While they surveyed all the equipment spread out in the sun, we laughed and joked and discussed my adventures. I showed them the solar still and the radio distress beacon, and explained their use. These men who live and die on the sea immediately appreciated such items.

I asked them to ferry my equipment round the rocky point and drop it on the beach. They agreed, but insisted on taking me as well. At first I declined, explaining that I had to walk; then I thought, what the heck, I've already climbed and swum around; so I threw my stuff into the *Crazy Pirate* and in a moment was on the other side.

They still insisted that the palms were just ahead. Thanking my friends and congratulating them on their timing, I waved goodbye and sadly watched them tear out into the Gulf. I wondered if I'd ever see them again.

Carrying my possessions to a suitably shady spot, I burst into song, 'Thank you for giving me this morning. Thank you for giving me this day. Thank you for every new day dawning. I'll be thanking you.'

My needs were simple. I had food, water, shade and stacks of driftwood. The way ahead was clear. I had much to be thankful for.

After making a fire and a cup of tea, I opened up the food box and made a valiant effort to put back some of the weight I'd lost – you can't beat carrying a heavy pack all day under a blazing sun for losing weight.

What a difference shade makes! I took a renewed interest in everything around me: the little fly that landed on my hand and obstinately refused to depart; the hummingbird that momentarily startled and delighted; the ever-present circling, soaring sea birds; the contented crows and vultures clinging to their shady nooks; and the far-off whale sending up its plumes of spray.

It was about 4.00 p.m. before I felt capable of moving again. The pack seemed ridiculously heavy. All my water containers were full and I still had a couple of pints that I couldn't drink. Reluctantly, I left it behind, buried in a heap of rocks beside the blackened remains of my fire. I fixed the location in my mind, just in case. . . .

The coast ahead loomed jagged, tumbling and defiant. It was going to make me pay dearly for every mile. In one hand I had the water bag. In the other, the canteen and a plastic bag full of food. I daren't fall with both hands full. Time after time I had to split the load, carrying one part over some awkward obstruction, then returning maybe fifty or a hundred yards for the rest. I felt I was walking Baja twice!

Guardian Angel Island appeared stark red and mountainous as I drew level with its northernmost point. The sea between was doldrum flat. Every splash and ripple could be seen and heard for miles. A shark fin rose and sliced ominously through the oily blue water. A large moray eel writhed and frolicked noisily in the rocky shallows. Like a stuttering machine-gun, a huge shoal of fish shot from the sea and curved back in again. The distant throb of a ship's engine carried from the middle of the channel.

The cliffs gave way to a stretch of flat coast where a vast wash came down from the mountains. Several cacti rose from its barren course, but no palm trees. A few miles in from the beach, the mountains leapt up beautiful in layers of salmon pink and cream, and hues of pastel green. I wondered if this was the mouth of La Asamblea canyon that Erle Stanley Gardner had explored and written about.

> Behind . . . [the rugged beach] . . . was a stretch of some five miles of deep sand running up a barren wash where some of the most colourful mountains I have ever seen were spread haphazardly on each side of the wash. Striated in a variety of colours – red, pink, green and various pastel shades – they were for the most part completely devoid of vegetation.

I recalled that he wrote about a spring of water in La Asamblea about twelve miles up from the ocean, of people who had reached it, and of others who lost their lives trying. He also described how two prospectors had landed on the beach and slogged up the sandy wash to the mouth of the canyons. One man agreed to take the food and water and to prospect. His companion returned to the boat to collect further supplies:

> On returning to the place selected as a rendezvous, the man who was laden with provisions and all the water he could carry found no trace of his companion. He waited patiently with time rapidly running out, then started exploring trying to find the tracks of his companion. Eventually he found his partner. He had been bitten by a rattlesnake and had died a horrible death. The story was pathetically told by the man's rolled-up trouser leg, the tourniquet he had contrived above the bite, and the knife slashes he had made in his leg . . . round the man's shoulder was a sack containing ore. Stories vary as to the richness of the ore. Some people say simply that it was very rich; others say that it was almost pure gold.

Just before sunset, I found my passage along the shore frustrated by a rounded pink headland which fell undercut into the sea. Walking on top was extremely dangerous. The smooth rock cracked and crumbled as if bursting from its skin. After sliding alarmingly close to one sheer drop, I backtracked to find a place to sleep on the beach below.

It was almost dark. I hated to make camp without knowing there was an obvious way ahead. My mood became as black as the once colourful mountains silhouetted against the lingering redness of the sunset. However, the peace and stillness slowly revived my spirits. Conditions were perfect for the run into Bahía de los Angeles. The full moon was approaching with the promise of extreme low tides. Perhaps the morning's low would enable me to bypass the point. Perhaps . . .

The spectacular sunrise tempted me to use one of my precious remaining photographs, but unfortunately the tide hadn't fallen sufficiently. The water was still much too deep beneath the smooth rocks. I climbed back on to the treacherously crumbling headland and reconfirmed my earlier assessment that it was too dangerous.

I walked back along the coast till I found a climbable gulley. With snakes uppermost in my mind, I ventured up to explore the possibilities. The contrast between the coal-black boulders and the bright pink soil between them, coupled with the complete absence of vegetation, produced a lunar or martian effect. Bouncing little green men wouldn't have looked too out of place. On top I was greeted by a series of barren, apparently walkable hills and ridges. The time had come to cut inland. I hurried back down for my equipment.

I kept off the ridges, while the deep valleys offered early morning shade which I would never have found on the coast. Glimpses of the sparkling sea reassured me from time to time that I hadn't wandered too far from its relative security.

I found a trail. It was only a few inches wide but well worn. I followed it with increasing admiration. Taking the line of least resistance, it marked the perfect pathway paralleling the coast, guiding me safely around rocky outcrops, across dangerous little gorges and through seemingly impenetrable brush. Every time I thought I knew better I got into trouble. Clearly it was the work of some cartographic genius who knew exactly where he was going and how to get there. But who could have made it and still be keeping it open? I bent down to examine the evidence. In several places it bore the unmistakable impression of paw prints. Coyotes! It could only be a coyote trail. Without quite realizing it, I had made one of the most important discoveries of the trip. The coyote expressway led me safely back to a relatively easy section of the coast.

Unfortunately, 'easy' meant little shade. And without shade there was no point in stopping, it always seemed twice as hot when I stood still. Like a figure in a nightmare, I dashed from one shadowy refuge to another. To anyone who couldn't imagine the difference between exposure to the blistering sun and the relief of a shady crevice, my antics must have looked ridiculous.

The water bag was almost empty. The bulk of its three gallons had been sweated through a myriad overworked pores. Tension rose in direct proportion to the lightening of the bag. I imagined the cool rustling shade of the palms and the prospect of unlimited supplies of water.

Ahead, rising from the heat haze, I could see what appeared to be the remains of a wood on some well-shelled sector of a First World War battlefield. What were they? Certainly not cacti. Can't be telegraph poles.

Bewilderment gave way to disappointment. I was staring at the leafless trunks of palm trees. Scattered around was the junk from a once thriving fishcamp – the usual assortment of shark heads, turtle shells, rusting cans, empty bottles and bits and pieces of metal and rope. So this was 'the palms'! It was such a far cry from the shady oasis of my imagination that I had to laugh.

The bare trunks offered no shade at all. Drawing short anxious breaths in the hot dry air, I searched around for a well or a source of water but found nothing. A broad, vegetation-choked valley stretched back into the mountains. That and the presence of the palm trees made it probable that there was water underground. But how far? I could easily sweat my way through the water I had left digging down two feet . . . four feet . . . who knows? Perhaps I'd find nothing.

Better to push on and find some shade. The air temperature must have been between 90°F. and 100°F. in the shade. Out in the mid-day sun it was hot enough to fry an egg.

Picking myself up and dusting off my disappointment, I thought back to the Desert of the Chinamen and those unfortunate Chinese labourers who wandered from one empty water hole to another. Beside each one another group would despair and die. Again I sensed the truth behind Alain Bombard's dictum that 'despair was the greatest killer of all'.

As I raced ahead to find a place to rest, I felt that the entire journey so far had just been a preparation for what was to come. If ever I needed faith in my survival skills, my stills and myself, it was then as I turned my back on the palms that had promised so much.

Chapter 14
Survival

I managed to find a sliver of shade in a coffin-sized hollow beneath a large rock. Lying down as comfortably as possible, I pulled out my maps and estimated my position. I was probably midway between the settlements in Gonzaga Bay and Los Angeles Bay, right in the heart of no-man's-land. Looking on the bright side, that meant I was no longer dashing ever further into the wilds. I could now see myself heading back towards safety.

The drawback, and the exhilaration, lay in not knowing what was ahead or whether I could make it. My maps only gave the general contour of the land and told me where the main roads and settlements were. Between Punta Final and Los Angeles Bay both maps echoed the opinions of Ed Wills and so many others – there was 'nothing'.

To reach safety, I would have to get as much mileage as possible from my half a gallon of water. I decided to ignore my thirst for as long as I dare. My rapidly darkening urine revealed that my kidneys had got the message – from now on every drop counted.

And every drop of sunscreen was going to have to count as well. I had just two tubes left. To save on sunscreen for my legs, I exchanged my shorts for a pair of jeans. According to the desert survival experts this would also help combat dehydration: 'On hot deserts it is a big temptation to take off a shirt and wear only shorts . . . this will do nothing but make you dehydrate faster. Clothing helps ration your sweat by not letting it evaporate so fast that you get only part of its cooling effect.' But I certainly didn't feel any cooling effect as I shouldered my pack and went in search of a more substantial piece of shade.

The backpack wasn't going to last much longer either. It had been badly mauled by the scraping rocks and tearing vegetation. The sun, the salt, the cactus, the granite, and the baking sand had also made surprisingly short work of my boots. Both of the Vibram soles were coming adrift. Thinking of all the climbing and rock work ahead, the seriousness of that sank in ever deeper with each step I took along the pebbly beach. I was just hoping that I could make everything last long enough to get me to Bahía de los Angeles.

To save on drinking water, as much of my food as possible would have to come from the juicy flesh of likely looking plants and cacti.

My first victim was a five-foot tall, base-branching cactus that rose up like a confused candelabra. Each of the almost square bright green 'candles' was as thick as a man's arm and crowned with a tuft of spiny hair. A line of sharp spiny clusters ran down each corner. In between the spines the naked walls sagged inwards as if enclosing a vacuum. Obviously it hadn't rained for a while. After a downpour the cactus would gorge itself and swell dramatically. It might have to store a year's supply of water in a few hours.

I cut hopefully into the avocado green flesh. It looked discouragingly firm and dry, and had the taste and texture of a hard, sharp, unripe peach. So much for the sumptuous juiciness I had imagined. I didn't eat much, just a nibble and a swallow.

The poorly protected plant showed little sign of bird or animal damage, only a few reddish-brown scars. Perhaps its defence was its very unpalatability? Perhaps it was poisonous?

Some time later, having suffered no ill-effects, I wandered up to a cardón cactus taller than myself but a mere baby of its species. Some cardóns grow to more than fifty feet.

I could just have linked my hands around the tree-like trunk. Not that I wanted to; rows of sharp spines ran along each of its many pleated edges. The cardón also was designed for considerable expansion when there was water to be had.

I cut off a piece of a spine-covered pleat. Again the supposedly water-bearing flesh was a disappointment. There was nothing thirst quenching about the cardón; its flesh was firm and gritty and left an unpleasant aftertaste. I had to drink more water than I could spare just to wash the taste from my mouth.

On a rocky slope I spied a small barrel cactus. It was reputed to be the best source of cactus food and water. Predictably, it was also the best protected, being covered with a densely woven network of curved orange-red spines so tough that only the most determined machete blows could break through. But having sliced off the top like an egg, it was easy to remove the spines and the dark green skin by chopping down and leaving a heart of white cactus tissue. Although bland and a bit like a rubbery apple, its taste wasn't objectionable. Nevertheless, I sampled it cautiously, chewing it to extract the liquid and spitting out the rest. Unfortunately, barrel cacti were few and far between along that stretch of coast, and more likely to be found on the higher slopes further inland where they might grow as tall as a man. In that baking heat, where one soon learns to curtail any unnecessary movement, I knew I didn't have the energy or motivation to do all the chopping and chewing, never mind the searching. Better to push on and find a shady spot to set up the solar still.

As cactus nibbling became a part of my routine, my conscience became filled with the imagined disapproving comments of nature-lovers and environmentalists: 'growing there for decades, centuries . . . part of a unique and fragile ecosystem . . . endangered species.'

At first I felt guilty, but my guilt gradually gave way to resentment: 'I'm the most endangered species around here,' I protested angrily. There in my 'desert cathedral' I didn't need anyone to tell me what was right and wrong. The land was sacred to me. I was a part of it. I wasn't one of a million careless tourists with their trucks, bikes and polluting toys. I was one in a million. The desert was special and my needs were special. There was no conflict. Besides, even if I'd deliberately set about to destroy everything in sight, I couldn't have made much impact on those vast, rugged, rolling vistas of cactus, mountain, and desert.

The sense of being special to a special place was very much part of the exhilaration and the experience. The desert seemed to be saying to me, 'Take what you need. All my grandeur is as nothing except that it be available for you.' Yet, to put it into words was to distort it. The feeling was the reality and the mystery. It saddened me to think that I might never be able to share it with another person. 'In what concerns you much,' wrote Thoreau, 'know that you are alone in the world.'

In my loneliness I could almost hear a voice whispering in the sea breeze, 'This is your land, your home, your destiny.' Why me? Why here of all places? Why am I doing this? Why? Why? Why?

I was convinced I was going off my rocker. Too much time alone. Too much time in the sun . . . The sun! I needed shade quickly.

The worst of the mountains had retreated a mile or two inland leaving a long, low, curving, shadowless bay. Before attempting to walk around, I thought it wise to take refuge in a sea-gouged shady hollow. There was room for both myself and the pack, but I tried not to move around too much as the abrasive rock had the texture of coarse sand-paper.

Feeling that every second was precious, I dug out the solar still, removed it from its plastic bag, re-read the instructions and, after sorting out the various tubes and cords, huffed and puffed till I'd blown it up. I almost fainted from the effort needed to inflate the main cone. After pouring in the recommended gallon of sea-water, I placed the still on a rock and angled it towards the sun. As the still needed the greatest possible exposure to the sun, and I needed the least, I prepared myself for a long stay.

Ten miles across the barely ruffled sea the outline of Guardian Angel Island seemed to rise up and float in the air. A small island off the northern tip slowly became two islands, then three, then disappeared altogether. Steinbeck had recorded the same phenomenon in his *Log From the Sea of Cortez*:

> As we moved up the Gulf, the mirage we had heard about began to distort the land. As you pass a headland it suddenly splits off and becomes an island and then the water seems to stretch inward and pinch it to a mushroom shaped cliff and finally to liberate it from the earth entirely so that it hangs in the air over the water. Even a short distance off-shore one cannot tell what the land really looks like. The very air here is miraculous and outlines of reality change with the moment. The sky sucks up the land and disgorges it. A kind of dream hangs over the whole region, a brooding kind of hallucination.

As neither brooding nor hallucinating would be the best way to pass the next four or five hours, I rummaged through my pack looking for something to do.

The torch! The batteries had become rather dim, and I had carried a spare pair since Puertecitos. Anticipating the saving in weight, I rolled out into the sun and threw the spent batteries as far out to sea as I could. It was as if I wanted to check my beleaguered sense of distance and reality. Half-expecting them to sail right over the island or pass through its ethereal solidity, I was almost relieved to see them plop into the water only fifty yards away.

I dropped the new batteries into the torch, screwed on the base and switched it on. Nothing! I opened it again to check they were in right. Still nothing. The new batteries were dead. There was a sinking feeling in my stomach as I thought of the consequences of not having a torch. Above all, I would need to make sure I took my contact lenses out before it got dark.

After directing a half-hearted tirade against all things Mexican, and vowing always to check my batteries in future, I began to see the funny side of it. It was just as well. The sea was rising fast. As it swirled and foamed along the sand, it became all too clear I was going to be forced out of my shady hollow.

With nowhere else to go, I took my pack to higher ground and then walked fully clothed into the warm water and made myself comfortable between two seaweed-covered boulders. As seaweed was supposed to be 'a godsend for the survivor', I began nibbling on all the various types floating around. I laughed as I pictured myself munching mouthfuls of the stuff. Absurdity aside, I was keeping cool and getting some nourishment while the beads of condensation were running down the inner wall of the still.

I thought about rigging up the kettle to boil seawater and condense the steam – there was plenty of driftwood – but I suspected that the plastic tubing would perish rapidly in use, possibly limiting me to just a few hours' production. I preferred to save it as a last resort.

It also seemed too much trouble to set up the hole-in-the-ground solar still. Digging a four-foot-deep hole in the blazing heat would be tantamount to digging my own grave. The yield wouldn't justify the effort unless I was going to stay put and do the digging at night. When the chips were really down, that would be the time to make a permanent 'survival camp' and get all my stills going full steam.

Not wanting to miss out on the rising tide, I put rod and reel together and enjoyed a spell of 'laid back' fishing. I managed to land a big fat bass. Getting my hands on him threw me into a dilemma. My hunger told me to enjoy my fish dinner. My thirst advised me not to. Convincing myself that I was going to need one last good meal for the trials ahead, my hunger won.

I soon had the victim cleaned, skewered and baking over a fire; but the fish wasn't the only thing cooking. Caught between the sun and the flames I was roasting myself too.

By the time I sat down to eat, my clothes were as dry as my mouth. I only managed to chew my way through so much fish with the aid of several long drinks of water. I had a feeling I was going to pay dearly for my protein treat.

Late in the afternoon, with the tide having fallen several feet, I left the sea for the last time to pack away my things.

Crouching down to inspect the yield from the still, I heard a rip! My jeans, the victim of continual immersion in salt water, had split up one leg from ankle to waist. But it hardly seemed to matter. If anything, the flapping leg brought back a feeling of comfort and coolness and was perhaps the perfect compromise between cover and freedom.

I paid more attention to the fact that Baja's relentless sunshine had, thanks to the still, given me over a pint of drinking water in just over four hours. It was warm, tasted disgustingly of plastic, and left a burning sensation in my throat; but it would be nothing compared to the sensation of having no water at all.

In the twenty-five minutes it took me to pack, I was totally dry. My watery 'siesta' was over. After smearing sunscreen on my grateful flesh, I resumed my cactus-nibbling progress, and for two days consumed my physical, mental and material resources.

I could delay setting up a 'survival camp' no longer. Looking for a sandy, sheltered, shady spot, I peered around yet another rocky headland, and my eyes popped in disbelief. Pangas! Three boats at anchor in a little sandy bay. Fishermen! My mind had to readjust. Becoming self-conscious again, I decided to take off and throw away my ripped and flapping jeans. After putting on a pair of shorts and consulting a mirror, I wandered up to the large canvas shelter the fishermen had constructed on the beach. I could tell by their blank stares and gaping mouths that passing gringos were not a common sight.

Six Mexicans sat on boxes and barrels outside their tent. The beds inside were covered with wet-suits and other diving gear. I bade them a cheerful 'Good evening' and managed to recall sufficient Spanish to provide a more or less coherent explanation of my presence. As I laughed and joked about my own absurdity, the tension eased and the Mexicans slowly reverted to their usual response of frontier hospitality. I was invited to share their evening meal of tortillas, beans, fish and coffee.

When I inquired what they were doing there, one of the Mexicans searched out the eyes of his comrades as if seeking permission to reply. 'We dive for oysters,' he said in English. Speculating that they were probably diving for pearls, I deemed it wise to inquire no further. If they had a horde of priceless pearls, I didn't want to know and they, understandably enough, wouldn't want to tell me.

The blue of the sea and the sky faded and became tinted with pink. It was as if the purple-pink mountains of Guardian Angel Island were radiating warmth and colour. The shimmering mid-day mirages had gone leaving just the soft pastel solidity of the desert evening.

As the fishermen slowly began to talk about their work and the trials of their way of life, they insisted I try another hot drink. It was made from a candle-like lump of brown-sugar candy called panocha. 'If ever there was an "industry" in Lower California,' Ann Zwinger has written, 'the making of panocha must have been it, for every town had its own panocha factory. Sugar cane harvested in the spring was cut into pieces and rolled to express the juice, which was boiled down until it reached syrup stage, then poured into moulds to harden.' The sweet drink was delicious by itself – if you have a sweet tooth – and even better with a little stick of cinnamon or a squeeze of lime juice. I tried it every way. My belly was distending like a rain-soaked cactus.

My hosts explained that they came from the old French mining town of Santa Rosalia, nearly two hundred miles to the south. They came out to fish and dive for a month or two every year. Except for brief supply runs to Bahía de los Angeles, they remained there in the wilderness out of touch with everything including their families. It must have been hard on them. Their faces all bore the same sad, resigned expression. I wondered if mine was beginning to develop the same look.

The English speaker joined the thumb and index finger of his left hand and bounced them on his lips. 'Do you have any pot?' he inquired hopefully.

'Well actually,' I replied, 'I'm British, and we're not really into that kind of thing.'

All hope disappeared from his countenance and the subject of conversation changed. I began to understand what they were trying to escape from when they started talking about the rattlesnakes they'd killed, the sharks they'd encountered and the scorpion stings they'd endured. When I commented on the precariousness of their existence and their inspiring courage, a finger pointed ominously towards a small hill. In mournful tones I was asked, 'Can you see the three crosses?'

As my eyes strained to pick out the silhouettes against the moon-bright sky, a surge of uneasy emotion rushed through me. I asked what had happened.

'A few years ago they were caught in a storm and drowned. We buried them on that hill. Now we call this place Campo Muertito – The Little Place of the Dead.'

Suddenly my eyes were heavy. The coffee couldn't keep me awake any longer. I said my goodnights and wandered off down the beach to make camp almost beneath the crosses.

Shark heads in various stages of decay were liberally scattered along the shore. A trickle of maggots wriggled rapidly away from each one as if determined to escape the stench.

Maggots and smell apart, the sand was clean, soft and inviting. Inside the tent I stretched out in the moonlight, but in spite of my exhaustion something kept me from sleeping. The distance I'd pitched my tent from the fishermen was a measure of my uneasiness. Pearls, graves, maggots – there was a vague sense of threat about it all.

About 10.30 p.m. – late by my standards – I fell into a shallow sleep, waking several times in the night and glancing in the direction of my wilderness companions. The incredibly bright moon and the piercing quiet combined eerily.

Breakfast was a real treat, a hot spicy mix of sausage and eggs, fish and tortillas; I stuffed myself shamelessly. On top of that, I was given some batteries for my torch, enough food for a day or two, as much water as I could carry, and the usual warnings about the cliffs and mountains ahead.

After expressing my heartfelt thanks, I exchanged goodbyes and dragged my bloated frame past the three lonely crosses. I was moved enough to make the Sign of the Cross on myself. I didn't know who they were and I didn't know their names, but I felt a strange kinship with them as if I, too, were heading for a little cross on some lonely Baja shore.

It was a later than usual start. With the sun high and my stomach full, the extra weight of all the food and water seemed almost unbearable. Only a massive dose of self-discipline kept me from stopping around the corner and returning to the relative security of my new found friends. As I resumed my battle with the rocks and boulders, I couldn't believe how much I was drinking. And no matter how much I drank, I couldn't escape the clutches of thirst. The foolishness of forcing down such a rich and spicy breakfast was becoming all too apparent.

I had walked over six miles before my conscience allowed me to call my midday halt. Making myself as comfortable as possible beneath some cliffs, I tried to sleep, but the ground was too rugged and stony, and a continual shower of clattering debris had me wondering if the background rumbling owed more to minor earth tremors than the pounding of the waves. A big earthquake would probably bring down the whole cliff on top of me. There always seemed to be something to worry about.

After eating lunch from the pack, I made a hot drink from a block of the panocha given to me by the fishermen. It was irresistible cut with the juice of a lime, and I had to fight the urge to have a refill. That would have been an unwarranted waste of water. Discipline! Discipline!

Ten miles across the sea, the 4,315-foot peak of Guardian Angel's tallest mountain shone majestically in the afternoon sun. If there was something mysterious and compelling about the coast of Baja, the island was even more so. I recalled its impact on Steinbeck:

> The long snake-like coast of Guardian Angel lay to the east of us; a desolate and fascinating coast. It is forty-two miles long, ten miles wide in some places, waterless and uninhabited. It is said to be crawling with rattlesnakes and iguanas, and a persistent rumor of gold comes from it. Few people have explored it or even gone more than a few steps from the shore . . . but there is a drawing power about its very forbidding aspect – a Golden Fleece, and the inevitable dragon, in this case rattlesnakes, to guard it.

I had enough to worry about on my side of the channel. The dragon which stood between me and the Golden Fleece of Bahía de los Angeles was Punta Remedios. Nearly all the coast ahead would be rugged, but judging by the way the contours of my map huddled menacingly around Punta Remedios, it looked as though I'd have to tackle a stretch of huge cliffs and massive mountains. But at least it would surely be the last barrier separating me from achieving the 'impossible'?

Underway again, the sullen, unfriendly shore tried every trick to thwart my progress. Every arm of every mountain seemed to fall barrier-like into the sea. Scrambling over one such wall of rock I slipped and crashed head-first to the boulders below. My arms shot forward to take the blow which, when it came, sent a painful jolt deep into my chest. I crumpled to the ground and lay there winded, bleeding profusely. The fall had opened several old wounds including a large gash on my wrist. I had an anxious time trying to stem the flow of blood.

Caked in blood, I warily edged towards another of the foothills of Remedios. It too seemed to have maliciously crashed down before me. I approached with a heavy heart. There seemed to be no way around. Then I noticed a black hollow just above the water line. My first thought was shade, but seeing it was quite a deep cave, my mind conjured up images of abandoned treasure and primitive artefacts. It's easy to do that in Baja where whole stretches of the country haven't heard the sound of human footsteps for generations. Then, seeing a shaft of light coming from deep inside, my mind turned to another possibility. Perhaps there was a way through to the other side.

For several minutes I stood at the entrance, asking myself, 'Is there danger?' 'Dare I go inside?' The answers didn't just come from analysing the information gleaned by my senses. Something seemingly irrational was creeping into my decision-making. It was a feeling, a knowing without necessarily knowing why. Call it intuition. Whatever it was, I had learned to trust it.

As I stood at the entrance of the cave there was no one impatiently pushing me to make a decision. I didn't have to explain myself. I would enter the cave because it 'felt' right. It was the same when I was about to dive off a rock into the sea, I would often stand and stare till it felt right to take the plunge. Of course, I'd be looking for sharks and jellyfish, and listening for anything unusual; but it was more than that . . . a sort of sixth sense I had discovered through being on my own. The certainty of my feelings intrigued me. It had been so ever since my first dramatic reaction to Baja. My thoughts were a fumbling rationalization of something I failed to understand, perhaps a futile attempt to make sense of something a little more mysterious than we can sanely acknowledge. Unfortunately, justifying your actions in terms of feelings doesn't normally go down too well. All the time we demand answers and reasons that make sense. But supposing intuition is a valid way of thinking? Perhaps being in tune with that sixth sense helps to explain why some people are 'lucky' and others go – for the best reasons – from one disaster to another. Perhaps Napoleon was right when he claimed that the most important quality for a general was luck.

And maybe prayer before any big decision isn't such a quaint absurdity. Perhaps one of the tragedies of modern life is our failure to find the time for such things.

Grabbing the torch and leaving behind the pack and the sunshine, I stepped cautiously into the blackness. Suddenly the myriad noises of the shore were muffled or cut out altogether. The stillness was both calming and threatening. The sweeping torch beam convinced me there wasn't a colony of rabid bats overhead or a nest of vipers at my feet. The floor of the cavern was about the size of a tennis court. Its roof was ridge-like, running in a line roughly from entrance to entrance. Both entrances seemed tiny when viewed from the centre of the cave. Stepping carefully over the boulders on the floor, I slowly worked my way towards the distant shaft of sunlight.

Daylight was streaming in from a 'porthole' halfway up the far wall. I was going to have to climb to reach it. All the walls of the cave appeared to be made up of a conglomerate of boulders embedded in mortar. Providing nothing came adrift it would afford a good climbing surface. I was able to pull myself up and peer out into the blinding glare; and I was elated to see that I was through to the beaches and cliffs beyond. It didn't matter that this might only be a temporary breakthrough. I was taking one step at a time and each successful step was a triumph. Climbing out, I saw I could get down easily and be on my way again. As ever, all that remained was to go back and do it all again with my pack.

I pushed on energetically. Amazed by my own stamina, I found myself almost running to meet my fate. Whether I conquered Punta Remedios or it conquered me, I had to find out and get it over with. The suspense was terrific. Remedios had become the focus of my existence. All that mattered was to get beyond it, to do the 'impossible' and walk my way to safety.

Zig-zagging and stumbling along the cliff-shaded rocky shore, I got my first glimpse of the point. It stood massive, brooding and contemptuous like an ill-tempered Goliath impatiently watching the laborious approach of his David. The most thunderous, blood-curdling roar could hardly have deepened my concern. In spite of my apprehension, I stood, stared and savoured the scene before me. 'Please there must be a way,' I said, 'I must get by. I must.'

With diminishing assurance, I crashed along a narrow stony beach, my eyes firmly on Remedios. Then Baja itself suddenly shouted in its own peculiar language: 'Ssschhh.'

I skidded to a halt. My boots dug into the pebbles. My darting eyes picked out the coiled, hissing and spitting rattlesnake. My heart was pounding almost in unison with his vibrating tail. He was just two yards to my left and perfectly camouflaged among the yellowish stones, I would never have seen him except for his giving himself away with so much racket.

Recovering my poise and ignoring the 'I've had enough, I want to go home, let me out' thumping inside my chest, I stepped back and picked up a large stone. Hurling the missile as hard as I could, it narrowly missed the serpent and shattered on a rock behind. I was astounded at the lightning speed with which the snake struck at the shattering impact. I reached down for more stones and threw them in rapid succession. The rattler, his heart probably pounding as fast as mine, decided to beat a hasty retreat. He had only half way disappeared beneath a large boulder when a plum-shaped pebble caught the unfortunate creature full on the belly. Even so, it managed to drag its shattered body out of sight, leaving just its erratically buzzing tail. I thought of grabbing the tail, pulling him out and whipping his head down on a rock; but common-sense, and my injunction about not taking unnecessary risks prevailed. I decided to get away and resign myself to another mundane meal.

As I did so my conscience dug in its fangs. I felt a curious sympathy for the rattlesnake. I should have left it alone or killed it cleanly and eaten it. Having condemned the unfortunate creature to a lingering death, I felt lower than a snake's belly myself.

Still, I didn't escape entirely unscathed; having been sensitized again to every scrape and rustle, the final stretch of the journey to Remedios exacted a terrible toll on my nerves. I approached the point more by the light of the rising moon than by the fading light of day. Its massive cliffs, silhouetted against the last colours of the evening sky, looked even more awesome and hypnotic than ever.

With the sea coming right up to the base of the cliffs, there was very little room to get by. My weary legs were called upon to make even greater exertion. I should have called it a day and waited for the morrow's dawn and falling tide, but now that I was so close, I had to get up to Remedios and see if there was a way around.

It was hard to be sure in the moonlight. I walked right to the water's edge, to where a towering wall of black rock slipped with an awful finality beneath the waveless sea. The barrier of rock shot out undercut and unscalable into deep water. There was no way around. The race was over. Standing there in the semi-darkness, I felt painfully alone and drained of everything except disappointment. As if to underline my despair, a large shark cruised menacingly just off shore, its dorsal fin slicing through the moon-lit water.

I sat on a rock in the warm evening air and wondered what on earth I was doing there. Why wasn't I at home, in the pub, downing a pint with the boys, talking about football or politics? Instead, I was hemmed in by so much danger and insecurity I had no idea what I was going to do next.

If ever I needed someone, it was then. The descending peace of the night fell gently around me. There was no friend or lover to hold me, but the universe itself seemed to put a comforting arm around my shoulder. I would feel better after a good night's sleep.

Unfortunately there was nowhere really safe to put up the tent. It was the usual choice – do I prefer to be crushed by falling rocks or washed away by the tide? The cliffs were so tall, there was no escaping the rockfall danger, so I satisfied myself with a tiny patch of stony beach which seemed to be one of the few not destined to be totally submerged. A pair of flanking fallen boulders served as both protection and a reminder of what I needed protecting from.

With the occasional slab of debris clattering down, I was, for once, in no great hurry to get inside the tent. When finally I retired, I placed the bulky backpack beside my head. It made me feel just a little more secure.

Every evening, I'd been estimating my position on the map, marking it with a little 'X'. From San Felipe the 'Xs' had run regularly down the coast, about an inch apart. There were four at Punta Bufeo, seven at Calamajué. Down the coast they went with a kind of inexorable inevitability. As I put my 'X' at Punta Remedios, I wondered if I was destined to mark my final campsite with the kind of cross I'd seen on the hill at El Muertito, or would the 'Xs' on my map completely ring the coastline? If my vision and my faith meant anything, I had nothing to worry about. I was going to write that book about Baja, and presumably I would do so from this side of the grave.

Chapter 15
Total commitment

At the first hint of light, I was up and out to assess the situation. Cutting inland was no easy option: I'd have to backtrack a mile or more to find a relatively safe place to climb, and wandering into the mountains with just over a gallon of water wasn't a particularly attractive proposition.

Noticing that the tide was much lower than that of the night before, I reconsidered the possibility of getting by under the cliffs. The problem was a grey, boot-shaped headland that seemed to have crunched down across the narrow pebble beach. The 'foot' was made up of a mass of huge, fallen boulders. They formed a potentially walkable platform, but they were all smooth, slippery and undercut; there was no way I could climb up.

A quick glance at my tide calendar revealed that I had arrived at Punta Remedios together with the lowest tide of the month. Feeling it might be an opportunity not to be missed, I stripped off and hurried down to the water's edge for an exploratory swim. In my enthusiasm, my foot slipped on a wet rock. Crash! Blood poured from a two-inch gash in my right shin.

Having spotted that shark the previous evening, I should have waited for the bleeding to stop but, more concerned about not missing the chance offered by the tide, I picked myself up and hobbled into the sea. Wading slowly out in the warm water, I studied each of the crannies between the boulders. Seeing no possibility of a way up, I breast-stroked around the point.

Just as I was thinking it was a long way back to the beach, a sudden, nearby splash and swirl of water had me trying to claw my way up a six-foot wall of wet slimy rock. Much to my surprise, I almost made it before calming down enough to slide slowly back into the sea. The swirl proved to be nothing more than the hasty retreat of a surprised fish.

I had to swim another fifty yards before finding a place to pull myself from the water. Leaping from rock to rock, I made a quick reconnaissance down the coast. The cliffs continued as far as I could see, but there was nothing as blatantly 'impassable' as the barrier I'd just swum around. Encouraged, I made my way back along the platform of boulders, racking my brains for a fast and certain solution to the problem of how to get my equipment up there with me. Again it was the pack that was frustrating my progress.

Back at the point, I noticed that, up against the cliffs, there was a two-foot wide gap between two of the less massive rocks. Peering down into the semi-blackness, I could just make out water rushing over pebbles a few feet below. Suddenly I had an idea. Plucking up the courage, I jumped into the sea, and squeezed my way into a grey-black world of claustrophobic tunnels. Every squashy thing I trod on conjured up images of giant eels and grasping tentacles.

One of my most important disqualifications for the task I had chosen was my over-active imagination. It definitely belonged with the list of major problems I drew up back in England – no money, unfit, no knowledge of desert survival, no Spanish, fair skin. The solution to those problems had been easily stated but what was the solution, if any, to the problem of an over-active imagination? Tranquillizers? As I had felt from the start, I was the last person in the world who should be doing this; but if I could, anybody could.

Like a wading potholer I followed the cool, curving walls of stone towards the base of the cliff. It was a tighter and tighter squeeze until I splashed into a more sizeable 'cavern' and there, six feet above, was the two-foot-wide gap through which I had looked down. The walls were too wet and smooth to enable me to climb out, but it would be enough if I could get my pack out.

I struggled back to the beach, tied my boots and water containers securely to the pack, wrapped the usual items in waterproof bags and stepped back into the watery semi-blackness.

Alternately cradling the pack in my arms, and carrying it over my head, I struggled back towards the 'cavern' with its promising skylight. As expected, I was able to squeeze the pack out and roll it on to the platform of rock.

Five minutes later, after swimming my way around, I too was safely on top, getting dressed and pulling on my boots. To make ten yards progress, I'd had to swim twice around the point, claw my way twice in and out of a dark, water-filled network of tunnels, and, even then, I only got by because of an exceptionally low tide. Walking around Baja wasn't going to be quite as straightforward as I'd imagined.

The sun was up. The tide was swinging from one extreme to another, going in one mad rush from the lowest to the highest of the month. I swung the rucksack on to my back, pulled its straps tight, and dashed on to see what else fate had in store.

My elation was short-lived. Apart from the fact that the sole of one of my boots was threatening to come off altogether, Punta Remedios and its problems seemed to go on and on, a never-ending round of climbing, wading, crawling and leaping. One rising wall of grey rock offered a single possibility: a cliff hugging, knee-knocking sidestep along a ledge forty feet above the swirling sea and the rocks. Death or serious injury would follow any miscalculation, but it was a risk I had to take despite the unbalancing pack and the wayward sole. Luckily the rock was solid and not crumbling.

Feet back on the ground, and with the coast opening before me, I had, at last, good reason to be ecstatic. Ahead I could see one of the familiar sights of the Bay of Los Angeles, the dramatic volcanic outline of Smith Island. It looked so close. Ten relatively easy miles, I guessed. An afternoon's stroll with a light pack and I'd have achieved the 'impossible'.

I made a cheerful, relaxed mid-day camp beneath the shade of a low line of friendly cliffs. My gallon of water suddenly appeared extravagantly generous, so I proceeded to dispose of half of it washing down all the food I could find in my pack with cup after cup of that delicious bitter-sweet drink made from panocha and lime juice. As I washed myself and my clothes in the sea, all I could think about were the joys of company and the comforts of town.

'The one cardinal rule in desert travel is to rest quietly during the day and hike only during the night, early morning or evening.' Guided by such sound common sense, I'd been typically taking four-hour mid-day breaks. However I was in no mood now to idle for so long. After halting barely an hour, I packed everything away, smeared myself with the last of my sunscreen and stepped out into the early afternoon heat.

At first, it didn't seem too bad. There was a pleasantly cooling sea breeze. But then the wind died, and before long it was blowing hot off the land.

A long narrow strip of stony beach separating the sea from a lagoon was an unpleasant surprise. I dashed along the thirty-yard wide pile of stones, dreading to think that up ahead the sea might be entering and leaving the lagoon through an unwadably deep channel. I didn't relish the prospect of going all the way back and along the inland edge of the lagoon, or having to sit for hours in the sun waiting for the tide to fall.

However, the level of the sea was clearly higher than that of the water in the lagoon. So they couldn't be connected; at least not through a single entrance. Rather, water was steadily seeping through the pebble causeway, much as it was seeping through the countless overworked pores of my skin.

My half gallon of water was disappearing alarmingly fast. I began to have my first doubts about contravening 'the one cardinal rule in desert travel'. I had even more doubts when, after two hours of hot and hard walking, Smith Island seemed as far away as ever.

After passing the usual assortment of dolphin, sea lion and pelican skeletons, I reached a deserted fishcamp. It was a relief to see a stack of rusting cans, broken bottles and sun-baked fish heads. I took a long gulp from my water flask. Civilization couldn't be far away, and the dusty track winding away from the camp would, no doubt, lead me to it.

The track ran along the flat monotonous bed of a dry lagoon, midway between a wall of stones holding back the sea and a forest of haze-distorted cacti apparently holding back the range of barren, red mountains.

As I dropped down to the sun-cracked bed of the lagoon, I was convinced this was Baja's version of Death Valley. The wind picked up, blasting viciously hot down from the mountains. My tired legs buckled as the shock took my breath away and set my head in a spin. It was like walking in a tumble dryer.

With thirst tightening its grip on my throat, I was now anything but complacent. But at least I had the road. It would surely lead me to town, and conceivably someone might appear. Those recurring cans of cold beer seemed to float before me to lighten my step and encourage me to keep going, by moonlight if necessary.

But, suddenly, the road did the unexpected. It cut inland away from the coast, almost in the opposite direction to Bahía de Los Angeles. According to my map it wasn't going anywhere, and I didn't dare head inland with just over a pint of water. It would have been a struggle to make that last through the night, and if the sun rose on me without water, my life expectancy could be measured in terms of hours. An agonizing, tragic end to my trip was all too plain to see.

As I headed back to the safety of the shore, more cliffs and mountains rose ominously before me. I had clearly greatly underestimated the distance to the town. All the rules of the survival game were back in force. Eating was out of the question, and every drop of water would have to count.

The sinking sun brought no relief. The west wind blew as if from a furnace. The need to drink was constant. I agonized whether I should stop and set up the stills, or whether I should push on in the hope of finding fishermen or reaching the town.

An extensive lagoon of black mud and long, probably snake-infested, grass forced me inland. Mosquitoes added their nuisance value to the dank odours and the oppressive heat. It was the last place I'd want to stop. Trying to escape the clutches of its many muddy arms, I was forced to take a wide arc around the edge of the lagoon. As it grew dark, my desiccated imagination saw mountain lions behind every cactus and rattlesnakes under every bush.

Columns of cacti seemed to be holding up the star-spangled sky as I followed a craggy U-shaped valley down to the shore. Just as I reached the beach, the moon peeped over the horizon sending a glittering torpedo trail through the water towards me. I might have appreciated the beauty and peace of it all a little more fully if I hadn't been so keen on getting my tent up and imbibing some liquid.

I had never been so thirsty in my life. My body hurt. My lips were cracked and sore and I could hardly swallow. As I looked at the moon, it was frightening to think that if I made the wrong move, death itself could be the next thing peeping over that horizon. I wanted desperately to down the single cup of water I had left, but I knew I had to string out the sips as long as possible.

Inside the tent I continued to debate the respective merits of 'running' for town or setting up the stills. Every instinct encouraged me to make one final headlong charge to safety. I croaked into my tape-recorder: 'If I set up my stills, I could be stranded. I may not be able to make sufficient water to carry on in this heat. So I'd just be getting weaker and more dehydrated. There's a ridge running to the sea in front of me. The Bay of L.A. is probably on the other side. My best bet is to go for it tomorrow. I'll try to snatch some sleep and get away before dawn.' When I played it back, I was amazed at how feeble I sounded; like I was mumbling in a drunken stupor.

Sleep was a welcome refuge from the agony and anxiety of thirst. I felt better on waking, though I was annoyed at myself for having left both ends of the tent wide open to the scorpions and rattlesnakes. The moon had marched some way across the sky. I guessed that dawn was an hour or two away. A breakfast of a couple of brittle, brown-skinned limes about the size of walnuts and a mouthful of water gave me the energy to take down the tent and pack everything away. Convincing myself that all I had to do was walk a mile or two and I'd be safe, I set off into the predawn silence.

The first part of the journey was the easiest, on the beach, around the curving bay and up a gently rising sandy arroyo to the steep rocky foothills of the ridge I had to cross. My imagination again ran riot with all the moonlit shapes and shadows. In the condition I was in, I wouldn't have stood a chance of surviving a rattlesnake bite.

Stepping over cactus and brush, with eyes and nerves strained to the full, I felt a sudden jab of pain in the back of my leg, I jumped and swivelled in instinctive horror. The pain intensified. Something was sunk deep into my calf. Looking down and seeing a snake-like shape, I shuddered and kicked wildly. A dead ocotillo branch flew through the air – my right boot must have kicked the wickedly spined stem into the back of my left leg.

Suitably spurred on, I dashed as fast as I dared towards the sanctuary of the hopefully nearby Bay of L.A. According to my map, La Gringa (feminine of gringo) would be the first outpost of town. It was named, so the story goes, after a beautiful American widow who used to live there on the beach. Almost certainly there'd be tourists at La Gringa. Any one of them would look beautiful to me if they had water!

I made it to the top of the ridge in time to admire the first glow of dawn. The spreading light revealed the coast to be the usual assortment of beaches, boulders and jutting masses of rock, but there was no sign of a town. Back at the water's edge, I watched the sky fill with light and colour. Then a burst of liquid gold appeared along the edge of the world. As the rising fireball assumed a mushroom shape I stood staring, as I might at the first exchange at Armageddon.

Sun or no sun, I made up my mind to carry on till I was out of water. The few sips I had left were strangely reassuring. I was convinced that salvation was just around the corner. When it wasn't, that could only mean it was around the next one. I became so wrapped up in my desire to reach safety that I wondered if I was being foolishly single-minded in pressing on. A voice inside me protested: 'Stop! For Christ's sake stop and set up your stills.'

There was a rocky headland a mile in front. I couldn't see beyond it. 'No more water till you get there,' I vowed. 'I mean it.' With the sun beating down from the brilliant blue, I worked myself into a trance-like determination to reach the headland and 'earn' my next drink of water.

When I got there, I peered around. Brutal disappointment. Another empty bay, more stony beaches, more awkward cliffs. I took the promised drink – taste would be more accurate – then closed my mouth firmly. A single breath in the hot, dry air was enough to undo the all too fleeting feeling of relief. Again I vowed, 'the next sip at the next point'.

My word had become the most important thing in the universe; the one power greater than the torment of my thirst. If I said I was going to reach an objective, I knew I was going to do it. The phrase, 'I mean it', was a signal to my brain that my word, my judgement and everything I held dear was on the line. I was playing a game with myself, a game I had learned to resort to when extraordinary effort was called for and there was every chance of giving way to weakness. Having been lazy and laid-back most my life, I was amazed at my ability to set an objective and totally commit myself to it. Having switched on to such a way of thinking, I knew I must not weaken. No matter what the pain or the exhaustion, I must not give in, I had to reach that point. . . .

I later confided to my diary: 'If I could give one piece of advice to anyone believing the world to be dull, it would be this – if you have the ability to set goals and value your word, then you'll never be bored. When you're absolutely determined to accomplish something you've committed yourself to, life suddenly becomes exciting and exhilarating. Look at the importance some people attach to sport, and how excited they get at such things as getting a ball over a line or down a hole. But what is a sport but some agreed upon goal and a set of players totally dedicated to its achievement? Yet, if you're able to set your own goals and go for them with everything you've got, then you're no longer a spectator. You're living out your own intense drama; you're the one playing in the Cup Final or the Superbowl. How can life ever be dull if you know where you're going and want desperately to get there?'

I wanted desperately to get to the Bay of L.A., but I suspected that I had reached the stage when stopping itself would have been dangerous. I would just have collapsed and died before getting a worthwhile drink from the stills.

Not daring to down my final thimble-full of water, I cut open the last of the small, sad limes I'd carried since Calamajué. They stung my cracked and raw lips, and there was nothing to wash away the sharp, burning taste. After eating all six in quick succession, my teeth were aching as if acid-washed to the roots. Even so, I would have eaten a thousand rather than endure the awfulness of my thirst.

There was no more sunscreen for my skin; no more balm for my lips; and both soles on my boots were now flapping at the toes. The pack had never been lighter but it cut cruelly into my sunburnt shoulders. Some corner of reason left inside my throbbing head watched in disbelief as I kept going.

Under the midday sun, I came to another long stony beach stretching between the sea and a lagoon. It beckoned like a trap. There was no shade if I was forced to stop and try to operate the stills, and I wouldn't have had the energy to plod back again. Instinctively I hesitated – thinking was no longer an accurate description of what was going on inside my head – before deciding to crunch my way along the shingle beach.

I was beginning to feel strangely detached from my decisions and my suffering. I remembered, with almost academic interest, the comments of a US serviceman who had experienced extreme dehydration: 'Something changes when your last water is gone. Things just seem to happen to you, and you don't feel responsible. You aren't in your right mind. Whether you decide to walk on for one more night, or lay down to die, it isn't you who plans any longer. You are only watching from somewhere outside.' Escaping into a kind of intoxication I stumbled on, becoming increasingly oblivious to everything except my rapid nasal breathing and the pebble-bashing rhythm of my boots.

Suddenly, I was conscious of another sound. Looking up, I saw a small, open fishing boat coming straight towards me, right beside the beach. Mexicans! Water! Rescue! From somewhere I found the energy to jump up and down and wave frantically. The two young fishermen looked doubtfully at one another before steering into the shore.

'Good morning, amigos,' I said, shocked at my own feeble croakings. 'I'm walking to Bahía de los Angeles and I need water. Do you have any to spare?'

The elder of the two held up a full half-gallon jug. 'We can spare some but we must keep a little as we're going out fishing.'

'Gracias, gracias,' I said impatiently as they poured about two pints into my empty canteen. I drank half of it immediately – closing my eyes to savour the experience – then forced myself to stop and keep the other pint to get me to town.

'How far is it to La Gringa?' I asked.

'Two or three miles, more or less.'

'No problems?' I inquired hopefully.

'No problems, amigo. An easy walk, and you will find many tourists between La Gringa and Bahía de los Angeles. Good luck.'

'Many thanks,' I said, 'Go with God.'

Unfortunately, they couldn't go anywhere. Their outboard motor refused to start. For fifteen minutes the confounded good samaritans sweated and cursed under the blistering sun. I couldn't just walk away and leave them, though they probably wished I would. At last, the knackered engine burst into life allowing us to go our separate ways with more exchanges of 'Good luck' and 'Go with God'. As I staggered onwards along the beach, and their sorry sounding motor whisked them out to sea, I suspect that God was in quite a dilemma about which way to go.

As the water percolated into my brain and clarified my thoughts, I wondered how I could still be two or three miles from La Gringa. I had already walked ten or fifteen miles since the day began; obviously I had badly mis-read my map. Then again, why hadn't I played it safe and set up a three-stilled survival camp? The questions were many, but there was time for the post-mortem (hopefully not a real one) later.

I was noticing the world around me again. I gazed out across a three-mile wide channel which now separated the Baja mainland from the precipitous volcanic slopes of Smith Island. Dolphins were leaping and a large whale was cruising a hundred yards from the shore. Judging by its size, it was probably a finback.

'While humpback and sperm whales are often sighted, the commonest species in the central gulf are the finbacks,' W. W. Johnson has written. 'Finbacks are streamlined monsters, second only to the great blue whale in size. They range up to 75 feet in length, up to 80 tons in weight... They seem to prefer to stay in the gulf rather than to roam the oceans of the world as other whales do. Specialists have estimated that there are perhaps 250 of these nonmigratory whales. Some believe that, in times past, finbacks found their way into the gulf and never found their way out. Others think that the richness of the food resources of the central gulf makes it too attractive for them to leave.'

I decided to take a quick, cooling swim. If anything, the water was too cool. As the tide raced up and down the gulf through the deeper channels it tended to produce great upwellings of cold water from the bottom. It was all this agitation and turnover that maximized the oxygen content of the water and supported the rich crop of plankton which, in turn, supported such a variety of marine life so close to one of the most barren deserts in the world.

To protect my lips, I wandered into the desert and sliced off the stem from a lomboy – a common, sprawling, spineless plant with large, luxuriously green, heart-shaped leaves. The cut stem immediately began exuding sap. I dabbed it on my lips, and as it dried, it formed a protective skin. 'The astringent sap is reputed to have medicinal properties. Some Baja California travellers swear by it as a preventive (or cure) for sun-cracked lips,' says the *Baja California Handbook*.

The breeze was still sweeping hot from the desert and my pint of water was disappearing alarmingly fast. It seemed a long two or three miles. By the time I reckoned I had done twice that distance, I started to feel angry. 'Where the hell is La Gringa?' I asked myself. Mumbling resentfully, I added, 'Why say two or three miles when you mean ten. "No problema". Like hell, no problema! You should try walking it!'

Still ranting away, and almost out of water again, I rounded yet another headland and forced my weary, sun-strained eyes to look up. After all the let-downs, I couldn't believe it. Motor homes, sunshades, swimmers. Just half a mile away. La Gringa!

A party of tourists from San Diego was surprised to see a heavily burdened, red-headed Englishman staggering towards them. I asked for water, drank nearly half a gallon, and needed little encouragement to follow that with four cold beers. That brought the smile back to my face and more sense back to my brain. When my appetite returned, I put away a ham sandwich and a bag of pretzels. As I told my story, I enjoyed the astonishment written on the faces of my hosts. One of them did his best to repair my boots with tape and glue. The warmth and hospitality were heartening. My strength and enthusiasm bounced right back. I was soon able to face the last few miles to Bahía de los Angeles. With more 'thank yous' flying around than seagulls, I was given water and fruit, and pointed in the right direction.

I passed several other campers as I made my way around the bay. I looked a sight: boots taped together; clothes blood-stained, sweat-soaked and tattered; lips cracked; wild carrot-coloured hair; unshaven; face as red as a beetroot and beaming elation; not the kind of thing you'd want to bump into with the sun going down. No wonder most of the other Americans I met treated me with cold suspicion.

As darkness fell, I left the shore and stuck to the dirt road heading towards town. For over an hour my way was lit only by my fading torch and the occasional, often blinding, car headlight.

The moon was rising over Guardian Angel Island as I wandered into the lights and the dusty streets of Bahía de los Angeles. Finding the bakery still open, I treated myself to some sugary cakes and a delicious cold pepsi. The proprietor found it hard to believe that I'd just walked along the coast from San Felipe, but my appearance helped convince him.

Exhausted, half-asleep, and wanting to be alone, I hurried through the town and headed towards a deserted beach a mile on the other side. The repaired boots hadn't lasted long – both soles were doubling over again – but they had made it and so had I.

Chapter 16
Bahía de los Angeles

Bahía de los Angeles is a place of extraordinary beauty. It is as if some monster had taken a ten-mile long, five-mile deep bite out of the coast, and then dropped a few chunks and crumbs to form the scattering of islands protecting the bay. Further out, the forty-two mile length of Isla Angel de la Guarda gives added protection. Multi-coloured mountains rise up in every direction making it easy to believe the bay is a land-locked lake.

That was how it struck me on my first visit in 1979 when, with no map and no idea where I was going, I hitched my way down to the sapphire blue waters of the Bay of the Angels. The place seems to inspire strong feelings. For me, it was love at first sight. John Steinbeck's reaction was slightly less positive:

> Angeles Bay . . . is land locked by fifteen islands, between several of which there is entrance depth . . . We entered through a deep channel between Red Point and two small islets, pulled into eight fathoms of water near the shore and dropped our anchor. The Coast Pilot had not mentioned any settlement, but here there were new buildings . . . and on a tiny airfield a plane sat. It was an odd feeling, for we had been a long time without seeing anything modern. Our feeling was more of resentment than of pleasure. We went ashore and were immediately surrounded by Mexicans who seemed curious and excited about our being there. They were joined by three Americans who said they had flown in for the fishing, and they too seemed very much interested in what we wanted until they were convinced it was marine animals. Then they and the Mexicans left us severely alone . . . Perhaps we imagined it, but we had a strong feeling of secrecy about the place . . . [it] breathed suspicion and no other place had been like that.

Steinbeck's visit took place in April 1940. Twenty years later, Erle Stanley Gardner was able to see the bay in a very different light:

> The Bahía de los Angeles is wonderfully photogenic. It stretches in a great crescent with islands out in the Gulf protecting the bay itself from most of the bad weather. The water is an intense blue, the sand a dazzling white and the entire place is soaked in an atmosphere of friendliness.
>
> The Mexicans who live there are dependent upon Antero Diaz for livelihood and Diaz is dependent for the most part on American tourists. The result is a friendly background of personal warmth which matches the balmy warmth of the climate.

Another twenty years on, in the early 1980s, Casa Diaz was not the only accommodation in town, though it was still the most famous. There were several trailer parks and a modern thirty-room hotel, the Villa Vita, complete with pool, jacuzzi and air-conditioning. There was also a launch ramp for trailered-in boats, a gas station, a desalination plant, some small restaurants and shops, a beer depository and a recently constructed paved airstrip just out of town (though most pilots preferred to land on the old 'downtown' dirt strip and taxi right up to their houses or hotel rooms). What with the new paved road running in from the highway, the Bay of L.A., as it is affectionately known among the tourists, has changed dramatically since Gardner's loving description. The fishing and the clamming aren't what they used to be and neither are the people. The friendliness and hospitality has largely come and gone. The wide open beaches have sprouted American homes, fences and property disputes. The almighty dollar has arrived.

Still, there wasn't a trace of sadness on my face as I opened wide the tent door and watched the sunrise. High above, a thousand pelicans were flapping their way north in their classical V-shaped formations. I had never seen them in such numbers or flying so high.

I was doing my own high flying. I'd made it. I'd done it. I'd arrived. The main part of town was a mile to my left. There were a couple of boats heading out between the islands, but close to me all was quiet. No one was in sight. The water was peaceful and the scene looked every bit as wonderful as I'd remembered. The mountains enclosing the southern part of the bay dropped gracefully into the sea at Red Point. It was those mountains that had called me four years before, and dared me to cross over. And there I was about to take up the challenge, to make real what most would have dismissed as an absurd fantasy. In a way I felt as if I had come home.

Steinbeck's and Gardner's descriptions were as vivid to me as my own memories. I pictured Steinbeck's Western Flyer pulling in between Red

Point and the Twins – the nearest pair of islands. I could see it anchored in front of the town. What would he make of it now? I wondered. If he resented a plane and a few huts, the booming little town of the 1980s would have made him do a quick U-turn and run to the 'rattlesnakes and iguanas' of Isla de la Guarda.

The low angle of the sun lent an imposing reality to the 3,400-foot mountain rising sharply above the town. I could hardly believe I'd climbed it two and a half years before with my girlfriend and a tall, gentle, bronzed, leathery-skinned, lean 'young' man of sixty, Mountain Man Mike. What a character he was. He first came to the bay in 1951 riding a motorcycle – 'in those days you had to make the road as you went along' – and finally decided to sell his business in Albuquerque and move down permanently in 1969. With so much empty desert around the bay, no one seemed bothered by his arrival with a half-ton truck and a trailer. Having been there ever since, he'd just become part of the scenery. He'd made the mountain his own, building a trail all the way to the peak and turning a cave on top into his second home. Over the years, he managed to carry up food, water and all kinds of camping equipment. The view from the top was breath-taking, assuming you have any breath left by the time you get up there!

There was a group of houses about a hundred yards away, just above the beach. It was all coming back to me. Mike's place was behind those houses. A VW bus, a pale blue trailer, and a hut surrounded by a corral containing tanks, chests, buckets, plants and other Mike-type paraphernalia. If Mike had a trait that separated him from his countrymen it was his reluctance to waste anything. Junk to him was the starting point for all manner of useful creations.

I knocked at the door of the trailer. 'Hello Mike, remember me?' Apparently not! I jogged his memory. 'Don't you remember, you, me and Janet, we climbed to the top of your mountain?'

'Janet,' he said, eyes lighting up, 'how could I forget Janet, that lovely, good-looking young lady.' He went on to recount every little detail of her appearance and every little thing she said. I still wasn't sure he remembered me though. Ah well, any friend of Janet's was a friend of his. After we finished nattering on about her, I explained what I was up to and related the drama of my dash to reach the Bay of L.A.

Mike knew someone who could repair my boots. He invited me to leave my things inside his trailer and accompany him on a walk into town. A Mexican working at the gas station said he'd nail and glue back the soles for six dollars – 'they'll be as good as new'. I had my doubts. The soles were worn almost flat and I couldn't see them lasting much longer no matter how well they were fixed. Nevertheless I handed over the boots and the money.

Mike showed me around town and introduced me to his friends. A couple of guys inside the Villa Vita hotel had just flown in from the States. As soon as I explained that I'd walked in, they insisted on buying the beers. Before I could polish off the ice-cold bottle of 'Bud', the hotel owner came over, heard the story and insisted on buying us another drink. The beer and my celebrity status were beginning to go to my head, but, back at Mike's trailer, a Baja wall-map helped tame my self-satisfaction. I looked at the distance I'd already walked and at what I still had to do. I scribbled in my diary: 'Arrival Bay of L.A. First feeling great satisfaction, then gradual realization that I'd just won round one; no, not won – survived! I had nine rounds to go and there was still plenty of time for the knock out punch.'

What to do next? Should I carry on down the Gulf coast with the June shade temperature soaring over 100°F., or should I venture over to the Pacific where the cold California current keeps the temperature anything up to 20°F. cooler? Or should I first go back to the States to re-equip?

Mike came up with an idea to give me time to think. He wanted to go back to California for a week or two and he needed someone to look after his place. I jumped at the chance.

Before he left, Mike continued to introduce me to everyone he knew. As well as picking up all kinds of useful information about what lay ahead, I went from one dinner engagement to another amazing everyone with my unchained capacity for eating and drinking: 'Invited to evening fish dinner on the beach. Drove over with Mike in the VW (only one brake working and that tends to stick). Great reception. Drinking Canadian whisky and 7-up, and lots of wine. Delicious fried halibut, yellowtail and bass. Lots of food and toasted marshmallow "smores". Invited to speak to them all (about 12–15) about my trip. Gave ten-minute account followed by question and answer session. Brief howling wind blasted down from the mountains then all peaceful again. Sing-along. I asked them to sing something patriotic. They sang Dixie! Got progressively more drunk.'

Next morning, Mike took me over to meet Antero Diaz – Papa Diaz as he was better known – explaining that I'd be looking after his place. I took up as much of his time as I could to question him about the history of the bay and about one of its most famous residents – Dick Daggett, the son of an English sailor of the same name. The town had briefly flourished as a gold and silver mining centre around the turn of the century, and one of the little locomotives that used to carry silver ore from the mine to the smelter had been put on display in the plaza and dedicated to the memory of Dick Daggett, jr.

Towards the end of the last century Dick's father had arrived at the bay aboard a German ship carrying a cargo of bricks for the mine. After falling out with the captain, he jumped ship and was hidden in a cave by sympathetic locals until the enraged captain and the search parties tired of looking for him. When the ship left, Daggett came out of hiding, got a job in the mine, married a Mexican girl and started a new life and family. Today he has left behind him quite a collection of grandchildren and great-grandchildren, most of whom could hardly imagine the English mists and lush green rolling hills that he was destined never to see again.

Mike took me to see Daggett's cave in the back of a rounded red mountain which rose from the gentler cactus-covered slopes dropping into the bay. From the cave we could see the route of the mini-railway which once brought trains of ore carts rattling down from the mine to the smelter which still scars the northern end of 'Red Mountain'. Even though it stood a stone's throw from the gently lapping waters of the bay, the old brickwork and rusting iron didn't seem to violate the stark beauty of the scene. If anything, the ruins added interest. I felt a kind of sympathy for them, so belittled were they by the confident power and enormity of the sea and the desert.

Four miles to the south, in the middle of a gradually encroaching cactus forest, the once booming little town of Las Flores displays even more extensive ruins; and there the Daggetts were buried side by side in the little cemetery.

Mike suggested walking over to Las Flores, but all I could think about was shade and a cold beer. I vowed to make the eight-mile return journey another day.

Having arranged his lift back to California, Mike explained what was what and delighted in showing me the simple efficiencies of his home. He got most of his drinking water from his home-made solar stills – five gallons a day in the summer, two in the winter. They needed topping up with sea water every three days. Two of the stills were on top of the hut and their yield fed directly into the trailer ensuring there was always drinking water on tap. Three more in the backyard fed into containers which could be used, stored or poured into the various water tanks as required.

Much of the water ended up in Mike's hydroponic garden. Hydroponics is gardening without soil, in effect growing plants in water to which the necessary nutrients have been added. Inside the coolness of a shelter built of ocotillo branches, Mike grew a range of vegetables including spring onions and Swiss chard. It was an every day task draining and topping up the nutrient solution.

A grove of prickly pear cactus grew outside in the sun. The water from the shower drained directly beneath them, so they rarely if ever needed watering. Mike seemed particularly fond of the slimy pads, swearing by their laxative powers. To me the exuding slime looked suspiciously like dripping snot, and I had no desire to touch a cactus again until I had to.

In the dunes by the beach, Mike kept a pair of ocean-going kayaks which he invited me to use. As my experience of such things was limited to a single excursion which ended with me rolling over in the middle of the Thames and nearly drowning, I couldn't really get up much enthusiasm for kayaking off into the sunset. More to my taste was his little library of books on Baja; I was looking forward to stocking the fridge with beer, getting my feet up and doing some reading.

One fine morning in June, I woke up and the place was all mine. After listening to the radio, I went out to water the plants, check the stills and familiarize myself with everything. Yet in spite of all my dreaming about the good, safe, lazy life, it soon cloyed. I got into my old bad habits of eating too much, drinking too much, and avoiding anything vaguely resembling exercise, physical or mental. With the sun almost overhead and the midday temperature shooting up to 115°F. in the shade, I couldn't be bothered to walk anywhere except into town for more food and beer. I brought $200 into Mexico and found few places to spend it till reaching the Bay of L.A., where I seemed to be making up for lost time. I was putting on weight so fast my joints were beginning to ache. I wanted nothing more than to throw myself back into the fray, preferably on the cooler Pacific coast. Having committed myself, however, I had to make the most of it.

As my lips healed and the burning redness faded from my face and hands, I ventured out more often. Morning and evening fishing sessions were usually fascinating and productive: 'Caught my usual 20lbs of bass and triggerfish, but amazed to catch a 15lb shovelnose shark in 3 feet of water right off the beach.'

I even took to swimming again in the heat of the day. It was too hot to do anything else. I had never seen so many stingrays – in places they almost carpeted the sandy sea-bed. Having spoken to a couple of tourists who made the painful mistake of treading on one, I always waded carefully into the sea doing the 'stingray shuffle'. Once I got my undercarriage up, I swam around splashing vigorously, more concerned about scattering rays than attracting sharks.

Late one afternoon when I was cleaning my fishing tackle, I noticed a large plane circling low around the bay. Stepping outside, I was amazed to see it was a US Coast Guard Hercules. Round and round it flew as if looking for someone in trouble. I wondered what on earth could be so serious as to bring the USCG into Mexican airspace. 'Oh God, my radio distress beacon!' I dashed inside and pulled it from my pack. However, the pin was still in place and the transmitting indicator light wasn't on.

When the Hercules landed, I wandered into town to see what was happening. Apparently a jeep had overturned, seriously injuring the three young men inside. A vacationing American doctor had rendered first aid and summoned an air ambulance to get them back to the States. The jet was able to fly out two of them. The coastguard plane had been standing-by waiting for permission to take out the third.

The drama had everyone in town buzzing. After picking up some shopping, I got dragged into an animated discussion on the porch of one of the better beach-side tourist houses. Clutching a huge rum and coke, I made my contribution to a group that consisted of a pair of Canadians, a couple of Cherokee Indians (one with notches on his knife supposedly for every white man he'd killed), a big, drunk, aggressive Californian who was continually chipping in with tactless comments about General Custer, a prim straight-laced, middle-aged lady who was a walking caricature of the indignant moral majority type that moviemakers love to offend, and Don, a young man from San Francisco who'd just sailed in with his elder brother. The brother had had to return to the States leaving Don to look after the yacht.

The young 'yachtie' had been to Alphonsinas resort shortly after me and heard all about my plans from Ed Wills. He said they'd kept an eye out for me as they sailed down the coast, but I must have been in Calamajué when they passed.

When the party broke up before becoming a war party, Don invited me to dinner aboard his yacht. We shared a meal of spam, Mexican beans, tortillas and beer, as he spoke emotionally about a brother who was killed in Vietnam. It was interesting to see the town from the water, perhaps from exactly the spot where Steinbeck had dropped anchor. The stars looked beautiful and clear above the gently moving mast. All was quiet except for the slops, slaps and splashes of the sea, and the odd sound or voice carrying way into the night. About 10 p.m. Don rowed me back in total darkness, hair-raising in such a flimsy looking inflatable. There was luminescence in the water again. Back on the beach, I had to walk 300 yards without a torch. I expected a rattle any moment. My eyes were straining for assistance from the star-light.

Having managed to acquire some film and sunscreen, and having picked up my repaired boots, I decided to visit Las Flores and pay my respects to the Daggetts. Setting off early and taking a gallon of water, I walked along the beach, past the ruins of the ore mill and up an old mule trail on the seaward side of Red Mountain. Two hundred feet below it was easy to pick out the stingrays and other flatfish resting in the shallows.

Further around the bay I came to a ranch and was offered a cup of coffee by an extremely friendly Mexican farmer. He said he'd lived there for thirty years. And with mules and chickens wandering freely around he talked about 'Dick' (Daggett, jr) with obvious respect and affection.

From the ranch I walked into a long broad valley. There was a mountain range a mile to my left and another a mile to my right. The valley itself supported a veritable forest of cacti. Bright green cardóns shot up tall and straight towards the unblemished blue sky. They were the biggest I had ever seen. It was best not to look up too much as groves of ferociously spined ocotillo, cholla and pitahaya were waiting to punish any misplaced steps.

Approaching Las Flores the desert thinned out dramatically. I managed to pick up a little dirt road which had been jokingly signposted 'The Las Flores Freeway'. The first indication that I was nearing what once was a bustling mining town were the huge piles of reddish coloured powdered rock that had been dumped on the landscape. There was no one around; just a sign saying that visitors were welcome but 'no digging'. Apparently some enterprising Mexicans were re-processing the 'tailings' to extract whatever gold and silver had been left behind.

I walked around the remains of the buildings and the sad abandoned machinery looking for anything that might have been 'Made in England'. Failing to find any identifying marks, I took refuge inside the cool, solid walls of the little jail where I enjoyed a long lingering lunch. Ironically, I had no desire to leave the jail. As incarceration seemed infinitely preferable to slaving away in the hot sun, I wondered if the whole Las Flores enterprise had failed because all the workers had conspired to be locked up!

Stepping out into the breath-taking heat and the blinding light, I searched for the graveyard. A white cross leaping out from the sparse green and grey vegetation marked the spot. There were several graves. Father and son lay side by side. Daggett senior had a comparatively modest, rusting and battered, iron cross; while the white cross which dominated the graveyard had been erected as a monument to the son. The inscription was simple:

RICHARD DAGGETT 1893–1969 REST IN PEACE

By all accounts 'Dick' deserved his striking white cross. He was 'a wonderful old character' with a mind 'as sharp as a cactus needle'. A man who 'could fix almost anything', and who 'helped many a gringo get going again'. He was always willing to 'come to the rescue – at any hour of the day or night'.

I stood by the graves a long time, one Brit taking time to remember another who found his final resting place half a world away from the chill greys and greens of his native land. Oddly enough, I felt quite sure that Daggett senior had no regrets about jumping ship that day.

In spite of the heat, I was now in no hurry to get back to the trailer. My eyes had been opened to all that there was to see. I was filled with enthusiasm to visit the mines, climb 'Mike's mountain,' scout down the coast and maybe do some kayaking. I had come looking for adventure on the cheap and I knew I'd be kicking myself if I missed the opportunities around me.

Next morning, with the sea dead-calm, I picked up a paddle and dragged one of Mike's kayaks into the crystal-clear water. My initial apprehension faded into fascination as I glided silently over scores of bottom-hugging stingrays and shovelnose sharks. A whole new world opened up to me. As my confidence grew, I went on longer and longer excursions giving my underused arms some much needed exercise. 'I paddled down to the southern end of the bay,' I wrote in my diary. 'Diminishing fear about deep water. Fascinating to see a whale break the surface and send up a plume of spray just fifty yards away. Sensibly resisted the urge to get closer. Just sat in the kayak admiring and mesmerized.'

Another morning: 'Scores of pelicans floating lazily on the surface. Directly beneath them, great massed shoals of small (3–6 inch), clean looking, big-eyed fish. Strange seeing pelicans just sitting on top of their dinner. Also passed through a big unhurried shoal of 10–20lb Jack Crevelle. Amazing! They were content to part before the kayak and give me a yard of room – otherwise not bothered. There seemed to be a truce. Everything seemed to be waiting for the carnage to begin. Thought about dragging a fishing line from the kayak but dismissed idea when I pictured being towed out to sea by an irate Jack Crevelle. The Mexicans didn't call them El Toro – the bull – for nothing.'

After a few false starts I eventually got up early enough to attempt to follow the route of the old railway up to the mine. Expecting Mike back any time, I left a note saying where I'd gone. I also took my radio distress beacon 'just in case'.

It was 5.45 a.m. but the sun was up and it was already too hot for comfort. I picked up the track at the base of Red Mountain and followed it as best I could through the town's rubbish dump. A group of vultures on top of some of the tallest cardóns eyed me with interest. Once past the piles of fish bones and rusting cans, the route was clearly marked by a five-foot wide, rubble bordered sterile track that ran as straight as a knife slash across the desert. For about a mile and a half it climbed gently with the slowly rising barren plain of cactus, brush and broken grey rock.

Approaching the mountains, I was amazed by the amount of glitter in the rock. Grey gave way to pink and yellow, and every stone seemed to be shot through with sparkling silver and gold crystals. Apart from one or two defiant bushes and cacti, the whole scene was one of dazzling sterile aridity.

I reached the base of the mountains and followed the track up a series of switchbacks to a little plateau that offered the most incredible view. It was so different seeing the mountains, the valleys and the islands from on high. Red Mountain looked like the dark back of a whale emerging from the landscape.

Having got to the top, I was surrounded by the abandoned refuse of the mining company – wooden railway sleepers, large steel bolts and plates, even a more or less intact wooden ore cart. I followed the carved out track around the back of the mountain eager to find the mineshaft, but a rockslide had fallen across the track beside a sheer 200 foot drop. It was too risky to try clambering over. Disappointed, I turned around and went back to the plateau to admire the view and take some photographs.

It was easy to summon up the ghosts of the mineworkers and imagine the scene at the end of the nineteenth century. I had to admire the engineering genius behind the railroad. It wasn't a slap that the hand of man had laid across the face of nature, rather a solid monument to human endeavour.

It took an hour and a half to get down. With the thermometer reading over 100°F., I went for a swim; then spent the rest of the day in the shade, reading, writing and recovering.

Next day, an immaculate silver-grey and white car pulled up outside. A casually immaculate gringo dressed in white hat, white shirt, silver-grey shorts and white socks stepped out. I thought I'd become used to the uniform striving for personal perfection displayed by the more solid citizenry of the United States; however, after a couple of weeks among the laid-back, hard-drinking, hard-fishing bullshitting Yanks of the Bay of Los Angeles, Ray's appearance was decidedly squeaky clean. I wondered how I must have looked as I stood at the door in tatty shorts and sweat-stained shirt.

That contrast aside, we had quite a bit in common. Ray was looking for Mike. So was I, he was a week overdue. Ray came from Los Angeles, close to where my friends Dave and Denise lived. Although he looked in good shape for his nearly fifty years, I was surprised when he said that he wanted to get advice from Mike about climbing his mountain. I told him that I was planning to go up, and we carried on our discussion over dinner that evening.

Ray had a beach-side trailer in the heart of town, next to the old runway. In spite of the excellent new paved airstrip three miles to the north, the majority of pilots still preferred the convenience of 'parking' close to all the amenities where they could watch their own planes and not have to worry about arranging rides in and out.

With the town expanding so fast and so many cars and pedestrians crossing paths with planes, it was only a matter of time before the old runway would have to close. I had almost got minced by a propellor on my first visit. A plane appeared from nowhere and landed alarmingly close amid a cloud of dust and flying stones. It was obviously a dangerous situation but old habits die hard.

I spent a great evening with Ray, eating hamburgers and drinking bourbon, brandy and beer. We were joined by Pepe Smith, a Mexican in every way bar the name. His grandfather was another English sailor who had jumped ship and married a local señorita. Predictably there are, today, many Smiths in and around the Bay of L.A. Ray and I agreed to make our assault on the mountain the next day. It would be a tough climb in the June sunshine. An early start was vital.

We set off at 5.00 a.m. It was just light enough not to need a torch. We found the beginning of the trail where Mike had indicated, but soon lost it again amid the tumble of brush, cactus and granite.

I was always amazed how few tourists ventured into the solitude of the desert. It was as if there was a wall around the town and along both sides of the road. Take away all those within the walls (and on the boats) and as often as not there'd be no one left. For that reason, you only had to wander a hundred yards into the desert to have it all to yourself.

We continued up a wash, picking up the trail which climbed through a series of switchbacks to a broad ridge. Gasping and sweating our way along the ridge, we came to Mike's 'Halfway House' – a hollowed-out shady overhang conveniently located halfway up the mountain.

Without Mike's guidance, we found and lost the trail several times. Once while searching, I kicked a ball of cholla cactus deep into the back of my calf. Despite my language I was full of begrudging admiration for the way nature ingeniously designed the cholla 'to be the scourge of the desert traveller'. Not only does the innocuous looking cactus seem to spring out and leap up at you, but its spines once in are obviously not meant to come out. I had about twenty of the barbed spines firmly embedded up to half an inch in my flesh. Each one needed a good tug to rip it free. Get careless and it will break off and fester. Every time I lifted one spine, the cactus ball rolled over and stuck in another.

Ray offered to help but, coward that I am, I insisted on removing the spines myself. So my companion cooed over the view and busied himself with his photography. I became naively irritated by the way he seemed to be pulling out cameras and lenses quicker than I was pulling out spines. In spite of our trials, however, we eventually made it to the top. It had taken five and a half hours.

Mike's cave, just beneath the peak, was twenty feet deep and crammed full of pots, pans, provisions, water, seats, sleeping bags, foam pads, etc. Outside, amid the huge white granite boulders, he'd rigged up rain collectors to funnel water into containers. Inside, he'd put together a little iron stove and a chimney. The floor of the cave was as flat as poured concrete. It ran out to form a ten foot wide ledge overlooking the bay. Ray and I pulled out some chairs and treated ourselves to the view. We could see the whole of Isla de la Guarda and even Isla Tiburon (Shark Island) fifty miles away on the other coast. Passing the binoculars between us, we pointed out the yachts entering the bay, the black strip that was the new airport, and a moving speck which was a car cutting across the desert.

The breeze at 3,000 feet felt refreshing. After a good lunch downed with coffee and beer, we alternately sunbathed, slept and explored. The late afternoon light lent an air of unreality to the scene. Like the Grand Canyon, it was almost too spectacular to be true.

Having decided to go down the next morning, we made our beds on the ledge in front of the cave. At one point we had to divert a trail of ants heading our way. A barrier of kerosene did the trick. I slept on and off watching the Milky Way move across the sky. I couldn't help thinking of Janet who had accompanied me on my first climb, and I wondered how she was faring on the other side of the world.

It took us three hours to walk down the following morning. Walking continuously downhill brings a different set of muscles into play. My legs were trembling by the time we reached the relative flatness of the coastal plain. Back at the trailer, I celebrated with a cold beer. Ray was shattered, but he must have gained some kind of masochistic pleasure out of it for he asked if he could join me for a week or two when I resumed my journey on the Pacific coast. I said I'd be glad of some company around the population centres of Tijuana and Ensenada. We agreed to discuss it again back in Los Angeles when I returned there to re-equip, as I had now decided to do. Once he'd got home to his wife and kids, I thought, I'd probably hear no more about it.

I hadn't heard any more about Mike. He'd been gone for three weeks, and I was getting worried. And not only about Mike. It was also about money. I was still eating, drinking and spending too much. I had just fifty dollars left from my original two hundred, and there was so much I needed to buy before starting stage two.

That evening I noticed a lot of unusual activity in town. There were a number of cars dashing around the runway and a flashing red light possibly on top of a police car. Then a plane took off by moonlight and headed north, but I was too tired to bother walking into town to see what was happening.

The following day I made a snap decision to venture up into the deep shady canyons behind the mine. The arroyo I chose had a series of dry waterfalls which I had to ascend. With no sign that anyone else had ever been there I, once again, experienced the indescribable pleasure of not knowing what was around the next bend. Knowing I was in mining country brought an additional thrill. Every vein and layer of rock lay brutally exposed, not concealed by either soil or vegetation.

Exploring one narrow squeeze of a side canyon, I came across what appeared to be the biggest motherload in history. A foot-thick vein of gleaming metallic gold ran through the sparkling light grey rock. Other veins of quartz ran beside it. I knew next to nothing about the geology of gold, but what I did know was that gold and quartz had some kind of association. And this stuff looked as golden as anything I'd seen.

Suddenly the idea of walking around Baja took second place to thoughts of claims, mines and making millions. I was overwhelmed by the strange mix of elation and insecurity typical of those who wrest the too precious metal from the ground.

Forcing myself back down to earth, I reasoned that it couldn't be gold. Surely the mining companies would have thoroughly surveyed the area? Then again, there was a lot of area to survey and the bright, gleaming vein couldn't have been better hidden. There was only one thing for it – I'd have to take a sample and have it analysed. Real gold or not, it was certainly an extremely beautiful rock. If it was fools gold, it had certainly fooled me.

I returned to the trailer to a great surprise. The sunshade was up. Mike was back. It was good to see him again. He explained his delayed return, saying a routine visit to a doctor had revealed a heart murmur, and he had to wait to see a specialist and have other check-ups. It was hard to believe that Mike's heart wasn't as stout as his mountain, but he was under orders to take nitroglycerine tablets, and try to relax.

He told me the reason for the commotion in town the night before. A thirteen-year-old boy was struck and killed by a landing plane. Apparently the youngster was speeding across the old dirt strip on a motorcycle when the plane's wing caught his head. He was flown back to the USA but he died in hospital. Not surprisingly, the tragedy had led to the immediate closure of the old runway.

Heart problem or not, Mike was determined to take a kayak out the following day, and I allowed myself to be talked into joining him on a trip to a turtle research station across the bay.

We paddled off into black, deep water. At first, it was calm, but halfway across we were hit by a very strong headwind. In spite of the gathering waves we managed to keep the two red kayaks close together. It was hard work but I had no intention of stopping till we reached the safety of the far shore.

At last, we pulled the kayaks up on to the beach and walked around the turtle tanks which were full of loggerheads two or three feet long. There was no one around to ask what the station was doing.

On the beach I found the dried head of a hammerhead shark. Thinking the jaws would make a fine souvenir, I decided to take the head back strapped to the front of the kayak. The wind had swung around, once again maliciously blasting into our faces and whipping up the waves in the open bay. Mike did his best to reassure me that the kayaks were safe but with the flimsy craft crashing and banging and rolling from side to side I wasn't convinced.

All the way across, I was forced to look at the wicked, toothy sneer stretched across the two-foot-wide head of the shark. I could almost hear it hissing: 'It'll be our turn in a minute, pal, just you wait.'

Even though I grew increasingly confident about the kayak's stability, I was happy to get my feet back on dry land. After surviving such a difficult seven or eight miles I would have felt confident to tackle any kind of coast-hugging expedition. Too late I realized I had missed a golden opportunity to explore the coast south of the Bay of L.A. Still, it's not always easy striking the right balance between boldness and timidity.

Having secured a lift back to the border, I left the bay with mixed feelings. Entering the United States, I went through the same kind of culture shock I'd experienced on entering Mexico. Feeling uncomfortable and out of place, I recorded my impression of the good life while waiting for a bus at the San Diego Greyhound Depot: 'I hate sitting around waiting. It's hard to concentrate on anything with the noise of traffic, buses, radios, space-invaders. All these people milling around ignoring each other – incredible! It's one big hassle. Give me the desert any day.'

Chapter 17
1533 and all that

It was good to get back to my base in Los Angeles. After digging out some clean clothes I was able to feel human again and relax in the company of my old friends from Sheffield. Even so, life in the big city seemed strange, unfamiliar, and vaguely threatening. I needed to mount another sponsorship drive, but just to look at a phone or a phone-book was enough to make me feel ill.

In need of inspiration, I buried myself and my money worries in the air-conditioned coolness of the local library. Unlike in England, there was no shortage of books on Baja. After all, the state of California shares a common history with the 'forgotten peninsula'. It was all part of the same California before the Mexican–American war of 1846–8 ended with Uncle Sam grabbing over half the total territory of old Mexico. As well as Alta (or Upper) California, the US helped herself to all of Nevada and Utah, most of Arizona and New Mexico, and parts of Colorado, Wyoming, Kansas and Oklahoma. What with the 1845 annexation of Texas the area of the United States was increased by over 900,000 square miles. Mexico was allowed to keep the 760,000 square miles it has today.

As a face-saving gesture America cancelled Mexico's national debt and made a token payment of $15,000,000 (about 5 cents an acre). Over the next ten years, the 'Forty-niners' extracted $600,000,000 worth of gold from California alone.

By some miracle of wheeling and dealing, Mexico managed to hang on to Baja (or Lower) California. The Americans had wanted the strategic peninsula enough to have offered $20,000,000 for it in 1843 and $40,000,000 in 1845; but in the face of Mexican resistance at the peace conference they decided to cut and run with what they had and leave the cactus and the rattlesnakes to their southern neighbours.

Even so, many people in the United States could never really accept the situation. In 1853 the self-styled 'Colonel' William Walker invaded the peninsula, claiming it for the United States. In 1866–7 John Ross Browne was sent into Baja by a company of wealthy New York capitalists, ostensibly to assess its development potential but, equally important, to report on the ways and means of reuniting all of California under the American flag. Browne wrote: 'I should be very glad to be the humble instrument of promoting, even in a degree, the acquisition by the United States of Lower California.'

American military spies were continually updating their plans for invasion and annexation. Luckily for the stark beauty of the wilderness, if not the material well being of its citizens, all such schemes came to nothing. Baja California remained part of Mexico.

However, historically this is to jump the gun. It is necessary, first, to consider the situation in Baja before the sixteenth-century arrival of the Spaniards.

The peninsula was sparsely populated by roving bands of hunting and gathering Indians as primitive as any on earth. An early missionary wrote: 'The Indians dwell, eat, sleep and live all the time under the free sky . . . They spend all their lives wandering unendingly, driven . . . by the necessity of collecting food . . . They lie down wherever night overtakes them.'

Reading about the original inhabitants of the peninsula, I began to realize just how far, in fact, I'd managed to 'go native'. However, I didn't want to go too far. 'The prehispanic inhabitants of Lower California lived in a disastrous cultural condition,' wrote Pablo Martinez, a Mexican historian. 'There is not found among them the least notion of writing . . . [and] . . . the majority could hardly count to five.' They cultivated nothing. They built nothing more than temporary rock and brush shelters. The men went about entirely nude, covering their bodies only with ornaments and paint. When not travelling, they went barefoot, but for excursions into the desert or the mountains they wore sandals of leather or plant fabric.

Marriages were conducted with little or no ceremony. Polygamy was general. The man with many wives lived in ease and comfort, as each wife did her utmost to bring him the best things to eat. She dreaded being abandoned because, owing to the continual wars and the hazards of the chase, there was a perpetual shortage of men. If she were cast aside as inattentive to his needs, the chances were no one else would want her.

Parental love did not reach edifying heights. Fathers thought little of killing any children they couldn't support. Education consisted of little more than teaching the young which grubs, plants, spiders and snakes were edible and which were dangerous. The Indians were commendably catholic in their culinary tastes. Virtually any potential food not protected by an ability to poison or assault the taste buds was seized upon with relish. However there is no evidence that these Indians resorted to eating human flesh. That seems to have been their one unshakeable food taboo.

Eventually history caught up with these simple children of the sun. The cruel and courageous Spanish conquistadors marched across Mexico determined to drag all its native peoples into the sixteenth century. Having crushed the Aztec empire by 1521 Hernando Cortés turned his forces north and south and forever westward towards the Pacific.

Nothing seemed impossible to his proud, disciplined, battle-hardened soldiers. They had seen with their own eyes the fabulous cities of the Aztecs and the Maya. The promises of wealth and plunder had proved true. What other barbaric empires were ready to ring with the clash of Toledo steel? What army could stand in their way? Every horizon was golden with the promise of El Dorado.

One of the most popular books of the time was the *Adventures of Esplandian*, a tale of chivalrous exploits by Garcia de Montalvo. Successive editions were printed in 1510, 1519, 1521, 1525 and 1526.

Rarely can such a work of imaginative fiction have had such an impact on the history of an age. Among other wonders, it tells of a fantastic island called California which is inhabited entirely by Amazons and ruled over by their queen, Califia.

> 'It is known that to the right of the Indies there exists an island called California very near the terrestrial paradise; and peopled by black women among whom there was not a single man since they lived in the way of the Amazons. They had beautiful robust bodies, spirited courage and great strength. Their island was the most impregnable in the world with its cliffs and headlands and rocky coasts. Their weapons were all of gold . . . because in all the island there was no metal except gold.'

The story took such a hold that among the instructions given to Cortés (by Velasquez, the governor of Cuba) on his assuming command of the expedition to Mexico was to 'inquire where the Amazons are, for the Indians that you are taking with you say that they are near there'.

Although no Amazons were found along the eastern seaboard of Mexico, there were promising accounts from the Pacific coast. In a letter Cortés wrote to the king of Spain in 1524, he states: 'there was brought to me a story from the lords of the province of Cihuatlan, who made strong assertions about an island that was entirely populated by women, without any males . . . and that this island is ten days journey from this province, and that many of them have been there and seen it. They also told me that it is rich in pearls and gold. I will labour at making preparations to learn the truth and will write at length about it to your majesty.'

In all probability the lords of Cihuatlan were talking about the Baja California peninsula which was indeed rich in pearls (if not gold) and blessed with a disproportionate number of women. No doubt the noble lords were happy to accommodate the wishful thinking of the Spaniards and tell them what they wanted to hear.

Cortés, restless as ever, and looking for some accomplishment to match his momentous conquest of the Aztecs, seems to have allowed his imagination to be seized by these tales. But his enthusiasm wasn't fully shared by the King of Spain or his more down-to-earth advisors. If Cortés wanted to go off in search of fabled isles he could do so at his own expense.

As agreed with the Crown, Cortés financed the building of ships on the Pacific (or the Sea of the South as the Spaniards called it). In 1532 he dispatched his first expedition in search of the Amazons.

Because of summer storms, one of the ships was sunk and the other, the *San Miguel*, was forced to the coast of Jalisco where it was confiscated by another conquistador, Nuño de Guzman.

While Cortés had been arguing for a free hand in sending 'armadas to discover islands and lands in the Sea of the South', Nuño de Guzman had proved himself as independent, ambitious and ruthless as Cortés himself. He had marched into the north-west corner of Mexico killing, burning and looting wherever he went. 'He was considered as one of the most cruel and despised conquerors.' Having inspired terror in all the lands where he set himself up as lord and master, he declared himself to be an enemy of Cortés and did everything he could to thwart his ambitions.

Cortés organized a new expedition to confront Guzman and recover the *San Miguel*. He financed the construction and outfitting of another two ships, the *San Lazaro* and the *Concepción*. The latter he placed under the command of a cousin, Diego de Becerra. In October 1533, the expedition set sail for Jalisco, but the two ships became separated on the first night of the voyage. The *San Lazaro* was forced westward while the *Concepción* continued northward along the coast. Diego de Becerra, 'a man of a very evil nature', lost the confidence of his crew. The pilot, Fortún Jiménez, led a mutiny which resulted in the 'evil' captain being stabbed to death in his sleep and his body being thrown overboard. Those still loyal to the captain were abandoned on the coast of mainland

Mexico, after which the mutineers fled to the north forgetting all about the private wars of Cortés and Nuño de Guzman. They sighted a rugged, unknown shoreline. Thus it was that Fortún Jiminéz, a murderer and mutineer, became in 1533 the first European to sight California which he assumed to be an island. Due to the circumstances of the voyage the exact date is unknown.

Jiménez sailed east around the coast and into what was to become the Bay of La Paz. 'It is known,' wrote Martinez, 'that they were fishing for pearls, which they were gathering by the handful when some of the men tried to violate the native women which provoked the fury of the natives, who fell upon the Spaniards, killing Jiménez and also twenty of his companions. Eighteen survivors of the massacre set sail, and the ship arrived at the coast of Sinaloa, where it was sacked by Nuño de Guzman.'

The *San Lazaro* had returned safely to port after discovering the isolated Revillagigedo Islands. Cortés waited patiently for news of the *Concepción*. When the story filtered back, he was determined once and for all to deal with Guzman. Civil war was in the air. But so were tales of pearls, gold and an impregnable Amazon island 'with its cliffs and headlands and rocky coasts'. Cortés was forced to wonder, had Jiménez discovered the fabled island of California? War fever subsided. The devil could deal with Guzman.

Cortés mounted another expedition which he elected to lead himself. Ignoring the fact that Jiménez and his men were killed by jealous and resentful tribesmen, the story circulated that they were off to the land of the bronzed Amazons where, 'All have strong perfect figures, are ardent lovers and insatiable sex mates.' No doubt it suited Cortés to feed the fevered, unfettered imaginations of his countrymen. Certainly he had no trouble enrolling volunteers for the venture.

Expecting hard fighting and eventual victory, he took along 300 well-armed men, 130 horses and 37 women to form the heart of a new colony in what he hoped was a rich and fertile land. Never one to miss an opportunity or shirk risks, Cortés ploughed much of his personal wealth into the expedition.

In the spring of 1535, the greatest of the conquistadors set sail with three vessels – the *San Lazaro*, *Santo Tomás* and *Santa Agueda*. Following a north-west course over a sparkling sea bursting with life, the expedition reached the Bay of La Paz where the cactus-covered sterility of the land must have come as a sobering shock. Nevertheless, Cortés took formal possession of the 'island' for the King of Spain, giving it the name Santa Cruz. With all the enthusiasm he could muster, he went about the business of establishing the first legitimate Spanish settlement in California.

Although there were pearls, there weren't as many as the Spaniards imagined and the land was totally incapable of supporting the colony. Two of the ships were twice sent back for supplies, but with men and animals on the verge of starvation it became painfully obvious that the colony would have to be abandoned. This was done at the end of 1536, and twenty-three dead were left behind.

Cortés, the audacious conqueror of the Aztecs, had, through pursuing the figment of a writer's imagination, played into the hands of his enemies and lost a fortune in Baja California. History stripped from him the privilege of giving the peninsula its name. Santa Cruz fell from usage. The ordinary soldiers who had gone there expecting so much, only to find thirst, hunger and death, gave vent to their bitter disillusionment by laughingly calling the land of promise, California!

As Martinez wrote, 'Can the reader imagine the humorous vein that was brought forth among troops that had set out for a paradise of gold and only women, troops that had read, or if they were not yet reading, had heard about the work of Ordonez de Montalvo?' So much for California; they probably wished they had sailed in order to do battle with Nuño de Guzman.

In July 1539 Cortés was able to put together another expedition of three ships under the command of Francisco de Ulloa. His orders were to advance and explore as far north as possible. Believing Santa Cruz (or California) to be an island they sailed north into the Gulf and were surprised to find it a dead end. At the head of the Gulf they took note of the enormous volume of material swept down by the great Colorado river. Then, sailing down the Baja coast they reached the very tip of the peninsula, which Ulloa named Cabo San Lucas.

Rounding the cape with its spectacular arch and dramatic line of rocks, Ulloa sailed into the Pacific, explored Magdalena Bay and, upon reaching Cedros Island in 28° latitude, he put together a detailed account of the voyage and sent it back with the other ship. Ulloa's ship pushed north alone and was never heard of again. 'So it was,' wrote Martinez, 'that the waves of the western California coast swallowed up the first European who dared to plough through them.'

To end the anarchy of the warlords the King of Spain had appointed his representative – the viceroy – to have full command and authority in New Spain. Cortés now had a new and much more powerful rival who had his own vision of El Dorado.

In 1540 Viceroy Mendoza sent a land expedition into the north-west under the command of Coronado. As ever, it was prompted by tales of fabulously wealthy lands and cities. To assist the army, Mendoza prepared a flotilla of two ships under the command of Hernando de Alarcón. Alarcón succeeded in getting his vessels over twenty miles up the Colorado river where he waited for news of the land expedition. Unable to make contact, he returned to Acapulco where he was at least able to confirm that California was a peninsula.

How eagerly the enemies of Cortés seized upon the name California, promoting it at every opportunity to embarrass their rival. The embittered Cortés returned to Spain to put his case and protest the erosion of his authority in Mexico, but he found few friends after the humiliation of his failed colony.

With Cortés out of the way, Mendoza could at last enjoy the full authority of his vice-regal office. He split the Pacific fleet, sending part of it across the ocean to the Philippines and the rest up the Pacific coast of America under Cabrillo. Juan Rodriguez Cabrillo was an expert navigator of Portuguese origin. As a young man he had served as a crossbowman with Cortés against the Aztecs.

Cabrillo set sail in June 1542. His little fleet consisted of two ships. They reached the southern tip of the peninsula on 3 July. Eleven days later Cabrillo entered and named the elongated, island-protected Bahía Magdalena. After anchoring five days off Cedros Island, he sailed north into unknown waters, noting the important details along the coast. On 21 August, he discovered the port of San Quintín, where he took formal possession of the land in the name of the King and the Viceroy. Accordingly, he called it Puerto de la Posesión.

On 28 September Cabrillo sailed into United States history by discovering 'a port enclosed and very good' to which he gave the name San Miguel. He had in fact discovered what is today San Diego Bay, the site of one of America's finest cities and home of a Pacific fleet infinitely larger and more powerful than anything Cabrillo's sailors could have imagined as they sailed back out into the Pacific in their tiny wooden vessels.

The two ships continued their explorations as far north as southern Oregon; but the commander of the second expedition to brave the waters of the Pacific coast of California fared no better than the first. He died of injuries as a result of a fall. However the ships returned safely to port nine and a half months after they set out.

One might have thought that the painstaking journeys of Ulloa, Alarcón and Cabrillo would have settled beyond reasonable doubt the peninsular nature of California. However the misconception that it was an island continued to circulate among those who gave too much credence to works of fiction and the perennial tall tales of sunbaked soldiers and sailors. Like a galleon stuck fast on the rocks, the frame of truth and facts became gradually ripped apart beneath a foaming swirl of wild imagining.

Island or peninsula, events across the Pacific were about to place a special importance on the land of California. The fleet which Mendoza sent across the ocean had discovered and conquered the Philippines. Manila became a centre for trade with China and the other countries of the east. The products of that trade were brought back to Mexico in the so-called Manila galleons which lumbered north across the Pacific usually sighting the Americas somewhere around Oregon or northern California. They were then steered down the coast of California to the safety and mighty acclaim of the port of Acapulco. The journey was long and arduous, many men died, several ships were lost, but the profits were enormous. Clearly such an important line of trade needed support and protection, but the Spanish authorities felt secure in their own 'private lake' – the Pacific. The depredations of the English corsairs Drake and Cavendish were about to make them pay dearly for their complacency.

Drake entered the Pacific through the Straits of Magellan in September 1578. With his little armada of three ships, he plundered ports and ships all along the Pacific coast of America. He found a safe place to unload and careen his ships in the Marias Islands, south of Baja California. Afterward he landed at the southern tip of the peninsula, took on water and sailed up the coast of California to Drake's Bay near present-day San Francisco where he took possession of the land in the name of his sovereign, Elizabeth I of England, and called it New Albion.

Unable to find a northerly passage back to England, he struck out across the Pacific, and made his way home by the Cape of Good Hope, becoming the first Englishman to circumnavigate the world. Back in England he was acclaimed a hero and knighted by a grateful queen.

Drake brought back much wealth and much valuable information but he failed to connect with perhaps the greatest prize, the fabulously rich Manila galleon. Thomas Cavendish, the second Englishman to circumnavigate the world, had better luck.

Cavendish set sail from England in 1586 with three ships – the *Desire* of 120 tons, the *Content* of 60 tons and another vessel of 40 tons. Having repeated Drake's plundering along the Pacific coast, he sank the smaller vessel for lack of hands and took up station at Cabo San Lucas, waiting for the Manila galleon. One of the English sailors thought the magnificent line of rocks marking the cape to be 'very like the Needles of the Isle of Wight'.

For a month lookouts on the peaks ashore and on the two vessels scanned the horizon, until on 14 November 1587 their patience was rewarded. A lookout aboard the *Desire* shouted: 'A sayle. A sayle. With which cheerefull word the master of the ship and divers others of the company went also up into the maine top, who perceiving the speech to be very true gave information unto our general of these happy newes . . .'

The great galleon *Santa Ana* was approaching Cabo San Lucas. She had been at sea with over 300 passengers for more than four months. With a fair wind they would soon be safely in port.

When her lookouts saw two sails, the captain, Tomás de Alzola, assumed they were Spanish. As they drew closer, 'it was seen that it was the admiral's ship of an English corsair and thief Don Tomás Candiens of Tembley, a young man of little age'. The alarm and the despair must have been terrible. Alzola distributed what lances, guns, swords and knives there were; and hundreds of great stones were pulled out from the ballast to help deter any attempt at boarding from the smaller vessels.

The English ships gave chase for over three hours before pulling alongside and 'giving them the broad side with our great ordinance and a volee of small shot'. The battle raged for six hours. The galleon was a veritable fortress. Every attempt at boarding was met by a shower of stones and lances being thrown 'overboord upon our heads and into our ship so fast, and being so many of them, that they put us off the shippe againe, with the losse of two of our men which were slaine, and with the hurting of 4 or 5'. However, the too-heavy galleon couldn't manoeuvre. The cannon were below the water line and couldn't be used. 'Our General,' wrote Master William Pretty, 'encouraging his men afresh with the whole noyse of trumpets gave them the third encounter with our great ordinance and all our small shot to the great discomforting of our enemies, raking them through in divers places, killing and spoiling many of the men ... their shippe being in hazard of sinking by reason of the great shot which were made ... set out a flagge of truce and parled for mercy.' Almost 200 of those on board the *Santa Ana* had been killed or mortally wounded.

The galleon was towed to the shelter of the great bay protected by Cabo San Lucas, where the jubilant English sailors found themselves in possession of a fortune in gold, pearls, silks and spices. With commendable propriety Cavendish presented Alzola with a signed receipt for the cargo and requested the pleasure of the company of the Spanish survivors at an on-board celebration of the anniversary of the coronation of Queen Elizabeth. The English cannon roared again, this time in salute.

With the *Content* and the *Desire* able to carry only a small fraction of the plunder, the rest was piled on the beach and burned. According to one of the English sailors, 'this was one of the richest vessels that ever sailed on the seas; and was able to have made many hundreds wealthy if we had had the means to have brought it home'.

Leaving behind the burning hulk of the galleon and a stock of supplies and materials for the 190 survivors, the two ships disappeared into the vastness of the ocean. The *Content* turned north up the coast of California and was never heard from again, whereas Cavendish steered the *Desire* across the Pacific, around the Cape of Good Hope and arrived off the Lizard on 3 September 1588. He was greeted by a Flemish vessel with the news of the recent defeat and destruction of the Spanish armada.

Some of the weird assortment of plants to be found in Baja's central desert.
The tallest are the cirios and cardón cacti.

The rugged Gulf of California coastline where the Sierra Giganta mountains drop precipitously to the sea just south of Loreto.

I carried all my essential supplies on my back and sometimes a gallon of water in each hand.

Beneath cliffs I would often wade in the sea carrying my backpack above my head.

The massive base of a cardón cactus which may be hundreds of years old.

The shark fishermen of Calamajué.

Making tortillas inside a fisherman's shack

Another day over, I would zip myself into the security of the tent.

With my telescopic rod I could take any number of
bass or trigger fish from the rocks.

Pouring a gallon of seawater into the inflatable solar still.
The device was capable of producing two or three pints of drinking water a day.

Cactus was an important part of my diet.
Removing the spines from a pad of prickly pear cactus.

Pelicans diving into the sea; an everyday sight on both Gulf and Pacific coasts.

A long abandoned Indian trail winds through the desert

Cliff-top view of the Gulf of California.

Mission San Ignacio: founded by the Jesuits in 1728 and completed by the Dominicans in 1786.

The first mission at Loreto, founded in 1697 by Jesuit padre Juan de Salvatierra whose bust stands in the adjacent plaza.

Gazing down at the southern end of Bahía de los Angeles.

The road to Bahía de los Angeles.

Walking beneath the cliffs on the Pacific coast was
a much more dangerous game.

The kettle still. Boiling seawater and condensing the steam was the most effective way of producing drinking water

Flowers carpet the desert after a heavy rainfall.

A young sea-lion surprised by my approach.

A vulture eyes me hopefully from on top of a cardón cactus.

I encountered scorpions on many occasions but only got stung twice.

The delicious fruit of the pitahaya cactus. From September to November it formed a major part of my diet.

A fisherman casts his net amongst the mangrove swamps of Magdalena Bay.

Another rattlesnake for the frying pan. The meat looks and tastes like chicken.

A ride that ended in disaster. I was fortunate to walk away from the crash with only a few cuts and bruises.

The ruins of Mission Dolores del Sur, founded
by the Jesuits in 1721 and positioned midway between Loreto and La Paz.

A rabid burro and the 1894 Winchester that killed it

Cabo San Lucas: sailing out from the sheltered bay
to round the southernmost tip of Baja.

Bonny the burro

The problems begin. It took time to learn how to pack my belongings securely on to Bonny's back.

The sun sinks into the Pacific. The camera self-timer was essential for photos like this.

Another beautiful Pacific sunset marked our last evening together.

The final painful step of the journey was saying goodbye
to my faithful companion.

'On . . . 10 September, 1588 . . . like wearied men, through the favour of the almighty, we got into Plymouth where the townsmen received us with all humanity.'

'As soon as the corsairs had set sail,' wrote Martinez, 'the Spaniards abandoned in San José del Cabo, headed by Sebastian Vizcaíno who voyaged in the role of a merchant, poured water on the *Santa Ana* and with great effort extinguished the fire in the ship and then, after making all possible repairs, they sailed towards the coast of New Spain.' Their reception was not quite as hearty as that given Cavendish in Plymouth.

The taking of the *Santa Ana* ruined merchants in Acapulco and Manila. Inquiries were set up, producing reams of regulations and recommendations. There were new calls to settle and secure 'the Californias'.

Sebastian Vizcaíno was by his deeds putting himself forward as the man for the job. In spite of being forced to watch the greater portion of his wealth going up in smoke, he more than anyone took command of the situation and ensured the survivors made it safely home. And undaunted by his losses, he again made the arduous and dangerous round-trip to Manila in 1590, making a profit of 2,500 ducats on an investment of 200 ducats. Although in the eyes of some of the Spanish grandees he was a 'mere merchant', his experience and personal qualities couldn't be ignored. He was put in command of another expedition charged with exploring the waters around California and establishing settlements there.

In March 1596 he set sail with three ships, four Franciscan padres, 'a goodly number of soldiers', and many of the soldiers' wives. Crossing to the tip of the peninsula, he came to the site where Jiménez and Cortés had landed before. The Indians received them with such warmth and hospitality that Vizcaíno gave the place its present name, La Paz (Peace).

Planting his colony, he pushed north into the Gulf to conduct his explorations; but the harsh and barren land proved a disappointment. However, in many places the sea was shallow and the waters crystal clear. Pearl oysters were plentiful. As one writer reported: 'The Indians dived with great facility for shells and having once taken them out, they cast them into the fire to open their valves. They gathered up the pearls, making in them a circular hole for running through a string, and thus they formed strings of pearls that were more or less long and valuable, with which they adorned their necks.'

All went well until, at one point half way up the Gulf, an over-zealous soldier struck out and incurred the wrath of the Indians. The landing party had to beat a hasty retreat. It was too hasty. Their longboat capsized spilling the armour-clad soldiers into the sea. Nineteen men drowned.

It was a demoralizing blow; and returning to La Paz, Vizcaíno found his colony in trouble. The soldiers constantly upset the Indians and undid the work of the padres. Storms had prevented them from fishing for pearls. Supplies were running short and, once again, it was apparent that the land was incapable of supporting such a colony. So, on 28 October 1596 the settlement was abandoned after just two months.

After such a failure, Vizcaíno's career as admiral and general, and his influence on the history of the Californias, might have come to an abrupt end. However, the King of Spain was still anxious to protect the weak link in his trade with the Orient, and also to ascertain whether there was any truth in the rumours of a passage between the Pacific and the Atlantic across the top of North America. Martinez writes:

> In 1599, Viceroy Count of Monterrey received an urgent order from Philip III that at the expense of the royal exchequer and without counting the costs, he was to equip an armada and place it under the command of Vizcaíno, not for the east coast of California but for the west one, with instructions to map out the ports and islands, sound the bays and explore all the territory possible to the north.

This time the crews were carefully selected, three ships were supplied of better than usual quality, and an expert map maker was taken along.

The expedition left Acapulco in May 1602. Three times it was blown back to the Gulf after trying to round Cabo San Lucas. At last in the Pacific, Vizcaíno encountered headwinds all the way. Like his predecessors, Ulloa and Cabrillo, he went days without making any progress at all. Tacking back and forth was a continual necessity. Even so, the coast was carefully mapped and explored and names were applied without much regard to those given by the earlier explorers. After four months beating up the length of Baja, Vizcaíno took shelter in Cabrillo's 'port enclosed and very good' and gave it its present-day name, San Diego. He continued as far north as Oregon where on 21 January 1603 he was satisfied sufficiently to turn around and take advantage of the fair winds back to Acapulco.

Largely due to the detail of his account, the skill of his map maker and the royal interest in his appointment, the names attached by Vizcaíno to the islands, points and bays of the coast are the major legacy of his expedition. One American historian has written: 'While monuments and parks have been named for his predecessor, Rodriquez Cabrillo, few monuments have been named for Vizcaíno, and the fact that almost all major place names along the California coast were given by him is often not remembered.' In Baja California, Vizcaíno's legacy has fared better. His name has been inseparably attached to the great flat 'awesome wilderness' of the central desert and the vast Pacific bay bordered by it.

Like so many before and after, Vizcaíno found himself captivated by California, and he was bitterly disappointed not to be allowed to conduct further explorations.

John Steinbeck wrote of Baja California: 'If it were lush and rich, one could understand the pull, but it is fierce and hostile and sullen. The stone mountains pile up to the sky and there is little fresh water. But we know we must go back if we live and we don't know why.'

The shock of the *Santa Ana* disaster had receded. The galleons continued to get through. The vastness of the Pacific was their best protection. The Spanish authorities gradually lost interest in a peninsula which offered no gold, no riches, no Amazons; just hardship, hunger and death. With so much of the world controlled by Spain, the level-headed bureaucrats found better places to spend money and lives.

It wasn't until 1683, eighty years later, that another major expedition was launched under the command of Admiral Atondo. It consisted of three ships, about a hundred men, and three Jesuit priests, including Padre Eusebio Kino who was another man about to fall under the spell of 'the Californias'.

The expedition reached La Paz on 1 April. Initially, the place lived up to its peaceful name. According to Kino:

> We were very much at peace with the [Indians], and they came to see us almost every day, bringing fruit and fish. But trouble soon flared. And then as the admiral was informed that an Indian had struck one of the soldiers with a dart but without drawing a drop of blood, he ordered the Indian to be put into stocks and hauled on board ship. This led to a violent disturbance among the Guaycura Indians who are most warlike.
>
> About 3 July, sixteen Guaycuras – their leaders and the bravest warriors among them – came to us; numerous others remained on the hill. It was feared that they came to capture one of our men or to free their own prisoner. Since they came in guise of peace and dissimulated their evil intent, the admiral ordered that they be given porridge, a dish they relish very much; and as they were seated eating it . . . the small artillery piece was fired . . . killing ten of them. The rest fled despite their severe injuries. Since then we are filled day and night with apprehension and anxiety . . . The last four days no Indian has been seen.

Once again, with supplies getting scarce, the La Paz colony had to be abandoned. Not surprisingly, the Guaycura Indians were less eager to welcome white settlers after the visit of Atondo. Nevertheless Padre Kino had become convinced that the basic, friendly, pliable natures of the native Californians would make them ideal candidates for religious instruction. Burning to bring the benefits of Christianity and civilization to these receptive souls, he passed on his enthusiasm to other Jesuits including Padre Juan Salvatierra who was eventually granted permission to found a permanent missionary settlement on behalf of his Order. There would be no help from the Crown however. The Jesuits would have to raise the money by private donation and run everything themselves. By 1697 they had accumulated sufficient funds to put together a modest expedition.

Apart from 1533, when Jiménez 'accidentally' became the first European to set foot on the peninsula, 1697 is the most important year in Baja California's history. In October, Salvatierra left the coast of Sinaloa with two tiny ships, a handful of men and his unshakeable faith.

Things went wrong from the start. Padre Kino, who should have accompanied Salvatierra, was withdrawn from participation by his superiors, who deemed that the mainland province of Sonora needed his services more. Salvatierra sailed nevertheless. He sighted the Baja coast the following day. However, the companion vessel was caught in a storm and not seen again for a month.

Salvatierra sailed along the coast looking for a suitable spot to build the first mission which was to be dedicated to 'Our Lady of Loreto'. They landed at a large arroyo flowing with a trickle of sweet water. Many Indians, including women and children, came to greet them. In spite of the warm and enthusiastic welcome, the number of Indians at the site inspired caution. A fort was constructed using the provisions as bulwarks. A small swivel cannon was mounted to command every approach. The statue of 'Our Lady of Loreto' was housed in a specially built shelter.

Salvatierra worked demoniacally in the first few days of the colony. He was priest, student of native languages, cook, governor and sentry rolled into one. In every way he was in charge. The soldiers took their orders from him.

The missionary initially handed out porridge to the Indians as a token of good will, then more as a reward for work done or religious instruction received, but the Indians showed increasing signs of resentment. They wanted and felt powerful enough to help themselves. Thus, on 13 November the natives attacked in force, showering the defenders with arrows and rocks. After holding back as long as he dare, Salvatierra reluctantly gave permission for the cannon to be used. As a light was brought to the powder, the artillery piece dramatically burst, injuring two of the Spanish soldiers. Salvatierra himself was nearly killed by a chunk of iron whizzing past his ear. Seeing this, the emboldened attackers pressed home to destroy the infant colony, but the uninjured defenders fired their muskets at point-blank range, killing several of the Indians and dispersing the rest.

Two days later, the missing boat turned up, bringing Father Piccolo and another handful of soldiers. The conquerors now numbered eighteen. Success was in the balance. Hunger, deprivation and danger lay ahead. But unlike the colonizing attempts of Cortés, Vizcaíno and Atondo, the Jesuits had different priorities. They had come in search of souls. They intended to win hearts through the power of love and example, not through terror and the sword.

These remarkable men – with their faith, dedication and common sense – succeeded where others had failed. Loreto became the first permanent European settlement in California. From Loreto, the Jesuits boldly explored in every direction, founding a chain of nineteen other missions which eventually, under the Dominicans and Franciscans, stretched along the entire length of California, both Baja and Alta.

Father Piccolo carried the Jesuit banner westward into the dauntingly precipitous Sierra Giganta mountains, setting up a second mission at San Javier. Padre Juan de Ugarte, arrived on the scene in 1701. He had begged to be released from a desk job in Mexico City procuring funds, in order to devote himself to the poor Indians of the peninsula. Salvatierra assigned to him the perilous post of San Javier, twenty miles from the still tenuous beach-head at Loreto.

He was escorted by a handful of wary soldiers to the site of the yet to be constructed mission. It was deserted. For several days not an Indian was to be seen. Suspecting the soldiers were the cause, he sent them back to Loreto and trusted his safety to divine providence. The Indians slowly returned, and the former professor of philosophy found himself teaching religious instruction in a language he laboured to comprehend to a people who, in the words of another Jesuit missionary, 'beside their physical shape and ability to think have nothing to distinguish them from animals'.

By example and sheer force of personality, he overcame every frustration and discouragement in acquainting the Indians with Christian beliefs and values, and accustoming them to the labour necessary to raise such crops as maize and vines from the craggy soil. Before long Ugarte was breeding horses and sheep, producing wine and generally acting as the main supplier for the garrison and the other missions. Moreover, he still had time to run a school and a hospital, arguably the first in California; and he was always willing to undertake any exploration, no matter how hazardous.

Ugarte took over all the California missions on the death of Salvatierra in 1717. Determined to find a suitable port for the Manila galleon, and to ascertain once and for all whether Baja was a peninsula or an island, he built a ship using a grove of timber from the mountains several miles inland. He wrote: 'While the wood was being cut I lived in the mountains under some reeds for four months in order to encourage the natives and create enthusiasm in those who worked there.' The padre's example so won the hearts of the Indians that they helped him both cut the timber and transport it to the coast.

On 16 July 1719, on the day when the Spanish church celebrates the feast of The Triumph of the Cross, Ugarte watched the sturdily constructed vessel being blessed by Father Piccolo and named *El Triunfo de la Cruz (The Triumph of the Cross).*

The ever-energetic Ugarte founded another mission at the site where the timber had been cut, and another at the promising but problematic site of La Paz, before embarking, at sixty-one years of age, on his examination of the coast up to the Colorado river. His pilot was an Englishman called William Strafford, who had behind him years of experience looking for pearls in the Gulf. Ugarte and Strafford together prepared a full report on all their discoveries which was 'transmitted to the King and the Council of the Indies through Viceroy Valero'.

Reaching the head of the Gulf, Ugarte satisfied himself that only the great river separated his missions from those in Sonora. Baja California was most certainly not an island.

Back in Loreto he equipped another expedition and took *The Triumph of the Cross* into the Pacific from where Ugarte and Strafford continued to send back reports. Clearly only death was going to stop the indefatigable padre. That came in December 1739, after he had given almost forty years service to the land and the people he loved. The American historian H. H. Bancroft wrote:

> Again and again had his courage, pertinacity and tact saved the missions from dissolution. Every crisis of distress and despair had found him ready. His heart had been strong when all others had been weak; his hand active when others were listless . . . he ever tempered the ruler's authority with the friend's affability, the gentleness of the priest with the dignity of the man.

In our liberal and sophisticated age, it has become fashionable to point out the deficiencies and the disastrous consequences of missionization – certainly it brought about a dramatic decline in the native population due to the introduction of European diseases such as smallpox – but any judgement has to take into account the character and the motives of the padres. The more I read about men like Salvatierra and Ugarte, the more impressed I became. Such men rise above the limitations of nation and religion to inspire us all. It was a source of pride for me to realize that, at times on my journey, I would be literally following in their footsteps.

My two-week sojourn in the library had been a journey of exploration and discovery every bit as fascinating and exciting as my journey along the coast. But I had read enough to draw the inspiration I needed; now there were preparations to make and problems to solve.

Chapter 18
Together and alone

I went to see Ray who lived in a quiet suburb on the edge of Los Angeles. Much to my surprise, he still wanted to join me for a couple of weeks in August or September – I had to wonder what drove him to want to participate in my ordeal.

Ray, like myself, was anything but the Rambo type. He was on the lean side of normal, and not much bigger than I was. Behind his glasses and his healthy Californian tan, he struck me as sensitive, intelligent and just a little squeamish. He had a small, pleasant kind of face. I wasn't sure if he reminded me more of Woody Allen or John McEnroe.

After meeting his charming wife, and teenage son and daughter, I did everything I could to put him off going. If anything happened and I had to bury him in the desert, I wanted to do it with a clear conscience.

Spreading out a map, I explained, 'I've decided to restart at Ensenada. The stretch from Tijuana to Ensenada is too developed – tourists, towns, a four-lane highway.'

I drummed my finger beside Ensenada, raising my voice to make sure Ray's wife could hear. 'This is not going to be like a hike along a trail in a National Park. We'll have a day or two to sort things out as we walk around Todos Santos Bay. Then when we get to La Bufadora, we'll be on our own. There's twenty miles of nothing but cliffs and mountains. I'm not even sure we can make it. I've got to try; but if you decide it's too much for you, there may be no easy way out. The main road is ten or fifteen miles inland.'

I ran my finger along the coast, 'O.K. There are ranches and trails here, but this is all rugged uphill and downhill cliffs and valleys. If possible, we'll be sticking to the coast. The cliffs will be as bad as those on the Gulf, but the surf will be much worse. Fishing, swimming and walking on the rocks will be a lot more dangerous.'

After pointing out the possibility of tidal waves, late summer storms and hurricanes, I pulled out some photographs of the Pacific coast desert. 'It won't be like climbing Mike's mountain or wandering through the desert around the Bay of L.A. There, at least, the cactus had the courtesy to grow up and out of your way. The cactus and brush growing on the Pacific is, if anything, even more fiercely spined, and it's spread thickly along the ground, making it difficult to pass through. It will be a bit like walking on a bed of nails with bush-sized sea urchins crossing spines everywhere. And more vegetation means more bugs, more spiders, more scorpions, more mice and more rattlesnakes!'

With Ray deep in thought, I added: 'The other thing we'll have to be careful of, are the people. In the villages and fields along the road, there'll be a lot of tomato pickers and other itinerant workers, many of them over from the mainland. They'll be poor and maybe desperate; we'll see more of them as we get nearer San Quintín.'

I couldn't be sure if I was putting Ray off or not, but I was certainly doing a good job on myself. With so many hazards to face, I was both surprised and relieved when he said he still wanted to join me.

'O.K., Ray, I've been averaging ten miles a day. If we start at Ensenada, and you last two weeks, that's 140 miles. Maybe we can make San Quintín. That's quite a big town. You should be able to catch a bus or hitch a ride to Ensenada.'

As Ray looked doubtful, I added, 'Don't worry. We're not going to race. We'll just take it easy. It'll take me a couple of weeks to get back into shape. Have you got a good pair of boots?'

'Yes,' he replied, 'I bought a pair recently, and I've been breaking them in; but what else do you think I'll need?'

After helping him draw up a list of essentials, we drove over to a monstrous – 'if we haven't got it, it doesn't exist' – camping and outdoor store. I felt like a penniless kid in a candy store as I helped Ray select his tent, backpack, water containers, knives, fishing tackle, etc. Money was no obstacle. As an afterthought, he bought a selection of gourmet dried foods. Considering the state of my equipment, and the culinary delicacies in store for me, I had my first doubts about whether the partnership would work.

Nevertheless, we agreed a start date; and with the few dollars I had left, I busied myself writing, phoning and chasing up every chance of sponsorship. It was an uphill struggle. Americans are a circumspect lot when it comes to someone without name or standing looking for something for nothing. The best I could do was persuade a major

Californian camping equipment manufacturer to offer me their goods at trade prices – a discount of 40%.

I placed an ad in the *Los Angeles Times*: 'Brit walking around Baja seeks sponsorship.' That brought in nothing but the wrong kind of ten-dollar bill, so trying a different tack, I took up some of the invitations to visit the Southern Californians who befriended me on the first leg of my journey. The resultant round of excellent dinners and good ideas did much for my morale.

Following up one suggestion, I contacted an American travel club called Mexico West. They were, I was assured, always looking for articles on Baja for their bi-monthly magazine. The club was run by Tom and Shirley Miller. Tom Miller, or Mr Baja as he was sometimes called, was the co-author of a popular Baja guidebook, and a profilic writer on peninsula matters. I gave him a call.

'Hello, Tom. My name is Graham Mackintosh. I've just set out to walk around the coastline of Baja, and obviously I'm bound to have some worthwhile experiences to write about. Would you consider accepting stories for *Mexico West*?'

His response was none too enthusiastic. 'Oh, we've had several stories from travellers off the beaten track. Besides, it has been done before. Jim Saylor and Alan Ehrgott, for example, walked the mission trail from Cabo San Lucas to the border.'

'Well, I'm attempting to walk all the way around the coastline, both sides, Gulf and Pacific. I don't think that's been done before.'

'It hasn't been done because I doubt very much if it can be done. You're biting off more than you can chew. There are places you won't get by – Punta Remedios for example.'

'Actually,' I said as tactfully as I could, 'I've already got by Punta Remedios. I've just walked from San Felipe to the Bay of L.A. right along the coast. I'm now about to try my luck on the Pacific side.'

'You walked down the coast to the Bay of L.A., past Punta Remedios? That's impossible!'

'Well, it was certainly very difficult; but it wasn't impossible.'

His attitude suddenly changed. 'Hmmm . . . O.K. It might be interesting. Send us 300-word reports. We don't pay a lot – forty dollars a piece, but that will keep you going a while.'

The opportunity to get something published and gain credibility certainly kept me going as I continued with my preparations. My problem was immediate cash. I could have put on my worn out boots and kicked myself for having blown nearly $200 at the Bay of L.A.

As the day of departure drew near and my Micawber-like certainty that something would turn up was being gradually eroded, I began to look lovingly at my Visa card. I had arranged with my bank manager that, in an emergency, I could use the card on the understanding that the bank would settle the account for me until my return. But hardly had my imagination conjured up images of wonderful new tents, boots and backpacks, than a letter arrived from England saying my Visa card had been cancelled. It was a misunderstanding, but I didn't have time to sort it out. I was going with Ray no matter what. I wasn't going to let him down.

One morning, I was sitting in the sun sewing up my old backpack when a letter arrived from my favourite city – San Diego. It was from the Andersons who gave my spirits such a lift in that first difficult week. Dick and his brother-in-law had clubbed together to send me a cheque for $200. 'To help you resupply for your return to Baja.'

I could hardly believe my luck. Or was it luck? Was everything going to fall in place because . . . because of what? Fate, faith, premonition?

The money arrived just in time. I bought clothes from a 'thrift' (second-hand) store; and I took advantage of the offered 40% discount to buy a sturdy backpack for $70. It was comfortable and spacious, though not the model I would have chosen if I had had more money. The major drawback was the sack design. The main body of the backpack wasn't subdivided into separately accessible compartments. What went in first, came out last. Filling it would require careful thought.

It wasn't easy deciding what I could and couldn't afford. I didn't buy a replacement plastic water bag. Instead, I picked up a couple of sturdy gallon chlorine bottles from the local pool store. At 25 cents a piece, they were a bargain.

After buying film, tapes, batteries, sunscreen and a dozen other necessities, I reluctantly dropped my plans for a new pair of boots, and a new tent.

Again, I elected to take just the inner tent, but, mindful of the possibility of late summer rain along the Pacific coast, I bought a can of waterproof spray and coated both surfaces of the permeable tent fabric. As for my boots, I'd just have to squeeze the remaining life out of the old pair. I had just 33 dollars left to take into Mexico!

The day of departure came. As I filled up my new backpack, David Bowyer suddenly remembered that he'd once been given a pair of hiking boots. He dug them out of a cupboard – brand new, excellent, expensive-looking boots with Vibram soles. They were two sizes too big, but I had to believe that this was a Godsend not to be sneered at. I could stuff them out with socks.

Ray drove up in high spirits. As I walked out of the door in my new boots, I called back to Dave, 'Thanks for the boots, and thank the previous owner. Tell him I'll be putting them to good use.'

'Actually,' he said, 'I can't. He's dead!'

'Who was he? What happened?'

'Well, he was a scientist and ... er ... he was killed in Baja.'

'Oh, don't give me that.' I thought Dave was pulling my leg till he produced a magazine article explaining how Dr Gerhard Bakker was killed when his boat was overturned by an angry gray whale in Scammon's Lagoon, midway down the Pacific coast of Baja. If the boots lasted, and if I lasted, I'd be wearing them as I came to the shores of the lagoon.

It was good to have a lift all the way to the border. Entering Mexico was, once again, a pleasant formality. We were waved across with a smile. Signs and posters welcomed us in Spanish and English, and offered suggestions as to how best to spend our dollars. Other signs directed us through Tijuana to Ensenada. The main road skirts the border for a couple of miles before turning down the coast. Driving by the border fence, you have an excellent view of Southern California to the right and the depressing shanty towns of Tijuana immediately to the left.

Crossing from one of the most affluent corners of the world to a third-world urban sprawl cannot fail to be disturbing. John Selby, a British military historian and former lecturer at Sandhurst, confessed that, before he had visited Mexico for the first time, he felt that country had been 'shamefully robbed' in 1846. However, after crossing from California to Mexico he wrote:

> California, at one time a Mexican state, is now, as all can see, one of the most advanced areas in the world. It is bursting with energy and activity; it manufactures sophisticated machines like Jumbo Jets and Space Modules; and it produces by skilful irrigation superb crops ... [In Mexico] the bus was besieged by a horde of young people, pushing and shoving to sell sticky cakes. The state of the men's room was quite disgusting. On the streets of the town ... female beggars were squatting with their bare-footed children around them. Everywhere were signs of abject poverty.... it would have been better for everyone concerned if, after the Mexican war, the United States had seized the whole country!

Scores of Mexicans who might have agreed were waiting patiently by the border fence for darkness to cover their attempt to break into Alta California. I thought of Margy, and wondered if he'd made it across, and how he was coping with the wonders of Los Angeles, San Francisco or wherever.

We joined the stream of cars with blue California plates heading down the impressive toll road meandering along the coast. With Tijuana behind us, the land to our left was now rolling, rugged and empty, coastal scrub rather than true desert. In between stretches of cliffs, the shore was largely occupied by bars, restaurants and clusters of American houses. It seemed ironic: Americans flocking to Mexico to idle around; Mexicans flocking to the United States to look for work; the former welcome, the latter unwelcome!

Ray and I were in good spirits. Our main worry was where to park the car. After failing to find somewhere suitable in Ensenada, we drove fifteen miles further south to La Bufadora, a small tourist spot built around a spectacular blow-hole in the cliffs. Ray paid two dollars a day to leave his car for two weeks. The $28 he handed over to the owner of a cliff-top campsite seemed like a fortune to me.

It was the start of an American holiday weekend, and little La Bufadora was gradually filling with 'get-away-from-it-all' gringos. By my standards it was crowded; by any others it was an insignificant little group of revellers sandwiched between the vastness of the ocean and the green and overgrown desert.

There was plenty of room for us to put our tents up on a bluff overlooking the Pacific. The sun was sinking, the air was still and the sea was calm apart from a long, rolling swell that crashed resoundingly against the milk-chocolate coloured cliffs.

The sightseers gathered around the blow-hole weren't disappointed. Every few minutes, an incoming wave funnelled into a 'canyon' in the cliffs. With a thunderous boom, the water shot upwards and backwards like a mighty geyser, leaving the air filled with a fine gentle mist, a rainbow, and the cries of the hovering gulls.

As the night drew on, the very different cries of carousing Americans echoed around La Bufadora. Ray and I preferred to talk quietly and watch the sky for shooting stars.

We woke to a grey and dreary morning. A bank of low cloud and fog had moved in during the night. Our tents were soaked inside and out by a heavy dew. While they dried, I polished and worked the leather of my new boots, studying their every stitch and fold.

With that done and the day warming, I stared at the ocean. I was back at the mouth of that cave at Punta Remedios, feeling and sensing what was in store. The only thing I managed to sense clearly was that Ray was in more of a hurry than I was. He couldn't understand my lack of urgency. The sun was rising. The cloud was burning away. We were missing the ideal time for struggling up the hills before us. Of course, he was right. We quickly packed, shouldered our burdens, and set off into the unknown.

Taking short, calf-aching steps and many breaks, we followed a little used track up a long incline. It was hard work. My boots felt heavy and uncomfortable. Ray had that 'what have I let myself in for' look on his face. The last of the morning mist and cloud soon disappeared, leaving a deep blue sea meeting a pale blue sky at a very distant horizon. We were both sweating and suffering under the midday sun. If the cooling Pacific breeze kept the temperature tolerable, nothing mitigated the burning fierceness of the sun.

The track degenerated into an animal trail and then disappeared altogether. The red cliffs ahead looked stark and awesome. The coast below was rugged and rocky. With the swell throwing up a powerful surf, I thought it best to spare Ray the perils of walking the water's edge.

We had to cut and weave our way up a series of steep, cactus-covered slopes. It was almost impossible to raise one foot above another without being ripped or impaled. The needle-tipped rosettes of the agave were particularly dangerous. I warned Ray: 'Whatever you do, don't fall on one of those bastards; they'll spike you to the bone.'

The agave is one of the most striking of the queer assortment of plants growing along the shores of the Pacific. In more ways than one it dominates the coastal scrub and the adjacent desert with the 'don't mess with me' spinal symmetry of a sea urchin or a porcupine.

The agave consists of a rosette of glossy green leaves anything up to two feet long and five inches wide, with each leaf ending in a rigid inch-long spine. To add to the viciousness of its appearance, the edges of the leaves are serrated with shark-like teeth. Put your hand in the centre of the plant, and you can imagine it snapping shut, drawing you down and impaling you on the spines.

In fact, the agave is a fascinating plant of many uses. After years of steady but unspectacular growth, it shoots up an asparagus-like stalk as much as fifteen feet tall and four inches wide. The upper half of the stalk produces a profusion of yellowish flowers which are pollinated by bees, hummingbirds and bats. That final burst of growth is followed by the death of the plant. The mistaken belief that this happens after a hundred years has lent another name to the agave, the Century Plant; but the average life-cycle is more like fifteen years. The young 'asparagus stage' stalks were an important source of food to the Baja Indians, especially in the dry season when there was little else. After the leaves were removed, the base of the stalk was roasted in a hole in the ground. Today it is more likely to end up being fermented to make tequila. The agave blossom also exudes a large amount of sweet nectar which the Indians used to collect and drink. They also made the seeds into flour.

Once we'd climbed the worst of the slope, and found a relatively flat outcrop of rock on which to sit, I gave Ray a few lessons in desert survival. We sampled the agave flowers, the nectar, the fresh-cut stalk and the leaves, everything except the heart. We weren't planning staying long enough to dig a pit and slow-roast it!

Instead, we wandered over to a grove of prickly pear cactus, where we tried the purple fruit and the flat 'beaver-tail' pads. Both were a prized food of the Indians. The Indians and the early pioneers also used to soak the split, fleshy pads in water and then bind them to wounds and bruises. As well as the large and obvious spines, one had to be careful of the glochids – the tiny, barbed innocuous looking hairs growing in clusters on the pads and the fruit. Several times I found my fingers, lips and tongue covered with them.

After a couple of days in the desert, both Ray and I were much more inclined to try walking the shore. With the breeze, the freshness, the mighty rolling Pacific, the sudden explosions of foam and spray, it was a different world from the Gulf shore. Wading around rocky points was a new and much more dangerous game!

Even fishing became hazardous. So, for food, I turned to the abundant supply of shellfish, especially mussels. In the inter-tidal zone, masses of purple-black mussels hung like bunches of grapes. As Ewell Gibbons wrote in *Hunting the Blue Eyed Scallop*, 'The mussel family probably constitutes the greatest unused seafood resource along the coast of America.' One reason for that under-utilization was that, during the warm-water months from May to October, mussels can be poisonous. Indeed, between those months, mussels are quarantined along the California coast. The coastal tribes had always known the danger. Part of their sea-lore dictated that mussels were not to be eaten when 'every wave carries a crest of fire', 'when the wake of a boat looks like a moonpath across the sea', and 'when schools of fish become displays of shooting stars'. The warm water encourages the growth of a dangerous dinoflagellate, Gonyaulux. While the rattlesnake warns of his presence through sound, Gonyaulux reveals itself through the phosphorescent light it imparts to the summer sea. As Rachel Carson explained in *The Sea Around Us*, 'Sometimes the meaning of the glowing water is ominous off the Pacific coast of North America, it may mean that the sea is filled with the dinoflagellate Gonyaulux, a minute plant that contains a poison of strange and terrible virulence. About four days after Gonyaulux comes to dominate the coastal plankton, some of the fishes and shellfish in the vicinity become toxic . . . mussels accumulate the Gonyaulux toxins in their livers, and the toxins react on the human nervous system with an effect similar to that of strychnine.'

I boiled my first mussel in seawater – it was so small I felt guilty about terminating its brief existence. Wondering if the miniscule mouthful would exact a terrible revenge, I forked it from its tiny shell and swallowed courageously. Suffering no ill effects, I ate a larger one at the next meal, then two, then three, until I was happily devouring dozens of the chewy morsels. All the time, I scanned the night ocean for any sign of phosphorescence.

If mussels were plentiful, so was seaweed. In places, it buried the rocks and choked the sea. For a while, mussels and seaweed became the heart of my diet, but Ray couldn't be tempted.

'Fancy some of this Gonyaulux, Ray?' 'No, no, you go ahead,' he'd reply in his inimitable self-sacrificial way, as he tucked into another plate of fried eggs. Ray couldn't be without eggs. At every farm, or from every passing tourist, he'd attempt to buy some more. In the main, he and I got on well. I was impressed with his stamina. For a man approaching fifty he was making an extraordinary effort. Although blistered by the sun and his boots, he pushed on with a gutsy determination, taking fear, thirst and exhaustion in his stride. In that sense, I couldn't have wished for a better companion. If there were misunderstandings, they were usually about money or time.

Late one afternoon we were strolling over some easy, rolling hills, and spotted an isolated ranch. Needing water, we wandered down to find a lively fiesta in progress. We were received with typical Mexican warmth and invited to join in the barbecue. Because I didn't have any money to offer, I suggested we decline and hurry down to the rocks to do some fishing. Ray, however, was insistent, and in the face of his reassurances, I relented and we tucked into a feast of barbecued steak and chicken, tortillas, beer, beans and salad. We were treated as honoured guests. One of the Mexicans spoke excellent English. He was taking a postgraduate degree in politics at the University of California, Los Angeles, and we had a long discussion about Margaret Thatcher and the Falklands war.

As the setting sun forced us to leave, Ray pulled out a $10 bill and went through the time-consuming task of getting our generous hosts to take it. Racing off to find a place to camp, my gratitude at Ray's generosity evaporated when he asked me for my $5 share. I was stunned, but put it down to a misunderstanding. It must have been hard for Ray to comprehend that I had only $33, and my journey was, hopefully, going to last a lot longer than two weeks. I was suddenly down to $28, the amount that Ray had casually paid to park his car.

Two days later, we came to a single croft-like cottage which nestled in an isolated bay. Change the cacti for heather, and it might have been in some remote and craggy corner of Scotland. The aging fisherman and his wife advised us against continuing along the coast, pointing out that the trails in the mountains were steep, washed out and rattlesnake-infested. I'd heard it all before, but, of course, it was all new and off-putting for Ray. When the fisherman's son offered to take us past the worst stretch in his boat, Ray jumped at the chance. I wasn't so keen. I reminded Ray that I was supposed to be walking, and if we took the boat ride we'd have to pay!

With Ray making even more reassuring noises about the money situation, I gave way to the responsibility I felt towards his getting as much as possible from our experience. It would certainly be fascinating to see the mountains and the cliffs from a small open boat tossed around on the ocean.

After a breakfast of shellfish, crab meat and water melon, we climbed into the boat and motored out of the bay, around the point and under the cliffs. Hundreds of seabirds watched us from the clifftops and the dozens of islands through which we weaved. Several house-sized rocks alternatively rose above and were subdued by the foaming sea. The young fisherman obviously knew every inch of the coast, but to my untrained eye we seemed to be steering perilously close to some of the masses of rock punching up from the depths. The water was deep, deep blue and crystal clear apart from streaks of white foam. The sunlight shafting down to the depths occasionally struck a rising rock or a swaying mass of seaweed. Looking at the steep cliffs and angular mountains, I could see how awesome they must have appeared to the first Spanish explorers, and how quick they would have been to believe that this was the island of the Amazons, 'the most impregnable in the whole world'.

The fisherman took us to a sheltered cove and, shouting above the noise of the wind and the waves raking the pebbles, said, 'there is a trail leading up the cliffs, and a village over the hills'.

Ray gave him 500 pesos ($3.50) and said to me, 'I think you should do the same.' I was astounded. The ride was worth every peso, and I didn't want to argue in front of the fisherman who'd risked his boat and his life to drop us there. So, I handed over my 500 pesos and jumped ashore.

Getting both boots soaked didn't do much for my temper. As the boat turned away I turned to Ray: 'For heaven's sake, I don't seem to be getting through to you. I haven't got that kind of money. I now have, $24 and 50 cents, and that is it! You put me in the position where I had to pay that guy. I didn't want to go on that boat ride. Remember, I said I couldn't afford it. You told me not to worry.'

'Oh I see, you expect me to pay for everything?'

'Maybe I do. If you make the bloody decision and it's going to cost money, then I do expect you to pay for it. I only ate at the ranch and jumped in that boat because you told me not to worry about it. We started at La Bufadora instead of Ensenada to suit you and your car. You come along to join me on my trip and now you're taking over!'

The tension dissipated as we realized that the trail up the cliffs had been washed away. For two hours we scouted the quarter-mile length of the cove for a safe way up. There wasn't one. So, returning to the remains of the old trail, we had to risk a dangerous climb above a sheer thirty-foot drop. I scaled it first, hauled up the packs, then watched anxiously as Ray climbed out. It was a timely moment to be reminded that we needed each other. Danger and hardship brought its own kind of camaraderie and understanding. Sitting around a campfire and watching a peaceful Pacific sunset, it was easy to laugh about the day's tensions.

Ray was an early-to-bed, early-to-rise man. I was more inclined to sit up staring into the fire and the night. Even inside my tent, I regarded it as an essential part of my day to scan the airwaves to find something worth listening to. The result was Ray was awake and wanting to get away long before me. One morning, he set his alarm for 5.30 a.m. I heard it and went straight back to sleep. I didn't come to Baja to have my life regulated by an alarm clock.

The next time I woke, Ray was standing by the tent door packed and ready to go. 'I'll walk on and see you down the coast,' he said.

'Down the coast! What! Where? What's the rush? You'll be shattered by nine o' clock.'

'I'll just wait for you to catch up.' And off he went. I couldn't let him go alone. With my morning contemplation rudely shattered, I packed as fast as I could and dashed after him. He wasn't exactly strolling. It took me over an hour to catch up. I wondered if I was worrying too much. He probably needed to get away from me.

Although Ray usually pushed himself far harder than I did, on occasions I'd dismiss his doubts and fears and obstinately insist on a certain course of action. One day when we were both almost out of water, we came to an impasse on the coast. Forced inland, I was confident we'd find a ranch or a fishcamp, but Ray, feeling his first brush with thirst, wanted to go back. I wouldn't entertain the idea. There was 'nothing' behind for miles.

We were down to our last sips of water, and hurting with thirst. An animal trail led us to a grove of dumpy barrel cacti, one of which we butchered and chewed to extract the liquid. It was getting dark and the creatures of the night were on the prowl. A brown tarantula as big and hairy as a hamster crossed the trail in front of us.

We came to a deep valley cut into the rounded hills. It was choked with bushes and trees. Hacking our way through, I was convinced there was water there. Ray was probably convinced he was in the hands of a madman leading him towards a fearful demise.

The ground became soft, then mushy, and then we found a trickle of water emerging as a spring from a little cluster of grey rocks. Filling our canteens, we thought it best to add water purifying tablets and wait the recommended thirty minutes before drinking it.

We both suffered blisters and discomfort from our new boots, but by the eighth day Ray had patches of skin missing from each heel and several toes. Although every step was agony, he insisted on carrying on. It pained me to watch him hobbling. On the ninth morning, we met a party of Mexican fishermen who offered to take him back to the main highway. It wasn't an easy decision but reluctantly Ray decided to call it a day.

The prospect of suddenly having to walk on alone, made me realize just how much I appreciated Ray's presence. I felt sad as we said our goodbyes over a final cup of coffee. We seemed to have packed nine years into our nine days together. Peering at my map in the early morning sunshine, I said: 'According to this, we've covered about 100 miles. It's been a real experience. Congratulations. You've done really well. I hope when I'm your age I can do half as well. I'm going to miss you. Take care.'

Ray's presence had made easier the transition from the world of supermarkets to that of self-reliance. He gave me most of his water and food. I shouldered my pack, shook his hand, thanked the Mexicans for the coffee and walked off alone down the coast.

Although I missed the security of having a companion, in another way I was much more relaxed and aware of everything around me: the lizard scampering across the trail, the distant coyote checking me out before ducking down into a little valley, and the curious sea lion following my progress along the rocks.

As I'd buried 'Seth' at the bottom of my backpack, I only had my tape-recorder to talk to; and with no shortage of tapes, batteries and things to observe, I rattled on at great length about anything and everything:

> I'm on my own and I've got to do a bit of adjusting. It's a beautiful day. The sea has calmed down and the swell isn't nearly as bad. I might try a bit of fishing later . . . I'm on a tiny trail going along the edge of a cliff. Every step has got to be careful and deliberate. One mistake and I'm as good as dead. There's a hell of a drop down there to the rocks . . . There are cacti all around, tiny barrel cacti, nothing more than a few inches tall. The soil is really poor, just stones with a bit of dirt in between. No wonder everything is so stunted. The toll on my boots has been awful, already the soles are showing signs of coming adrift . . . I feel I'm in no-man's-land. I'm not on the coast where I could walk fairly straight and level, and I'm not way into the mountains where I could try to follow the easier ridges, I'm on a plateau with arroyo after arroyo cutting across in front of me; and that means up and down, up and down, all day. The vegetation is also much thicker in the arroyos. So I think I'll work my way in closer to the mountains to see if I can find some easier walking . . . I'm following a coyote trail now, about half a mile in from the sea . . . There's so much cacti and spikes around here, I really can't imagine a rattlesnake crawling along. He'd be better waiting in ambush for some poor mouse weaving his way between the spines . . .

Tiring of hearing my own voice, I slipped on the headphones, turned on the radio, and tuned into a slightly crackly Californian station. Its familiar 'golden-oldies' music lightened my step as I watched the sun sink into the Pacific. It was my first time listening to the radio while I was walking.

There was an annoying hissing noise. As I spun the dial to tune the station a bit better, something started moving just in front of me. Probably just another lizard. Finding myself looking at what appeared to be a writhing, vibrating cowpat, I stopped with all the shocked suddenness of someone walking into a glass door. I was a step away from a very unhappy looking rattlesnake.

I hadn't heeded his warning. I hadn't backed away. I'd just kept right on coming. I was a threat. I was in range. The rattler slowly raised its head. For whatever fraction of a second I stared, it was like looking down the barrel of a gun knowing the trigger was being slowly squeezed.

There was a sudden blur as the snake struck. I pulled my feet away with such force that I lost my balance and went tumbling forward. Somehow, I managed to twist in mid air and land pack down, on top of the snake. I shook off the shoulder straps, sprang to my feet and disappeared in a cloud of dust. The equally disconcerted serpent slid off in the opposite direction as fast as his wriggling ribs would carry him.

I had learned my lesson. I put away the radio and tuned back into the sounds of the desert.

Chapter 19

Coyote trails and lobster tails

All I could hear was the howl of the wind and the roar of the surf as I enjoyed the exhilarating feeling that I had one of the world's most beautiful beaches all to myself. However, I soon realized I was not alone on my sandy patch of paradise. Through the mist-like spray drifting in from the tops of the waves, I could see a couple of vans up on a bluff and a group of people splashing around in the sea. As I approached, one of them came rushing out of the water to greet me like a long lost brother.

'Hi, my name is John,' he said with a slur and some difficulty in standing up. 'Where are you going?'

I explained. He became even more excited and called his friends from the water. 'Come and meet this crazy Limey. He's walking all the way around Baja.'

Big, pot-bellied, balding, long-haired, John was clearly a character and a half. He absolutely insisted I camp with them. It didn't seem to matter what anyone else thought. I was the entertainment for the evening and that was it. His three companions – a guy and two topless gals – left the water with a conspiratorial, 'what has he dragged us into now?', look on their bronzed faces.

John was outrageous. Seeing the girls' discomfiture at my presence, he said, 'Don't worry. He won't grab your tits. He's British and a gentleman.'

I was soon by their fire, beer in hand. The evening was warm and pleasant. We had a commanding view of the beach and a sunset as colourful and outrageous as big, bad John. The drinks flowed freely. The girls put together a delicious Mexican meal of burritos and salad. We laughed, and joked, and sang, and got increasingly drunk. This was the other side of the story, the fun and the friendship. It was worth recording.

'O.K. You guys,' I shouted, 'I'm making a tape for a radio station back in England. How about a few words to give them the idea of what it's like walking the Baja.'

Archer and John, showmen to the end, jumped at the chance to say their bit and preferably everybody else's. The ladies – Judy and Donna – could hardly get a word in; but laughing virtually non-stop, they didn't seem to mind.

GRAHAM: 'As you can hear we're having a great party on the beach. I'd like to introduce you to four of the loveliest people I've ever met, and they are going to tell you what they think about the most beautiful and exciting place in the world.'

JOHN – [loud and drunk]: 'Before there was any type of highway, it was all dirt road. They had to try and get down there in their old Chevies . . .'

ARCHER – [impatient with John]: 'O.K. Cut! Cut! you Limey, cut. I'm from England myself . . .'

JOHN – [increasingly incoherent, with Archer clucking away in the background like a chicken]: 'The older guys would drive their big Chevies down when there wasn't a road. It was all dirt, cactus and rocks. It's bad enough driving the thing. Nobody in their right mind would try to walk the thing! They'd have to be absolutely ludicrous. They're dead meat.'

GRAHAM [trying to stop laughing]: 'Now here we have a big handsome chap from San Diego, California, though he's of English descent. Archer, what do you think of Baja?'

ARCHER: 'How can you describe the Baja? All you can think of is you take a desert, and you put an ocean up against a desert, and that's the Baja. You're totally by yourself and you can do anything you want because there's no one down here. I feel that if I had the time . . . if I didn't have to work for a living, the one thing I'd love to do, is put on a backpack and walk to the tip of Baja. And I wish I had that kind of freedom in my life because I think it would be the greatest.'

JOHN: 'The idea of trying to walk the peninsula! Anybody should be shot for even thinking about it; put out of their misery before they even attempt it.'

GRAHAM – [trying to get Donna and Judy in on the act]: 'Maybe we can get the views of these two lovely Californian girls.'

ARCHER: 'What is it like to be a Californian girl?'

JOHN – [in his best 'dumb blond' accent]: 'I love the sweat and the sun. But sometimes I get too hot and the boys excite me . . . I mean not all the boys, just the hunky ones.'

We just cracked up. The tape degenerated into a farce. Wondering what the Radio Kent listeners would make of it, I staggered towards my tent marvelling at how much living can be packed into twenty-four hours.

A few days later, I was enjoying some Mexican hospitality. I had been racing the sunset looking for a fishcamp which my map suggested was just ahead. It was almost dark when I spotted it on a low sandy bluff. It detracted from Baja's expansive emptiness by a dozen well scattered shacks and an assortment of battered vehicles and beached boats. I could hear laughter, singing and the mellow strumming of a guitar as I slid unseen down a rubble slope towards their fires. Little more than the moonlight lit my way as I wandered up to the largest group of revellers. They were sitting around a fire on the usual assortment of barrels, boxes and old car seats. Suddenly, a pack of dogs woke to my presence and barked out their disapproval. A stout and balding Mexican with a bandit-like, drop-handlebar moustache directed a few choice curses at the dogs who went cowering off into the night. Then he stood up and motioned for me to take his seat.

'Welcome my friend. Where are you going with such a heavy burden?' he said in English.

There were the usual exclamations and whistles when I explained my plans. I was given a can of beer. 'What are you celebrating?' I asked.

The chap with the long moustache – everyone called him 'Pancho Villa' after the Mexican revolutionary leader – said proudly, 'This day is a fiesta in all of Mexico. Our country celebrates its independence from Spain. Our 16 September is the same as your 4 July when you kicked out the British.'

'Actually,' I said, 'I am British.'

'Oh,' he said with a smile. 'You are far from home, my friend. Do join us and drink tequila to La Independencia.'

He passed me a bottle. A woman emerged from the shadows to offer me a plate of tortillas and fried fish. One of the first things one notices in the camps and ranches of Baja is the way the women and girls tend to stay smiling shyly in the background. While they looked on, I joined the menfolk eating, drinking and singing to La Independencia.

As we all got progressively more drunk, I pulled out my tape-recorder again and said: 'Amigos, I am making a tape to send to my friends in England. I want them to know how you celebrate this night that is so special to the good people of Mexico. Perhaps you can sing your National Anthem?'

The fishermen were happy to oblige. The singing spread throughout the camp, almost drowning out the background whistle of the wind and the roar of the surf.

'Pancho Villa' asked me if I'd like to try a spot of fishing off the rocks. Why not? I was given a handline, a hunk of bait and an escort of six or seven very happy, very drunk, Mexicans. We walked carefully out along a narrow point of rock and took turns at casting the line into the moon-sparkling sea. No one caught anything, but it didn't seem to matter. It was a good excuse to carry on laughing and celebrating beneath a heaven that was smiling approvingly.

When bed-time beckoned, I grabbed my pack and walked to a clean, sandy, spur overlooking the ocean. I was too drunk to figure out how to get my tent up. In the end, I just threw the poles and pegs aside, crawled in and fell immediately asleep.

The next day, hangover and all, I joined my new friends on a handline fishing trip out in the ocean. The party continued as we motored out of sight of land. The first fish I caught was a perch-like thing about two inches long. The boat nearly capsized as the fishermen rolled around laughing. However, I soon got the hang of it, dragging up a variety of fish up to 10lbs in weight. The celebrations continued in the sea. One of the Mexicans jumped overboard. The rest followed like lemmings. Before long, I was the only one left on the boat. Everyone was swimming around ten miles from shore, shouting, 'Shark! shark!' They invited me to join them, but I wasn't that drunk.

Although I had never been seasick in my life, I soon tired of bobbing up and down on the ocean. One second the beer in my stomach seemed to be dropping to my feet, the next it was rising to my head. I was beginning to have some idea how the fish felt when they were dragged up from the depths with their eyes bulging, and their swim-bladders hanging from their mouths. I was more than glad when we called it a day and headed back to shore.

After being treated to a fine, fry-up lunch, I spent the rest of the afternoon engaged in such stomach-settling pursuits as sewing up my clothes, washing them in the sea, sharpening my knives and polishing my boots. As my clothes dried on the tent, I caught up with my journal and studied my maps.

The evening found me back around the campfires questioning the Mexicans about the coast ahead. They all agreed that my journey would change dramatically at El Rosario. They talked about that little town as if it were the end of the world. One of the older fishermen said, in words reminiscent of those used by Ed Wills in describing the Gulf south of Punta Final: 'After El Rosario, señor, there is much danger, many coyotes, snakes and lions. There are many cliffs and mountains, and only one or two very bad roads. Sometimes they are passable, sometimes not. If there are fishcamps you must travel many days from one to another. There is no water. It is not good to walk there alone, señor. It is better you take the road.'

The old fisherman was talking about the main highway. Unfortunately it left the coast at El Rosario and wandered into the mountainous heart of the peninsula. I explained that I had to walk down the coast. He couldn't understand: 'Today, it is possible to take a bus to Cabo San Lucas. Why must you walk, señor?'

Before leaving, I thanked them all for their kindness and hospitality. They refused to take a peso in return.

At first, the coast was more awkward than difficult; a tiring combination of sandy bluffs, low cliffs and steep pebble beaches. Thirty or forty miles inland a series of peaks made up the backbone of the peninsula. The tallest was the 10,126-foot Picacho del Diablo – the Devil's Peak. Its great mass of grey-white granite sometimes floated eerily above the thinning morning mist; at other times, with the rest of the sky bright blue and clear, the mountain top would be lost in a puff of cloud. In a month or two, the first snows would fall on its precipitous slopes, transforming it into a glistening white beacon visible from far out in the Pacific. It was often the first indication that land was near. And sailors did well to heed its presence. Ever since the mysterious disappearance of Francisco de Ulloa, the first European to explore these waters, the fog-prone Pacific coast of Baja, with its islands, reefs and relentless onshore-breezes, has been exacting its steady toll of victims.

I was walking along the margin of a steamy lagoon. The mists seemed to rise from the shallow pools and hang ten feet in the air. Above that the sky was bright blue. Through the mists something was taking shape; something monstrous that didn't belong. As I got closer, it looked like Noah's Ark abandoned after the flood. It turned out to be the *Isla del Carmen*, a freighter which had run aground on a beach beyond the lagoon. It was resting in shallow water, half on its side, bow to the shore. It wasn't the first wreck I'd seen, and it wouldn't be the last.

Approaching San Quintín, I had to be careful not to go wandering down a narrow ten-mile peninsula between the sea and a bay which was perhaps the only safe anchorage for a hundred miles to the north and two hundred miles to the south. This was where, in August 1542, Cabrillo had landed and taken possession of the land in the name of the Viceroy and the King of Spain. It was an excellent port; its position identified by a distinctive line of volcanic cones marking the western margin of the bay.

Taking my bearings from the peaks, I cut inland and followed the highway towards San Quintín. Most of San Quintín is spread out along the highway, a growing town at the centre of an increasingly important agricultural region. It has a permanent population of about 20,000, but its streets are often filled with migrant workers, usually colourfully clad Indians shipped in from other parts of Mexico. From the highway, one sees mile after mile of lettuce, corn, tomatoes, and chilis. The land has been made fertile by extensive irrigation using underground water.

It wasn't always so productive. In the 1880s the International Company of Mexico offered the land for sale. It was bought by a group of American investors who attempted to colonize the region. But, in the words of the American writer and Baja enthusiast, Mike McMahan: 'only the searing sun greeted their efforts . . . the colony disappeared – many of the colonists returning to the States. The next year, natives say, came the biggest winter rainfall in all Baja memory . . .' He goes on:

> When the next spring came to the valley, it was aglow with wild flowers. The cacti put forth their vivid blossoms of red and yellow; the century plants grew high with their once-in-a-lifetime regal crown of blooms . . . a land promoter's dream . . . The Americans, no dummies, brought the British in for a look. They jumped at the bait. So British colonization took over where the Americans had failed . . . The British soon discovered the fraud. But, with Anglo-Saxon reserve, they went ahead with their plans, quietly, figuring that one good fraud deserves another.
>
> To give the appearance of truth to their claims for the valley's productivity the British began to build a flour mill at San Quintín to process all the wheat that was to be grown on these fertile fields.
>
> The entire mill had to be constructed with imported materials, of course. And to entice the next crop of suckers it was put into operation . . . with imported wheat.
>
> So the land was sold again . . . And most of the people who bought were Bajacalifornios. Perhaps they knew that the wheat mill was a fraud, but also they knew the land was not.
>
> With Mexican ingenuity, the new native owners looked for a new source of water and found it – in the upside-down rivers and underground springs beneath their lands.

The mill was recently demolished, but the remains of the old English cemetery can still be seen on the eastern shore of the bay, a poignant reminder of what failure in Baja often meant.

I made my way back out to the coast, south of the bay. The beach was magnificent. The white sand and the surf threw back the sun's rays in a blinding glare that made sunglasses a necessity. Beyond the wall of sand dunes to my left, there was an extensive lagoon. I wasn't particularly bothered by its presence till the wind dropped. Then I was hit by a swarm of hard-biting mosquitoes. Quickly I smeared my face, arms and legs in repellent. That merely sent the mosquitoes angrily crawling into my ears, up my nostrils and wherever they could find a repellent-free area to bite. My shirt was almost black. They were biting me through the thin material. I slapped and swatted furiously. My shirt and hands were soon spotted with red. At one point, I nearly ran into the sea screaming but, feeling the breeze picking up, I pulled out a spare shirt and lashed myself on, twisting and turning and shouting obscenities. The assault lasted barely fifteen minutes, but I spent most of that night in sleepless misery, rubbing and scratching and wondering how I would fare among the vast mangrove swamps along the bays and lagoons further south.

Two days later, I was making my way down into the broad, steep-sided El Rosario valley. Beyond it, there would be all the loneliness, thirst, hunger, excitement and adventure I could possibly want. The town itself was at the bottom of the valley, a few miles in from the sea. It was a small, unremarkable fishing and agricultural community which was well known, prior to the completion of the paved transpeninsular highway, as the last outpost of civilization before the foolhardy plunged into the depths of the Baja desert. And south of El Rosario the desert certainly changed dramatically.

As the American Automobile Association (AAA) handbook describes it:

> Leaving El Rosario, Highway 1 turns east and follows the wide, cultivated Arroyo del Rosario for a few miles, then crosses the valley and climbs into a region of low, deeply eroded hills. Soon cirio trees and giant cardón cacti appear alongside the highway, as the terrain begins to conform to the armchair traveller's notion of Baja California. With its blue skies, expansive views and abundance of unique vegetation, this is one of North America's most fascinating desert regions.

Looking across the valley, I thought back to the time I had first seen that sensational cactus garden. The tall branching cardóns were spectacular enough, but it was the cirios that seized my imagination. They stood like 50-foot tall tapering candles or squid taking headlong, panic refuge in the ground. Some grew straight, some branched, some doubled over and coiled; I walked between them as moved as if I were walking between the hairs on the back of the hand of God.

With the highway disappearing, and my journey about to change as dramatically as the desert, I splashed out nearly $5 on rice, flour, coffee, powdered milk, fruit and vegetables. It was a large chunk of what I had left, but there probably wouldn't be another store till I reached the town of Guerrero Negro some 250 miles to the south.

Carrying my pack, and my burden of anxieties, I walked out to the coast and a fishcamp at a place called Punta Baja. It was there, while weathering a storm, that I wrote my first piece for *Mexico West* on the back of an old well-worn map. The local fishermen kindly allowed me to erect my tent inside one of their disused shacks.

When the storms passed, I mustered up the courage to go. My 60lb pack was securely on my back. Each hand held a gallon water container. As I took my first steps away from Punta Baja, a woman called after me. 'Are you not afraid?'

'Of what?' I replied.

'Coyotes.'

'No, they are my amigos. At night we sing together.' I howled for emphasis.

She laughed and muttered to herself, 'Inglés es loco.'

I wasn't entirely joking though. After just a few days I was able to write in my diary:

> They may be only three inches wide, they may branch and disappear, but coyote trails can do a lot of thinking for you. I hardly noticed them at first, but now I think like a coyote. My advice to anyone lost off the beaten track in Baja, especially if you want to parallel the coast, is to find a coyote trail, and think long and hard before leaving it. Go with nature. You might come face to face with the occasional coyote. If so, thank him, he will almost certainly guide you safely around cliffs, through steep arroyos and difficult brush.

My initial apprehension slowly gave way to a more relaxed appreciation of the beauties of Baja's Pacific coastline:

> Came across a lovely, sheltered, sandy beach, which went out shallow for over a hundred yards. Several V-shaped formations of pelicans flew overhead. Tried fishing. Quickly caught two six-inch silvery fish with underslung mouths – probably 'croakers'. They certainly croaked enough when I tried to remove the hooks. You can keep your tropical paradises. Nothing can beat this – warm, clean, bursting with life. If this beach was anywhere else in the world, it would be packed with hotels and tourists. Viva isolation! Viva Baja!

The fishing was steadily improving as I headed south. Fish, shellfish, seaweed and cactus, there was certainly food in abundance. But one never knows what Baja will dish up next.

One morning, I was searching for something to eat when I came across a seal pup. He was high and dry and all alone, looking up at me with his big innocent eyes. I was so hungry, all I could see was forty pounds of seal meat roasting on a stick. Fingering my machete, I looked guiltily around. I should have hit him hard, quick and clean. Instead, I kept staring at those eyes. They seemed to be saying, 'Are you my daddy?' I thought of all the Seaworld seals I'd seen and I couldn't do it; or rather I wasn't quite desperate enough. I reached forward to pat him on his chestnut-brown head. He rose up hissing and honking and showing his

Alsatian-like teeth. I didn't think the beach was the safest place for him. So, using a bit of gentle encouragement from my boot, I manoeuvred him back into the sea and carried on with a good conscience and an empty belly.

A little while later, the low tide invited me to find my lunch in the pools and crevices of a rocky platform reaching well out to sea. It was there that I first made the acquaintance of the abalone – a large limpet-like shellfish that grows as big as a breakfast bowl. They cling to the smooth rocks with a powerful muscular 'foot'. Once they pull the shell down tight, it's almost impossible to get them off. Speed and surprise are what counts. I learned to thrust the blade of my machete under the shell and lever them off before they sensed what was happening.

The ear-shaped shell has a characteristic line of holes along one edge. Inside, it is a beautiful blue-grey, iridescent, mother of pearl. Even more beautiful to me was the sight of the large, muscular foot. After a few minutes boiling, the creature easily came away from its shell, and a quick pull separated the meaty foot from the innards. It was as delicious as a piece of prime steak.

One day, with just two pints of water left, my mouth dry and my throat parched, exhilaration and excitement reverted once again to apprehension and fear. I began preparing myself for the ordeal ahead. The falling tide enabled me to walk on a narrow stretch of fine-gravel beach beneath a line of low, yellow cliffs. I stepped over yet another rivulet of water draining back to the sea. 'Strange!' I thought. 'Where's all that coming from?' It couldn't have been left by the tide. I walked back, scooped up a handful and tasted it. It was fresh! Fresh water, coming from a spring at the base of the cliffs. Hardly able to believe my luck, I threw down my pack, made a fire, filled the kettle and sat drinking cup after cup of coffee. I dug a hole in the beach and diverted the trickle of water into it. The fresh water pool that formed was perfect for washing myself and my clothes. Water! What marvellous stuff it was. I left a gallon of it warming inside one of the chlorine bottles, then I enjoyed the sheer sensual delight of pouring it slowly over my head. With hardly a care in the world, I relived my water-loving childhood as I wandered among the rockpools playing with the crabs and the anemones, and looking for lunch. With an unlimited supply of fresh water I could eat as much as I wanted. It was a terrific feeling.

About 5 p.m., however, the rising tide forced me to leave. Struggling with the weight of three gallons of water, I was able to cover another four miles before dark. I made camp in a little side canyon cut into the cliffs, and slept well. Three gallons of water meant another three days walking and another thirty miles closer to Guerrero Negro.

A fishcamp saved me from the next water crisis. Gone was the 'don't drink the water', and 'get out of camp before dark', mentality. Usually I couldn't wait to get in!

The camp was situated on an arc of beach in a beautiful, sheltered south-facing bay. There was an abnormal amount of mid-day activity, for most of the fishermen had just arrived for the opening of the lobster season. I was offered a cup of coffee and a place to sleep in a little shack bashed together against a wall of sand and gravel. It wouldn't have looked too out-of-place in a trench on the Somme.

I preferred to put my tent higher up overlooking the Pacific. The coast ahead was intimidating. A great rounded block of mountain fell precipitously down to the water. I was in the mood for enjoying myself while I could, and was helped by the arrival of a group of middle-aged Americans who'd braved the thirty-mile drive in from the main highway. They were surprised to see me. One of them, looking up and down the coast said, 'You've certainly got balls', in a way suggesting that he didn't think I'd have them much longer.

Promising a 'special treat', they invited me to join them for dinner. One of them had bought a sack of lobster from the fishermen. I'd never eaten lobster before and I was quickly disillusioned about how to prepare them. I had always assumed that you simply drop them into boiling water. Instead, one of the Americans pulled a bewildered looking specimen from the sack. Holding it down on a block of wood, he took a heavy knife and cut off the twelve-inch-long feelers at the front. Then he chopped away the wriggling legs down one side, and then down the other. The poor creature hardly had time to come to terms with this loss before he said goodbye to his tail, got a knife in his back, and was cut down the middle, smeared with butter and popped on a grill.

With the remains of the lobster twitching and sizzling away, we all stood around the fire, pouring drinks, swapping stories and reflecting on how wonderful life can be. I didn't think it was quite so wonderful when I was given the knife and a particularly lively lobster, and invited to prepare my own dinner.

I held the strange beast as if it was a creature from outer space. The Pacific lobster, unlike the more familiar Maine lobster, has no claws. It relies on its tough, spiny shell and its snappy, sharp-edged tail for defence.

'Watch your hand!' someone shouted.

Just in time, I shifted my grip as the tail snapped viciously. As I chopped and stabbed away, I had no idea that this 'special treat' was about to become a very familiar part of my diet.

The following morning, I wrote some letters and gave them to the Americans to post. They gave me a stock of chocolate chip cookies, candy bars, oranges and all the water I could carry. Some of the

Mexicans gave me a bag of tortillas and a detailed account of what lay ahead. If I could get beyond a bad stretch of about four miles of cliffs I would find several miles of 'easy' walking – low bluffs, rounded hills and sandy beaches. They warned me to keep an eye open for a wild and savage white-tailed coyote with a reputation for attacking people.

After waiting for the tide to start falling. I strapped my machete to my belt, picked up my heavy load and walked off towards the daunting line of cliffs. I was able to walk several hundred yards in the desert before being forced down on to the stony beach. It was very difficult walking. The beach dropped steeply into the sea. I was sliding down so much with the pebbles, it was like continually walking uphill. And any flat stretches tended to be covered with an awkward tangle of driftwood, bones and barrels.

At least on the rocks under the cliffs, I was able to make faster, less exhausting, progress. But then I started falling. I dented the kettle; I banged my knee; I landed on top of one of the water containers, splitting it wide open and losing over two pints of water; and last, but not least, I dashed my shin against a sharp rock leaving behind a not very pretty mix of skin, hair and blood. Luckily, I was able to hobble on. Being on rocks beneath cliffs with the tide rising was a great anaesthetic.

Working my way around the final barrier of rock before the promised stretch of beach, I surprised a pack of a dozen or more coyotes feasting on a dead seal. I whipped out my machete as they scattered in every direction. One was having his after-dinner nap and didn't realize he'd been deserted by his buddies till I stood over him and coughed politely. I don't think he stopped running till he got to Cabo!

A few days later, I was following a coyote trail along a particularly difficult bit of coast. In spite of the trail, it was slow, painful progress, a dangerous series of ups and downs on loose, crumbling rock. I had just two pints of water, and was sweating and drinking continuously.

At one point – where the trail ran along a short, boulder-strewn stretch of stony beach – I found a washed-up lobster trap. There was a large lobster still alive inside! No point leaving him there to die in the sun. I popped him in a plastic bag and looked forward to a lobster dinner.

The coyote trail led me up on to a ledge sandwiched between a sheer wall of red rock rising to vulture-circling heights on my left and a line of sheer cliffs falling away to the gulls gliding two hundred feet below. The ledge seemed to be narrowing all the time. Yet I pushed on. Coyote trails always went somewhere.

The trail wound confidently and purposefully along the ledge. If I lost it, I'd circle and zigzag till I picked it up again. The trail was a guide and a friend, a laid-down direction that kept at bay that chilling sense of being lost and alone.

The unscaleable slope above came closer and closer to joining that below. The trail just ended. It had to. The wall of rock fell almost sheer from the mountain peak to the sea. Not even a coyote could get by. I sat down and tried to come to terms with adding the pain of retreat to the unpleasantnesses of fear, thirst and uncertainty.

A mile back down the trail, I was faced with a dilemma. I could either go all the way down to the rocks and try to make my way under the cliffs, or I could climb a ridge to the top of the mountain and try to find a way down the other side.

As the climb down to the shore looked too dangerous, I decided to go up. After an hour I made it, legs trembling, to the peak. The view was spectacular. As if he were anxious to have a look, the lobster started wriggling around in the bag and, in a moment of frivolity, I held the curious crustacean aloft to give him a glimpse of life at 2,000 feet. But my mood turned a little more serious as I searched for the best way down. Apart from leaping off, the only certain way was the way I'd come up. The backside of the mountain had just fallen away into nothing. In spite of my exhaustion, fear gave me the strength to backtrack down the ridge and climb down to the water. I was certainly seeing Baja from every angle.

With renewed optimism I pushed on beneath the cliffs. The waves of crystal clear water rolled in, exploding against the rocks. With water rushing and cascading all around, it was a hopeless task trying to keep my feet dry, so I put on my tennis shoes and tied my boots around my neck. Learning from the many crabs dashing and clinging, dashing and clinging, I edged along the base of the cliffs, throwing myself at the wall and holding tight as the worst of the waves threatened.

After half an hour I was beginning to think that I might make it past that awkward mountain when I came across a deep channel of water surging into a cave in the cliffs. Shit! There was no way over; and there'd be no help from the tide. It was already at its lowest.

I stood staring at the limpet-studded wall of rock on the other side of the channel. Ten feet away! It might as well have been ten miles. Inside, I was a boiling mix of disappointment, anxiety, frustration and anger. The tide would soon be rising. I had to get out from under those cliffs quick.

I made my way back along the rocks, and climbed up to the coyote trail. The retreat continued. I abandoned all thoughts of making progress. Desperately thirsty, the only thing that mattered now was water. I followed the trail back for two miles looking for a suitable beach to set up my stills. The narrow sandy floor at the mouth of a steep-sided canyon was perfect. There was no time to lose. I swallowed my last mouthful of water and pulled out my stills. It was too late in the day to get much from the solar still. For the first time, I would have to boil seawater. Looking at the cheap, battered aluminium kettle and the flimsy plastic tubing, I felt a rush of panic. Supposing it didn't work? Supposing I'd damaged the kettle in one of those falls? Supposing the tubing melted or my matches were wet?

With my life on the line, I looked back in disbelief at the cavalier way I'd tested the kettle-still in Los Angeles. I had played with it for fifteen minutes, got a little drinkable water, and jumped around in naive satisfaction. Someone should have banged me on the head, to remind me of what I'd read in the survival literature: 'fear, panic and distress can kill in hours' . . . 'How many castaways through the ages have become stiff and sudden corpses, killed, not by the sea, not by hunger or thirst, but by their own terror?' . . . 'The cure for panic is a thorough knowledge of your survival equipment and the confidence that this brings.'

So much had gone wrong that day, it was hard to imagine anything going right. I clambered over the dam-like barrier of pebbles that had been dumped across the mouth of the valley. The stones dropped steeply into the sea; so steep there was hardly any surf, just a powerful rise and fall of water. Standing knee deep, I immersed the kettle and a water container. The bubbles rose for a few seconds, then the sea dropped, leaving me surrounded by tumbling pebbles. When the sea rushed back, it rose in a great explosive surge that lifted me off my feet and carried me away. The kettle was torn from my hand. I watched in horror as it slowly sank in the foam before me. Releasing the water container, I sent both hands slapping and slicing through the sea till I got hold of the handle and held on for dear life. I was also able to grab back the water-bottle before kicking furiously towards the beach. The sea several times pushed me to within touching distance, then raked me back like a cat playing with a mouse. Eventually, I got my feet down and, running faster than the pebbles were tumbling, scrambled up to safety.

The experience didn't do much for my nerves, and swallowing a mouthful of seawater didn't do much for my thirst. Shaking deep down, if not visibly, I went off in search of a rock pool.

I quickly got the fire going, then put the kettle on to boil. As the steam came blowing through the plastic tube, I passed it into my aluminium water bottle which soon became 'boiling hot'. Most of the steam was rising and escaping, so I placed the water bottle in a saucepan of cold sea water. Every minute I shook it to see how much water had condensed inside. At last, I seemed to be getting something. I poured a mouthful into my cup. Ugh! It was salty. My life depended on it being fresh and it was salty. Trying to stay calm, I threw away the yield and tried again.

For ten thirst-tortured, nail-biting minutes, I waited for more water to condense. It was still salty. Why? Steam is pure water. Where was the salt coming from?

Panic and dehydration were wringing my brain for a drop of water. I couldn't think straight. In a moment of madness, I almost kicked the still across the beach. I shut my eyes and clenched my fists as I struggled to compose myself. Remember, 'killed not by hunger or thirst but by their own terror'. Suddenly the sergeant was back beside me, not shouting and bawling but calm and reassuring: 'Come on. It'll work. Let's try again.' I looked up into the sunset and just for a second I thought I saw him in his scarlet tunic. My mind was playing tricks, but it was the distraction I needed.

I picked up the still. All I could think of was, maybe the kettle was too full; maybe boiling water was being carried through with the steam? I poured out half the seawater, and put the kettle back on the fire with the spout end raised a bit.

I scalded my lips in my anxiety to test the next batch. I didn't care. I could have drunk a gallon of it. It was fresh, beautiful, life-sustaining, brain-clearing, fresh water. Having got things sorted out, I began producing water at the rate of a cup an hour.

Unable to sit still, I left the kettle simmering on a low fire and went, machete in hand, to explore the little canyon. After a hundred yards it opened out. The sheer walls gave way to rounded yellow hills. Apart from the very few desiccated bushes and cacti, the dusty, washed-out slopes wouldn't have looked out of place on the moon. Further inland the mountains looked mauve in the evening light.

The floor of the valley was sterile sand, easy walking. It seemed the obvious route into the mountains and hopefully around the impasse on the coast. I wandered up one of the slopes looking for a barrel cactus, and found one a bit bigger than I would have liked; but there was no point worrying about conservation now. I managed to unearth the cactus and carry it by its roots back to the camp. I almost ran. I couldn't shake off the feeling of anxiety. Supposing a coyote was running off with my still, supposing the plastic tubing had caught fire? You name it, I saw it happening.

Having slaked my thirst, I allowed myself to think of food. I had as much barrel cactus as I could eat, but lobster was beginning to sound very tempting. Before dispatching the strange looking beast, I studied him carefully. With his armour plating, jointed appendages and spiny back he didn't look nearly as good as he tasted. I hated the idea of chopping him up or dropping him in boiling water, so I resorted to another method I'd seen the Mexicans use – I grabbed his tail, bent it over, then twisted and pulled. All his armour made no difference. There was a horrible cracking sound as the lobster broke in two. I'm not sure if it was any more humane, but once I'd thrown the head end in the sea, I was left with a hunk of meat in my hand. I cut it down the middle, pulled out the string of gut, then dropped both sides into a pan of boiling seawater. Lobster followed by barrel cactus, followed by coffee, satisfied my hunger and my thirst.

I sat by the fire tending the still until the early hours of the morning. When I'd made about two and a half pints of water, I felt relaxed enough to crawl into the tent and get some sleep. A coyote sent up a chilling howl from deep in the valley. Perhaps it was White Tail. I slipped the machete beneath my pillow and stared up at the stars through the tent. My heavy eyelids flickered, then brought down the curtain on a day I wanted to forget.

Chapter 20
Pitahaya madness

Imagine lying on your back inside a tent in the middle of nowhere and listening to two or three hours of: 'Two on and one out for the Dodgers. We're in the bottom of the sixth. Sax is up hitting two-eighty seven. The count is three and one. Fast ball! Strike! Three and two.'

Baseball, for someone like myself who tends to freeze when confronted by a mass of figures, is not an easy game to decipher. However, having taken a perverse delight in trying to make sense of America's national game, I found myself hooked. I adopted the Los Angeles Dodgers as my team. Their season was building to a dramatic climax as they struggled to clinch the National League West title. I wrote in my diary:

> Sept. 28, 1983. The days are getting shorter. It was almost dark when I made camp in a wide arroyo just above a pleasant sandy beach. I quickly cooked the last of my porridge, then disappeared inside the tent to listen to the big game – The Dodgers and the San Diego Padres. It was a real thriller. 4–4 in the fourteenth when it was rained off. Disappointed, I went for a walk along the beach. The air was warm. The sea was calm. The stars were beautiful – like a million home-runs disappearing into eternity.

Before retiring to my tent for the night, I looked south and saw a glow and a flash. A car headlight? A fishcamp? I had been a week alone and was looking forward to some company.

I awoke to the sound of pit . . . pit . . . pat . . . pit. I couldn't make it out. The pit-pat pace picked up till it sounded like a racing Geiger counter. There was a flash; then another, closer and brighter. A fine, cold mist seemed to be descending on my skin. Half awake, I fumbled for my torch, looked at my watch, then grabbed my tape recorder:

Well, that's a real surprise at half past four in the morning. It's raining! And all around flashes of lightning and the occasional clap of thunder. It's a bit like being under artillery bombardment. I'm just waiting for one to strike one of the aluminium tent poles.

It was a beautiful clear night. I looked at the Milky Way before I went to bed. I could see the stars so clearly; there was no hint of this. What I've got to be careful of, I've pitched the tent in the mouth of a river, a dry river, an arroyo. If it's raining up in the mountains there's a possibility of a flash flood coming sweeping down that water course. I visited the grave of an English lady at the Bay of Los Angeles who was killed along with her American husband by a flash flood. They were in their car and were swept away. These things are not to be fooled with.

I've got nearly an hour and a half till dawn. I don't fancy getting up and moving the tent. I don't fancy going to higher ground with lightning flashing all around. I'll just have to keep my wits about me, and if I hear a distant roar coming down the arroyo, I'll probably have thirty seconds to do something quick.

[With the rain getting heavier] Well, this has really caught me out. I didn't bring the outer covering for this tent. I just sprayed it with waterproof spray and it has obviously not worked. I can feel the water coming through. And being short of water with all this rain falling, I'm obviously feeling very silly that I haven't thought up some idea for running water into a container. But my first priority is to get everything put away into my backpack which is waterproof – I hope!

Boy! This is really pelting. The lightning's getting closer. I'm going to be washed away here. I don't mind confessing this is scary. The water is pouring through the tent. I'll be washed away inside it if this continues much longer. I have everything packed away in the backpack, and as soon as I feel any water hitting the tent, then I've got to get out quick or I'll end up in the sea, struggling inside this thing.

[Fifteen minutes later] Well, I've adopted the ostrich tactic. I've pulled myself into my sleeping bag and I'm lying on the mat, the foam pad I've got, and if lightning does strike the tent I just hope *[chuckles]* there's enough insulation under me . . . I don't suppose it will do much good. I'm a bit worried about those poles just sticking up.

It was still raining at daybreak but the lightning and the thunder were drifting away. The inside of the tent was one big puddle. I was able to suck up over a pint of water by putting my lips to the groundsheet. My sleeping bag was soaking wet but at least it was warm. Before radio reception faded, I tuned in to a Californian news station where I belatedly heard that there was a major tropical storm moving off the coast of Baja California. More worrying, there was a hurricane watch in Hawaii and another in Acapulco. I was sandwiched right in the middle.

Around nine o'clock it stopped raining and the sun came out. The inside of the tent became steamy hot. I crawled outside and spread everything out to dry. How different the desert was after rain. Pools of water were being rapidly absorbed by the rain-pocked sand. The normally clean, dry, sand was heavy and clinging. So was the air. There was a hot, jungle humidity. The steam visibly rose up to chase the blue-grey clouds tumbling inland. The cacti looked beautifully incongruous against such a backdrop.

I tried to start a fire. First problem, I'd left my matches out. I had to dig deep inside the pack to get another box which I'd carefully wrapped in polythene. Second problem, of course, everything was wet. A frustrating thirty minutes later, after I'd sacrificed strips off maps, a letter I'd written to a friend in England and a few precious pieces of toilet tissue. I managed to stoke up a few smokey flames and get a cup of tea. No need to worry about water now, there were pools of it on the rocks.

Two hours of hot Baja sunshine was enough to dry out everything, including my enthusiasm for walking. I felt exhausted. Perhaps it was the stress of the night. Perhaps my 'healthy' seafood/desert diet had caught up with me. I was craving something sweet. My mouth watered at the thought of a cold pepsi and a hot apple pie.

I found a road, or rather a pair of tracks cut into the rubble of the desert. Because of the rain, it was hard to tell when it had last been used. I followed it for several miles, before tiring of its wide and, from a walker's point of view, unnecessary detours around some of the steeper valleys. Also, it was too easy. It was boring. I preferred the more direct coast-hugging coyote trails. Back seeing the seabirds and the sea lions, I recovered a sense of exhilaration.

Still craving something sweet, I crested a small coastal hill, and was amazed to see a trio of motor homes lined up on a beach. Looking down, I saw two wet-suit clad gringos clambering out of the ocean on to the rocks.

I wandered down unnoticed as one of them, a big man with a large sandy beard, rifled through his wet-suit and pulled out his pecker to take a piss. I was laughing to myself as I walked up to say hello. The poor guy was suddenly pissing in all directions. Surprise over, we soon got to know each other in the way that off-beat travellers do.

'Come over to the camp and we'll see if we can find you a beer and something to eat.'

I was the guest of three adventurous gringos from a remote mountain resort in Southern California. They'd been on the beach for nearly a month spearing fish and lobster, and generally saying muchas gracias to

Mother Nature. They had dared to venture so far off the main highway because they had everything necessary, including the know-how, to cope with any likely situation. In their workshop of tools and spares they had generators, winches and welding gear. Their camp was well laid out. Beneath a large awning they had tables and chairs and all the comforts of home. A rubbish pit had been dug fifty yards away; and just over a rise and behind a bush a portable toilet sat offering a pleasant view of the low rounded hills rising a hundred yards from the beach.

As I sat in the shade of the awning, drinking beer and eating apple and raisin cake, it seemed that all my wishes were coming true. The 'gringos' helped me retie some of the eyes coming away from my fishing rod, oiled and serviced my reel, lent me an awl to sew up a split in my backpack, attempted to glue back the soles of my boots with a rubber compound used for plugging tyres, and, when it started raining again, they gave me a tarpaulin to stretch over my tent. Then for dinner we had lobster, and cake, and coke and tequila. I couldn't believe my luck!

As soon as it was dark, the rain became torrential. The awning above us rapidly filled with water and threatened to collapse. They had to knock a hole in it to let the water drain. We sat drinking and talking while the mini-waterfall slowly filled a five-gallon bucket.

It was still raining next morning. Worried about the roads being washed out, they decided it was time to get back to the highway while they still could. Naturally I said 'yes' when they asked if I wanted some food they were going to throw away. They brought over enough food to feed an army. From a precarious hand-to-mouth existence, I suddenly found myself with rice, spaghetti, potatoes, several bags of crisps and chips, bottles of tomato sauce, tartare sauce, prawn cocktail sauce and cucumber sauce, tins of fruit, fruit juice, beans, green beans, mushrooms, ham, sardines, and peanuts, not to mention margarine, jam, onions, garlic, tomatoes, tortilla flour, sugar, pancake mix, syrup and powdered milk.

As an afterthought, they gave me batteries, a lighter, three packs of film, a can of charcoal lighter, a waterproof poncho, the tarp on my tent and half a dozen white T-shirts proudly emblazoned with '*Iran sucks*'. It was beginning to feel like Christmas. I was also given a small folding stool with a toilet seat on top, some old magazines and a selection of buckets and containers.

I shouted my goodbyes as they drove away. 'How can I ever thank you guys?'

'Send us a copy of the book.'

'You've got it. Safe journey.'

'Same to you. Good luck.'

The three motor homes disappeared over the hill. Suddenly I was alone. The rain stopped. I started to make myself comfy. I brought up a bucket of seawater for the dishes and built a table out of some of the other stuff left behind. The toilet seat was an incredible luxury. I felt like a king on a throne as I sat and read a month old copy of *Newsweek*. Although I explored the beach and the rocky point, and did some swimming and fishing, I spent most of the afternoon stuffing myself. In between I had much to write in my diary:

> Towards evening, the sky was a little brighter. Is this unusual weather coming to an end? Will the rain return? I sat by my campfire looking at the misty stars through breaks in the clouds. Thought of home, friends and loved ones. If they could see me now. I listened to the radio, mostly news and country music. Otherwise I could be the last person in the world.
>
> Oct. 1, 1983. Woke to sound of rain. Raining off and on all morning. Impossible to get fire going. Whilst shaking the tarp, saw a black widow in a bush next to the tent. Killed it with a stone.
>
> Oct. 2, 1983. Rained all night. The sand is covered with stinkbugs. Probably brought out by the rain. Threaten one and he immediately raises his rear end! I don't mess with them. Killed a large scorpion I found under a log by impaling him with a stick.
>
> Oct. 3, 1983. Off and on rain, but less than previous days. Washed all my clothes, final rinse in fresh water.
>
> Oct. 4, 1983. Dry when I woke about 4.30 a.m. but soon the sound of rain on tarp. Stopped. Up for breakfast of peaches and muffins. Got lovely log fire going. Drank lots of hot chocolate. Then rain heavier, everything away then retire to tent. Maybe I'm going to need all this food to sit out this weather. I want to get back into the battle – it brings out my best. I'm not cut out for all this lazing about. I get lethargic, lazy and think only of my stomach. I wish some Mexicans would appear. The food has become a problem. I hate to waste food, but I don't mind giving it away.

An hour after writing that, a passing panga with a pair of young fishermen pulled into the beach. In spite of the rain, the sea was almost flat calm. I invited them to join me for some hot chocolate and blueberry muffins. One of the Mexicans carried up two big lobsters by their long spiny feelers. The ugly looking creatures expressed their displeasure by a few wicked tail snaps. I put them in an empty bucket. As a token of my gratitude I gave the Mexicans a 3lb-bag of rice and a 5lb-bag of potatoes, a pack of spaghetti and some assorted sauces.

'Weather permitting, we shall return tomorrow, señor.'

'Go with God, amigos.'

After a delicious lunch of fried lobster-tail and tartare sauce I went down to the rocks to do some fishing. I caught three sweet-looking, docile, flabby pufferfish. As they all looked so similar, I wondered if I'd caught the same fish three times.

Gullible, guileless, gormless, at first sight this big-eyed fish looks the picture of perfect innocence, God's gift to predators. However he's not as innocent as he looks. Behind his sweet smile lies a vicious set of chisel teeth. A small 1lb-fish is quite capable of biting a hook in half; a 2lb-specimen would have little trouble removing the end of a finger poking around for a lost hook. But, more important from the puffer's point of view, 'Eating him almost invariably causes death in agony.' His flesh is shot through with a tasteless, odourless alkaloid reputed to be five hundred times more poisonous than cyanide. A lethal dose would be smaller than a grain of salt.

Thousands of years before Christ, the Chinese and the Egyptians were aware of the unique danger posed by the puffer. The figure of a puffer fish has been found on the tomb of one of the Pharaohs. Yet, I was amazed how few tourists in Baja were aware of the dangers. Puffers are common all around the coast, especially in warm shallow waters. It was the first fish I ever caught in the Sea of Cortez. Luckily, I only used it for bait. Shortly before my arrival in the Bay of Los Angeles, a young Frenchman had been taken violently ill after catching and cooking a puffer. He was flown out to the States, but he died later in hospital. There is no known antidote. According to one of the medical accounts of ciguatera, pufferfish poisoning, 'The poisonous flesh acts primarily on the nervous tissue of the stomach, causing violent spasms of that organ and, shortly afterward, of all the muscles of the body. The frame becomes wracked with spasms . . . the eye fixed, the breathing laborious, and the patient expires in a paroxysm of extreme suffering.'

Some species of puffer, the so-called porcupine puffers, have another trick enabling them to avenge themselves on their would-be predators. They are capable of ballooning up and erecting spines like a porcupine when threatened. Any pelican or other sea bird slithering a porcupine puffer down his throat would receive a very nasty shock. Live specimens have been found lodged in the throats of dead sharks. And Darwin, in *The Voyage of the Beagle*, states: 'I have heard from Dr Allan of Forres, that he has frequently found a Diodon [pufferfish] floating alive and distended, in the stomach of the shark; and that on several occasions he has known it eat its way, not only through the coats of the stomach, but through the sides of the monster, which has thus been killed. Who would ever have imagined that a little soft fish could have destroyed the great and savage shark?'

With the sea so calm, I was able to enjoy fishing from a rock with my feet dangling in the warm sea. Something touched my foot. At first I thought it was a piece of sea weed. Then I felt a tightening, a muscular movement. My instinct was to kick out wildly, but instead I bent forward to see a pair of inch-thick purplish tentacles caressing my leg. I slowly lifted it up. The suckers gripped and held. A tug of war was in process with my foot as the prize. When another tentacle started to kiss its way around the back of my leg, that was enough. I stood up and pulled. The body of an octopus – the dreaded pulpo – lifted half out of the water. One look at me was enough, he let all his suckers slip, and dashed back to his underwater cave.

Staying in one place for several days enabled me to get to know something about the other creatures sharing my patch of paradise. It soon became apparent that a system of apartheid operated on the beach. The seagulls had their patch and the crows had theirs. Only insults and threats flew between them.

Among the gulls, one individual stood out, or more accurately was kept out and apart by his gully companions. He was old and tatty and easily the biggest of the bunch. He had somehow lost a leg and an eye. Nevertheless, he supported his enormous seagull bulk with great dignity on his remaining leg. The younger sleeker gulls ganged up on him and chased him across the driftwood and the seaweed. But one to one he was a match for any of them. He seemed capable of opening his mouth so wide that there was nothing to attack but an enormous chasm surrounded by a beak that meant business.

I called him Nelson. Whenever I went down to the rocks to fish or down to the beach to swim, he'd be there. Poor old thing. I spent quite a bit of time talking to him and feeding him. He trusted me and came closer than any of the other birds. Hatred of Nelson seemed to be the only thing that united the crows and the gulls.

> Oct. 5. Rain before dawn followed by a bright promising sunrise. A lovely 95% clear day. Hot again! I spread everything out to dry and took the tarp off the tent. The Mexicans returned with three more lobsters. Enjoyed some more fishing in the afternoon. The tide fell very low. My eyes popped at the number of abalone studding the rocks. For dinner I had a delicious onion, tomato, potato, abalone fry-up with Thousand Island dressing. Retired bloated to a dry, clean tent to listen to the Dodgers beat Philadelphia 4–1.
>
> Oct. 6. No rain! Woke just before dawn, listened to radio before it fades. Floods in Arizona. So much for arid regions! If it's a good day I should leave this afternoon.

It turned out to be a perfect day, sunny and breezy. The fishermen appeared but the surf made it too dangerous for them to land, so I waved goodbye and shouted out my thanks. It wasn't easy deciding what to take and what to leave behind. In the end I decided to say adios to the tarp, the toilet seat, the 'Iran sucks' T-shirts, the buckets, and several gallons of water. I took all the food. The weight was almost impossible. I left that camp with a bag of food and a gallon of water in each hand. The problems of affluence!

I pushed on a hundred painful yards at a time. The coast was fascinating walking. The retreating tide left many long patches of beach replete with large clams lying there for the taking. There were other beaches of beautiful, polished, marble-like stones full of veins and subtle colours. I had to negotiate headlands of barren red and black rock peeling and cracking in the sun. I passed several pterodactyl-sized nests perched precariously on top of sea stacks or little islets. One stony beach was white with the shrimp-like skeletons of lobster krill, a favourite food of whales often seen drifting on the surface of the ocean in bright red swarms.

The rain had brought out a rush of life. The mountains inland looked a kind of mouldy green, and some of the valleys seemed even more densely choked with vegetation. Spiders' webs ran in and between every bush. I got used to having spiders and webs all over me. They were a necessary evil.

At last, with my arms feeling like they were half way down to my ankles, I reached a deserted fishcamp and called a halt. There were shells everywhere, but I found an acceptable place to put my tent. As I was looking up at the stars, a large flying insect hit me in the face and fell inside the tent. It took half the night to chase him out.

Next morning I was walking along a beautiful, apparently never-ending beach when I started wishing I had somewhere clean and dry to sit down. Up ahead was what appeared to be a table. It was a cable drum. The perfect place to sit and place my pack. 'Wishes are powerful things out here,' I wrote, 'they seem to come true.'

Every new experience convinced me that something incredible was happening. It couldn't be just a coincidence. No wonder the high and dry places of the world have been the traditional sources of spiritual inspiration. Perhaps that is why Jesus said: 'Come ye yourselves apart into a desert place, and rest awhile.' [*Mark* 6, 31.] For it is there that one senses the truth of the claim: 'What things soever you desire, when ye pray, believe that you receive them, and ye shall have them.' [*Mark* 11, 24.]

It wasn't long before I was once again short of water, and therefore severely restricted in what I could eat. I was then less keen on listening to the baseball games – I couldn't stand all the ads for beer made from Rocky Mountain spring water, or foot-long Dodger dogs made from corn fed hogs. In the midst of my despair, Baja provided yet again.

I was in an arroyo, hacking my way through a sprawling grove of pitahaya cactus. Something red caught my eye, a large fruit, like a cricket ball covered in spines. It had burst and the oozing red pulp was full of black seeds and ants. I knocked it off with my machete, sliced away the open part, then cut it in two and spooned out the middle. I knew the pitahaya produced edible fruits but they were bigger and better than I expected; delicious; sweet and juicy, satisfying both thirst and hunger.

I decided to abandon the beach and zigzag my way across the desert checking out every clump of pitahaya. The branches of the pitahaya are like thick, ribbed cucumbers covered with a profusion of stiff, dagger-like spines. They twist and turn in every direction without order or symmetry, producing impenetrable thickets sometimes as much as ten feet tall. Almost every plant bore fruits in different stages of development. The smaller fruits had a somewhat more tart, acid taste but they were still refreshing. The bigger ones were the sweetest and, as far as I was concerned, the best. When fully ripe, they are much easier to knock from the plant, and then the clusters of spines can be easily brushed off. 'Look!' it seems to be saying, 'I have shed my spines and fallen at your feet. Take me, I'm yours.'

Dr William Butler, a contemporary of Shakespeare remarked of the strawberry: 'Doubtless God could have made a better berry but doubtless God never did.' After sampling the fruit of the pitahaya I could only conclude that doubtless Dr Butler never tried it.

James Bull, the son of a Pennsylvanian clergyman journeyed through Baja in the fall of 1843. He wrote: 'Today we frequently stopped along the roadside to gather the fruit of the sweet petalle [pitahaya]. The fruit when ripe is of a deep red colour, covered with a thick husk or shell from which also project thorns in bunches. When the fruit is peeled it almost melts in the mouth, indeed, it is the most delicious fruit that I think I have ever tasted.'

The fruit of the pitahaya was so important to the Baja Indians that its appearance towards the end of the summer was a time of great joy and celebration. Much to the chagrin of the early missionaries, their new converts would up and leave the missions and go wandering through the desert eating pitahayas till they could eat no more. They would then dance, sing and satisfy their sexual appetites in a protracted orgy of indulgence. The good padres tried to stop the excesses by warning that such conduct would whisk them away to the fires of hell, but the Indians were unrepentant. They confounded the padres by asserting that such a hell must be a fine place as there was obviously no shortage of firewood.

The Indians had their own vision of heaven and hell. Hell was a land without pitahayas. Whereas the slopes of heaven would be eternally crimson with big fat fruits, and in the shade of the tall cardóns there would be never ending days of laughter, dancing and copulation. I must say it sounded a hell of a lot better than any images of heaven propounded by the Jesuits.

If the padres had a bit of trouble getting aspects of their theology across, they were able to utilize some Indian beliefs to explain the mysteries of Christianity. Indeed, some of the parallels are striking! The Pericu, the main Indian tribe in the south of the peninsula, held that a great lord called Niparaja had made the earth, the sky and the sea. He had three sons, one of whom, Cuajaip had been sent to earth as a man to help people and teach them how to live. But the ungrateful people of the earth killed him and placed on his head a wreath of thorns. They also believed that a great war had been fought in the sky when the evil Tuparan rebelled against the supreme creator Niparaja. Niparaja had triumphed in the end. He took from Tuparan the pitahayas and the fruits of the desert, cast him from the sky with all his followers, imprisoned him in a cave near the sea and created whales to guard him and keep him in his place.

The Indians measured their year by the season of the pitahaya. They rejoiced at its coming and lamented its passing. However, they prolonged the feast in a peculiar way. There was a 'second harvest' to be gathered. The fruity pulp contains thousands of small black seeds. They pass through the digestive system without destruction. During the pitahaya season the Indians would defecate on carefully selected, large, flat rocks. When the fresh fruits were no more, these impressive deposits were broken up and the seeds picked out and ground into flour or toasted. The story is told of how the Jesuit, Father Piccolo, was presented with a sample of this flour. In blissful ignorance he baked with it much to the satisfaction of his flock. When other missionaries met with Father Piccolo they used to joke about the 'second harvest' with much amusement.

As for the first harvest, I wandered from cactus to cactus like a lotus-eater. Some days I made hardly any progress, but it didn't seem to matter. My diary relates something of the mood that the pitahaya season induced:

> I chose to walk the inland valleys in the hope of finding more pitahayas. Soon found a grove and helped myself to the ripe, red balls of fluffy sweetness. Juice oozing out. I ate 5 or 6. Progress slow. I had to force myself to go on, leaving many behind. . . . More pitahayas. I indulged in pitahaya madness. No detour, no risk, no tangle of thorns or spider's web was too much trouble to get at the delicious fruits. Perhaps only the presence of the fiercely spined cholla made me hesitate! . . .
>
> I walked around with a machete in my hand and a spoon in my back pocket . . . Made camp and indulged my fantasy – pitahaya flan. I fried up a mix of flour and water then spread the scarlet fruit on top. Hmmm! Looked and tasted great. I admired a pitahaya red sunset, then sat by my fire in the moonlight, very content with things. A good day behind me. I felt no fear; I just took great pleasure from the rests, and the bounty of the desert. Will these be the best days of my life?

Chapter 21

Jap, One Eye, and Blondie

One day, I breezed into a fishcamp and introduced myself to the fishermen in the middle of their lobster lunch. They were a delightful bunch, quick to offer me a chair and a plate, and all the usual gloom and doom about the coast ahead. Undeterred, I laughed it off and downed a delicious meal of lobster, tortillas, beans and coffee.

It quickly became apparent that two of the Mexicans were, like me, total strangers to the camp. And they were a pretty strange pair. They said they were from a town two hundred miles to the south, and they had come looking for work. One was short and stocky and had his left eye so badly mangled I doubted if he could see anything out of it. The other was tall and lean with an almost aristocratic bearing, and he spoke quite decent English. But, hard as he tried to be helpful and polite, there was something about him I didn't like. Perhaps the piece of cloth hanging from the back of his buff-coloured baseball cap made him look too much like a sadistic Japanese army officer. Also, he seemed excessively interested in my possessions; and the more questions he asked the more paranoiac I got. I christened the two strangers Jap and One Eye, and had to laugh at my own irrational suspicions as I left the camp looking over my shoulder.

About 4.30 p.m. I came across a small boat on a sandy beach. Nearby, an untidy shack sheltered in the mouth of a little red-rock canyon. Sensing there was someone inside, and not wishing to drop in too unexpectedly, I shouted, 'Ola! Ola, amigo!' Out stepped a jolly looking, dumpy old Mexican followed by two familiar figures: Jap and One Eye!

The old man asked if I wanted a cup of coffee. I said yes, and sat down uneasily. He said he lived there alone, he preferred it that way. On one wall there was a slab of wood on which had been carved the words: 'Take time for thought and education.'

Pleasantries aside, Jap continued to question me about my equipment: my cassette recorder, my camera, my knives . . . He wanted to know how I carried my machete, my fish knife, and did I carry a gun? I tried to answer as evasively as possible without seeming rude.

There was a bowl of pitahaya fruits on the table. I mentioned how I'd been enjoying them. That brought surprised looks from all three Mexicans.

Jap held up one and said, 'See how easily they can be peeled once the spines have been removed.' His assistant nodded approvingly. I glanced anxiously at the sun.

I had to wonder what the old man was thinking. Probably something along the lines of, 'Caramba! I live out here for years and never see anyone, and today they all arrive. They must have opened the asylums.'

'How far will you get before you make camp?' Jap asked still peeling his pitahaya.

'Oh, a long way, I do most of my walking in the cool of the evening. I must go.'

I thanked the old man for his hospitality, picked up my pack and raced away. I walked as much as possible on the wet sand; weaving in and out with the waves like the nimble little birds pursuing the sand fleas. That way, the sea obliterated most of my footprints. About two miles down the coast, when it was almost dark, I took a final glance back to make sure no one was following me, then disappeared into a maze of dunes, covering my tracks with a clump of twigs.

The dunes weren't entirely sterile; they were a series of ridges and troughs held together by scattered clumps of grass and brush. I placed the tent in the bottom of one of the deeper depressions, made a small fire, had a cup of coffee, warmed some beans then extinguished the flames.

I was glad to see the sliver of a new moon. Brighter nights were ahead. Every evening the moon would appear bigger and make a larger sweep across the sky, till it rose in its full glory, ranging across from one horizon to another. Then would come the times of moonrise; the contracting moon would rise later and later till the nights were once again black.

New moon, full moon, waxing, waning, up until then it had all been words and vague notions. An indoors existence back in cloudy old England had hardly helped me to take an interest in the lunar cycle. There in Baja, it was so easy to see the pattern. The young moon fell gently into the Pacific leaving the stars to shine alone.

The jewels of the night gave away to those of the morning. The inside walls of the tent sparkled with condensation as the sun tried to break through the morning mist. Trying not to disturb the water droplets, I stepped out on to the cool sand, and began gathering up firewood. Suddenly I saw two sets of boot prints. They were recent, perhaps in the night. Jap and One Eye! Looking for me? I dropped the wood, returned to my tent and packed hurriedly. It was no good trying to reason with myself. I just wanted to put that pair of characters as far behind me as possible.

Miles later, I relaxed again. The coast was beautiful; a magnificent mix of headlands and beaches. Some beaches were buried beneath tons of blinding white clam shells. As well as the usual sea lion and dolphin skeletons, I began seeing whale ribs, skulls and vertebrae. Whenever I got too hot, I went for a swim. With the shorter days, I was less inclined to take a long midday break. The air was as clear as any in the world. I could see points and headlands thirty and forty miles distant.

Mention the word desert and people usually think of vast, sterile, Saharan-type, shimmering sand dunes. Although most of the Baja desert isn't like that, there are, along the Pacific coast in particular, long stretches of wind-blown, silvery-white sand – dune after dune, ripple after ripple, beautiful, untouched, maybe just the odd coyote print.

No matter how straight I thought I was walking, I invariably looked back to see a wildly meandering line of boot prints; shallow on the firmer tops, deep and shadowed where the sand had cascaded with me down the slopes. My desert survival guide warned that sand dunes should be avoided if possible – they were difficult, strength-sapping, shadeless and devoid of life. However, I saw them more as fascinating, fun places to walk, especially towards the cool of the evening when the sand reflected the pinks and golds of the sunset.

One awesome-looking rocky point forced me to ascend a long, draining, sandy slope towards a saddleback ridge. That wasn't much fun, but there was a fine grove of pitahaya on top, so I took it easy, enjoying the fruits and the view, before working my way down the other side.

There I was surprised to see, first a lighthouse, then a beached panga, and then two young fishermen repairing their wire lobster cages. They sat on barrels beside their temporary home – a large igloo-shaped blue tent beneath a wall-less wooden sun shade. It was a good arrangement – it kept off the sun and kept out the scorpions. I was invited to share the shade and given a cup of hot chocolate and some biscuits.

My hosts turned out to be two brothers from Santa Rosalillita – a sizeable permanent camp one or two days further south. Jose Luis was in his mid-twenties and Alberto about eighteen. They were out there for the lobster season from September to November.

The brothers were both dressed in jeans, and wore T-shirts that appeared dazzling white against their brown skin. Alberto's hair displayed a curly wildness that was unusual among Mexicans. In spite of being unshaven, they had handsome, pleasant faces. They were quick with their smiles and their generosity.

I was amazed when they said their surname was MacLish, and that they were descended from a Scottish great-grandfather. Today, they said, there were many MacLishes scattered around Baja. They had seven other brothers and a sister, a protestant enclave in a Catholic world. They talked of their church with pride, relating how they both contributed to their church services with their guitars.

I took photographs of them repairing their traps; and apart from the colour of their skin, I could almost picture them, ruddy and well wrapped, on a building site in Glasgow. We talked a bit about Scotland and why there were so many Macs in the world. They insisted I stop by in Santa Rosalillita and convey their regards to their family. I was looking forward to meeting them.

Shouldering my pack and stepping back into the sun, I said my goodbyes to Jose Luis and Alberto; but I wouldn't have looked quite so cheerful if I'd known that one of the three of us would be dead by Christmas.

Punta Rocosa – Rocky Point – lived up to its name. The cliffs dropped at an angle of 60° into the sea, where many brown and grey islands leaned at the same angle back to the coast. Between the islands, patches of emerald and torquoise revealed where the bottom was sandy. A sea lion twisted, turned and glided immediately below.

A coyote trail ran across the steep drop. I followed it for a while before chickening out and climbing up towards the mountain to pick out my own pathway. The slope of the mountain came down like a ski-jump, steep at first and then levelling out before the cliffs fell sharply away. Along the narrow, dangerously eroded ledge the stones and boulders were mostly flat, angular and golden yellow. In several places landslides of the beautiful rock had fallen over the cliff leaving trails like golden waterfalls down to the sea.

As I made my way along the edge of the 60° drop, I confided to my tape recorder:

> I'm going to have to be really careful; the surface is covered with slates, crumbly rock and sand; if I go down, it will be all the way to the sea. It certainly looks beautiful down there but I don't fancy joining the seal under those circumstances . . . I'm carrying all my water in one bottle. That's a worry. If I trip – natural instinct hands out, drop the bottle, no water and I'm in trouble. Climbing, there's also the possibility of coming across a snake, no room to manoeuvre and the shock could send you over the edge . . . There's a trail here running

around the top of a sheer drop. Beyond, it all looks comfortable again. I have a decision to make: do I take a 100 to 1 risk with death? No way! I'm 99% certain I'll make it. But those odds aren't good enough. I might be doing something like that five times, six times a day, so 100 to 1 is too risky. After a while, I'll go over and that will be the end of me!

South of Punta Rocosa the desert changed quite markedly. As well as the pitahayas and the tree yuccas, there were suddenly more cirio trees, cardóns, elephant trees and ocotillos; and the air bore a different, more pungent, fragrance. There were also beautiful, narrow, sheltered beaches, perfect for fishing and swimming. But with not quite enough water to feel secure, I kept my halts to a minimum.

Even so, I enjoyed that stretch of coast more than any other. I felt privileged to be there, away from it all, at peace, following the coyote trails, living off the land, just concerned enough to be energized, but not so concerned I couldn't relax.

I was almost disappointed when I came to a track. It didn't seem to have been used for some time, but the inroads of civilization were sad to see.

I didn't quite make Santa Rosalillita that day. Approaching a wide, low headland, I cut inland and was surprised to see a little lagoon. I tasted the water and, much to my surprise, it was fresh!

I made camp beside it. There was just enough daylight to boil the kettle and prepare a dinner of oriental noodles. The waxing moon gave me a little more light as I sat by the fire eulogizing to my tape recorder about the pleasures of pitahaya: 'Today, it's been more pitahayas. Every mile or so I'd hunt around and find one or two. When you eat a bunch together, they're good, but to eat one when you're thirsty is just heavenly. I've eaten nothing but pitahayas all day. I'd better shut up, I could go on raving about them all night.'

Next morning was fine and sunny. The birds were singing merrily, while a nearby sea lion colony started honking madly. Just occasionally I caught the distant rumble of traffic. I was in no hurry to leave my campsite. I built a fire and sat naked beside it, brushing up on my Spanish and catching up with my journal. When I felt able to face civilization, I put on my least smelly three pairs of socks and my least dirty shirt, then I brushed myself down and clambered back over the dunes on to the beach.

Coming around the point, I saw Santa Rosalillita nestling below a little coastal ridge. It was bigger than I expected, about fifty houses and a small factory building that was probably the fish plant. I walked in to the strident acclamation of a large crow and the jubilant fluttering of butterflies. I asked someone where to find the MacLish house.

I knocked on the door of the blue-green house and introduced myself as an amigo of Alberto and Jose Luis. Mr and Mrs MacLish, their daughter, and their three youngest sons were in the house. The other six sons were either out fishing or away at school in Guerrero Negro.

I was whisked inside and immediately surrounded by warmth and hospitality. Would you like coffee, something to eat, a shower, a place to sleep, some lemonade? I opted for the latter.

I explained that I too was a Mac-something and my father was from Scotland. Fascination filled their faces. They were a well-read family. Among their many books, there was a set of encyclopedias – in Spanish of course. I found a map of Scotland, told them what I could about the clans, the country, and its political relationship to England. They said they had never heard of any other MacLishes. Suspecting it might be because they spelled their name differently, I flicked through the encyclopedia looking for a world famous-MacLeish. There was just one: Archibald MacLeish, the American poet and Pulitzer prize winner. I explained that their ancestor was probably MacLeish spelled with an 'e'. Everyone present seemed delighted by this revelation.

I asked if there was a store in town.

'No, what do you need?'

'Just a few basics, some flour, a bar of soap.'

Immediately, cupboards were opened, and tin lids too. I was given 2lbs of flour, half a pound of milk powder, 1lb of dried potato, a small jar of oil and a bar of soap. I felt that, if I hadn't stopped them, they would have given me everything in the kitchen. As ever they wouldn't take a peso in return.

While we were still talking about Scotland, who should come in but Jose Luis and Alberto. They had driven to town to sell their lobster catch. That was cause for more merriment and lemonade. After a couple of hours, I thought it best to go. The strain of speaking Spanish and only half understanding what was being said had drained me. Besides, I had a lot of miles to cover, and I was becoming acutely aware that if I didn't shift gear, I'd still be walking for another year.

I took my parting shot with my camera, asking everyone to line up by the side of the family truck. It had the name MacLish on the red door. Click! Click! Maybe I couldn't get them to take any money, but I could certainly send them some photographs. Very few of the fishermen were able to afford cameras.

I passed the lobster skeletons and the shark heads on the beach – mostly hammerheads – and made my way back to the desert and the pitahayas. Although the pack felt very heavy, I pushed on in good spirits. It was a glorious sunny day. There was a small 'road' running along the coast, about a hundred yards inland. I tried walking it, but found it boring. I preferred to take it easy by the shore or wander up in the hills looking for pitahayas.

That evening I had trouble finding a suitable campsite. There was a long stretch where the rocky foothills ran down to the boulders by the shore. With just the crescent moon and a blood red band lighting the blackening sky, I was on full rattler alert as I searched anxiously for a patch of sand or gravel. At last I found a place. Someone had used it before, and kindly left a circle of stones and a little collection of firewood. I got a fire going and sat there, merrily cooking some delicious pitahaya pancakes.

It had been a hard day but I was learning to revel in the simpler pleasures: food, a cup of coffee, a rest, a sunset, companionship, a swim in the sea. Life was good. Inside the tent I listened to a radio talk show and briefly participated in the lives, loves and problems of ordinary Americans.

Resuming my travels I came to a lagoon. Usual problem – does it have a mouth? Suspecting it might, I chose the inland route around and passed a struggle in a spider's web. A black and tan butterfly had been caught in a black widow's web. The spider was trying to get close enough to deliver its fatal bite, and the butterfly was struggling to break free. I thought about intervening, but the victim seemed hopelessly ensnared. I pushed on feeling an absurd sadness.

Beyond the lagoon, there was a wide arroyo half-choked with washed-down cactus and brush. If I was still feeling any guilt about my impact on the desert, I soon forgot it as I gazed at literally hundreds of barrel cacti, pitahayas and cardóns left behind by what must have been an incredible torrent of water.

A washed-out trail led me back to the coast where I was surprised to see some shacks and a trailer. As I passed the trailer, I heard a woman's voice call in English, 'Hi! Where are you going?'

Thus I made the acquaintance of 'Blondie', a personality-packed middle-aged Californian who had chosen to vacation alone in a fish camp. Fascinated by my journey, and asking lots of questions, she was quick to pull out maps, books and articles to supplement the goldmine of information she had about Baja. She had been visiting Baja since she was a child. Her father had been conducting a long, passionate love affair with the peninsula.

We got on famously. She asked me to stay for dinner. I couldn't resist. I helped her dispose of a lobster and a large bottle of excellent Californian wine. She gave me two new things to worry about: centipedes in the driftwood and wild dogs in the dunes. I listened carefully. She knew what she was talking about. When she retired early, she left me on the porch of her trailer with several books, a hurricane lamp and the remains of the bottle of wine.

I woke to a grey day and quickly packed away my tent in case it rained. Then I was treated to a fine breakfast, given some pens, film, paper, and firelighters, and invited to stop off in San Diego to stay with her and her husband. I left determined to cover as many miles as possible before having to return to the United States.

The first mile was stony beach, then there was sand. Above the high-tide mark there was a washed-up wall of cactus and brush, where the sea had returned to the land the outpourings of the arroyos.

The beachcombing was fascinating. Apart from millions of shells, there were tree trunks and whale bones everywhere. I found a quarter-full bottle of Canadian whisky to bring cheer to my campfire. Using a whale vertebra as a stool, I sat under a half moon staring at the flames. Nothing could spoil my good spirits, not even a ripped back muscle or a pitahaya spine that had broken off and festered in my finger. I forced it out with not a little blood, pus and pain.

Next day I passed a massive lagoon, a bird watcher's paradise with curlews, egrets, herons and all manner of long-legged, long-beaked wonders. The lagoon was separated from the sea by totally barren islands of white sand. Catching the sun, they looked ghostly and unreal. The air was full of squawks and grunts as an osprey flew overhead clutching his still wriggling fish. Sunset and the threat of mosquitoes sent me scurrying away from the lagoon and into the sandy wastes of the desert.

Putting up my tent, I felt something touch the back of my leg. I turned around and nearly died of fright. A tarantula was crawling over my calf. Oh God! It looked horrible, but I thought it best to let him pass unmolested. He crawled down and disappeared under a lomboy bush. After that we left each other alone, but I made sure I zipped up my tent every time I got in and out.

The dunes were surprisingly full of life. I sat on the sand frying up my pitahaya flans while birds hopped from one barren bush to another, apparently singing out their delight to see me. A snake wriggled up to say a less welcome hello. It wasn't a rattler, but a small-headed, handsome, orange and brown diamond-patterned snake. He was very docile and slow to anger. I picked him up with a stick and examined him closely. He wasn't interested in biting anything, certainly not the stick.

The worst harassment I received was from the slow, stupid, common as muck, rear-raising stinkbugs – the pufferfish of the dunes. Their peculiar zip-like trails criss-crossed the sand. They were fascinating to watch. Whenever two met, they broke into a desperate tussle until one beat a hasty retreat with his tail more between his legs than up in the air. I was never sure if they were fighting or making love. I don't think they knew!

The following day I walked into Guerrero Negro, one of the world's leading producers of industrial salt. Most of its 5,000 inhabitants are dependent upon one company – Exportadora de Sal – as witnessed by the number of company houses, stores, roads and black and yellow vehicles. There are thousands of evaporating ponds just south of town. The desert sun quickly evaporates the pumped-in sea water leaving a residue of almost pure salt.

However, in spite of its importance to the economy of Baja, I couldn't find a place in Guerrero Negro to repair my boots. And I had just ten dollars left. It was time to think. I bought some fruit, got some water and made my way out to an old disused port on the shores of a lagoon. And there I waited. I wrote to a friend: 'I'm halfway down the Pacific coast of Baja, 700 miles from my base in Los Angeles, 10,000 miles from home, I've got the equivalent of about £5 in my pocket, yet, funny enough, I'm not worried. I know something will turn up.'

Two days later, a motor home arrived. It was Blondie returning from a beachcombing expedition. We chatted awhile, then she asked if I wanted to do some work.

'I've got some friends coming down to see me in a few days and I want to tidy up the fishcamp, get rid of all that rubbish in the dunes and on the beach. I was going to pay the Mexicans but if you need the money, it's up to you. It'll take two or three days but I'll give you 100 dollars and feed you, of course.'

'Sounds O.K. Are you sure the Mexicans won't mind?'

'Don't tell them you're getting paid for it.'

We returned to town where she bought food and other presents for her favourite families in the camp. That eased my mind a bit. Everyone would surely be willing to indulge the wishes of this generous woman.

Back in 'Blondie's Camp' I wandered around gradually appreciating the size of the task before me. There were several mounds of rubbish to be cleared and there were old cans and bottles everywhere. The shore was a palisade of driftwood and trash. Whatever virtues Mexicans possess, being fastidious about their rubbish is not one of them.

I made a start beneath Blondie's trailer. In one corner a bitch was suckling fourteen puppies. No sooner had I bent down to have a look than I started scratching. Fleas were crawling up my white socks like Mexicans scaling the walls of the Alamo. There was a visible mist of them around the dogs.

Then came the scorpions and the centipedes and the black widows! The surest way to find such nasties is to start picking up rubbish. But for my thick gloves I would have been stung and bitten several times.

After cleaning under the trailer, I started ranging farther afield. Most of the Mexicans sat inside their dingy shacks looking at me with total incomprehension. There was an unmistakable air of resentment. In a way I sympathized. This was their camp, their homes, yet here was I dashing around and implicitly insulting them by picking up paper and bottles and other things that they had seen fit to leave lying around.

The only Mexican not to treat me with cold suspicion was a young boy of about five. Once he got the hang of what I was doing he seemed very keen to help. I sadly missed his moral support when his mother came out to pull him away from the madman wandering around making stacks of rubbish.

Blondie wasn't exactly a model of tact. Some of the Mexicans – especially the men – resented her imperious attitude. I felt obliged to give more and more of my time over to P.R. and building bridges. However, for all of her warm and generous nature, if Blondie wanted something done, she wanted it done now. I began to notice her noticing if I stood around chatting too long. Her go-getting aggression was totally foreign to these Mexicans, and a bit alien to me as well.

The job itself was bad enough, the atmosphere I had to work in became impossible. Stepping over the dunes to take a piss, I looked up to see the beautiful mountains of Baja. They seemed to represent freedom. I couldn't wait to get back. How much better to do your own thing and be your own boss. It seemed ironic: I didn't want to clean up the camp; the Mexicans didn't want me cleaning it up. What was making it all happen. Money! What peculiar stuff it is.

To ease my boredom, I combined my cleaning duties with the excitement of hunting widows and scorpions. Every day I kept score: the widows are winning 3–2. What's under this rusty sheet? A scorpion! Squash! 3–3. It looks like extra time.

It took me four days to get all the trash burnt or hauled out to the arroyo. But it all finally seemed worth while when I had $100 in my pocket. I thanked Blondie sincerely, but I confided to my diary: 'I remember wondering on the plane, what will be the worst part of the trip – now I think I know.'

Chapter 22
Whales and whisky

I stood at the turn-off for the Bay of L.A. for over an hour before a vehicle appeared. It was a motorhome bigger than a fisherman's shack: a palace on wheels, equipped with everything from a bathroom to the proverbial kitchen sink. A middle-aged man and woman sat up front in armchair comfort. They had probably just come down from the supermarkets and freeways of Los Angeles.

Whereas in the 'old days', before the completion of the paved highway in 1974, the journey might have taken a week or two, it was now possible, if the road hadn't been washed away, to drive from the border to the Bay of L.A. in one or two days. But that gave no time to adjust to the different pace of life, to a new way of thinking and new responsibilities. As the fishermen had so often said, 'out here we are all brothers'. There I was, a fellow gringo, thumb out in the middle of nowhere, along comes the only vehicle I've seen for an hour, and they just drive by as if I didn't exist.

An hour later, a second motorhome approached. Same story. With only the vultures, circling high overhead, showing any interest in me, I picked up my pack and started walking. It was about forty miles to the Bay of L.A. I could do it in two days, and do it I would, if necessary.

The air was still and hot; there was no cooling Pacific breeze. A magnificent forest of cirio and cactus rose from the rolling red and yellow desert while mountains ringed the horizon.

The ribbon of black tarmac was not the best walking surface. I could feel its heat through the soles of my boots. Nevertheless, happy to plod on without need for thought or decision, I stuck to the road; sometimes literally.

After walking four miles in the hottest part of the day, the simmering silence was cut by the noise of an approaching vehicle. I glanced back. Another motor home. Surely this time they had to stop, if only to check that I was all right. I was miles from anywhere, purple-faced and probably looking as desperate as I felt. Without water I could be dead in a few hours.

Mike McMahan tells the story of how, in July 1968, he was with his son exploring the desert south of Gonzaga Bay. Entering a camp, they discovered that a dead woman had just been brought in: 'The desert had taken its toll. Their truck had broken an axle and the man, about fifty, and the woman, about thirty, had tried to walk the seven miles to this camp.

'He had finally stumbled in . . . alone, and almost delirious. Three men went out to search for the woman and found her – just half a mile from camp — crumpled under a bush. Dead. Seven miles later. Dead.'

I stuck my thumb out. The driver smiled as he drove past in his cosy, air-conditioned, beer-swilling, stereo-wafting, comfort. I threw my arms up in a gesture of disgust. My face turned a little more purple. I plodded on fuming quietly. 'You shouldn't come down if you aren't willing to help a person in need. It's easier for a camel to get through the eye of a needle . . . You can keep all your space shuttles and jumbo jets. I'll bet my boots the first Mexican will stop.'

Another two miles down the road, a dirty, spluttering pick-up emerged from the heat-haze. I only had to turn and look, to know that the good samaritans had arrived. They slowed to a stop and asked if I needed a ride. The smiling, caring expressions on the faces of the poor Mexicans were beautiful to see. I climbed in the back of the truck and made a home for myself between the picks and the shovels and buckets of tar. The rugged desert and the warm air rushed by as I stood up and admired the scene. The drive into the Bay of L.A. was as spectacular and beautiful as the Bay itself.

I left my boots with Patricio at the Gas Station – estimate $6 – then wandered over to see Mike. It was good to be back, and to enjoy my celebrity status. Mike dragged me off to a dinner party where I was treated to sweet and sour duck, and endless drink and dirty jokes. A dozen Americans were now my greatest buddies. They marvelled at my tales, patted me on the back and generally puffed up my ego. I wondered if any of them had driven past me on the way in.

There, at the Bay, I had time to ponder the question of how to get by Scammon's Lagoon. It was an enormous body of water, forty miles long and up to ten miles wide, occupying the centre of a vast salt-sterilized sandy depression in the heart of a desert so desperately poor that not even the padres bothered with it. Only dunes, salt flats, swamp and quicksand bordered the lagoon. To get safely around would involve a hazardous and monotonous detour of over a hundred miles. I would very likely see no one. In places, I wouldn't be able to get to the water. It was a fearsome prospect, and one I would have done almost anything to avoid.

The alternative was to cross the lagoon by boat and virtually maroon myself on Malarrimo beach — reputed to offer the finest beachcombing in the world. The first ten miles of the beach was practically an island. Ten miles west of the entrance to Scammon's Lagoon the sea had broken through the dunes and created a new lagoon which was, according to one of my maps, only separated from Scammon's Lagoon by an area of salt marsh. I almost certainly wouldn't be able to cross the mouth of the lagoon and there was no guarantee I could walk around.

I spent four days at the Bay of L.A. before hitching a ride out with the same Mexican roadworkers who picked me up on the way in. Patricio had done a good job with my boots. He'd glued and nailed back the soles, and even sewed up some of the stitching from the heel. It was $6 well spent.

Back in Guerrero Negro, I plucked up the courage to approach the works manager of the salt company. The place was so big, a car had to be sent to take me from reception to his office. However Señor Bremmer seemed genuinely interested in my plight. Pointing to a map on his office wall, he explained that the company had no boats capable of approaching the beaches on the far side of Scammon's Lagoon. The boats were ocean-going salt barges. But he did offer me a ride in a company vehicle fifty miles to a worksite near the southern end of the lagoon. I explained that I had to walk, so that was out of the question. I asked for his permission to visit the company port of El Chaparrito where the salt was loaded for its journey over to Cedros Island. 'Perhaps there will be some fishermen there who can help?'

'Of course. Feel free to mention my name.' A plane flew low overhead. 'I'm sorry, I must go, I have some visitors from Japan. I must meet them at the airport. If you have trouble getting over, come back and see me anytime. Good luck!'

I made my way out to El Chaparrito, where one of the company managers tried to arrange a ride first of all aboard one of the many shrimp boats using the port; and when that proved fruitless, he arranged for a truck to take me along the lagoon to find a fishcamp. I couldn't believe the trouble everyone was going to for me.

The driver approached a little camp consisting of two shacks, and explained my needs to the camp 'boss' who seemed horrified by my request. It is too dangerous over there, he said, listing the whole gamut of dreads from coyotes to quicksand. But in the end he relented. If the loco gringo wanted to kill himself what business was it of his? I was left in the camp, and in the hands of the three brothers who had lived and fished there for fifteen years.

Once these amiable brothers had taken responsibility for me, they did their best to make me feel at home in their simple half-open plywood and tar-paper shack. At first glance it would have been easy to dismiss them as down-and-outs living in poverty; but as we sat around their only source of light – a small can filled with a mix of gasoline and oil – it was easy to see through the holes in their clothes and come to respect their unpretentious dignity.

I was treated to a lobster dinner while my hosts tried to enlighten me about what I'd find on the other side of the lagoon. They confirmed that, if I chose to go by way of Malarrimo beach, I would come to mouth of the new lagoon and, unless I built a raft, there was no way I could get across. And if I couldn't find a way over, I'd have to work my way around, through fifteen miles of soft, sodden sand. It would be very unpleasant. One of the fishermen said, 'In the dry sand you sink to your knees. In the wet sand, maybe you sink to your doom.'

They gave me lots of tips and advice. One of them sliced open a couple of cloves of garlic, bent down and began rubbing them on my boots. 'This will keep the rattlesnakes away,' he said.

I stared into the smoky flames from the burning can thinking of how the lamps of America were once fuelled by the whale oil from Scammon's Lagoon.

About 7.30 p.m. I felt tired enough to want to retire. I sat at the mouth of my tent, rear inside, while I removed my boots. The camp dog approached convinced that I was playing some kind of game. He started pulling at my laces, leaping in the air and kicking sand in my face. Suspecting that the flea-bitten son-of-a-bitch would run off with my boots, I thought it wise to take them into the tent with me.

I couldn't sleep. I was too excited. Tomorrow I'd be 'hitting the beach'; and what a beach it was. In spite of the danger of quicksand, and the risk of being stranded, I felt the call. I had to go over.

Malarrimo is situated where the coast of Baja hooks sharply out into the Pacific, cutting across what oceanographers have called – 'the longest river in the world' – a variously named ocean current that runs for 9,000 miles from the Philippines, past Japan, across the northern Pacific, down the coast of California to Baja California and Malarrimo. It was this current that carried, for 250 years, the Spanish galleons from Manila to Acapulco.

There was a good chance that anything cast adrift in the northern Pacific would end up on that beach. But Malarrimo is extremely difficult to get to. Access by sea is almost impossible because of the continually crashing surf and the dangerous onshore wind and current. Access by land, through deep cactus strewn canyons and over continually shifting trails and dunes is risky. If you break down you may not see another soul till the hereafter. Pilots of small planes are sometimes tempted to land on the broad sandy beach at low tide, but a forest of washed-up tree trunks and treacherous, soft sand make it extremely hazardous.

I had read many tales of Malarrimo. The beachcombing sounded too good to be true. I dropped off to sleep dreaming of masts and wooden hulls and treasure ships and crates of whisky.

After a leisurely breakfast we left at 9.30 a.m. It was cloudy and cool, indeed almost cold, as the panga picked up speed and leapt and crashed off the waves. I looked at my repaired boots and thought of Gerhard Bakker whose life had ended there in the lagoon. I thought how, in two months, thousands of gray whales would be entering the lagoon at the end of their 5,000-mile journey from the Arctic seas between Alaska and Siberia, arguably the longest migration in the world.

After four months summer feeding in the plankton rich waters of the Arctic, up to 10,000 gray whales take three months to make it down to Baja where they winter and calve in her warm, shallow lagoons. Scammon's is only the largest of several lagoons along Baja's Pacific coast. With the return journey taking another three months, the gray whale spends up to half its life commuting between the Arctic and the desert lagoons. But the tremendous effort is worthwhile because the calm, buoyant waters of the lagoons are perfect for ensuring that the newly born calves have the maximum chance to reach the surface and take their first breath, usually with a helping lift from mother.

The California gray is a medium-sized whale of up to fifty feet in length and weighing forty tons. At birth the average baby gray weighs a ton. Yet it is poorly covered in blubber. Before it can survive the freezing waters of the Arctic, it needs to double its weight. The mother's milk is extremely rich, its fat content eight times higher than human milk.

From the end of December to March, hundreds of tourists camp on the accessible shores of the lagoon and watch the spectacular sight of a closed body of water packed 'like sardines' with whales.

The pregnant females move to the most protected and shallow parts of the lagoon to give birth. Mexican guides are licensed to take spectators out to observe the whales at close hand. Many of the whales are known to be friendly, and quite happily come up to the small open boats for the excited tourists to pat their barnacle-encrusted heads.

These magnificent, highly intelligent creatures were not always so friendly. In the mid-nineteenth century American whalers discovered the lagoon and mercilessly hunted them to the point of extinction. The cornered, nursing mothers turned on their tormentors with such violence that the whalers called them 'devilfish'.

Scammon's Lagoon was named after Captain Charles M. Scammon, the first captain to gain access to the lagoon and start the slaughter. Scammon, like so many of the San Francisco-based whalers, had long patrolled the migratory pathway taking whatever individuals came his way. Scammon was convinced, however, that the whales had to be congregating somewhere. Even though his lookouts were searching for an appropriate channel or a bay, they sailed right by the entrance to the lagoon. From the ocean all that could be seen was endless surf and blinding dunes. Then, a masthead lookout was amazed to see several whale spouts rising from the desert.

Scammon ordered two whaleboats lowered. But so well concealed was the entrance that the oarsmen pulled for two days along the breakers before they spotted the channel. By a combination of skill and luck Scammon got his ship inside the lagoon, where the whalers could hardly believe their eyes. They took two whales without incident.

The next day, 'word had got around'; the whales were aware of the threat. They tried to avoid the boats, and when that was impossible they turned around and attacked, smashing boats, breaking bones and throwing the sailors into the shark-infested waters.

The 'devilfish' began to earn its reputation. The men refused to man the boats. Scammon spent two days trying to figure out how to take the creatures tantalizingly spouting all over the lagoon.

They tried anchoring the whaleboats in shallow water next to some of the deeper channels. As the whales came by, a gun would fire a bomb-lance hoping to hit a vital point. The lances exploded inside the whales. They took some like that, but, to get at the mass of whales, the crews had to take to the open water. They refined their techniques, but whaling inside the lagoon remained a hazardous business. As Scammon wrote later: 'the casualties from coast-whaling are nothing to be compared with the accidents that have been experienced by those engaged in taking the females in the lagoons. Hardly a day passes but there is upsetting or staving of boats, the crews receiving bruises, cuts, and in many instances, having limbs broken; and repeated accidents have happened in which men have been instantly killed, or received mortal injury.'

In record time Scammon had taken his fill of whales, perhaps more than his fill, for he had trouble getting the ship out over the shoals at the mouth of the lagoon.

Back in San Francisco the crew was sworn to secrecy. The other whaling captains assumed Scammon had been lucky. But when he returned yet again with a record catch in record time, the other whalers followed him out. He managed to lose them in the vastness of the ocean. But according to Erle Stanley Gardner:

> The baffled hunters cruised everywhere trying to find where Scammon had disappeared, and in the end it was the wind which betrayed Scammon's location. A lookout on one of the whaling ships which had been cruising off Cedros Island noticed the tell-tale taint of whale blubber drying out, and reported to the captain, who promptly turned the ship into the wind and started following the scent which of course kept growing stronger until, to his amazement, the captain beheld the spars of Scammon's ship apparently moored in the middle of a sandy desert; and surrounded by the spouts of whales.

The whalers then arrived en masse and the massacre began. Between 1846 and 1874 an estimated 10,000 gray whales were slaughtered, many there in Scammon's Lagoon.

As our little open boat raced towards the far shore, I tried to take a photograph of my Mexican companions, but the boat was crashing too much. The shocks shot painfully along my spine. Instead, I stood up and gazed out across the broad lagoon and pictured the scene as described by Scammon:

> The slaughter was exceedingly picturesque and unusually exciting, especially on a calm morning, when the mirage would transform not only the boats and their crews into fantastic imagery, but the whales, as they sent forth their towering spouts of aqueous vapour, frequently tinted with blood, would appear greatly distorted. At one time the upper sections of the boats, with their crews, would be seen gliding over the molten looking surface of the water, with a portion of the colossal form of the whale appearing for an instant, like a spectre in the advance . . . Numbers of them will be fast to whales at the same time, and the stricken animals in their efforts to escape, can be seen darting in every direction through the water, or breaching headlong clear of its surface, coming down with a splash that sends columns of foam in every direction, and with a rattling report that can be heard beyond the surrounding shores.

The ride across the lagoon had taken forty-five minutes. Approaching the other side, the tension was exhilarating. The sun was shining. The shore was blinding white and sterile. To the whales it must have looked like the Arctic wastes they knew so well. The boat glided through the beautifully clear shallows, then touched with a gentle hiss.

I took a mighty leap from the side of the boat trying to clear the water. However, the sand was so soft, my leading boot sank in ankle deep. I 'hit the beach' with all the grace of a breaching whale, and fell flat on my face. A wave washed over me. In trying to keep my boots dry, I'd managed to soak myself from head to foot. I had to laugh. We all laughed. It didn't seem the best start to my attack on Malarrimo.

I was a mile inside the lagoon, and the fishermen assured me that I could work my way around the water's edge to the main beach. When I asked how much I owed them, they kept repeating 'nothing'. I waved a ten-dollar bill till my wrist was tired but they were resolute, hurriedly disappearing back across the lagoon to get on with their fishing. I waved goodbye, vowing one day to return with a bottle of tequila.

All alone, I took stock of the situation. The tide was high and right up against the powder white dunes coming down from the desert. There was little walking room between the water and the steep slopes of sand.

Although my boots were wet and getting wetter, I preferred to keep them on as the broad soles had an almost snow-shoe effect on the frighteningly soft surface; and there was so much debris around, it would have been asking for trouble to go barefoot.

Even inside the lagoon, there was evidence of interesting beachcombing: glass bulbs, bottles, crates and containers of all kinds. I found a large, stainless steel vessel, probably intended for a laboratory. It would have made an excellent cooking pot, but it was too heavy to carry.

I tried walking the dunes, but the dry sand was like talcum powder. I was sinking up to my knees in sudden soft patches. It was exhausting and nerve-wracking.

Relieved to see the tide falling fast. I made my way down to the broadening band of sand and shallow pools. I couldn't escape that horrible sinking feeling. There were soft patches where the weight of a step sent out jelly-like waves. Remembering the warning the fishermen had given me, I cautiously pussy-footed my way over the wet surface where the wind had whipped up patches of sand-coloured foam. Lying on top of a pool of water, they looked deceptively solid. I stepped on one and immediately collapsed in muck and water. I thought I'd fallen into quicksand. I pulled myself out, took a few deep breaths and tried to pull myself together before making my way slowly and steadily towards the main beach.

Once out of the lagoon, I found firmer sand. The receding tide exposed a band of beach being battered by two hundred yards of rolling surf. The breakers reached across the mouth of the lagoon. It was easy to understand why the whalers had so much trouble finding the way in.

Malarrimo wasn't a disappointment. For every mile I covered on the shore, I must have zigzagged five along the beach and into the dunes. The scene was incredible. It was as if some terrible and destructive battle had taken place off the coast. The shore was littered with planks, buckets, tree trunks, helmets, hatch covers, bits and pieces of boats and planes, and all kinds of military and medical equipment.

I picked up a plastic bottle containing a hundred Tetracycline antibiotic tablets, a phial of nerve gas antidote, 'for use in nerve agent poisoning' – I wondered if it might be useful to keep in case of scorpion sting or snake bite – and a litre plastic bag of 5% dextrose and 0.9% NaCl supposedly for intravenous injection, but it occurred to me it might be worth drinking if I ran short of water.

There were other things I preferred to keep away from: a cylinder containing phosphorus, with a warning for the finder to contact the police or the military immediately; and some kind of missile with wires hanging from the back.

I could have done with a supermarket trolley as I wandered along the beach picking up cans of beer, coke, and dried milk, lifeboat rations, shampoo, sunscreen, contraceptives, spray cans of pasteurized cheese and cream, not to mention biscuits from Spain, dried snacks from Japan, and chocolate syrup from Hersheys.

The newly washed-up stuff was close to the shore, but the really old and possibly valuable material was back in the dunes. There were several wrecks; and fascinating items such as hatch covers and an old sailing mast. I found the wooden hull of one ship covered in copper sheeting. A piece of it flaked away in my hand revealing the mark 'Shears of London'. I ripped off the coin-sized stamp and took it as a souvenir. It was heartbreaking to think of the treasures I had to leave behind.

I had learned to check out any bottle with a top on. Some contained drinkable quantities of spirits. A surprising number contained messages:

'I was on the MTS Daphne and threw this overboard. Please send postcard to Jeff Friedlieb . . . Chicago, Illinois.'

'Cecilia Abad on Azure Seas. Age 6. Cerritos, California.'

There was a bottle from the Scripps Institute of Oceanography. The message inside asked the finder to send details of the find to help in a study of ocean currents.

There was also a bottle from the Catalina Island Museum, Avalon, California. Inside the message read:

'FRIEND: I AM GLAD YOU FOUND ME. I CARRY BEST WISHES FROM ALL THE CITIZENS OF THE CITY OF AVALON, ON SANTA CATALINA ISLAND. WE ARE LOCATED 40 KILOMETRES SOUTH OF LOS ANGELES, JUST OFF THE COAST OF SOUTHERN CALIFORNIA, IN THE UNITED STATES OF AMERICA.

'ON 4 JULY OF THIS YEAR, 1976, OUR COUNTRY OBSERVES HER 200TH YEAR OF INDEPENDENCE, THE BICENTENNIAL. THIS BOTTLE WAS CAST INTO THE PACIFIC OCEAN AT LATITUDE 30°33'20" NORTH, LONGITUDE 118°14'30" WEST, ON 4 APRIL, 1976, BY CHARLES COLLINS, AS A PART OF THE BICENTENNIAL CELEBRATION, AND AS A SCIENTIFIC EXPERIMENT.

'WOULD YOU PLEASE COMPLETE THE ENCLOSED FORM AND MAIL IT TO US IN THE SELF-ADDRESSED ENVELOPE? WE PROMISE UPON RECEIVING IT, TO SEND YOU A THREE-PIECE 1776–1976 COIN SET.

'WE WISH YOU PEACE, HAPPINESS AND PROSPERITY. YOUR NAME AND THE INFORMATION YOU SEND US WILL BE RECORDED IN THE SANTA CATALINA ISLAND MUSEUM, AND IN THE OFFICIAL RECORDS OF THE BICENTENNIAL.'

I wrote down details of all the messages. And as soon as I could get a letter out, I wrote to Avalon to claim my coin set and my place in American history, requesting that the coins be sent to my parents in England. They arrived with the following letter:

Dear Mr. Mackintosh:

We were delighted to receive your note about bottle no. 1865, which you found on Malarrimo Beach while beachcombing. Thank you for taking the time to respond, and (considering your nationality), for so graciously congratulating us on the occasion of the Bicentennial of our Independence.

Charlie Collins is now a student at the University of California at Davis. In 1976, he was a young teenager in Avalon, one of 200 persons who contributed two dollars apiece to sponsor a Bicentennial bottle. On April 4th these 200 sponsors sailed forth in an island ferry donated for the occasion and threw into the sea their bottles numbered from 1776 through 1976 and containing messages in English and Spanish hand-written by Avalon school children. Soon after, a storm blew many of the bottles to Baja California. However, two did make their way across the Pacific Ocean to the Marshall Islands. Others, of course, may still be lying on isolated beaches waiting to be found by beachcombers such as you.

Your walk around the coastline of Baja California must be an exciting challenge. We wish you the best of adventures.

CATALINA ISLAND MUSEUM SOCIETY, INC.

Making camp, I had tons of firewood, and plenty of food and drink. I enjoyed a can of beer followed by a couple of warming swigs of Bacardi. My campsite, with all the bottles gathered around looked like a well stocked bar. Half-pickled, I sat there pondering some of life's deeper questions, such as how does all this booze get in the ocean and how am I going to drink it all?

Before breakfast, I went for a half-an-hour walk to see what the tide had brought in. I picked up a can of beer, several cans of soda, a bottle of Martini, a coconut, another message in a bottle from the Geographical

Society, a baseball cap, and more nerve gas antidote. I started my breakfast with a can of beer, a swig of Bacardi, a hefty swallow of Martini and shot of brandy. Best start to the day for a long time. To save weight I mixed all my booze together and carried it in a large vacuum flask I'd found.

As I staggered along the crest of the dunes, I saw the new lagoon gradually filling to my left. It was an enormous body of shimmering water. I was on a rapidly tapering peninsula, deliberately doing what I had always dreaded – approaching the broad mouth of a lagoon I could not possibly pass over.

I followed the wet sand of the beach around into the lagoon. As expected, the mouth was wide, and the water was deep. A powerful surf was crashing just beyond the entrance while the relatively calm blue water inside the lagoon was alive with fish and crabs. The setting was beautiful. There was a little, half-dilapidated shack, half-buried by the white, wind-blown sand.

Struggling to come to terms with my predicament, I spotted something . . . I couldn't believe it. There, upside down and under water was the unmistakable shape of a boat! A small rowing boat. Could I paddle it across?

My elation was premature. The aluminium boat must have been there for years. It was badly corroded and full of tiny holes. I raised it from the bottom. drained the water, pushed it from the shore, leapt in, paddled around with a plank, and timed how long it took to sink. Within minutes the little fountains of water shooting up from the flimsy hull became eddies as the boat began to go down. Caught by the wind and the current, I found myself paddling in vain. I was being swept out to sea. Close to panic, I nearly jumped over the side and tried to swim back, but eventually I managed to paddle back weary and wiser.

As the tide fell and the lagoon drained, the mouth got smaller and smaller until just one hundred yards separated me from the other side. I stared and stared, psyching myself up, willing myself to pick my moment and go. If I could balance the wind and the current I could probably paddle over before sinking.

I tied my pack to the boat, took a swig of Dutch courage, and was ready to run the boat down the sand into the water . . . when a sudden huge splash halfway across changed my mind. The water was probably full of sharks. With the current trying to sweep me out into the Pacific, and the wind trying to blast me into the lagoon, I realized I'd be casting off in a sinking boat with downward my only certain direction. It was crazy.

I paced up and down the beach thinking of the horrors of having to walk around the lagoon. The current was slacking. I was missing the one brief moment when it might be possible. I saw another message in a bottle. It turned out to be a religious tract entitled – Help from above! That was exactly what I needed, so I read it carefully. There was a section on the evils of strong drink. Suddenly I knew what I had to do. I threw away all the booze, then pulled the boat towards the narrowest part of the channel. As I was about to leap in, a mullet shot from the water and went sliding up on to the sand. A sign! I pounced on the wriggling fish and threw it into the boat.

With adrenalin pumping and dinner flapping, I pushed the boat out, leapt in and paddled furiously. At first, progress was exhausting and painfully slow. Then the current seized me and took me away from the bank into deep water.

When I noticed my fish dinner swimming contentedly around my feet, it seemed like a good idea to stop paddling and start bailing. Ten more agonizing minutes paddling and bailing and I was over, clenching my fists in relief and exultation.

While searching for a campsite, I stubbed my toe against a bottle of very old, very excellent Japanese whisky. A reward for my faith! The mullet was delicious. The sunset and the stars seemed even more beautiful, and I was more than ever convinced that someone up there was watching over my little walk around Baja.

For three more days I made my incredulous way westward without seeing a soul. I was struggling on, weighed down with bottles of Bacardi, Scotch, brandy and Japanese whisky, when I spied a nearly full bottle of London gin. 'Please, please, let it be seawater,' I implored. Unfortunately it was pure gin. Grabbing it and walking on, I joked to myself that what I needed now was some tonic. Five minutes later, I found a can all the way from Australia!

After toasting Queen and Empire I continued my even more wobbly path along the beach to a point where Malarrimo changes from sand to rocks and cliffs. I quickly discovered that too many gin-and-tonics on the rocks was not a good idea. I fell heavily. Bottles flew everywhere and I was lucky to escape with just a twisted ankle.

Then came the sobering realization that I was in danger of being trapped by the rising tide. Mile after mile I could find no way up. For my sins I spent an uncomfortable night perched on a ledge, the sea washing away beneath and the cliffs towering ominously above.

From Malarrimo to Punta Eugenia and down to Laguna San Ignacio I was treated to more fantastic hospitality. The kindness of the lobster fishermen is something I will never forget. In every fishcamp they did their best to fatten me with as much lobster as I could eat. Most of the fishermen were from Bahía Tortugas which gradually became my favourite Baja town. When I got there, I stayed two days with one family who treated me like a king. Even my prodigious appetite couldn't cope with the platefuls of lobster they kept dishing up.

It wasn't all easy living. There were some bad stretches and nightmare days bent anxiously over stills. With the pitahaya season coming to an end, I became reacquainted with hunger. Once, while up in the mountains, I was attending to cuts and bruises after a fall, when a vulture alighted on a nearby rock and eyed me hopefully. For a while it was touch-and-go who was going to eat whom. In the end we both went in search of something better.

In the midst of my troubles, for some reason I thought of arrowheads. I started looking. Within ten minutes, I'd begun my collection with two arrowheads, a flint scraper and other bits of worked stone. Admittedly, one can find Indian artefacts throughout the peninsula, but it was yet another extraordinary coincidence to ponder.

I walked into one town just as it was getting dark. While waiting for the moon to rise and help me find a suitable campsite, I sat outside the little town-store enjoying a cold beer. First the town drunk came over, insisting that we were in Mexico; then, in case I had any doubts, I was approached by three, gun-toting policemen. They asked if I wanted somewhere to stay the night. I naturally said yes, thinking I was on to a good thing. They bundled me into a pick-up and drove several miles out of town to a lonely, half-built house overlooking the ocean. It was pitch black and miles from anywhere. I could sense something wasn't right. While I was wondering if I was about to be used for target practice or pushed off the cliffs, one of the cops asked me, 'Do you have any weed, any marijuana?' I assured him I didn't. They all seemed very disappointed, and drove off into the night leaving me stranded in the middle of nowhere.

Laguna San Ignacio was almost as much of a barrier as Scammon's Lagoon, and this time there was to be no boat-ride across. All the fishcamps were on the other side. To stay clear of the treacherous salt flats I had to take a long, exhausting hundred-mile detour to get around. I wrote in my diary:

> The pack unbearably heavy. Much stopping and bending over to ease the weight. As darkness descended I felt a few spots of rain. I pitched the tent in a gap between two red, rocky hills. Black clouds were sweeping by. It started belting down. I spent most of the evening mopping up water with socks and shirts.
>
> Next morning, I put everything out to dry, and climbed one of the red rock hills to see what was ahead. The rocks were very dangerous, loose and crumbly. The place smelled of rattlers. I was assaulted by

apprehension when I thought how much of this I'd have to face on the other coast. Not just one brief climb, but days and weeks of it. Tremendous risks lay ahead. I saw it so clearly. I thought of Jesus saying, if only this cup could pass from my lips.

I marched through the desert singing cheerfully: 'Amazing Grace', 'When Johnny comes marching home', 'One day at a time', 'The last farewell'. Funny how some songs just seem appropriate and start themselves. How strange my shadow seems. One moment a Roman soldier, the next a Civil War soldier, then a Samurai warrior. The cap and pack lending themselves to various interpretations.

I had been forced so far inland it seemed sensible to go a little further and visit the oasis town of San Ignacio. There I met a pair of young guys from New Zealand who were travelling around the world, and an eighteen-year-old girl from California who was hitching down to Cabo San Lucas hoping to get on a yacht. She was a delight to talk to: open, optimistic, affectionate and very amusing.

We sat around the campfire, chatting, laughing and drinking. She made me wish I had a yacht anchored down in Cabo. How different it would be to travel with someone so lovely. Even after I crawled half-sloshed into my tent, I kept picturing her wide-open adventurous eyes, I was in love. I'd definitely been too long in the desert.

From San Ignacio, I made my way out to the southern shore of the lagoon. In a few weeks the whales would arrive, but I'd made up my mind to return to the States. My boots were going again and I wanted to prepare myself properly to tackle the Gulf coast. I could spend Christmas with my friends in California and then, fattened and refreshed, attempt what was probably going to be the toughest, most dangerous and most demanding stretch – south from Bahía de los Angeles.

Chapter 23
The sting

It took me four days to hitch back to California where I was delighted to learn that two of my articles had been published in *Mexico West*. I read them over and over again. It's a delicious feeling seeing your first piece of writing in print. The book seemed that much closer.

Emboldened and inspired, I turned my attention towards other markets. Most American newspapers have Sunday Travel sections. After perusing some in the local library, I hurriedly put together some articles and sent them off to the *Los Angeles Times, San Diego Union, San Francisco Examiner* and *Valley Daily News*, but not having the money or the time to send enlargements or copies, I gambled and sent some of my best colour slides and black and white negatives. If I could just get a couple of hundred bucks for one article, my financial position would look a lot healthier. My money had run out and I was slipping into debt.

I had dinner with Ray and we discussed our experiences after parting the previous September. After all his sufferings, I was amazed at his enthusiasm to join me for a stretch on the Gulf; perhaps at Easter. However, I pointed out that the Gulf was a whole new ball game, rugged, daunting and much more dangerous than anything we encountered on the Pacific coast. Even meeting up would be a problem. Who knew where I'd be in March or April? The only thing we could do was stay in touch by mail. He could write to me 'Lista de Correos'. So I'd pick up my mail at the post offices in the towns. If he still wanted to try the Gulf, we could 'discuss' it nearer the time.

I studied the films I'd shot on my previous trips and tried to sort out which techniques worked and which didn't. Being on my own so much, it was a problem putting myself in the picture. How often did I get an acceptable photo when placing the camera on a rock and using the self-timer? How were the Mexicans doing when they took a picture? Which was best – colour or black and white? Every shot had to count.

The photos of the MacLish brothers were good, so I sent a couple of prints to their mother and father. 'Many thanks for your hospitality to me in Santa Rosalillita. I hope you like the enclosed photos of Alberto and Jose Luis. Give them my regards. Wishing you a happy Christmas and a prosperous New Year.'

I spent Christmas with Dave and Denise, and couldn't have wished for better presents – film, camping equipment, food, diary, a sweater. The $80 I got from the *Mexico West* articles I invested in a pair of boots, sunscreen and batteries, a new saucepan and kettle (and some aluminium tubing and corks to turn it into a more efficient still). Then, early in the New Year, I took off again.

I crossed the border at Tecate, a small town thirty miles east of Tijuana, picked up my six-month entry permit and walked out along the Ensenada road looking for the first of the many rides I would probably need to get me back to the Bay of L.A.

Before I'd even begun hitching, a small pick-up loaded with Mexicans did a U-turn and the driver offered me a ride to Ensenada. Congratulating myself on my good fortune, I climbed into the camper shell on the back of the pick-up and squeezed myself between the three persons already in residence. This journey wasn't going to take long. These guys were in a hurry.

I was a little surprised to be asked, 'Do you have lots of money?'

'No, no,' I replied, 'I'm from England. We're still paying for the Falklands War; the gringos have all the money.' They eyed my backpack and new boots and didn't seem totally convinced.

Racing downhill a few minutes later, we started to take a left-hand curve. Even from where I sat in the back, it was obvious we were going too fast. Suddenly, everything jumped wildly as we left the road then . . . Crash! Bang! We were over on one side and then the vehicle went into a spin. I found myself sliding along in the roof of the camper, watching the rest of the pick-up rolling and disintegrating around me.

When we slid to a halt, I was soaked. A moment of panic! Blood? Gasoline? No, one of my water jugs had burst.

By the time I had gathered up my senses and belongings, and checked the damage to myself and my equipment, I realized the Mexicans were gone. I was on my own. They must have stopped a passing car and cleared off while they could. I suspect they were in no hurry to deal with the local police.

My thumb, my knee and my left elbow were grazed, my lip was cut and my back was sore, but I could move around O.K. And I had enough sense to jot down the vehicle's licence number and take lots of photographs.

Some ranchers appeared as I patched myself with bandages. They were clearly under the impression that I was responsible for the scene before them. In case the police arrived and reached the same conclusion, and not wanting to spend the forseeable future trying to argue my way out of jail, I too decided to disappear. When in Mexico, do what the Mexicans do!

I hitched my way back across the border to San Diego and presumed upon the hospitality of the Andersons who were making a habit of coming to my rescue. I had to replace the kettle and the broken water bottle, but apart from cuts and bruises there didn't seem to be anything wrong with me that a box of bandaids and a few hours in a jacuzzi couldn't put right. Two days later, I was ready to try again.

I returned to Tecate and stuck out a bandaged thumb at the same spot where I'd picked up the previous near-disastrous ride. Three nail-biting days later I arrived safely at Bahía de los Angeles.

Getting stage three of my journey underway wasn't going to be easy. It would have been horrendously difficult following the finger-like promontories around Red Point, the southern hook which enclosed Bahía de los Angeles. So I toyed with the idea of by-passing the worst of the ins-and-outs by climbing over the top. Peering through a pair of Mike's binoculars, I examined a steep gulley rising from the bay to the top of the ridge. It seemed to lie along a fault between red rock on one side and grey rock on the other.

Next day I left the town and made my way around the bay. I tried the ascent first without the pack, taking just a gallon of water. After an hour of breathless, nerve-straining, leg-aching, sun-baking suffering, I crawled up on to the ridge. The view was magnificent, back over the bay to Mike's mountain and, looking east, out over the Gulf to Guardian Angel Island. The way down looked as tricky as the way up. I explored the possibilities and selected a steep-at-first gulley that eventually eased to a gently meandering sandy-floored arroyo snaking its way to the sea three or four miles away.

It had been a tough climb even without the pack. Now I was asking myself to go all the way down, and then, weakened by the first climb, pick up an extra 70lbs and climb all the way back up in the worst of the afternoon's heat! What amazed me was that I was willing to do it. I had come a long way since the days when I used to join my girl friend on her walks through the Kent and Sussex countryside. I'd go out of duty. It all seemed a lot of hard work for nothing. Fields, flowers, houses, hedge-rows, the same old well-worn paths; quite honestly, it had bored me silly. I switched off because so many other people were doing the same thing. I didn't belong to that world. I knew it and I couldn't pretend otherwise.

Leaving the gallon of water on top, I made my way back down the 1,000-foot gulley. To cool off, I dived from the rocks into the shallow, ultramarine waters of the bay. The surprised stingrays shot from their sandy hideaways like wriggling dustbin lids.

It was 2 p.m. before I felt rested enough to attempt the real climb, and 4 p.m. before I threw down my pack on top of the ridge. There was only time for a ten-minute breather before I began working my way down into the shadows on the other side.

I camped in the arroyo just in from the sea, and enjoyed a dinner of porridge and dried apple. It felt strange using my new kettle and pans. An owl flew overhead. A moon was on the rise. I was surprisingly relaxed. Ironically I felt safer in the wilderness than I ever did on the road.

It was good to get back to the tranquil waters of the Gulf, and the familiar routines of wading waist-deep and waiting for the high tides to fall. After the mists and greenery and thunderous rolling white of Pacific cloud and surf, the Gulf gives an overwhelming impression of calm, crystal clear, sterile, pink and purple and blue upon blue. In the still evening light, the islands have a pastel beauty beyond description. At a distance, one would think there wasn't a living thing on mountain or island. I loved it. It fascinated me. It energized me. I belonged to it. And I wasn't lonely. I would have felt more lonely walking down an English country lane.

The fishing was generally relaxing and productive. I could take any number of bass or trigger fish from the rocks. Sometimes it was downright exciting. The sea would explode at my feet. Fish and birds would be leaping and crashing everywhere. Carrying my folded-down telescopic rod, with reel and lure attached, I could be fishing in seconds. Casting into the frenzied carnage one could catch anything from a cormorant or a pelican to a barracuda or a jack.

The ospreys were doing equally well. I saw several returning to their cardón-crowning nests with helpless fish in their claws. One bold or brainless osprey didn't even have to reach the sea for his dinner. He was flying overhead with a still wriggling rattlesnake in his claws.

A similar event had been enough to make the Aztecs choose Mexico City as their capital. Huitzilopochtli, the Aztec god of war and sun, had appeared to their High Priest, Quahcoatl, and commanded: 'Go at once and find the cactus on which the eagle sits joyfully devouring a snake. That is where we shall settle; where we shall rule; where we shall conquer with our javelin and our shield. That is where our city Mexico-Tenochtitlán shall be; there where the eagle cries, opens its wings, and devours the serpent.'

After years of wandering the Aztecs reached the marshes around Lake Texcoco. There, exactly as the High Priest had predicted, they saw an eagle landing on a cactus with a serpent in its beak. The cactus was on an island in the middle of one of the lagoons; and to build their city according to the prophecy they had to create a marvel the equal of Venice.

The eagle devouring a serpent on a cactus has become the emblem of Mexico, reproduced on the national flag and the coinage.

Although the coast was rugged and rocky in places, I was pleasantly surprised by the number of beautiful beaches with calm blue-green water. The water was on the cool side, though the air temperature rose to a pleasant, dry, 80°F. At night, beneath clear skies, the temperature could plummet to a biting cold. Sometimes I slept fully clothed; and in the morning I was never in any hurry to leave the snug warmth of my sleeping bag till the sun rose to warm the tent.

Bahía de las Animas is one of Baja's most beautiful bays; like the Bay of L.A. but minus the people, or at least the tourists. I came across a single 'casa' in a clump of trees; just a simple half-open fisherman's hut built against an old crumbling adobe wall. A fire was burning but no one was around. Hoping to pick up some water, I sat beneath the shade of a tree and waited. My crash wounds were healing nicely but the new boots were causing problems. One toe, in particular, was a mess. I got out the first-aid kit and tried to clean it up.

After a while an old pick-up motored slowly in along the rutted, washed-out road. A young fisherman and his wife were surprised to see me. His name turned out to be Ricardo Cristobal Romero Daggett. He was a grandson of Dick Daggett, jr, and great-grandson of the Englishman who jumped ship to work in the mines of Bahía de los Angeles. His wife came from Santa Rosalillita. I mentioned that I had been there and knew the family MacLish, and how I met Alberto and Jose Luis at El Marron. When she told me that Alberto was dead, I couldn't believe it.

'No, young Alberto, he was only seventeen or eighteen.'

'Yes. He was killed in a car crash near San Vicente. Alberto and his uncle were both killed when their car left the road and exploded.'

I was shocked. 'He was so young. I was laughing and joking with him just . . . three or four months ago. Poor Alberto! And his poor family! His family were so good to me. I sent them some photographs for Christmas, a picture of Alberto and his brother smiling, repairing their lobster traps. When did it happen?'

'The accident was two days before Christmas. They were driving up to see some relatives near Ensenada.'

'His poor family! What a Christmas.' I tried to imagine what they felt when they read my letter.

'Yes. It was very sad.'

I was treated to a meal of fried halibut, tortillas, eggs, goat-cheese, and fruit juice, and given a bag of tortillas and two gallons of water. As much as I tried and protested, they wouldn't accept any money.

The load felt almost unbearable as I cut and hacked my way through the green and fertile patch of desert at the southern end of the Bay. It was a short-cut that went wrong. There was so much grass and vegetation, it seemed just a matter of time before I stepped on a rattlesnake.

The following day I found myself in a broad U-shaped valley feeling I was taking the most beautiful hike in the world. Between the well dispersed cacti and ocotillo, the desert was in fantastic bloom, a carpet of purples, oranges, yellows and whites. If the explosion of colour had been sound, it would have been deafening, and the loose boulders would have come tumbling down from the barren red slopes above the valley.

I strode carefully through the flowers not sure whether to look up, down or around. A score of hawks, buzzards and ravens vied for space in the sky. Hummingbirds and flying insects added their notes to the magical air of the lost valley. It was a place to return to. I marked it on my map and searched through the viewfinder for the best way to capture it on film. Holding the camera at arm's length, I took a close-up of myself in my white sun hat surrounded by the showy white petals and golden yellow stamens of the tall prickly poppy. Its seeds, which contain a narcotic stronger than opium, are much prized by the desert birds. I wondered if the cawing, soaring parade circling above were all 'as high as kites'.

If so, I was certainly getting a vicarious buzz. There was a pleasant dream-like quality to the place. And it seemed a strange coincidence that the 3,800 foot peak dominating the valley was called Pico Alberto.

I made camp just after sunset on a gravel wash at the bottom of the valley. There were plenty of fallen branches and old dry cactus to feed a blazing fire. Lots of birds appeared on the bushes, and as darkness fell, there was movement beneath them. I shone a light and saw nothing; but the rustling and scrapping continued. I was sitting by my fire ill-at-ease about the mystery until the culprit moved boldly out to look at me. Just two feet away, a mouse stood sniffing and staring; then as if deciding he didn't like the smell, he retreated under his bush. Next thing, his whole family were out for a look. Four of them came close and wrinkled their noses in disbelief. I threw more wood on the fire and sent them scarpering. The valley was certainly a paradise for rattlesnakes. There were lots and lots of bold, stupid mice to eat.

I studied my map while a far-off coyote had a good throat-clearing howl. I was south of Bahía de las Animas, south-west of Punta de las Animas, east of the 4,600-foot Cerro de las Animas, and west of Isla las Animas. I sat out marvelling at the moon and the fire-lit stillness assuming that Las Animas was Spanish for 'The Animals'. The name seemed appropriate. However, next day, when my sleep-refreshed brain thought about it, I recalled that the Spanish for animals was 'animales', so I looked up Las Animas. It meant the ghosts or the spirits. That name seemed just as appropriate. Even without the map, I had the feeling that there was something strange about that patch of desert. Perhaps others felt it? Perhaps the names had been given for good reason?

The following day I had good reason to wonder if I was going crazy. I tried to work my way back to the sea. Taking my bearings from the sun, the main peaks and my compass, I was convinced the coast was just a mile or two due east. Yet mountains stretched as far as the eye could see in that direction. I was surrounded by mountains. I checked and double-checked my reasoning; the sea had to be due east but, plain as day, I could see that I'd be wandering into a maze of peaks and valleys. It was a frightening sensation. Nothing made sense. Going in the wrong direction could be fatal if I wandered inland.

I left my pack, took a quart of water and climbed a nearby peak. Half way up, the problem was solved. The coast *was* just two miles away. The mountains were on a group of islands ten, fifteen, twenty miles offshore. I climbed back down shaking my head in disbelief.

After making my way to the water's edge, I used the cool of the evening to dash around the sandy sweep of Bahía de San Rafael. I was short of water. Fifteen or twenty miles ahead, there was a fly-in resort at a place called San Francisquito. If I pushed myself hard I could probably get there before having to use my stills. I was always looking for a crisis to put some go into my weary legs. Suddenly I had one. It was San Francisquito or bust! The tide fell, giving me a broader band of firm, silvery-white sand on which to walk.

I was exhausted as I put up my tent and made camp. There was no shortage of driftwood on the beach and I soon had a blazing fire. The beautiful Salsipuedes Islands – the name means 'Get out if you can' – looked strikingly unreal in the fading light. I sat drinking coffee, staring into the flames and dreaming of missionaries and conquistadors.

I was barely conscious of my hand reaching down to feed a log further into the flames. Suddenly . . . Shock! Pain! I dropped the wood and leapt to my feet cursing and trying to brush off what I assumed to be a red-hot ember. Then I saw the culprit in the firelight. A two-inch long, dark yellow scorpion was still swinging his tail wildly.

I'd been stung on the side of the knuckle of my right index finger. The burning pain continued and there was a deadening sensation in my arm. Anxious thoughts flashed through my mind. Maybe I'm allergic or hypersensitive, maybe I'll react badly, maybe, maybe, maybe . . .? One hard fact burst into consciousness: in Mexico you're ten times more likely to be killed by a scorpion than by a rattlesnake.

I played with the scorpion and considered taking him away from the camp and letting him go. For a minute or two I watched it taking up its revolving, claws-out tail-up defensive posture while I shepherded it with a piece of twig. A lot might depend on what type of scorpion it was, so I reluctantly skewered it into the ground and kept the remains of its shattered body for possible species identification.

Otherwise there was nothing to be done but crawl inside the tent and wait to see what happened. After the initial shock I was now totally calm. I had confidence in my health and fitness. My main worry was being short of water. If I became ill and unable to move, dehydration might prove to be the final straw for my over-stretched system. I unpacked my stills while I was able.

I could feel the venom spreading up my arm as a wave of tingling numbness. The key question was what would happen when it reached my chest. I hurriedly left a message in my diary and on my tape-recorder just in case. Lying on my back waiting, I tried to recall what I'd read about scorpions.

Not all species are equally deadly, but some of the world's most dangerous scorpions are found in Mexico . . . They are normally yellow in colour . . . Stings delivered in self-defence usually contain a maximum dose of poison . . . The dangerous scorpions produce a neurotoxin causing partial paralysis and destroying red blood cells. Species that are neurotoxic produce intense local pain at the site of the sting . . . the tongue feels thick and the throat feels tight . . . speech becomes difficult. There might be twitching of the muscles, sneezing and a continuous flow of fluid from the nose and mouth. Convulsions follow, the arms are flailed about and the extremities become quite blue before death occurs in anything from 45 minutes to 12 hours.

My nose started running, my throat got tight, my tongue thick. The more I lay thinking about it the more symptoms I developed.

I started shivering. It seemed to be a bitterly cold night. Still wearing my socks, shirt and sweater, I sank into the comfort of my sleeping bag and lay there waiting.

Still alive an hour later, I was beginning to relax again. The tingling sensation reaching my shoulder was feeling almost pleasant, and the worst of the burning pain had passed. If I was about to die tomorrow, I thought, I might as well get a good night's sleep.

Next morning, 14 February 1984, I woke feeling fine, and wrote in my diary:

> Just a slightly stiff arm. Valentine's Day. Life I love you! I had my eve of Valentine's kiss from a scorpion. (On the 13th!) I opened the tent to a beautiful morning. The sun was up, the sea calm. Lots of fish leaping. The islands are clear and sharp, and reclining in an eternity of blue.

I was able to carry on and marvel at the number of dolphin skeletons on the beach – there must have been one every hundred yards – and the profusion of pufferfish in the shallows. At first there were only a few rocky points to negotiate, but then the rocks and cliffs began to crowd the shore and make things difficult. The fishing was superb, but I did not dare hang around too long or eat more than one good-sized bass, cooked in foil and sprinkled with lemon juice.

Approaching a jutting, convoluted rocky point, I decided to cut a straight path over the hills just inland. At a guess I was five miles from the resort. The race was on. Struggling up and down, and through the tearing vegetation, I began to think I'd made a bad mistake. I lost sight of the sea. I was surrounded instead by wave after wave of rugged, barren, granite rock. I had no food, and I was carefully watching the sun and my water-level sinking. At times I felt like I was a million miles from anywhere. Up down, up down, it seemed never-ending!

I was scrambling down the dirty white, crystalline boulders on one side of an arroyo when I slid to a crunching halt. Hearing the unmistakable 'hiss' of a rattlesnake, I might have jumped six feet in the air had I known in which direction to leap. The sweat cleared from my darting eyes. When I saw the coiled serpent, my only fear was that he'd get away. I threw down the pack and showered him with rocks. It was a big snake. I could hardly miss. After three strikes his flat head was considerably flatter. Although still twisting and rattling, he was almost certainly dead, but I picked up a large hunk of granite and brought it down twice more shattering the fangs and squeezing out the clear, almost colourless venom on to the gold and black speckled white rock. I very carefully cut off the remains of the head and tossed it aside. Headless, the snake was still wriggling and squirming for all he was worth. I popped him into a black plastic bag and dashed on knowing that at least my food problems were solved.

I'd come a long way since the first rattler I'd seen in the northern Gulf. Then I'd almost jumped out of my skin. Now my mouth watered as I planned removing this guy from his skin and getting him into a frying-pan.

It was almost dark by the time I reached San Francisquito. It consisted of little more than an airstrip, a beach-side 'primitive' hotel, and a few bungalows and thatched sunshades.

No one knew what to make of this cactus-mauled, red-headed Englishman staggering out of the desert with an empty water jug in one hand and a dead rattlesnake in the other. I enjoyed the puzzled looks. Surprising people had become my private joke.

Still, frontier hospitality to the fore, I was given a great reception and was soon swapping stories with Ed Studley, a big friendly American married to a delightful Mexican lady. I could have listened for hours to his Mexican stories and wartime exploits flying P-38s.

Nothing could have been easier than cleaning and skinning that big snake. The skin simply peels back. The innards are out quicker and cleaner than with a fish, then it is just a matter of chopping and frying. I shared this deliciously different snack with one or two of the bolder guests. We all agreed that fried rattlesnake looked and tasted something like rabbit or chicken.

The journey was hotting up. I wrote in my diary:

> One night I am on my own in the wilderness nursing a scorpion sting. The next I am in the company of wonderful people munching away on fried rattlesnake. Yes, 24 hours in Baja has a lot to offer. Who would want to be anywhere else?

Three days later, I was in the wars again, up in the mountains above some impossible cliffs. Cactus and brush conspired to thwart my progress. My long socks, my legs, my shorts, my pack – nothing emerged unscathed as I battled with the vegetation and the terrain. The stillness of my desert cathedral was rudely shattered by a few frustrated curses as I tried to remove a clump of cholla from the side of my knee. No sooner had I managed that than the fishhook spines of a barrel cactus ripped open an old wound.

It was getting late and I was leaving a trail of blood as I cut and crashed my way down a steep gulley into a sheer walled canyon. Halfway down, I realized that something was following me; something big enough to make almost as much racket as I was.

At the bottom of the arroyo I made camp and surrounded myself with three blazing fires as the full moon rose and the unseen 'thing' crept around in the shadows. Seeking comfort from my radio, I switched it on only to hear Michael Jackson telling me, 'Nothing's going to save you from the beast about to strike'. I fell asleep that night cuddling my machete like a teddy bear.

I had been told that there was a ranch at Punta Trinidad. I pushed myself hard to get there before my water ran out. I didn't make it. I was thirsty. It was almost dark. I'd have to boil sea water. A palm tree on the beach ahead seemed a good place to make camp. There was shade, plenty of firewood, and, if the still didn't work, the possibility of water in the ground.

With a strong breeze rustling the black, sunset-silhouetted palm fronds, I hurriedly pegged out the tent and went through the normal anxieties as I put together the still, and made several fires; a small one for the kettle and the larger ones for warmth and light. The kettle took an eternity to boil. At last a vigorous rush of steam came through the plastic and aluminium tubing into my aluminium belt bottle. In minutes I had a pint of water. That was too quick. It was salty. The sea water had bubbled over with the steam. I made the necessary adjustments. A quick taste. That's better. It was working this time, but it took an hour to obtain the next pint. I lifted the kettle carefully off the fire while I dug out my little plastic container of instant coffee. After putting a spoon of it in my mug, I reached for the aluminium bottle containing the hot drinking water. There was nothing in it! The water had gone!

For a few seconds I sat there wide-eyed and open-mouthed . . . Then it dawned, the cooling kettle had sucked back all the water. I burst out laughing. If I could have spared the tears, I might have cried. I had it all to do again.

It is a mistake you make once. In fact I began using the suction effect to refill the kettle quickly and save playing around with the delicate cork which was already showing signs of breaking up with the steam. I only had three corks. I should have brought more.

Next day, that particular water crisis was over. After picking up a network of cattle trails, I followed one into a broad valley green with trees, bushes and palms. Rancho Trinidad had to be somewhere down in that maze of fertility. Hobbling along with my boot-skinned feet cripplingly sore, I found myself being sucked into an impossible whirl of vegetation. I was going round in circles. I got angry at the stupid cows and began to long for a nice, rational coyote trail.

Eventually I squeezed my way out and headed for open country. A deep estuary blocked my path. However, I was saved from despair by the sound of voices. Heading towards them, I came across four Mexicans standing by a rowing boat. I introduced myself. Three of them were probably in their twenties, one about sixty. They were all courteous and jolly, shaking my hand and listening with interest to my story, before inviting me to their ranch for lunch. They had an old jeep parked nearby. Rancho Trinidad was about half a mile away against the base of a barren red mountain rising above the valley.

The older man introduced himself as Lorenzo Aguilar. He had been living there with his large family for fifteen years since leaving Santa Rosalia, some forty or fifty miles to the south. The younger men were his sons and son-in-law.

The ranch was exceptionally clean and well kept. Nothing fancy, almost everything – house, corrals, fences – made of cane, cactus, thatch or piled rock. The sounds were warm and familiar: the chickens clucking and scratching and occasionally taking to evasive action, the donkey braying, the goats bleating, and the occasional 'moo' echoing around the valley. Even the hum of flies had a cosy familiarity. Jeep and a radio antenna apart, there was nothing obviously modern. I might have stepped back two hundred years.

They invited me inside, and gave me coffee and then a lunch of chili, cheese, rice, beans, tortillas, mayonnaise, and vegetables followed by fruit salad and pumpkin cooked in a heavy syrup.

Only the men ate with me. The women and the children stood around happy and smiling, and occasionally laughing at my poor Spanish. But I listened very carefully as the men told me what the coast was like ahead and where I could find water.

Before I could reach Santa Rosalia, I would have to get by the mountain mass of the Tres Virgenes, something I had long been dreading. 'The Three Virgins' were three extinct volcanoes rising dramatically from a great upwelling of volcanic rock sitting right on the coast. The tallest was 6,547 feet. James Bull recorded his impression of the area in 1843:

> We came across a country that had evidently been subjected to strong volcanic action. In places the whole face of the country as far as the eye could see was one black mass of stone and cinder and lava . . . We had in view the whole of this day two lofty peaks of the volcano Las Virgenes (The Nuns). This volcano was in active eruption in the year 1811, and at that time some of the inhabitants of the mission of San Ignacio were destroyed by the earthquake.

Although the volcano has been dormant since the beginning of the nineteenth century, the landscape remains red, black and inexpressibly barren. The great sheets of lava still look as if they had cooled yesterday. There is little soil or vegetation between the rugged craggy rocks. And for fifteen or twenty miles, huge cliffs fringe the seaward side of that volcanic excrescence.

'You cannot walk under those cliffs. They are very bad. If you want, we will take you to Santa Rosalia in our boat.'

I wanted that very much, but I explained the problem.

'In that case, it is better you climb through the mountains.'

I was told about a trail that wound its way up between the two tallest peaks. It was beginning to sound very tempting until . . .

'If you don't know where the trail is, it is not easy to find or to follow. And in the mountains, there are many mountain lions. Do you have a gun?'

'I'm afraid not,' I said, keeping my amusement to myself.

'Then it is best not to stay the night there. It is safer to start early, rush like the wind and try to get down to the other side before dark.'

The family invited me to stay the night with them. I slapped my stomach and thanked them but said they had fattened me up sufficiently for the lions.

'Amigos,' I said, 'it has been a pleasure to meet such a wonderful family. Thank you for all the food and the advice. I shall mention your hospitality in my book.' Judging by their smiles, they had about as much faith in my book as I had in their mountain lions.

Chapter 24
The Three Virgins

I dug a hole in the gravelly floor of a palm-studded arroyo. Beneath the hot, dry stones, there was dampness; and then, about three feet down, cool water! Exactly as the Mexicans had said. Water was seeping into the hole almost as fast as I was scooping it out. The palm trees were the key. Palms mean water! I filled my containers and then flavoured the rapidly warming pool with my feet.

For almost a year now I had been walking around the coast of Baja, step by painful step. But thanks to my boots, I was no longer walking, I was hobbling. They were the worst pair I'd worn, threatening to break apart before I could break them in. The rugged terrain, the heat and the salt water soakings were once again separating the soles from the uppers. I battled my way along the coast trying not to look down at the depressing sight of my boots, nor up at the Tres Virgenes rising ever larger and more menacing.

Standing at the base of the mountains and seeing the huge cliffs stretching as far as I could see, I made up my mind to cut inland. Mindful of the warnings I received at Rancho Trinidad, I set off at first light, hoping that everything would go according to plan and I'd be able to make camp that night on the other side of the mountains.

I followed a trail, sometimes in boulder-strewn, tree-lined arroyos, and sometimes across sunbaked volcanic ridges from one arroyo to another. Up and up I went, muscles aching, breathless, shirt soaked with sweat, my thirst insatiable; sweaty palms clutching the security of a gallon and a half of water; a security that disappeared alarmingly fast!

On one ridge I stopped to draw breath and inspiration from the savage scene of sun-seared rock and sparse, thorny brush. Far below, a tiny speck of a white sail moved imperceptibly across a lightly stirred sea.

Eventually the open vistas of sea and sky gave way to rocky layers of white-pink and rust as I followed the trail into a broad sheer-walled canyon. Having walked at the base of so many cliffs, I was used to being flanked by a wall of rock, but there, deep in the canyon I had the claustrophobic feeling of cliffs on both sides.

I lost the trail among the water-smoothed boulders but there was only one way to go. All the side canyons were too rugged and steep to climb. The lower arroyos had led to this one 'grand' canyon. It had to be the pass the Mexicans told me about.

At last the floor of the canyon began to rise more steeply, lifting me once again into a broadening sky. I was confident I was nearing the top. Coming across a grove of tall palms with their leaves glistening green in the afternoon sun, I slipped off the pack and scrambled up to investigate. Water! A hot-spring emerged from a fossil-encrusted wall of red rock. A little steaming stream flowed for just fifty yards before disappearing beneath the gravel of the canyon floor.

It was the perfect spot to have lunch. I dashed down to fetch my pack. My jaw dropped. The neat pile of possessions I'd left against a rock had been scattered around the arroyo. One of my water jugs had been rolled twenty yards, and water was seeping out. A tin of beans had been carried an equal distance and heavily dented. I pulled the machete from my rolled-up sleeping bag and looked nervously around.

Suddenly, from the slope above, there was a scurrying and a rattling of displaced stones. Fearing I was about to be floored by a couple of hundred pounds of snarling cougar, I whipped the machete from its sheath and held it with both hands like a mighty broadsword.

If ever two creatures stared at each other in disbelief . . . For seconds that seemed like minutes we just looked one another up and down, before the beautiful animal leapt from his bushy hideaway and hoofed it down the canyon. A white horse! Whatever next?

I carried the pack up to the hot spring and settled beneath the shade of the palms to enjoy lunch and a hot shower. As I dried myself in the sun, the horse returned and stood staring intently as if he were trying to tell me something. Perhaps he wanted his waterhole back?

Thinking I'd soon be down, and being a bit suspicious of the strange smelling water, I took just a couple of pints from the spring and pushed on. But I was surprised and disturbed to discover that, instead of going down, the valley continued upwards between steep, rising walls of rugged, crumbling, pitted, gouged and unscalable red rock. The ascent got more difficult as the valley floor became choked with boulders, thorny bushes and trees. Tall cacti stood like eerie green figures against the red slopes and the blue sky.

All afternoon, I worked my way up with no sign of the top. Fearing

I'd taken a wrong turn and was wandering into a maze of unknown canyons, my nerves received a temporary respite from – of all things – a rusty beer can. What most people would have regarded as a desecrating piece of rubbish, I saw as an exciting find. I picked it up, studied it, and thought how beautiful it looked, and how much pleasure the contents had given a fellow human being. I wondered who he was and where he was and what he had been doing so far up in the mountains. I dared to hope, against all reason, that I was still on the trail.

But when I reached a steep, dry waterfall I knew I'd gone wrong. It was almost dark. Climbing up would be a major task, better tackled in daylight. Backtracking a hundred yards to a tiny patch of gravel between the boulders, I set up my tent and collected sufficient wood to fuel a couple of blazing fires.

I was covered in scratches, not so much from the cacti as from the small trees lining the arroyos, the mesquite, the palo verde and the well-named cat's claw. Its branches were covered in viciously hooked thorns which seemed to take a delight in ripping and raking my arms, legs and face.

Sandwiched between the comforting, crackling fires, I sat on a rounded boulder and thought of how I'd been warned to 'Get down from the mountains before dark!' The plots of a half-dozen Dracula films came back to haunt me as a pair of bats swooped and fluttered overhead.

When the vultures rose with the sun to reclaim the sky, I would have another much more pressing problem than the – I hoped – remote possibility of meeting a hungry mountain lion. I was probably 4,000 feet up and ten miles inland with just half-a-gallon of water. If I couldn't find more, or make my way back down to the sea, I could count my life expectancy in hours.

I tried to get something on the radio, but the canyon was too deep; and I doubt I would have been able to listen much anyway, my mind was too active. Should I go back to the hot spring? Or should I carry on? The top couldn't be far away; then I could take my bearings and select the best route down. Should I eat? Should I drink the sulphurous spring water?

While my mind worked over the options, my eyes nervously scanned the fire-and-star-lit slopes above for any sign of movement, and my ears sifted the noise of the wind for the fierce scream of the mountain lion. In spite of the two blazing fires, the mountain air was chilly. I carried on my anxious musings inside my sleeping bag.

At daybreak, I climbed the dry waterfall and continued up and up through the tearing vegetation. There seemed no end to it. Tension and frustration overflowed into anger. 'This is fucking ridiculous,' I shouted. 'How can I still be going up? How?'

'How . . . How . . . How . . . How?' My baffled, embittered voice echoed around the dividing canyon. I took the right fork. It led me into a nightmare of more boulders, thorns and brush. Feeling I'd passed the point of no return, I wasted no more energy thinking about retreat. I had to hack and push my way up to the top.

The sun poured its heat into the still air of the valley, forcing me to drink continuously. All too quickly I was down to the sulphurous spring water. Supposing it was poisonous? Being already dehydrated, I knew if I got the runs and started vomiting, the water loss would be almost immediately fatal.

The American novelist Tom Robbins once wrote: 'The principal difference between an adventurer and a suicide is that the adventurer leaves himself a margin of escape.' There, in those deep canyons, my stills were useless; my radio distress beacon was probably useless; and I was drinking water that might kill me. I was fast running out of escape clauses.

Weariness, thirst, the pain of my boots, nothing mattered but going up. Not another sip till . . . no rest till . . . the old familiar game was back in play. My word was more solid and constraining than all the rock and desolation around me. Having given it, I knew I could call on reserves that most of us only sense we possess.

I came to another series of dry waterfalls. Climbing up I could just picture how, after the rains, the cool water would come cascading down. Then I was amazed to see something not quite so spectacular but most certainly real – a pool of green water about the size of a small-garden goldfish-pond. Wasps danced across its surface while other bugs floated in and out of view beneath.

The water had probably been there months concentrating in the sun. It might be good. It might be poisonous. But I had no choice. I filtered a gallon through a handkerchief, then raced on, trying to mark the route back in my memory.

Eventually the floor of the canyon rose as steep as its own side walls. I'd had enough of being trapped. Wanting out, one way or another, I gambled, and threaded my way up the tumbling rock and falling rubble of the southern slope. The only relatively secure handholds were cacti and brush. By the time I got to the top, my hands were bleeding and full of broken cactus spines. But I hardly noticed. I was on a plateau. There was nothing above me but blue sky and, a few miles to the west, the two larger volcanic cones of the Tres Virgenes. I must have been on top of the smallest virgin, which rose relatively flat-chested, a mere 4,600 feet above the sea which sparkled five miles to the east. What a view!

At my feet canyons and ridges radiated down to the desert and to the town of Santa Rosalia less than twenty miles away. I could see Isla

Tortuga (Turtle Island) and Isla San Marcos. And I could even see Highway One snaking down a mountainside ten miles due south. I watched what looked like a motorhome slowly tackling the descent. Safely down the gradient, the occupants would probably give their full attention to the magnificent spectacle of the Tres Virgenes basking in the Baja sunshine. Little did they know that someone up there was watching them. I thought about pulling out my mirror and sending them some greeting flashes, but then thought better of it. They might see it as an SOS. With a bit of luck now, I could make my own way down to the highway and to town.

To see where I was going I kept to the ridges and avoided the valleys. With the pressure partially lifted, pain demanded expression. The descent was murderous on my feet, but at least I got down a hell of a lot quicker than I got up.

I made camp in a relatively shallow arroyo beneath an outcrop of white rock. The predominant tree in that valley was one I hadn't seen much north of the Tres Virgenes – the palo blanco which, with its ghostly white trunk and branches, somewhat resembles the eucalyptus or silver birch. Indeed, there was a noticeable difference between the vegetation north and south of the Tres Virgenes. There were no more cirios, and a different type of pitahaya was more in evidence, the taller base-branching, vertical-stemmed pitahaya dulce (sweet pitahaya). As they weren't in season, I helped myself to the fruits and flesh of the barrel cactus. One or two monsters grew as fat as dustbins and stood twice as high. But only the cardóns, the tallest cacti in the world, could dispute the sky with the palo blancos.

I boiled the green water I'd carried from the mountain pool and tried to revitalize and rehydrate myself with a few cups of sweet, weak coffee.

The next day, after picking up water at a ranch, I crossed the highway and made my way down a deep V-shaped valley towards Santa Rosalia. All around there were fragments of blue-green minerals. Copper!

Arriving at Santa Rosalia was a bit like finding that old rusting can in the mountains. It didn't belong; but looked at in the right way, it wasn't entirely ugly or devoid of interest. Imagine a piece of the industrial heart of Sheffield or the Ruhr dropped along one of the world's most unspoilt, sun-soaked coastlines and you have Santa Rosalia.

Following the discovery of rich copper deposits in the surrounding hills, the town was founded by the French-owned El Boleo copper company in the 1880s. Indian labour was imported from Sonora. A pipeline was built to bring in water from a source in the mountains. A port was constructed to handle the shipments of processed ore. And up went all the dirty, dusty paraphernalia of smelting and processing.

The French company remained until 1953, by which time the most profitable deposits had been worked out. Shortly afterwards, however, a Mexican company took over and resumed operations on a smaller scale utilizing newly discovered deposits of ore.

The town still bears its peculiar French stamp. Steinbeck wrote in his *Log from The Sea of Cortez*: 'It looked, from the sea at least, to be less Mexican than other towns. Perhaps that was because we knew it was run by a French company. A Mexican town grows out of the ground. You cannot conceive its never having been there. But Santa Rosalia looked "built".'

Although some of the great engines and cranes have been put on display as a 'museum', the great tourist invasion down Highway One has paid Santa Rosalia only passing interest. It still remains a business-like town of about 12,000 souls mostly packed into the narrow parallel streets at the bottom of a broad arroyo. The summer heat in the valley must be unbearable. Most of the French bosses and engineers used to live on the north plateau above the arroyo. Today, many of the houses there are still distinctly French and colonial in style.

One of Santa Rosalia's claims to fame is its prefabricated iron church designed by A. G. Eiffel (of Tower fame) for the 1898 Paris World Fair. The flat, galvanized sections of iron were then shipped from France around Cape Horn. There is certainly nothing quite like it in Baja. Joseph Wood Krutch hated it: 'It would be difficult to find even faint praise with which to damn the iron monstrosity at Santa Rosalia. It is the acme of the inappropriate and of sheer ugliness. Just possibly, it is blasphemous as well.' Personally, I couldn't help feeling it seemed very appropriate amongst the steel and girders of the copper smelters. One shouldn't damn the church without damning the whole town.

The Mexican historian of Baja California, Pablo Martinez, described Santa Rosalia's El Boleo mine as 'notable for the merciless exploitation of man . . . The owners . . . formed on their property a Dantesque kingdom, a description of which causes nausea. There, paying tribute into the pockets of Rothschild, the father of this writer ended his existence.' Martinez does not elaborate.

A week later I entered Mulegé, a little oasis town in a green and fertile valley surrounded by barren desert hills. Situated on the north bank of the Rio Mulegé, about two miles from the Gulf, this town of 5,000 inhabitants was the site of one of the earliest Jesuit missions – founded in 1705, just eight years after the 'conquest'. Dates, from trees planted by the missionaries, are still the town's principal crop, if one doesn't include tourists! Since the completion of Highway One, sleepy 'tropical' Mulegé has become one of Baja's most popular tourist destinations, with trailer parks, hotels and gift shops.

I approached the town on a different highway, one made by coyotes! Descending from the coastal hills, I stepped over a low fence and headed towards a cluster of smart-looking huts and houses. Passing a building where there were a dozen Mexicans in navy-blue uniforms, I realized I'd walked into the marine barracks. I smiled confidently and asked to be directed to town. Pointed in the right direction, I passed through the impressive, impregnable-looking entrance to the barracks, with its sandbags, observation posts and steel-helmeted guards clutching their Belgian FN automatic rifles. The soldiers all looked at me, then at each other, as I sauntered past bidding them a cheery 'Buenas dias'. I tried not to laugh when I heard them whispering, 'Who is he?' 'Where did he come from?'

Mulegé was one of my mail pick-up points. I was hoping to have a letter from home waiting in the post office. If so, it would have to wait an hour longer. It was siesta time. I wandered up to the hill-top mission, wanting to step inside and say a few prayers but, amazingly, it too was closed. Siesta time in heaven no doubt! I carried my burden back into town, where at least one or two small shops were open. I bought a packet of biscuits and a coke, then sat in the plaza writing postcards and marvelling at how expensive Mulegé was compared to Santa Rosalia, when I was suddenly aware of someone saying, 'Excuse me, are you English?'

I turned around to see a handsome, middle-aged American with a warming smile. He elaborated, 'I've just been reading about a red-headed Englishman walking around Baja. Is that you?'

'Yes, I'm English; and I'm walking around Baja. Where did you read it?' I asked excitedly.

'In the *San Diego Union.* We've just been looking at it, my wife and my brother-in-law. It was good. You haven't seen it? I'll bring it over.'

A minute later, he returned with his family and friends, a can of beer and the Travel Section of the *San Diego Union*. And there was my story on the front page, complete with two colour photographs. My spirits soared. I was maybe 150 or 200 dollars richer, which translated into a new pair of boots and several more months walking. And there was still the *Los Angeles Times, Valley Daily News* and *San Francisco Examiner.*

On my way out of town, I was approached by another American couple who asked, 'Are you the Scotsman we heard about?' While chatting, yet another pair of tourists approached and showered excited congratulations on me. They'd read my story in Los Angeles. Perhaps it had been published in the *Los Angeles Times* as well! I allowed them to drag me over to a hotel bar and top me up with beer and iced Pepsi. One of them insisted on giving me $20. I couldn't make him take it back. I was touched. What a morale boost.

Immediately south of Mulegé, the hospitality continued along the shores of the 26-mile-long Bahía Concepción, an increasingly popular winter destination for the 'snowbirds' from Canada, Washington state, Oregon and Idaho. Joseph Wood Krutch, who hadn't thought much of Eiffel's Santa Rosalia church, found Concepción Bay more to his liking: 'Surely one of the great beauty spots of the world . . . Nothing else on the whole of Baja's spectacular coast is quite so fine.'

It's a beautiful bay all right, but the explosion of tourism in recent years has taken away some of its magic. The main highway skirts the western shore of the bay. There are many places to camp. And every recreational vehicle coming to Baja seems to end up there. Nowadays, the only way to see Concepción Bay at anything like its pristine best is to come in the summer, when the oppressive heat guarantees you'll have the beach and the bath-warm water all to yourself.

Still, I shouldn't say too much about the tourists. Mustn't bite the hand that feeds me. I was certainly well fed and 'watered' as I made my way down the magnificent length of the bay, and I was given sunscreen, film, tapes, maps, advice and everything else I needed. Americans are some of the world's most wonderful people – when they're not scared to death of you! I found it quite bewildering, the number of people who wanted to shake my hand and take my picture. Everyone should be allowed to experience the feeling of being a celebrity at least once in their lives.

At the southern end of the bay, the main highway disappears into the mountains. I had to face the prospect of leaping back into the wilderness, and heading 26 crow-flying miles north along the eastern edge of the bay and an equal distance down the Gulf shore. It's amazing how one side of Concepción is packed with people, while the other is totally empty except for the odd fishcamp and ranch.

At the very end of the bay, I bumped into a couple of big Oregonians – at least their pick-up had yellow Oregon plates. They were enjoying a lunch of fresh dug clams and beer. As they might be the last tourists I'd see for a while, I went over to see if I could get a top up with water.

'Hello there! How are you doing?' I said, bubbling away like a bottle of beer.

Silence.

'Pleased to meet you. My name's Graham. I'm walking around Punta Concepción and down the coast to Loreto. Could I get a couple of pints of water from you?'

'We haven't got any to spare,' one of them said coldly. They turned their backs on me.

'Umm . . . Excuse me. Do you know if there are any fishcamps ahead?'

'They won't have any water either. They go to a lot of trouble to truck it in, and they can't afford to give it away.'

'Well, I'd better go. I've got a long walk to Loreto.'
'You won't make it.'
Why are some people so damned negative? They had me weighed up as a no good, sponging, drop-out, drug-dependent parasite before I'd even opened my mouth. I was down to earth with a bang. It certainly made me think. The fishermen couldn't afford to spare food and water for me, but they gave it, and in their giving they had changed me. The bond I felt to Baja had been continually deepened by their hospitality. The bonds of a hundred friendships had been forged. I couldn't pay them back, not now. But one day, I knew I'd give something back to those who'd given me so much.
Ten miles later I arrived in a small temporary-looking fishcamp just as three Mexicans were returning in their panga with the results of their morning's diving – several sackloads of shellfish. There was nothing negative about these characters. They smiled and offered me a cup of coffee and some shellfish tacos.
When one of them said he had been there for eight months, I asked, 'What, all the time?'
'No, occasionally I go home to milk the cow.'
'You have a cow?' I asked naively.
They all laughed loudly, leaving me in no doubt what he went home for.
I was told about a waterfall in a palm-lined canyon about fifteen miles ahead. It sounded beautiful.
With empty beaches to my left, and the mountains to my right the colour of the Mexican flag – red, white and green – I continued north along the cactus-covered, alluvial plains on the eastern side of the great bay.
The sun was setting as I ascended what I hoped was the correct canyon. A couple of miles up, just when I thought I'd reached a sheer walled cul-de-sac, I saw the palms in a steep little extension to the main canyon. And there was the stream flowing between the palms and down a smooth rock face before disappearing in the valley floor. Though not perhaps as spectacular as I'd imagined, it was every bit as beautiful. The air was still and clear; and the mellow evening light lent a mood of mysterious unreality to the scene.
After putting up my tent, I sat outside admiring the moon and the stars, and drinking cup after cup of coffee. The caffeine must have excited my brain. I began to see and hear things. A towering wall of silver and shadow began to take on a disturbing shape. I tried not to look, but the more I tried, the more insistent was the image. A face was taking shape. I'd spent enough nights alone not to fear the dark, but I knew something was going to happen . . . I was going to see something terrible, something that would shock me to the core.

Even after removing my boots and crawling inside the tent, I couldn't escape the compulsion to keep looking back outside. And every time I did so the face crystallized, and I averted my eyes just before . . . before an image that would be the embodiment of horror itself. Then I thought I heard a voice asking, 'Are you afraid to see?' Oh God! Here we go, voices! I couldn't blame the hallucinations on being too long alone. It was the first night I'd been on my own for almost a week.

I heard the voice again, 'Are you ready?'

Lying sweating on my sleeping bag. I kept struggling with the voice in my head . . . 'No. No. I'm not ready. I'm not ready,' I insisted.

Suddenly there was a rattle of stones in the valley. I almost died of fright. Something ponderous and relentless was moving towards the tent. I held my breath and, it seemed, my heart too. Whatever it was stopped outside the door of the tent. I slowly undid the zip and shone my torch out. Oh my God! I shuddered. A nightmare. I found myself staring at an enormous pair of white eyes enclosed between two ghostly silver horns!

'Shoo . . . Go on, piss off!' I couldn't think of anything more appropriate to say, to try to persuade a beefy-looking, black bull to take his carcass elsewhere. He hesitated, then trotted off down the canyon. If he hadn't, I would have.

I left the bay, rounded Punta Concepción, and found myself back on the open Gulf, and back to my stills, my fishing rod and my survival skills.

Walking the wilds of Baja for any length of time is likely to bring trouble. Walking at night is asking for it. Normally, after dark, I would be safely zipped up inside my tent listening to the radio, but as my confidence grew, caution gave way to curiosity and I started exploring further and further afield.

One night I wandered off to a background of howling coyotes. Using my torch, it was fascinating to watch a praying mantis licking his lips after devouring a meal and a large tarantula still searching for his. Then my flashlight revealed two huge scorpions holding claws. I crouched down to observe them. Unconcerned by my presence, they were content to spend the night gazing lovestruck into each other's eyes, occasionally dancing round and round to break the monotony. Supposedly, these dark monsters aren't as dangerous as their smaller yellow cousins, but I had my doubts. Just seeing one crawl up your leg could give you a heart attack! Like a voyeur, I waited to see how their romance would develop. How do you make love when your partner has a lethal sting in his tail and a pair of pincers capable of ripping your head off? Obviously very slowly! Their patience exceeded mine and I decided to call it a night.

A few steps later, I came to a shocked halt. My foot was hovering over a coiled rattlesnake. A mouse sniffed innocently inches away. He was the luckiest little mouse in the desert that night. A few more seconds and he'd never have known what hit him. The unfortunate snake had a pretty good idea though. All his evil sounding hissing and rattling was to no avail. Holding the torch in my left hand I threw rocks as fast as I could. At first, the bewildered rattler tried to dodge and back away, but seeing there was no escape he moved on to the offensive, chasing and striking viciously at the light until a timely throw almost decapitated him.

I removed the remains of the head with one quick chop of the machete and carried the body of the snake back to my tent for breakfast. I wrapped it in a black plastic bag and brought it inside for the night – I hadn't risked my life to feed some opportunistic coyote. It was hard to fall asleep after all the excitement, especially with a writhing, rattling snake wriggling up beside you. I cut the tail off. That, at least, quietened him down a bit.

A few days later, I was in a desolate place which, apart from being about forty miles north of Loreto, might most safely be described as in the middle of nowhere. I was coming to the end of a day of cliffs and climbs when, on a beach below, I spotted what appeared to be camping equipment. I climbed down. Sure enough, there were bags, backpacks and other bits and pieces. But no one in sight. I put down my pack and explored. Around the point there was a small fishcamp, complete with dogs and three big turtles lying on their backs, but no people. The situation had a sort of 'Marie Celeste' quality about it.

I made the mistake of sitting beside the upended turtles and getting to know them. At first they flippered nervously, but soon resigned themselves to my presence and their fate. I fancied I saw a look of terror in their eyes which seemed to flow with tears. I thought of righting them, letting them go, and disappearing. 'Don't be so bloody stupid and sentimental,' I said to myself. 'There are millions of creatures suffering and dying all over the world, and probably hundreds of turtles lying on their backs in fishcamps all around Baja, and you get emotional about these three. Idiot.'

'Yes, but they're not there in front of me, "weeping" and struggling. I'm not holding their flippers or stroking their throats.'

The sun was setting when the pangas appeared. The fishermen were a little surprised to find me sitting beside their turtles. Still they insisted I dine with them, and explained that the camping equipment belonged to a group of kayakers who had gone off to soak in some hot springs down the coast. I gratefully polished off a plateful of fried fish and tortillas.

Just before dark four kayaks pulled around the point. The party of eight Americans were equally surprised to see me, and I found myself with a second invite to dinner. Loosening my belt, I accepted the kind offer. Who knows, tomorrow there may be only seagull and seaweed.

At first glance the kayakers – who included a mother and daughter, a young couple and a very laid-back hippie – looked a bit out of their depth there in the wilds. The leader of the group, Trudi, was a quiet-spoken, kindly, attractive Californian lady in her late twenties. Although she looked the epitome of the sweet young housewife, she clearly knew her trade and every inch of the coast from Concepción Bay to La Paz. Sitting by the firelight, she marked on my American Automobile Association map, which showed vast areas of nothing ahead, every problem, waterhole, farm and fishcamp. She had kayaked the coast many times. What a stroke of luck meeting her.

She wrote on whole sections of coast such comments as 'easy', 'fairly difficult', 'low cliffs', 'high cliffs', and, worst of all, 'Good Luck!' Pointing to one section midway between Loreto and La Paz, just south of the long abandoned Jesuit mission of Dolores del Sur, she said, 'I don't want to worry you but I don't see how you can get by this. For miles you've got huge cliffs dropping into deep water. There's no way up, and the mountains look horrendous, really steep and jagged.' She triple-underlined her 'Good Luck' on that stretch.

Next morning, Trudi wouldn't let me walk off alone into the wilderness with just information. I was given a stock of dried fruit and milk, granola, oatmeal and oranges, and a gallon of water made doubly precious by the fact that the kayakers were short themselves. I wasn't the only one moved by the tears of the turtles. Before parting, we tried to buy their release, but even chipping in together we couldn't afford the $75 they were worth to their captors.

Resting under cliffs a couple of miles ahead, I waved as the kayaks passed a hundred yards offshore. The breeze picked up and I was amazed to see those little canoes running up sails and drifting effortlessly along. Unfortunately I had to continue bouncing from rock to rock, and sweating my way over beaches of every type. As ever I had my crusties for company.

A week later I arrived in Loreto blistered from the sun and my boots which were falling apart again and almost certainly beyond repair. The awesome, intimidating peaks of the Sierra Giganta Mountains towered above the narrow coastal plain around the town.

Loreto was the first capital of the Californias, and the site of the first permanent European settlement founded by the Jesuit Salvatierra in 1697. It remained the capital of Baja California for 132 years, until 1829 when the town was devastated by a hurricane, and the capital was moved to La Paz.

When Steinbeck visited Loreto in 1940 he found the mission partially destroyed by earthquake and hurricane:

> The roof had fallen in and the main body of the church was a mass of rubble. From the walls hung the shreds of old paintings. But the bell tower was intact, and we wormed our way deviously up to look at the old bells and to strike them softly with the palms of our hands so that they glowed a little with tone . . . The bells on the tower were the special present of the Spanish throne to this very loyal city . . . The Virgin Herself, Our Lady of Loreto, was in a glass case and surrounded by the lilies of the recently past Easter.

Today, the mission has been beautifully restored if one disregards the rather tasteless clock that has been added to the tower. The inscription above the double wooden doors proudly reads: 'Head and Mother of the Missions of Lower and Upper California.' Passing between those doors into the cool half-light I stepped back a couple of centuries, and once again sensed that brotherhood with those others who had felt the call and given their lives to this land – the brotherhood of the believers.

Much of the town of Loreto is lost in a maze of palms and greenery. Every garden seems to overflow with natural shade. I had been given the address of an American couple who had retired to Mexico and had a house on the beach near the centre of town. I hesitated to just drop by, but I'm glad I did. Dick and Sandy were fascinated by my wanderings and made me feel very welcome. With my tongue lubricated with kahlua and gin, I soon had the maps and the stories flowing before them. They invited me to stay the night and share their dinner. Having somewhere to wash, clean myself up and leave my pack, encouraged me to visit the town and look around.

One of the main thoroughfares is called Davis Street. And many houses had the name Davis by the front door. Sensing a story, I made inquiries and was directed to the Pescadero Supermercado where, in a wheelchair, I found Manuel Davis, a delightful, helpful old Mexican. He said that his family was descended from three Welsh brothers who had jumped ship in Loreto in the nineteenth century. Two had stayed, married, raised families, and well and truly mixed up the Welsh dragon with the Mexican eagle.

Loreto also had sizeable groupings of Greens, Cunninghams and Drews. I bumped into one of the Greens in a bar. He told me that he was descended from a British sailor. If I wanted to know more, he advised me to contact his brother, Ildefonso Green, 'the family historian', who ran a little stationery store on the edge of the town.

I walked into the store 'Papeleria Green', and found Señor Green more than willing to tell me about his heritage – after he'd expressed his opinions about adventurers. 'They are all running away from something, often themselves. They are all crooks, pirates, bad people; and too many of them are gringos.'

Ildefonso Green was obviously quite a character. He said his family was descended from Stephen Green who jumped ship in Cabo San Lucas in the 1820s. He had two sons. One went to the United States. The other married and stayed around the tip of Baja.

He was Ildefonso Green Ceceña, the great-grandfather of my informant, and apparently a man handy with the gun. He liked to bring the señoritas down to earth by shooting away their high heels. Even so, he must have had a way with the ladies; he had 52 children! And he still found time to take part in every war and revolution that affected the peninsula. Miraculously, he lived to be 105 years old. He was in his eighties when he fought in the 1910 revolution. On his one hundredth birthday he turned up at the wedding of his grandson, my informant's father, on a horse. He died in 1931.

In case I was becoming understandably sceptical, he added: 'In La Paz, in the Governor's Palace, there is a wall mural of a flag bearing four faces, the first face is that of Ildefonso Green.'

I dined with Dick and Sandy. Dick, hearing of my boot plight offered me a pair of his walking boots. I couldn't believe my luck. They seemed so soft and comfortable. I accepted and left town wearing my fourth pair of boots.

I had to hurry because I was due to meet Ray on a beach twenty miles south of Loreto. I found him asleep in the back of his pick-up. We had a 'party' on the beach, and were later joined by a young American backpacker who looked, with a red scarf tied around his head, like an Apache Indian. He had come to Baja after reading my story in the *San Diego Union*. I think he was amazed he'd actually bumped into me. But that's Baja; in so many ways, such a small place. He asked if he could join us on our journey down the coast, but I had to say no. It wouldn't be fair on the Mexicans for three people to descend on a farm or fishcamp and ask for water. It was bad enough two of us arriving.

Ray was in a strange mood. I suspect the rugged mountains around Loreto had come as a shock, and he was wondering what he'd let himself in for.

Almost immediately we had to face tough cliffs. After climbing 2,000 feet we were rewarded with a view of the coast ahead that was both spectacular and forbidding. There was no obvious way down or along. Ray was very quiet.

'Don't worry, Ray. According to Trudi this isn't even a "Good Luck" stage.'

The joke wasn't appreciated. He picked up his backpack and said, 'I'm sorry, Graham. I can't handle this. I'm going back. I've got a wife and kids, and I want to see them again.'

Suddenly I was back to being alone. Giving up was the one option that never entered my head. I was going to finish the journey or it was going to finish me. Life was so refreshingly simple.

Chapter 25

Baja bites back

Agua Verde is an interesting little settlement about sixty miles south of Loreto, with a fine anchorage. The ranchers and fishermen there had long been accustomed to the comings and goings of yachts, and now many were bracing themselves for the different kind of tourist traffic likely to follow on the new road being run in from the paved highway. I didn't fit into either pattern as I struggled along the beach with my pack but, as ever, I was warmly received and given lots of sound advice. This time it was a dangerous donkey I had to watch out for. It made a change from man-eating coyotes and mountain lions. Out of politeness I tried not to reveal my scepticism.

However the dangerous donkey (or 'burro') was the 'talk of the town'. He had already chased several fishermen and been seen running around crazed and foaming at the mouth. The word 'rabia' was mentioned. This was different. I asked why someone hadn't shot it.

An hour later, I climbed into a fishing boat with three obliging Mexicans; our weapons were a .22 rifle ideally suited for rabbits, an 1894 Winchester left over from some war or revolution, and a battered Konica camera.

We left the shelter of Agua Verde Bay, rounded the imposing cliffs of Punta San Marcial and headed down the coast. And what a coast it was – red cliffs and mountains separating the blue of the sea and the sky. I revelled in the excitement of the hunt and the opportunity to scan the coast that I had to walk. The fishermen kept close in to the cliffs to give me a good view. There was deep water lapping into one cave. No way could I pass it at sea-level. I'd have to climb up and over.

A V-shaped flock of pelicans flew overhead. But one bird was different – a gannet had slotted perfectly into the formation. Still, he looked no more absurd than I did in a panga full of Mexicans with rifles and cowboy hats.

After a run of hot, dusty days ashore, it was always a treat to get out to sea with the Mexicans. Such journeys were never uneventful. Maybe my tight budget precluded the more normal tourist joys of marlin fishing down at the resorts around Cabo San Lucas, but I wasn't complaining. The fishermen had treated me to all the excitement and exhilaration I could possibly want.

The sea was full of life. For a while we followed in the oily wake of a whale, then we had an escort of dolphins, and in the distance a marlin screwed vertically right out of the water and dropped back with an almighty splash. The greatest spectacle of all, however, was passing under the boat, a school of effortlessly gliding manta rays. They were so close to the surface I hung on in case we collided with one of them.

About ten miles from Agua Verde we landed at a beautiful oasis which would have made a perfect campsite among the desolate hills and mountains. While wading ashore, the seriousness of the hunt hit me. Forget rattlers and sharks, a rabid animal is the most dangerous creature alive. An untreated bite is invariably fatal. Just to come into contact with its blood or saliva is enough to doom you to a terrible lingering death.

As we edged into the broad valley with its clusters of palms and bushes, I kept close to the guy with the Winchester. He had the knock-out punch. For several minutes we nervously shouted and called. Just as I was beginning to wonder if we were on a wild burro chase, a black burro dramatically stepped out from behind some bushes a hundred yards away. The plan was clear. We walk up, shoot, burn the body and that's the end of it.

The victim had other ideas. He charged like a wounded rhino. I raised the camera and waited for the shots to ring in my ears.

With the only sound that of approaching hooves, I cast a glance to either side. My comrades had gone! There was a lot of splashing as they ran through the water and jumped in the boat. Needless to say, I wasn't far behind, running for my life.

As suddenly as he had charged, the burro stopped and began browsing contentedly. Again we cautiously left the boat. The quarry was standing quietly in the shade. At fifty yards, the man with the .22 started firing. After each hit the burro shuddered, shuffled around, then stood frightened and staring in disbelief. There was a sudden, long, heart-rending hee-haw. Rabid or not, my heart bled for him. I was glad to hear the heavy report of the Winchester. Bang! Bang! He went down, got up, then agonizingly slowly sank to his knees and rolled over. Still alive as we approached, his eyes followed us, then gazed into nothingness.

I looked at his sad, expressive face. How terrible to kill such an animal, even though it was necessary. There was blood everywhere. As we piled logs on the body and fetched gasoline from the boat, I just wanted to get away.

Ten days later I was doing some collapsing and staggering of my own. Massive cliffs midway between Loreto and La Paz, exactly where Trudi had triple-underlined her 'Good Luck' on my map, forced me to climb inland. Experience had taught me that leaving the coast was a dangerous game, but local fishermen assured me that there was a trail leading up the cliffs that would take me through a maze of mountain canyons back down the other side.

I began the climb with a gallon and a half of water. Things went wrong from the start. I couldn't find the trail, and I left my own trail of blood as I cut and crashed my way up the cactus-strewn slope, an insignificant speck among the huge boulders and rock walls.

It was hot and still. I had drunk half my water by the time I stood on top, and the way down was far from obvious. No trails, no clues, just a maze of arroyos dropping into sheer-walled canyons going nowhere, certainly not going back to the coast. A great block of mountains barred the way.

I had no option but to venture further inland, and my water bottle seemed like an hour-glass slowly draining. The sweat dripping from my sunburned face and soaking my shirt had to be replaced.

After anxious hours battling the unbelievably rugged terrain, I at last found myself in an arroyo falling towards the coast. In the race to safety, I scrambled down the steeply dropping, dry waterfalls and over stacks of rounded boulders. Descents I wouldn't normally have tried had to be attempted.

My tongue was thick and dry. My head was pounding. Inexplicable aches and pains were spreading through my body. I'd pushed myself too hard and rationed the water too strictly. Collapse now, I thought, and it's 'adios'. My only hope was down, down to the sea. No matter what the risk, I had to keep going down.

I came to a T-junction; the canyon before me was deeply set in the mountain but at least it wasn't dropping precipitously. Ironically, its floor was so level, it was hard to tell which way was down. To the left or to the right? My eyes started to play tricks. I walked a hundred yards to the right then swore I was going up. I retreated and went a hundred yards the other way before becoming convinced that too was up. I had to go some way. I chose to the right, at least that was south, the direction I wanted to travel.

Sometimes I was sure I was going down, and then I was sure I wasn't! There was no way of climbing out of the canyon. It was like being trapped in some frightening Victorian alley or backstreet. In places I was sandwiched between two vertical walls of rock 150 feet high and just 30 feet wide. A lone, wild fig tree clung tight and flat against one of the walls as if breathing-in to let me pass.

Forcing myself to use every last moment of light, I came to another, much wider, cross canyon. There at the 'T', where the 'backstreet' spilled on to a major thoroughfare, I thought I was seeing things. In the middle of an arid, rocky, wasteland that probably hadn't known rain for months, there was a pool of water deep enough to dive in and swim around. The water was stagnant and green but pure gold to me. After filtering and boiling, I sat drinking endless cups of coffee beneath a heaven slowly filling with bats and stars.

The immediate crisis was over, but the pool was just a life-raft; I was aboard, but still lost at sea in an ocean of rock. A more terrible struggle was about to begin.

The confluence of the canyons was sufficiently open-skied to allow me to pick up a distant, crackly radio station. A southern preacher was passionately pouring forth on the word of God, the coming tribulation, the certainty of judgement, the need to be saved, and the importance of sending contributions to keep the programme on the air.

For over a year I had listened to the ayatollahs of America pumping out their incredible interpretations of Christianity. Although possibly facing eternity sooner than most, I had no qualms about expressing my own increasingly strong opinions on the subject. I wrote:

> Why do so many Christians use their religion to look down on and condemn others? Where is the humility and compassion? Why are so many Christians paranoiacally concerned about their own salvation? What would Christ have to say about such arrogance and selfishness?
>
> How can men be so blind as to miss the whole point of Christianity; to use the doctrine that bears Christ's name to further their own prejudices, insecurities and hatreds? Much of scripture is contradictory and confusing. Coherence and clarity must come from our hearts and our sense of what's right and wrong, from our sense of what's sound in Christ's teaching.
>
> Christ's teaching is a guide for life. The Sermon on the Mount, the parable of the good Samaritan, the injunction to turn the other cheek, forgive and forget, rather than go in all guns blazing, blindly seeking revenge – isn't that the core of the message? Wasn't Christ's mission to teach us how to rise above the worst aspects of our potentially evil human nature; and to sow love, trust and mutual understanding rather than hate? To do unto others as we would have them do unto us.

Maybe God gives us such an unclear, contradictory message – an eye for an eye and turn the other cheek – so that we reveal what is really in our hearts by the doctrines we adhere to and cherish. That would be a good example of God's wisdom and justice; come the day of judgement the false and unworthy would have revealed themselves by their reading of His word. They would have spent their lives wasting time with the ego-massaging desire to judge, and their fundamentally selfish concern about their own salvation. Maybe the saved are those that say to the God which is being erroneously presented to us, 'You are wrong. I will not serve you. My God should be and is a God of love and compassion.' When Christians are willing to risk their eternal souls for what they believe in, then there is true faith, courage, and hope for the world.

I am a Christian. I made sense of much that I saw and experienced in terms of Christianity. My faith has been deepened, but I would rather be a Christ-like Moslem than an un-Christ-like Christian.

Next morning, I realized my problems were just beginning. Ahead there was an impossible drop, no way down or around. I returned to the water hole to have a cup of tea and think about what to do. The rest of the day was spent exploring one canyon after another, vainly looking for a way out. A grove of prickly pear cactus satisfied my hunger. The slimy pads were better than nothing.

By late afternoon, I found an over-the-top animal trail that seemed to head towards the coast. Loading up with water, I reluctantly left the security of the pool and followed the trail through a maze of ridges and valleys. Eventually it led into a broad U-shaped valley which drained inland! Dilemma! Do I follow it down and away from the coast or up and towards the coast? I headed east directly to the Gulf. The climb up was gentle enough.

I began to look for a place to spend my second night in the mountains. Exhaustion was overtaking me. For two days I had been pushing myself to the limit, and beyond. Something was wrong.

The sun was sinking and I still felt hot, painfully, uncomfortably hot. The inexplicable aches returned. Columns of cacti started spinning faster and faster. My legs buckled as I struggled to put up the tent. Inside it I alternately shivered and sweated. All through the night a thousand images and ghosts raced through my mind – a white horse, the crack of a rifle, and a donkey calling in pain. Then I was alone, at night, by my fire, and a voice said, 'You want to know if you can stand the pain of a rattlesnake bite?' The glowing embers of the burned down fire suddenly coalesced into a hissing snake and shot into my leg. I woke sweating and groaning and frightened before drifting again into delirious oblivion.

The sergeant was back. 'I'm here. It'll be all right. We'll go through this together. You're not alone.' There he was, in that scarlet tunic as large as life. This time I knew him. Of course! I'd conjured up an image of something I hadn't seen for years, the portrait that used to fascinate me as a kid, the grandfather I'd never known except looking proudly down from the wall with his ribbons and medals – my grandfather with the red hair and the red moustache, Colour-Sergeant-Major Mackintosh of the Seaforth Highlanders. He died before I was born. But I knew him through that golden framed painting, through his medals and the stories my father told me of his deeds 'holding together a tottering empire' from his first action at Omdurman in the Sudan to his last on some bloody First World War battlefield.

His service to King and Country was cut short by a piece of red-hot shrapnel ripping into his back. All day the kilted warrior lay groaning and delirious beneath the summer sun, while the battle raged around.

I found myself floating away from my body. I could see the tent below. I was rising out of the valley and into the starry, peaceful sky. It was a beautiful feeling but I didn't trust it. I didn't want to let go. I was fighting desperately to resist, and clung on as if clinging to life itself. A calming voice urged me not to struggle. It was his voice. I floated away then looked down, I was high above the ground, but instead of my tent below, there was a figure in a shell hole. A sergeant! I woke up shouting: 'You're not alone. You're not alone.'

In between periods of feverish babble, I pondered my predicament. My life depended on being able to walk and I couldn't even stand. Suspecting that I hovered on the brink of heat stroke, I drank freely and licked salt from boots white-ringed from wading in the sea. Not able to face another slimy bit of cactus, I swallowed a multivitamin instead.

No matter what, I had to pack and get away before sunrise, to take my chances with the rattlesnakes rather than the heat of the day.

An hour before dawn, I eased on my backpack and struggled weakly along fighting the desire to sink to my knees and lie down. I kept thinking of that poor burro. How valiantly he tried to keep his feet. He knew that if he went down it would be forever.

Wherever possible I used my machete to cut through the thorn and brush. Otherwise I would simply crash through. Nothing mattered except climbing to the head of the valley. I had convinced myself that the ocean and a fishcamp were down on the other side.

The stars disappeared. The sky went through its rainbow range of colours before settling to its brilliant blue. At last, I was coming to the end of the valley. Fresh air and sea birds ahead. Summoning all my strength and will-power, I made it to the top and looked beyond my boots to see a 500-foot sheer drop. There was no way down to the sea except by jumping. The disappointment was such, I had to laugh.

With the enormous morning sun staring me in the face, I backed away and collapsed on to a pile of loose red stones. A hummingbird darted in for a quick look at the strange creature crumpled, chuckling on the ground. A frigate bird swooped down. A vulture circled.

I began psyching myself up to use the Radio Distress Beacon. Would anyone pick it up? Could they find me? Could they get up to me in time? Nothing was certain. I had to try to save myself first.

Both sides of the valley were steep and rocky. Should I go north or south? I started up the marginally easier-looking north wall, and then changed my mind and headed south. I was nearing the top when I thought I heard someone calling me. It was beyond belief that anyone else was up there. I was obviously hearing things. But the sound continued, the only real thing in my whirling mind.

I called back and thus made the acquaintance of Francisco, a young Mexican boy up in the mountains looking for his goats. Seeing my condition, he took my pack and escorted me down those impossible-looking cliffs into his fishcamp where his family looked after me for a couple of days, till I had recovered sufficiently to be able to carry on.

I was relieved to reach the incredibly beautiful little bay of San Everisto, a popular Gulf anchorage. After pitching my tent on the beach, I looked out at the rising moon and the four or five yachts which had pulled in for the night.

The pelicans were executing their last dives of the evening. Just the occasional splash and the hum of a generator broke the descending silence. No more walking for me, sailing seemed the way to go. Then one sailboat chap climbed down into his dingy and rowed towards a large motorboat bathed in light. How nice, I thought, he's probably going over to party.

Under the stern of the big powerboat he engaged the skipper in a conversation that went something like:

'Please, your generator is very loud.'

'Sorry, we need it now.'

'But we're trying to sleep!'

'And we're trying to have a party!'

There was soon a heated argument. The partying skipper was accused of being a bad American. Indignant, he clutched his cocktail, stood by the stars and stripes and drowned out the generator with a vigorous rendition of his national anthem. The poor 'yachtie' rowed away in disgust. I was laughing too hard to pick up his final comments. Next day, I appreciated anew the joys of being alone in the desert.

A few days after that, sweat was stinging my eyes as I pushed my way along a narrow, pebble beach between the sea and the cliffs. I heard a motor. Probably a panga. I turned around. Sure enough it was a Mexican fishing boat, but standing up in the bow was a well-bronzed, totally naked, young lady with the most captivating smile I'd ever seen.

My eyes cleared even more, and I realized there was a big, smiling, equally bronzed gringo steering the boat to the shore. He was modest enough to wear a pair of underpants. I'm not sure which of us was more surprised. I explained my presence and Dwayne explained how he'd bought the boat at the head of the Gulf and set off to motor down to Cabo San Lucas. He'd met Irene in a motel in Mulegé and persuaded her to join him. She was Dutch and had just headed down to Baja in search of adventure.

'You're certainly getting a good tan,' I said. She was perfectly proportioned and quite happy to stand there totally naked in the middle of nowhere talking to two men. 'Could I ask a favour? Could I get a photograph of you? No one's going to believe this.'

'Certainly, how do you want me?'

'Well . . . Perhaps you could just sit up there on the bow of the boat.'

She was happy to oblige. They gave me a couple of oranges, then disappeared down the coast, leaving me with second thoughts about the advantages of travelling alone.

I walked maybe another mile before coming to a tricky point. The tide was too high to let me pass, so I retreated to a shady overhang, threw down my pack, and tried my luck fishing. Nothing doing, I stripped off and waded in for a cooling swim. Suddenly, there was the growl of a motor. The panga reappeared around the point. This time Irene and Dwayne were dressed. I was the one who was caught naked. They had done a bit of snorkeling and had come up with a large fish, some oysters and a couple of lobsters. We made a fire, warmed the coffee, and fried the seafood in garlic butter. Delicious! We ate so much we all dozed off in the afternoon heat.

I had more success with my own fishing and foraging as I made my way down towards the city of La Paz. The increasingly long, hot days ensured that I had a steady supply of rattlesnakes for my frying pan. As a general rule, the rattlers I encountered miles from anywhere were more likely to buzz loudly and reveal their presence, while those I saw near settlements tended to be more silent and therefore dangerous. Perhaps a form of natural selection was occurring. Those that revealed themselves too readily were the most likely to be killed.

Although I regarded myself now as an increasingly efficient hunter and fisher, Baja was always capable of biting back.

Falling asleep on the beach one star-twinkling, balmy night, I was rudely dragged from my dreams by the feeling that someone had applied an oxy-acetylene flame to my foot. I knew immediately what had happened. I sat up and fumbled for the flashlight. Seeing the scorpion, I picked up a piece of wood and slapped it down on his head. That just seemed to make him more angry and inclined to sting everything in sight. I hit him again. The end of his tail fell off. Nevertheless, I didn't feel safe till I'd crushed the crazily running arachnid into the dirt.

'I have been stung on the ball of my foot near my big toe where the skin had built up thickest over the previous months,' I recorded in my diary. 'Burning pain! Again the question, how will I react? I can feel the venom travelling up my leg . . . After 15 minutes, it's as if a long needle has been rammed up the inside of my left leg. The burning pain at the point of entry, being joined by a deep throbbing ache that continues to spread. . . . It's interesting to follow the pathway of pain. At my groin, it seemed to spill over and pour down the other leg . . . Real pain gave way to uncertain pain. A tightness developed in my stomach and pressure seized my heart. Probably just tension. This sting seems much worse than the last one.'

Belatedly inside my tent, I slipped into an uneasy sleep. My leg seemed to be glowing and pulsing with light. The star-burst dots flowing before my eyes became a nightmare scene of scorpions moving in locust numbers over and under and through the tent. They were crawling over the sleeping bag, over my arms and face, stinging and stinging. I was trying to beat them off with a shirt, but they flowed back till I was overwhelmed, disappearing beneath a greenish-yellow quicksand of two-inch-long avenging scorpions.

Hardly had my foot recovered from the venom when I very foolishly allowed it to be bitten by a shark.

It was about 7 a.m. A beautiful morning. The two fishermen turned up on the beach clutching a bottle of tequila. We pushed the boat into the sea and conveniently headed south, enabling me once again to survey the coast I'd shortly have to walk. Although it had felt warm enough on the beach, as the boat raced into the stiff morning breeze, I was wishing I'd brought my jacket. The two fishermen kept themselves warm by passing the bottle between them. I couldn't believe how much they were drinking. At least the sea was warm. I dangled my hand over the side.

The boat curved to a halt beside the net. While it was being raised, a large fin appeared amid a powerful vortex of water just thirty yards away. One of the Mexicans nearly fell overboard as he stood up too sharply. He shouted, 'Shark.' His companion shouted, 'Marlin.' Carrying on the debate, they hauled up the net. It appeared to be a good catch. Over eighty percent of it was shark, mostly hammerhead, but there were one or two big 'sardineros' (mako sharks). By the time the end of the long net had been reached, the boat was full. There was no place to sit without resting your feet on shark.

The net was put back in the rapidly roughening sea. I'd had enough, and wanted to get back to land and feel warm again. At last, we picked up speed and headed towards the fishcamp. My inebriated companions laughed as bucketfuls of water sprayed back over the boat, landing mostly on me.

Huddled against the cold and the spray, I failed to notice that one of the few lively sharks had slid from the top of the pile down to my feet. While the half-pickled Mexicans were commenting on how beautiful the clouds looked, the shark sank his teeth into my foot. There was a sudden crushing pain around my toes. I sat up smartly and began kicking the three foot juvenile 'jaws' till he'd released his bite. He had bruised me and left the imprint of one or two of his teeth, but my leather shoes had protected my foot from anything worse.

After cleaning the catch we all joked about it over breakfast. We were joined by another Mexican, the brother of one of the fishermen. He was even more drunk, hardly able to stand up. After lamenting that he had nothing more to drink, he was given a small bottle of pure rubbing alcohol. What a family of alcoholics! I finished my breakfast watching the fishermen and his wife picking nits from the head of one of their little boys who sat blissfully picking his nose. It was enough to drive anyone to drink.

After so much time alone in the desert one gets used to hearing voices from above, but walking along the beach in the centre of La Paz I was surprised to hear: 'Hey, you crazy Limey, get yourself up here.' I cast my eyes to heaven, to see a bunch of familiar faces hanging from a window of the Los Arcos Hotel. By one of those strange Baja coincidences, just about every 'yachtie' I'd met along the Gulf was up in the hotel bar talking about me. To the consternation of the immaculately dressed hotel staff, I walked up to the large, posh bar, plonked down the pack, and then packed down the plonk, as I joined in the laughter and reminiscing!

La Paz has come a long way since it was the scene of the massacre of Jiménez's men in 1533, and of the failed colonies of Cortés, Vizcaíno and the trigger-happy Admiral Atondo. It is a beautiful city of about 150,000 people, sandwiched between cactus-covered foothills and the great sweep of La Paz Bay. Backed by mountains to the east, the city is well sited to appreciate the spectacular sunsets over the bay to the west. It has been the state capital of Baja California Sur since the destruction of Loreto in 1829; and today, with its excellent airport, fine sport-fishing, abundance of shops, restaurants and tourist facilities, it is fast becoming one of the most popular tourist destinations on Mexico's west coast.

Even so, the city retains a certain tranquil elegance. On beautiful evenings, and most evenings are beautiful, thousands of Mexicans join in the customary stroll beneath the palm trees along the sea-wall, and above the placid blue-green waters of the bay.

The boots I had picked up in Loreto had got me to La Paz. They had been a delight to wear, but they weren't going to last much longer. I went shopping, and bought a new pair. They were the wrong size, much too big and devoid of laces; but they were the right price, much too cheap to resist. I was so pleased to get what looked like a $100 pair of boots for $28 that I splashed out on an $8 mask and snorkel. That was the one extra thing I always would have been glad to carry. The undersea life in the Sea of Cortez gets more colourful and spectacular as you travel south.

After months of small towns and vast deserts, La Paz seemed so cosmopolitan, hectic and exciting. Who should I bump into but Dwayne and Irene? They invited me back to their cheap but comfortable hotel. There I met Ron from Berlin, Tuck from Japan, and Nick from England. I had a room for the night and somewhere to leave my pack. Together, we wandered around the narrow down-town streets eating tacos, drinking coke and generally having a good time.

Dwayne and Irene had seen enough of each other and the boat. He was trying to sell it and get on a yacht to the south seas; she was negotiating a ride on a Dutch yacht to Hawaii. The others were all wondering what to do next and not sure where they were going. I seemed to be the only one who knew exactly what his plans were.

My new boots felt awfully heavy. I was praying they weren't going to cause me too much pain as I followed the coast past beautiful coves that once were the safe hideouts for Dutch and English pirates who were always willing, on the slightest pretext, to fall upon the poor old Spaniards who just wanted to be left alone on their private lake – the Pacific.

Chapter 26

Uphill against wind and current

The Baja California peninsula is at its narrowest and easiest to cross in the region of the Bay of La Paz. There a mere thirty miles separates the Gulf from the Pacific. Further south, the peninsula rises and broadens again around the grey-white granite mass of the Sierra de la Laguna. The arroyos and the beaches around these mountains are so dazzling and white that, under a midday sun, one is as much in danger of 'snowblindness' as sunstroke.

The sand imparts an astonishing blueness to the sea. And when I slid beneath the surface with my new mask and snorkel, I couldn't believe the colours of the fish. It was like swimming in a tropical aquarium: blue and green parrot fish; spotted, yellow-fin surgeonfish; vividly striped moray eels; white-spotted, purple puffers that were changing colour by stages to a pure golden-yellow; king angel fish, and even little cleaning-wrasse who had the endearing habit of nibbling at my freckles and pulling my hair when I entered their cleaning stations.

I spent many hours fishing underwater, dragging a baited hook over the rocks behind me. I had one or two exciting battles. When I hooked a moray eel or a barracuda, I was generally out of the sea like a shot. Otherwise, I'd play the catch under water, with fish charging around, appearing or disappearing as their alarm or curiosity dictated. I saw some fine lobster in their rocky crevices, but without a spear I never managed to catch any.

More than ever I hated leaving the security of the coast, but another long line of towering cliffs and the presence of a beautiful sandy arroyo twisting into the mountains seemed like a seductive invite to try my luck again.

I began my ascent on the coarse, crystalline, granite sand which formed the sterile bed of the arroyo. It was as if the beach had suddenly turned right and cut inland. Flash floods ensured that nothing much had a chance to grow.

I came to a ranch. A cane and palm thatch building with fences and corrals of dried cactus and brush, and sad, shade-hugging mules and cattle. Only the penned-in goats showed any sign of life, and only the noise of their bleating rose above the background hum of the flies.

'Hello! Anyone home?' I shouted. A middle-aged, serious-looking Mexican appeared and invited me into the shade of his shack. His skin was almost of the same colour and toughness as all the home-made saddlery lying around. I asked his opinion about getting through the mountains. He shook his head, saying there was an old burro trail, but it was 'muy malo' – very bad. My heart sank. I had heard the same words used to describe two other trails. They both turned out to be nightmares.

However he was quick to point out that the coast was even more 'muy malo'; and when he realized that I was serious about heading into the mountains, he offered to go with me and guide me through.

'I have a mule you can ride,' he said.

'Thank you, señor, you are very kind, but I must walk; and I'm afraid I don't have any money to pay for a guide.'

His face dropped. He scratched his head. Part of him very much wanted to get away from the ranch and indulge in a little adventure. Another part wondered if he should venture out alone with the loco gringo who travels with no money and would rather walk than ride.

He looked towards his wife and children who sat absolutely motionless across the room, then left me with a cup of coffee and went to fetch a miserable looking mule. The animal was no pet. Its back was dotted with pink patches of raw flesh.

A few old blankets and a saddle were thrown on to the tender back, and cinched tight. The Mexican jumped up, cradled my pack across the front of the saddle, tied the water behind it, introduced himself as Torino, and off we went.

The poor mule looked at me with hate in his eyes. Sensing that I was the cause of this extra work, he seemed to go out of his way to kick sand over me, tread on my foot, and once he suddenly sneezed in my direction covering me with streaks of snot.

We made our way up the sandy floor of the valley till we came to a grove of palm trees, where we helped ourselves to the hazelnut-sized fruits that Torino called 'tacos'. There wasn't much taco left between the large central stone and the hard, crisp shell, but what one could scrape off was date-like and tasty.

The near-naked, white-rock canyons were unbelievably beautiful with their surprising groves of palm trees, and springs of water. Torino was an excellent guide. All the time, he was pointing out the things I might have missed: 'Look! See that bees' nest in the fig tree . . . And that is an alamo tree, very good for shade.' Alamo! Of course! The Alamo, Los Alamos, Los Alamitos – all place names derived from the tree known as 'el alamo' in Spanish. How much I enjoyed that beautiful granite country, and how different with a guide, no anxiety, not one drop of blood. Just fascination.

The trail snaked up and out of the canyon, and meandered for a mile or two along a series of rough granite ridges before taking us down to another palm grove, and more tacos.

We stopped for lunch at an old, abandoned ranch, sitting splendidly on a commanding bluff. Torino had lived there as a boy. He pointed with pride to the remains of the palm-thatched roof that he had helped construct all those years ago.

We carried on up the valley, making it to the top just before the sun sank behind the tallest peaks. Ahead there was a steep descent, then a great plain stretching to the sea. The worst was over. We made camp by the final glow of a magnificent sunset and then sat by the fire talking and drinking coffee.

In between checking on his mule, Torino told me of his encounters with rattlesnakes, mountain lions and skunks. I was surprised to be warned about skunks, but then I recalled the words of Walter Bryant, an American who came to the southern mountains of Baja to study and collect birds in 1890. 'Skunks,' he wrote, 'are more feared by the inhabitants than drought, yellow fever, small-pox or cholera.' Torino explained, 'Skunks, squirrels, chipmunks, you must be very careful, sometimes they are crazy with rabies.'

I was so delighted to be over what was probably the last dangerous block of mountain, that I offered Torino $8 which was more than I could really afford, but it was scant payment for his services. He had guided me through a long day, and it would take him another day to get back.

I made my way along an exhausting stretch of beach with the wind howling and the onshore breeze whipping up a rare old surf. Through the drifting spray and the eternal heat haze, I was surprised to see a yacht almost on its side surrounded by frantically moving figures. As always it seemed to take forever to reach the scene. An American yacht had run aground in the night. The deck was facing the sea and being washed by waves. The unfortunate family were trying to rescue what they could.

I threw down my pack, took off my boots and raced up to help, collecting what I could of what was being thrown, dropped or slid over the side and down the hull, and then piling it high and dry in the dunes.

Throughout the morning, other gringos arrived. They had driven out from La Paz after hearing the SOS on the radio. Luckily a driveable trail led right to the scene. We were all needed. There seemed to be tons of personal possessions and equipment to save – books, maps, instruments, clothes, food, furniture, anchors, sails, generators. I was amazed how much stuff you could cram aboard a 41-foot yacht.

Having salvaged what we could, we carried it over the dunes and down to a circle of vehicles waiting to transport the goods back to a house that someone had put at the family's disposal. It was heart-warming to watch all the yachties rally round to help one of their number in need. As well as Americans, there were Canadians, a couple from New Zealand and a tall young man from Edinburgh.

As the tide rose, the cabin and the deck took a pounding. Glass broke, woodwork smashed. The owners, Dave and Sandy from Ventura, California, watched their beautiful ketch being battered to pieces. Poor Sandy broke down and cried. She recovered her poise, then came over to say: 'Thank you for helping out today. I thought you were a yachtie. I've only just realized you were just walking by.'

'You yachties have helped me countless times. I was glad to be able to do something in return.'

It got dark. I put up my tent. Fires were lit. Out came the booze and the guitars. It was only when someone stuck a plate of food under my nose that I realized how hungry I was.

A young Californian who had spent four years crewing his way around the world, came over and said, 'I've just put two and two together. You're that Irishman walking around Baja, aren't you?'

'Well, I'm half Irish.' I explained, 'Name's Graham Mackintosh, that's the Scottish half, and I was born in London. Where did you hear about me?'

'I read a story in Los Angeles. Did you write something for the *L.A. Times*?'

'Yes, I did,' I said excitedly. 'But I'm not sure if it's been published.'

'I guess it must have been,' he said. 'Here's something to help you celebrate.' He gave me a bottle of rum.

The *L.A. Times*! How I wanted to see that story. It wasn't just for the money or to keep my Angelino friends informed about my progress, it had more to do with my feelings about Los Angeles, the city of my youthful dreams.

Next morning, the wind and the sea dropped considerably. A large tug-like motorboat, the *Esperanza Viva* (Long Live Hope), came around and a line was tied to the stricken yacht. The guys with their loud walkie-talkies had everything under control. Nothing more I could do. I wished them good luck and went back to my long and lonely beach.

Although I was walking what should have been one of the easiest stretches of Baja's varied coastline, the humid, increasingly tropical heat, and the months of bouncing from rock to rock with my too heavy pack, were finally catching up with me. Every muscle in my back seemed to be ripped and crying out for a chance to recover; the new boots were taking their pound of flesh; and without the adrenalin rush of fear and the anaesthetizing effect of heart-pounding danger, I found myself barely capable of putting one foot in front of another.

As luck would have it, on my birthday, I bumped into a hotel owner, the grandson of a former president of Mexico. He was so impressed by my story and my shattered looks that he offered to put me up in the exclusive Palmilla Hotel for a few days on condition that I prop up the bar and entertain the guests with tales of the Baja.

The hotel, the first and arguably the best on the cape, is situated on a low rocky point a few miles west of the town of San José del Cabo. I walked through the white arch and into the hotel grounds. Tasteful, low, white, red-roofed, Spanish style buildings stood peacefully amid a mass of swaying, shining coconut palms. I was shown my room, strategically located beneath the palatial bar and dining-room, and opening out on to the swimming pool terrace overlooking the ocean. It seemed unreal after what I'd been used to.

After a deliciously long shower, I selected my least blood-stained clothes and wandered a little self-consciously up to the bar. But the atmosphere was so intimate, I quickly got to know everyone in the hotel.

Rodolfo the barman was a large, genial, pleasant-looking chap. Suspecting that he wasn't altogether Mexican, I inquired about his pedigree. Surprise, surprise, his grandmother was a MacLish. Another hotel-worker came in with the unlikely name of Eligio de la Peña Collins. He told me how in the early nineteenth century, five Collins brothers jumped off an English whaling ship and settled in the area.

Many Mexicans living in the cape area were descended from English sailors. 'They tend to live to a ripe old age. Many are over a hundred,' Rodolfo said as he mixed me up a piña colada.

When the other guests found out it was my birthday, I had the time of my life. I was given a clean shirt and pair of shorts, and everyone wanted to know about the trip. So, true to my word, I told my tales of six-foot rattlesnakes with three heads. The number of heads miraculously increased with each piña colada.

What a day it turned out to be! I was treated to a fine steak dinner complete with banana margaritas and the most delicious strawberry tart I've ever tasted. I only had to compliment the chef to find another large slice on its way while everyone sang 'Happy Birthday'.

Suddenly the dining-room lights went out, and we late revellers assumed it was just a subtle hint; but the lights were out in the bar and even in the town. It was a power cut. The hotel staff lit enough candles to enable us to see what we were drinking. The mood was perfect. When everyone else crashed out, I sat on the low wall of the bar terrace and listened to the surf below and looked at the stars above. The Southern Cross was well above the horizon.

I recalled my previous birthday in Calamajué, and the simple Mexican kindness I received there. I thought of home and friends and felt a deep contentment. 'What a birthday,' I wrote. 'No doubt about it, I'm a lucky bastard.'

For three days I graced the bar and the dining-room of the beautiful hotel, kept in the shade except to snorkel among the rocks, and left a new, if slightly heavier man.

A couple more days out in the midsummer sun was enough to cancel out the weight gain. I struggled over yet another headland and at last, there it was, three or four miles ahead – Cabo San Lucas. The unmistakable Needles-like line of rocks and the famous arch. A spectacular end to a spectacular peninsula. Fly, sail, drive, walk, however you arrive, there's a kind of, 'you've made it' symbolism about those 'Stately Stones'.

It seemed a fitting end to my Gulf journey to climb out along the granite rocks and rest awhile with my memories. The tallest was La Vigia – 'the crow's nest' – a 500-foot block of grey-white granite affording an excellent view of the ocean around and the bay below.

I was surrounded by ghosts. English pirates and privateers had sat, perhaps on the spot where I was sitting, searching the horizon for a Spanish sail. To the west and south they would have seen the vast Pacific stretching across almost half the globe, and to the east, the Gulf of California beginning its ascent to the Colorado river.

Many pirates came to the cape to try to seize the Manila Galleon, but only twice did the great ship fall to the guns of a foreign power. In 1587 Cavendish had seized the *Santa Ana*; and it wasn't till 1709 that that feat was emulated by his fellow countryman Woodes Rogers.

During the War of the Spanish Succession, Woodes Rogers left Bristol with two ships, the *Duke* and *Duchess*, carrying a total of 62 cannon. Following the Prize Act of 1708, they had no trouble in raising finance from Bristol merchants who sensed there was more money to be had from privateering than honest trade. Spain's ability to prosecute the war depended in large part upon the profits she received from the Manila galleons.

Rogers stopped at a small island off the coast of Chile, where he picked up a sailor named Alexander Selkirk who had been marooned there four years earlier after falling out with his captain. Back in

England, Selkirk's story was to inspire Daniel Defoe to write *Robinson Crusoe*.

Rogers arrived off Cabo San Lucas at the end of November 1709. As well as sending look-outs up to the 'crow's nest' he stationed his ships to scout the seas around the cape. Seeing fires on shore one evening he found a large encampment of Indians near a source of fresh water. They were seen to be: 'the poorest wretches in nature, and had no manner of refreshment for us . . . a dull musician rubbing two jagged sticks across each other, and humming to it, to divert and welcome their new guests'.

A month passed. Rogers had to use all his powers of leadership to keep the increasingly restless crews from fighting among themselves. There was no sign of the galleons, which usually travelled in pairs ever since the debacle of the *Santa Ana*. The decision was taken to sail for home: 'we have prolonged our cruize to the utmost Extent, in hopes to meet the rich Manila ship . . . Fortune has not favour'd us . . . 'tis my opinion that now our time is so far spent, we ought to attempt nothing more in these seas, lest our too long stay might be the loss of all, because the worm has already entered our sheathing . . .'

While preparations were being made to leave, the *Duke*'s lookout spotted a ship: the *Encarnación*. Rogers gave chase and, after a bloody battle in which he was shot in the jaw and the heel, his men boarded the great galleon. They learned of a second and probably richer prize, the *Begoña*. A few days later she too appeared off the cape. The wounded Rogers directed the second battle from the shelter of San Lucas bay using a signaller perched where I was standing. After another fierce struggle, the *Begoña* escaped and limped gratefully into Acapulco.

On 21 January 1710 Rogers set sail for England, arriving a year and half later. The profits of his voyage had been enormous.

I camped on a beautiful sweep of beach close to the town, with yachts and cruise ships in front of me, some buildings under construction to my left, and a line of splendidly sited and comparatively inexpensive hotels and restaurants to my right. Cabo was booming. It was the tip of the peninsula, and the tip of the iceberg for what was to come.

A group of campers had gathered around the shade of a washed-up yacht, which had been blown, along with a dozen others on to the beach. Cabo is well protected from the prevailing north-west winds, but totally open to the south from where that storm came.

Some of the campers looked like they'd been washed up by the storms of life. There was a hard-looking young American who was a walking parody of paranoia; he talked about everyone as if they were murderers and robbers; suspecting that he had the inclination to be both I steered clear, leaving him to the comforts of his knife and his marijuana. There was a Mexican from Tijuana who confessed that he too was once into drugs; so much so he ended up in a mental hospital, where he said he'd found Christ. There were a couple of far-out punk girls from Denmark; and a pioneering young lady from San Francisco who insisted on greeting the sunrise by walking along the beach topless practising some Kung-fu-like movements. She wouldn't listen to those who cautioned that such antics weren't really acceptable in conservative Catholic Mexico. The last I saw of her she was being led away by a Mexican policeman, screaming: 'Why is it all right for all those men to go topless?' Cabo was making progress, but it wasn't quite ready for such liberation.

However, there were people that I had more in common with. Carlos from Spain was a comedian, very likeable and easy-going. He was trying to get aboard a yacht as a cook. He watched my tent for me while I wandered back along the beach to an old graveyard situated behind the dunes on the eastern side of town. I wanted to pay my respects to Thomas Ritchie, another Englishman, who had – you guessed it – jumped ship in the nineteenth century.

John Ross Browne, who had been sent to Baja California to report on the possibilities of its annexation by the United States, wrote about his meeting with Captain Ritchie in 1866:

> Captain Ritchie, an old Englishman, lives here; he is the only European on the cape . . . one of the institutions of the country. Forty years ago he was a cabin boy in a vessel belonging to his uncle. Becoming fascinated with the charms of a dark señorita at San José, he ran away and secreted himself till the ship sailed. Ever since, he has lived at or near the cape . . . He has been the host of all the distinguished navigators who have visited the coast during the past forty years. Smuggling, stockraising, fishing, farming and trading have been among his varied occupations. He now has a family of half-breeds around him, none of whom speak his native language. He has made and lost a dozen fortunes, chiefly by selling and drinking whisky. No man is better known on the Pacific coast than 'Old Ritchie'. He has suffered martyrdom at the hands of the Mexicans. They have robbed him, taxed him, imprisoned him, threatened to kill him, but all to no purpose; and they now regard him as an inevitable citizen of the country. At one time they confiscated his property and carried him over to Mazatlán, where they cast him into a prison; but he survived it all. An English man-of-war got him out of the difficulty, and threatened to bombard the city if they ever maltreated him again. The various injuries inflicted upon him would have destroyed any other man on earth. It will be a marvel if he ever dies.

The white headstone was framed with yellow and red flowers. The inscription in Spanish read:

TOMAS RITCHIE
Born 23 March 1809.
Baptized in the church of Santa
Maria Woolnoth, Lombard, London
Died 13 November 1872

You have died dear husband
and adored father.
I have lost my repose.
We have lost our protection.

Weeping at our misfortune
we are inconsolable orphans.
We cry at your memory
for all eternity.

I was a couple of dollars short of being penniless and my boots needed repairing. It was time to return to the United States. But after the crash on the way down, I didn't fancy hitching a thousand miles along Baja's roads, so I began frequenting the harbour and the yachtie joints looking for a ride north. The uphill journey against wind and current is not as popular as the downhill run to Cabo. There are usually a few desertions.

Although I didn't have any real experience, I had other things in my favour. There was a 44-foot ketch, *The Debonair*, sailing for San Diego. The Dutch owner had put the yacht in the hands of a skipper to sail her back. Skipper Bob was about thirty, a lean, swarthy, jolly chap with a distinct Mediterranean, almost Arab, appearance; but he was as American as apple pie and rock 'n'roll.

'I heard you might be looking for crew' I shouted from the harbour wall.

'Aren't you the guy from England who is walking around Baja?'

'I guess so. There can't be too many of us.'

'Hey, we were just talking about you the other day, in La Paz. Sandy, my girlfriend, read about you in the *San Diego Union*. Get your stuff. Yes, we'll take you. I've got a feeling we're going to need your sense of humour.'

The yacht had a few problems, the engine was suspect, the toilet wasn't working, and the survival equipment was basic to say the least. My Radio Distress Beacon and Solar Still were looked upon as valuable additions to the emergency bag to be grabbed 'if the yacht sank'!

The good news was, I was promised $100 on arrival in San Diego, and while that was sinking in, Bob and Sandy rowed ashore and came back with 'some last minute supplies', five cases of beer and seven blocks of ice. 'I don't like to eat when I'm at sea,' Bob explained, 'I usually just drink beer.'

I was talking to Sandy as we motored out from the harbour into the bay. Shapely, tanned, attractive, early twenties, she seemed a very likeable girl, confessing that this was her first sailing experience. Suddenly the sky darkened, it became cooler, but there wasn't a cloud in the sky. An eclipse! It was almost total, and lasted for ten minutes. I watched it through the sextant hoping it wasn't an omen.

We anchored in thirty feet of water about 150 yards from shore. Bob put on a mask and snorkel and slipped over the side to inspect the bottom. 'We'll have to scrape her, she's really fouled. Can you give us a hand, Graham?' I donned mask, snorkel and flippers, stepped down the ladder, slipped beneath the crystal-clear warm water and started earning my pay.

It was easy enough scraping off the green and brown 'moss', but there was a lot of hull and the keel went way down. Watching the fish rising to investigate the cloud of scrapings reminded me of an incident which the Atlantic oarsman, John Fairfax, describes in his book *Britannia*.

> I dived into the pleasantly warm water and with my knife began to scrape away the hundreds of barnacles that had managed to attach themselves to the bottom of *Britannia* . . . Zestfully scraping away, I was soon surrounded by a slowly sinking cloud of cirripeds . . . I was suddenly overwhelmed by an unaccountable desire to look behind. I turned and as I did so, my heart thumped in mad crescendo – then stopped cold. Hardly twenty yards away, stealthily rising from the depths . . . one of the biggest sharks I have ever seen was coming straight at me, slowly but steadily.

My eyes nervously scanned the clear blue water lest the noise and the cloud had attracted a similar unwelcome visitor. With all the twisting and turning and swimming upside down, it was easy to become disoriented and light-headed. After half an hour we had the cleanest bottom in the bay, and I was glad to climb out of the water and grab a beer.

We sailed out to sea past two big cruise liners, one Dutch, the other British. If only their pirate and privateer forerunners could have seen these monstrous white pleasure boats!

We passed the famous arch. Bob took a hefty swallow of beer and smiled broadly. The wind ripped into us as we lost the shelter of the bay and headed into the Pacific. The contrast between one side of the rocks and the other was unbelievable. The Pacific surf was crashing thunderously against the arch and shooting twenty or thirty feet into the air. The boat was leaning so much, I thought for one horrible moment that we were going over. A wave washed along the deck. Crash, bang! Suddenly I realized why the uphill run was not so popular. Bob shouted above the hiss of the sea and the scream of the wind, 'We'll take turns at the wheel. Two hours on, four hours off.' I began to wonder what I'd let myself in for.

Sandy seemed to have similar misgivings. The colour and the confident smile slipped from her face. She threw up on the deck. I had never been seasick in my life, but when I went down into the cabin, I came close. I was glad to get back up.

At sunset we saw a whale to port, a ship to starboard. The land disappeared. The stars came out. I finished my watch and went below. After a miserable twenty minutes with my head buried in the 'honey-bucket', I too threw up. Feeling a little better, I went back on deck and got hit in the face by a flying fish. People do this for fun, I marvelled!

Feeling O.K. in the morning, I tried a bowl of granola and immediately threw up again. Bob stuck to his beer. I gave it a go, and after two days I had my sea legs, and was better able to enjoy watching the blue-footed boobies following us above and the dolphins following us below.

As the days went by, I began to feel totally secure. I loved being alone on watch at night – the Southern Cross behind, the mast moving across the Milky Way, the noise of the wind and the slap of the wires on the metal mainmast, and, if the engine wasn't running, the comfort of my radio. But it was a dangerous game taking a piss over the side, especially with the others asleep. While unclipping and clipping the safety harness one was vulnerable to a slip or a rogue wave.

After a week at sea we were barely a quarter of the way up the coast. Bob, who was irritable at our lack of progress, decided to motor into Bahía Santa Maria at the southern end of Magdalena Island. The dirty-looking water bore a strange, foul smell. I wondered if there was a red tide in the bay; but even if we had anchored in a sewer, it would have been worth it to be able to eat and drink properly, get a good night's sleep, and escape from the endless crashing and crazy leaning.

When we left the following night, I volunteered to take the first watch, having to be really careful rounding Cabo San Lazaro in the dark – many ships had come to grief there. With that first miserable day at sea now seeming like a year ago, I sat in the open cockpit clutching the wheel, watching the heavens, and the Stars and Stripes fluttering from the back of the mizzen mast.

Bob became really ratty and depressed when we ran out of beer. To cheer him up I sacrificed the bottle of tequila I was taking back to Dave and Denise Bowyer. We had a few slugs, then, with Sandy at the helm, we sat together inside the cabin listening to the short wave radio. The trouble in India between the Sikhs and Hindus was making the news.

First we tuned into the BBC and listened intently to the account of the terrible events. Then we picked up an American station and the newsreader kept talking about 'Sicks'. Bob and I rolled around the cabin laughing.

One day I had just come off watch and was down in the cabin alone. I kept staring at the portholes which were just too small to squeeze through. I recalled vividly one of the most horrendous photographs I ever saw. In the summer of 1970, a fire aboard a German freighter had trapped several sailors below decks. One tried to squeeze out of a porthole headfirst and became stuck at his hips. The photograph showed him hanging arms down and face up to heaven while the flames roared inside. The horrified rescuers could do nothing.

All I could think about was fire. I walked up front and checked that the forward hatch was unobstructed. It wasn't. It was full of ropes, sails and junk, so I cleared it a bit and familiarized myself with how to open it. A fire at the rear of the boat, I thought, and that would be my only escape. I checked around for the fire extinguishers and made absolutely sure I could find them in the dark.

It was 2.00 a.m. I felt a hand shaking me. 'Your watch, Graham.' I struggled out of my bunk and into my foul weather gear. As my brain cleared, I noticed that the enclosed cabin was anything but clear.

'What's all that smoke, Bob?'

'It's just the motor running.'

'No, there's too much smoke; and I can smell diesel.'

Something seemed to change on Bob's face as if he too felt something was wrong. He opened the engine-compartment door and crawled in with a flashlight.

Having been brought up with a fine sense of how to underplay a crisis, I was a bit perturbed to hear Bob scream, 'Oh no! Shit! Fuck it! Grab this. Get rid of it.'

A few seconds later he shoved out a five-gallon plastic drum of diesel. I looked at it bewildered.

'What do you want me to do with it?'

'Take it away. Throw it up on deck.' He disappeared back into the smoke-filled compartment. More screaming and cursing.

'Shall I kill the engine? Do you want a fire extinguisher?' I asked, trying to be helpful.

The only reply I got was a loud long, 'Shhhit!' Then another five-gallon container of diesel was pushed out along with the warning, 'Fire hazard! Fire hazard!'

Something had burned a hole through the container. Diesel was slopping out with the roll of the boat. The plastic was bubbling and smoking, and the cap and the container had fused. I took it up on deck with my heart beating as loud and fast as the still throbbing engine.

Bob came out looking ashen and shaken. 'God! That was close.'

We sat down on the bunk, and I felt a belated surge of shock, as I heard how one of the diesel containers lashed inside the engine compartment had worked loose and fallen on to the engine, on to the red hot manifold. The plastic had burned right through and the diesel was spilling out over the engine and down into the bilge.

'We were lucky', he said. 'We would have had burning diesel sloshing from one end of the bilge to the other. In seconds we would have been a fireball, another mysterious disappearance in the Pacific.'

I went up on deck, took the wheel and pondered why I'd thought of fire all day. The moon sank into the ocean, leaving the Milky Way as a glowing arch across the heavens. We seemed to be sailing right beneath it. As a new day showed its promise in the east, I looked up at the Stars and Stripes trailing from the stern and found myself singing, 'Oh say, can you see by the dawn's early light what so proudly we hailed at the twilight's last gleaming.'

I tried to forget that the American National Anthem had been written during an incident in the British–American war of 1812, when a prisoner aboard a British warship saw that, in spite of the British bombardment, dawn revealed that the Stars and Stripes was still flying above the besieged fort. It seemed so appropriate: the 'flag was still there', and so were we. We had come 'through the perilous night'.

The next day the Pacific fell to a flat calm. What appeared to be a floating log turned out to be a large shark. Great patches of the sea were blood red with shrimp-like rock lobsters, a favourite food for whales. The colour intrigued me. Not the best camouflage in the world.

Needing diesel, beer, ice, bread and sleep, we decided to motor into Bahía Tortugas (Turtle Bay). 'You'll love this town,' I said to Bob and Sandy. 'If you remember the article I wrote for the *San Diego Union*, I described it as my favourite town in Baja. The people were really great to me.'

We all looked at the 'Baja California Cruising Notes':

> A citizen of Turtle Bay who has been important to visiting yachtsmen is Adan Geraldo Talamantes, a mechanic from La Paz who moved to Turtle Bay with his wife and three children in 1956. Since then his family has increased to eleven healthy children. If you want fuel, if you want water, if you want advice or if you just want to chit-chat Adan is your man in Turtle Bay. The American yachtsmen have nicknamed him Gordo.

Bob stepped ashore and greeted Gordo and one of his sons with hugs and handshakes, asking them to come aboard for a few beers and some 'chit-chat'. The Mexican said he would love to but was not allowed, pointing to two armed marines standing overlooking the harbour.

'There's been a bit of trouble, and it's best we wait till it dies down.'

Bit by bit we pieced together the story. Just a week before we arrived, two American yachtsmen had been murdered in the harbour. It all began when Robert Kavaney, an experienced single-handed sailor, arrived on his 41-foot ketch and dropped anchor. The divorced father of four went ashore, met a pair of young Mexicans, and invited them aboard his yacht. After a lot of drinking, a fight broke out and Kavaney was overpowered and stabbed to death.

After unsuccessfully trying to start Kavaney's yacht, the two Mexicans took to the dinghy and headed towards another yacht riding peacefully at anchor in the bay. Bob and Marlene Pugh were returning to the United States after spending almost six years sailing around the South Sea Islands and Hawaii. They were almost home. When the Mexicans reached their yacht they asked for beer, and when their request was turned down they forced their way on board, pulling knives and bundling the hapless couple below. For forty-five minutes the American couple were tied up and hideously assaulted until Bob Pugh was stabbed and shot in front of his wife.

While the assailants were trying to start the motor, Marlene Pugh managed to break free, leap over the side and swim screaming towards shore. She was pulled from the water by a woman on another yacht, and the alarm was raised.

The two Mexicans had managed to up-anchor and motor towards the open sea. As they were leaving, a trimaran entering the bay, picked up the distress call and gave chase. They were shot at several times for their trouble. However, they forced the sailboat on to the rocks at the entrance to the bay where the Mexicans made their way ashore and ran off into the hills.

Meanwhile officials in the town were asking the distressed and shocked Marlene Pugh if she could give any clues to the identity of her attackers. One of the men, she recalled, had several tattoos including a very distinct one with a message in a scroll. Hearing this, the interrogating official turned white and almost collapsed. 'You have just described my son,' he said.

The two fugitives in their twenties were soon hunted down and cornered by the Mexican marines. A few bursts of automatic fire persuaded them to surrender. They were taken into police custody and charged with murder.

When Marlene Pugh was being driven out to the airport, to be flown back to the US together with the body of her husband, the whole town turned out along the streets. They offered flowers and apologies. Many were in tears.

In spite of her terrible ordeal Marlene Pugh was still able to say: 'They were just a couple of bad eggs. I bear no ill will towards the people of Turtle Bay or Mexico.' Although she seemed willing to forgive, I sensed the town would be a long time forgiving itself.

I wandered through the streets happy to see so many familiar faces, but the light had gone from their eyes. The town had lost its innocence. The very soul of Bahía Tortugas had been shocked and shamed.

After another week of two hours on, four hours off, we sailed past the submarines and battleships into San Diego Bay. It had been an unforgettable, exhilarating three weeks. I was $100 richer, and had thereby recovered more than half of the money I took into Baja nearly six months earlier. I was keen to get back to Los Angeles to see how much money the various newspaper articles had brought in.

Chapter 27

Newspaper business

Three large envelopes were waiting for me in California, one from the *San Diego Union*, one from the *Valley Daily News*, and one from the *Los Angeles Times*. The *San Diego Union* had sent me a couple of copies of the article I'd already seen and a cheque for $200. I opened the envelope from the *Daily News* to find that they too had published the article and sent me a cheque for $50. Full of enthusiasm and optimism, I opened the envelope from the most prestigious West Coast newspaper, the *Los Angeles Times*. All it contained was the returned manuscript and a letter from Jerry Hulse, the Travel Editor.

> Dear Mr Mackintosh:
> Early on in your writing career you'd better get one thing straight: you don't pitch the same story to two different newspapers in the same circulation area. I had fully intended to use your story and pay you well, but then I saw a similar piece appear in the *Valley Daily News*. This completes our journalistic relationship.

I was stunned; not just at the financial loss, which was bad enough, but at the loss of the *L.A. Times* as a market, and the aggressive reply. I wrote back:

> Dear Mr Hulse,
> I have just returned from Cabo San Lucas to find your letter censuring me for offering an account of my walking adventures in Baja to both the *Los Angeles Times* and the *Valley Daily News*.
> Clearly, I have offended against a basic journalistic principle. Please accept my apologies. I am not a journalist or travel writer. My purpose

in walking around Baja is – hopefully – to inspire the unemployed youngsters I taught back in my native England, and to open their eyes to possibilities beyond the street corner.

Try anything new and you're going to make mistakes! How often I've said that hoping to reassure and embolden my students.

I apologize for being wrong on three counts.

(1) Never having tried to write for newspapers before, I had little expectation that there would be any interest and was far too pessimistic about my chances of getting even one article published.

(2) I mistakenly assumed the articles were sufficiently different in content to pose no problem.

(3) Not being a 'local' I also failed to appreciate the local geography and circulation areas involved.

You have certainly put me 'straight'. Thank you for returning the article and photographs.

Sincere apologies.

As there was no reply at all from the San Francisco *Examiner*, I was concerned enough about the photos I enclosed to give them a call.

'I sent you a story and some photographs last January, and I haven't heard anything since.'

'Did you send a self-addressed, stamped envelope?'

'No I didn't.'

'Well that's why we didn't return it.'

'What happened to the photos?'

'Oh, we'll have thrown them away by now.'

'What! For the sake of a twenty cent stamp, you've thrown away my negatives?'

I was quickly learning the rules of the newspaper game. The $250 was nevertheless a godsend, but it didn't last long. It cost me more than that to process my film. A cheque for $80 arrived for my last two *Mexico West* articles, but that soon disappeared on phone calls and correspondence and living in L.A. Once again I was penniless.

I wrote to everyone from the *National Geographic* to the *National Enquirer*. I rang the Los Angeles *Herald Examiner* and the *Valley Daily News* asking if they'd like to interview me or take a story. They said they'd call back. They never did. I began to wonder if the *L.A. Times* had blacked me. With desperation overcoming my natural shyness, I approached every potential sponsor I could think of, and those I approached before I approached again.

Persistence paid off. I got the break I needed from a company that had already turned me down. Trying a slightly indirect approach, I wrote to them to complain about the 'bargain' boots they had sold me, and enclosed a newspaper cutting outlining my trip. Amazingly, they agreed to supply me with all the footwear I'd need to finish the walk. I chose two pairs of modern, lightweight, comfortable boots, and two similar pairs of hiking shoes. I expressed my gratitude by arranging for a local newspaper to cover the story.

The half-page feature, which included a photograph of the enormous range of boots on offer in the store, began:

> Graham Mackintosh was always telling his students back in England to go for a walk. Practically none of them did, so he took his own advice. He is still walking. All the way around the coastline of Baja California. Alone . . .
>
> With his flaming red hair, complementary fair skin and pale blue eyes, Graham is not well suited to spend most of the year walking the perimeters of torrid Baja – and he's the first to admit it . . . Graham found his largest expense to be hiking boots. To date he has gone through five pairs . . . Hearing of his boot problem, the Sport Chalet of La Cañada stepped in . . .

Thanks to the publicity, I managed to arrange another sponsorship deal with Pacific Mountain Sports of La Cañada. They agreed to kit me out with a new tent, water-containers, kettle, cooking vessels, flashlights, sunscreen, insect repellent, snake-bite kit and all the other bits and pieces I needed.

Before taking off again, I wrote follow-up articles for the *San Diego Union* and the *Daily News*, a couple of articles for a new magazine called *Viva Baja*, and my old, $40-a-story, staple, *Mexico West*. In spite of their initial cool response, they had published all my articles and made my adventure well known among regular Baja travellers. And they even arranged a lift back to San Ignacio with one of their Travel Club members.

Chapter 28

Assistant

The final leg of my journey from Laguna San Ignacio along the Pacific coast to Cabo San Lucas would be relatively flat, but there were other problems. The worst being the hundred-mile-long, mangrove fringed, steamy expanse of Magdalena Bay, and miles of empty beach north and south of the bay might sound great, but walking on soft sand with an enormous load on your back is unbelievably tiring.

I had one of my brainwaves. Thinking my back had taken enough punishment, and I'd spent too long alone, I made up my mind to finish the journey with an assistant. I had said I was going to walk around Baja; I never said anything about carrying my own pack!

After the lift down, I found myself in San Ignacio with twice as much equipment as I could possibly carry, including ropes, old leather belts and an assortment of bags and containers. It seemed appropriate to step inside the cool, four-feet thick, lava block walls of the beautiful old Jesuit mission and offer up a few prayers before going in search of a suitable companion. I wanted to call him 'Rabies'; but my mother insisted I call him Bonny. Considering the worry I was causing her, it seemed the least I could do to defer to her wishes.

There are several little ranches on the road from San Ignacio to the great lagoon of the same name. I remembered seeing some burros when I walked along that road the previous December. A Mexican in town suggested I try Rancho Batequi.

I stood at the beginning of the road waiting for a vehicle. An hour later a truck approached. It was weighed down with hay. A good sign, I thought. The Mexican driver was a little surprised when I explained, 'I need a ride to somewhere where I can buy a burro. Do you know any ranches where they have burros for sale?'

He thought deeply, 'No! I can think of no burros on this road. We all have pick-up trucks now.'

'What about Rancho Batequi?'

'We come from Batequi and we have no burros. You are better off searching in San Ignacio.'

A group of kids approached and one of them said his grandfather had a burro for sale. Leaving all my equipment at a nearby house, I went to see the beast.

Granddad was obviously in no hurry to part with his donkey. 'It is a good clean burro and it is not for sale. I need him for many tasks.' Then he seemed to have afterthoughts. Any gringo crazy enough to want to buy a donkey might be crazy enough to part with lots of money. The old boy suddenly said $50. That was far too much, but I wanted to see him anyway. I wandered down to the bottom of his garden with half of San Ignacio trailing along.

He was huge, more like a horse; but far from being calm he ran around the garden kicking out and crashing into all the man's fences and fruit trees. Three Mexicans tried in vain to hold him. I'd seen enough. He was too powerful for me. 'Thanks for letting me see him. I need time to think about it.'

The donkey hunt continued. 'There's a man with donkeys near the school.' 'Try Señor Rodriguez in San Lino.' 'See Martin who runs the trailer park near the Hotel Presidente.' At the end of a long and frustrating day, I was directed to the house of a tall, serious, dignified, typically rustic and unshaven Mexican: 'I hear you might have some burros for sale?'

'Why do you want a burro?' he asked suspiciously.

I told him.

He shook his head in disbelief. 'It is very difficult and dangerous, señor, only the crazy would attempt such a thing. It is better to go to Cabo San Lucas by bus. I have no burros.' I was learning the ways of Mexican trading. First deny you have the object desired, then gauge the disappointment, and set the price accordingly. I must have looked as shattered as I felt.

'Come to think of it,' he said, 'I have the perfect burro for you. Just $70. He is strong, clean and very docile. Come back in an hour and I will show him to you.'

'But I don't have $70. I have just $30 and no more.'

'Come back in an hour and I'll show you a $50 burro.'

An hour later I returned to see him holding a sweet little white burro. It was love at first sight. It was Bonny.

'He is perfect for you, señor, very clean, very strong and very tranquil. $50.'

I offered $30 and not a peso more. I wanted him badly but I guessed the Mexican wanted the money just as badly. When the sun was sinking it was down to $40. I insisted I only had $30. I pulled the money from my pocket and waved it in front of his face.

It had been dark over an hour before the weary vendor realized I wasn't kidding; it was $30 or no sale. He seemed pleased enough to be stuffing the money into his pocket as he gave me the lead rope and a receipt. 'Sold to Señor Mackintosh, one white donkey.'

'Are you sure he is calm, healthy and strong? He will be carrying all my equipment. If he collapses or runs off into the desert, I'll be in trouble.'

Never having owned anything bigger than a hamster before, I accepted his assurances on faith.

'You crazy limey, you've done it now,' I chuckled to myself as I walked Bonny back to my tent secreted amongst the palm trees. Above the rustling palms a half-hidden explosion of stars twinkled across the desert sky. As I turned around, alternately singing 'Little Donkey' and laughing, my new amigo looked at me dumbfounded, unaware that he was the last element in a scene that was biblical in its simplicity.

I tied him to the trunk of a palm tree, gave him what I hoped would be the first of many goodnight hugs and watched him contentedly wrapping his lips around the fallen dates. Like so many called to greatness, he had no idea of the dramatic changes about to befall. 'You and me fella, we're going in search of adventure.'

Next morning I walked into town to buy a scrubbing brush. I found the man who had sold me the burro in a store buying a big bottle of tequila. He smiled and disappeared with suspicious haste.

Trying to load Bonny was a problem. He refused to stand still and wasn't averse to the odd little kick. I placed some old sacking and a few bits of cardboard across his back. Then I put on the 'burriqueta', a saddle-like frame made of wood and bits of car-tyre and seat-belt which I'd bought for 50 cents. It was crude but effective.

I placed my backpack on one side of the frame and a counterbalancing kit-bag containing the tent, sleeping bag, foam mattresses etc., on the other. Three smaller canvas bags attached to a pair of belts slipped over the top. They contained such items as food, kettle, and pots and pans. I also had six white water jugs (chlorine bottles) tied together in pairs and placed front and back of the main load. With the water, and food and the 'rubbing alcohol', I guessed Bonny was carrying about 120lbs.

With everything loaded and secure – or so it seemed – I dragged my wheezing and groaning amigo to our first ordeal. To get on the road back to the coast we had to walk through San Ignacio.

We had barely gone a hundred yards when the town drunk came over and, vampire-like, attached himself to the neck of a burro convinced the world was going berserk. Shaking him off had the unfortunate effect of shaking loose the pack. It slipped as I tried to hurry unnoticed past the busy plaza. We had to stop. A crowd gathered. Mexicans smiled sympathetically. Tourists asked me to pose. Cameras clicked. Then . . . 'Oh no! Here come the police. Behave yourself, Bon. If I get a ticket for disturbing the peace, I'll be tempted to add another for assault.'

The threat seemed to sink in. He stood as good as gold while the kindly officer helped me repack, and sent me on my way with just a friendly 'Good luck'.

Around the corner, it all proved too much for Bon. Rearing, kicking and dragging me round in circles, he terrified a family of Mexicans who took refuge over the nearest wall. I would have done the same had I been able to get by the whirling vortex of white. At last he calmed down. I flashed an embarrassed smile at the family emerging like shell-shocked soldiers from their fox holes. I had a feeling 'good luck' was the commodity I was going to need most.

Both Bonny and I had a lot to learn as we made our way out to the surf-lashed shores of the Pacific. Like convicts chained together, we eyed each other warily. Not wanting to hazard everything on the whim of my four-legged friend, I carried a small backpack with water and other essentials.

The donkey's load was tending to slip to one side. I had to stop several times to adjust it. This pleased Bonny enormously. The only thing he seemed to prefer to a snail's pace was no pace at all. I had to drag him up all the hills. He was better downhill, merely threatening to collapse and die if forced to take another step. We didn't get far that first day, just three miles, a fraction of what I could have done alone.

At sunset, I tied him to a tree. While I attempted to untie the load, Bonny collapsed and looked a picture of total exhaustion. He spent the rest of the evening rubbing himself against a branch and scratching with his teeth. Trying to win his trust, I ran the brush through his hair. Little things kept springing out on to my arm. I examined them closely, dropped the brush and leapt back. So much for being clean! He was crawling with lice.

All my old squeamishness returned. I stripped and washed myself thoroughly, leaving my hair caked with soap. I hesitated to get into the same tent as the equipment that had just come off his back. Several of the bags were covered in what looked suspiciously like white eggs. Sure enough, every hair I pulled from the donkey had several of the eggs attached.

I had no appetite as I lay in my tent. With lice on the brain, I couldn't stop scratching. After spending half the night agonizing about the problem, it seemed the only sensible thing to do was cut my losses, put it down to experience and carry on with what I could carry. Calm, clean and capable! I'd been done. The donkey was about as calm as a stepped-on stingray, covered in parasites and easily capable of being overtaken by a snail.

I woke to a beautiful sunrise and the sound of Bonny scratching with his teeth. I examined him again. More lice sprang out. No way could I get on top of them with a brush. Before dumping the donkey, I decided to seek advice at one of the ranches ahead. I still had no appetite. And Bonny wasn't eating or drinking either.

It took me an hour and a half to pack and secure the load. As I was putting the finishing touches to it, he kept trying to move off. I pulled him back. He kicked out and just missed me. I slapped him hard. He took off into the desert with baggage flying everywhere, and me hanging on desperately with rope-burned hands.

I stopped at a ranch set in an oasis of date palms. 'There is a special powder, señor,' the kind old rancher said. While he went to fetch it, I tied Bonny to a post. The rancher mixed the powder with some water and attempted to spray away the parasites. In return the ungrateful donkey tried to kick the ranch down. We sprayed the pack and the burriqueta. The spray did the trick. As I brushed, dead lice were falling from his coat by the thousand.

I left the ranch a lot happier than when I entered it. Then I met two young Mexican boys on the road. They walked with me for a while telling me about what burros like to eat, and did their best to show me, a knot moron, how to tie the most useful knots. I noticed that if they walked behind him, Bonny suddenly quickened his pace. No longer hanging back, he was actually overtaking me. I wondered if I should hire a Mexican to walk behind all the way.

That night, I tied him to the type of tree the youngsters recommended, and was delighted to put up the tent to the sound of munching.

Next morning, back on the road to the lagoon, a truck approached from behind, I pulled Bonny to one side and held him firmly. The truck stopped and out jumped two mean looking Mexicans with rifles.

'What are you carrying?' they asked, obviously meaning business.

'Just camping equipment, food and water,' I replied.

One stood back threatening with his rifle while the other went through the side pockets of my backpack.

'Is there a problem?' I said, wondering if I was being mugged. I was shown a card. Federal Police! Federales! They're normally after guns and drugs.

The searcher pulled out an unmarked kilo of white powder wrapped up in a black plastic bag. His companion pointed his rifle at my heart.

'It's for tortillas. It's flour.'

He tasted it and wrapped it up again quite disappointed. He pulled out everything else that looked suspicious.

I explained politely that those are water-purifying tablets, and that's just a roll of plastic bags.

'Show us your passport and papers.'

They were buried deep inside the pack. To unearth them, I had to tie Bon to a tree and unload him.

'Here are my documents.' The federales took a cursory look, lowered their weapons, walked back to their battered old truck and drove off into the sunset.

I was having trouble getting Bonny to drink. He wouldn't touch water in the cut-off plastic jug I'd fashioned. He didn't mind drinking from the stream at the ranch but any kind of container scared him to death.

By the time we arrived at the lagoon Bonny was pretty thirsty. He raced up for a drink. Ugh! He looked at me as if to say, what have you brought me to? Even the water isn't drinkable.

Along the shore of the lagoon, I came across a deserted fishcamp. Among the stuff lying around was an old tartan blanket and a wide, blue metal bowl, exactly what I needed. The bowl even had convenient carrying handles. I filled it with water and sat under the shade of a tree by the lagoon waiting. For two hours Bon approached with interest then stood uncertain before retreating. He put his nose in, then backed away. His fear was amazing. I fed him almost half my dates over the water bowl, some I 'accidentally' dropped into the bowl. In the end I left him alone tied close to the water. After a while, like a genteel old lady sipping tea, he protruded his lips to make contact. Suddenly panic, the noise of his own slurp had him trying to uproot the tree in his effort to get away.

He had to drink. All afternoon I waited. He returned for another sip, then I watched with almost as much satisfaction as Bon himself, when I saw the water-filled waves running up his throat. He polished off two gallons.

We picked up six gallons of water from a fishcamp and then disappeared into the wilderness – very, very slowly disappeared. Bonny knew how to pace himself. At times I felt I was dragging a reluctant whale from the lagoon.

We followed a soft, sandy road along the edge of a salt flat that stretched away to a shimmering, uncertain horizon. Sometimes the road meandered through a sandy desert of low hills and stunted lomboys and ocotillos. Sometimes it took us across boot-crunching salt.

It was a dead, dreary, monotonous landscape. Apart from a circling crow and a passing bird of prey, nothing moved, nothing disturbed the sunbaked silence. Nothing, that is, except Bonny who knew how to break a man's heart with pathetic coughs and wheezes. I was still expecting him to drop dead any moment.

A remarkable coincidence gave my spirits a boost. That morning, while opening a can of beans for breakfast, I broke my imitation Swiss Army knife. Not just the can opener; but all the blades were loose and threatening to fall out. I hadn't gone two miles before I found a real one, half-buried in the salt-sand by the lagoon. It was tarnished but perfectly serviceable. Once again, I felt that someone up yonder was looking after me. I walked on singing the song that was fast becoming the anthem of my trip, 'How great Thou art'.

At last, after a couple of days we came to the real desert with cardóns, cholla and pitahaya. And the pitahaya were once again in season. There were many big fruits. I shared some of the best with Bon, trying to win his heart with kindness.

One evening we came to a valley containing a pool of water. Was it fresh? Bon was willing to hazard a delicate sip and, after a moment's thought, suck up a couple of gallons.

Pleased by the way he was settling down, I made the mistake of taking my eye off him while I perused my map. Bon found a nice patch of powdery dirt, sank to his knees and tried to roll over, crushing two of my precious water bottles and a good deal else beside. I shouted for him to get up but he didn't seem able to with the heavy load. When he finally struggled to his feet, he was very frightened. I had to steady and reassure him.

Making camp, I tied Bonny to a mesquite tree. The stillness of the night was punctuated by hearty munching and the ghostly noise of battle. Grasshoppers sounded like distant bursts of machine-gun fire, while the far away surf thundered like the barrage of a thousand guns.

Next morning, Bonny stopped and kicked over a little round cactus, which he ate spines and all. He went for it as if he'd recognized a special treat. He was definitely desert wise.

We saw our first rattler during the hottest part of the day. My guard was down. I was too busy looking up admiring the beautiful cactus forest we were walking through. I stepped innocently over the big red diamondback. When snake and burro came eye to eye all hell let loose. My arm was wrenched from its socket as my amigo decided he'd had enough adventure and took off back to San Ignacio. Dragged over the evil-sounding serpent, I had to dance my way out of trouble before dashing after everything I held dear. Burros can really shift when they want to. When I finally caught him, I tied Bon to a cactus, grabbed my machete and went back to see if dinner was still there. He was, coiled under a bush, and quick to hiss as I approached. I picked up a pair of sticks and tried to pull him out by the tail.

Apart from the hissing, the snake seemed unusually docile, almost inviting me to get complacent. Only when a rock thudded into the sand by his head did he start rattling. I used the sticks to retrieve the stone. As I did so, the snake struck out with a viciousness that almost sent me running back to San Ignacio. In a moment he was transformed from a sluggish, timid creature into one defending its life with surprise, power and speed. I threw the stone again and missed. The snake almost screamed as he struck again. With the racket reaching a fearsome crescendo, I threw once more, and caught him square on the neck, a few inches below the head. Even so he was still striking feebly. I raised my machete and sliced off the head. With great care, I eased out the fangs from their fleshy sheaths. As I squeezed, a lot of clear yellow venom oozed out. The venom sacks were loaded.

Despite instinctive revulsion, I picked up the still wriggling body of the snake and, with it dripping blood, curling up and wrapping itself around my arm, I went back for Bonny. He backed away nervously.

For the rest of the day I remained charged with adrenalin, looking for snakes everywhere. As I made camp, Bonny seemed restless too. I had to tie him securely. I boiled the snake in fresh water, then ate the stringy white meat off the comb-like ribs.

I enjoyed better fare when I reached San Juanico, a beautiful town which sits proudly on a bluff overlooking a long, splendid beach set in a gently curving bay. It was bigger than I expected, there were several streets, a couple of restaurants and stores, and even a church a bit like the 'prefabricated iron monstrosity' at Santa Rosalia.

As I passed the newly opened restaurant Estrella del Mar, the proprietor ushered me in to chat. I tied Bonny to a lamp-post, stepped inside and ordered a beer. Price 50 cents. And a full lobster dinner was on offer for just $3. I was tempted but I needed the $3 more than the meal.

Susano, the restaurant owner, pulled out a letter he had just received from a friend in California. He asked me to translate: the writer said how much he liked Susano's family, his town and his country, and he thanked him for his assistance with the broken down dune-buggy, and wished his wife a speedy recovery.

Susano explained that she had fractured her skull while performing in the circus in La Paz.

I was asked to help with one or two problems Susano was having with his English. As he was now in the restaurant business, he needed to discriminate soup from soap, and warm from worm. He offered me a lobster to take on my journey. 'I shall mention your hospitality and your prices in my next article for *Mexico West*,' I said. Then I headed toward the local store. As I paced the streets of town, I had that 'arriving gunfighter' feeling. Children followed at a respectful distance, curtains moved, people woke from their siestas to stand and stare. Real *High Noon* stuff.

Inside the store, a small business with next to nothing on sale, I somehow ran up a bill for $2.50. I was presented with the bill on headed paper. As I tried to pay, the owner of the 'Mini-Super' gestured for me to put away my money. 'It is a present for you,' he said.

When I asked where I could buy tea, he disappeared around the back and returned with a handful of some dried herb. 'This makes good tea.'

'What is it?'

'Damiana.'

Damiana is a herb that grows only in the south of the peninsula, where it was revered by the local Indians as a powerful aphrodisiac. Today, it is more commonly sold as a liqueur which is taken either neat or added to the tequila in Baja Margaritas.

As I stepped back out on the street, a group of men approached who seemed the worse for drink. The oldest, a man about fifty, didn't seem to know what planet he was on! His companion, a stocky fellow in his twenties, threw his arms around me and hugged me with such emotion that I wondered if he'd been drinking damiana. 'My house is your house,' he said, taking my arm. 'Please have lunch with my family.' He was so insistent, I went along not wanting to insult his hospitality.

I was introduced to his wife and mother, and then fed the traditional fare of lobster, tortillas, beans, coffee and beer. While I was dutifully stuffing myself, another fisherman entered the house and was equally insistent I have my next meal with him.

I took some photos and promised to send them when I finished the trip. I was given the names and addresses of other family members I'd likely meet in the fishcamps down the coast. I turned down an offer to stay there the night, by pointing to my patiently-standing, still-loaded burro, saying I had to find a place for him to graze.

On the way down to the beach, I stopped at a cervezeria – a shed serving as a beer depository – and bought a litre bottle of beer. It was for the burro, I joked. Before I knew it, a basin of water was on the ground for Bonny. The merest hint that he was thirsty was enough. Unfortunately, he wouldn't touch it, so I used the water for my jugs and thanked the smiling Mexicans for their thoughtfulness.

Back in the street, another man approached and offered me a place for the night, and some alfalfa for Bon. What incredible hospitality! I could stand it no longer. I wandered down to the sanity of the dunes, convinced they'd mistaken me for somebody else. Perhaps they had been expecting a guru with a burro?

I made camp on the lovely beach and, as there was no grazing in the dunes, I took Bon into a nearby arroyo and tied him to a cactus.

Back at the tent, I tried some damiana tea. There was music in town, a dance or a celebration. I found it strangely sad. Hoping Bonny was O.K. I picked up a couple of cookies and walked up the arroyo by moonlight thinking I'd give Bon a hug and whisper a few sweet nothings into his big ears. I carried my flashlight, but the moon was so bright it was hardly necessary. A hundred yards up the valley and just twenty from Bon, I heard a barely audible click. It stopped me in my tracks. I shone the light. Just a yard ahead and to the right, a rattlesnake was coiled and ready, and beautifully camouflaged in the moonlight.

I shouted my goodnights to Bonny, and made my way back to the tent munching his cookies.

Chapter 29
Mag Bay

It was another beautiful Baja morning. The sea was calm. The wide beach was flat and firm, a treat to walk. I was leaving San Juanico in excellent spirits and Bon was excelling himself. He seemed in a hurry to get somewhere. Probably he was nervous of the surf.

The waves rolled in, rising like windows into the crystal-clear blue sea. Shapes and shadows and silvery flashes chased one another through the water, till the whole lot came crashing down in a wall of blinding foam.

Every time I stopped to fish or swim, Bon would look at me suspiciously. He was a funny old donkey. He didn't seem to like it when I was around, and he didn't seem to like my leaving him either.

The water remained comfortably warm and the surf fishing continued to improve as I went south. I was back to my Gulf-like ways of hooking one for the pot and another dozen for the sheer fun of it.

I came to an apparently never-ending wall of sand cliffs, up to two hundred feet high. The beach became softer, and Bonny's little hooves were sinking in alarmingly deep. All the time the rising tide was forcing us closer to the wall. And there was no way up, certainly not for the donkey. We both grew increasingly anxious. Bonny would go wild if the surf caught us against the cliffs. I put strength into his tiring legs by taking him closer to the waves. Convinced that they were reaching for him, Bon suddenly found the energy to trot while I ran alongside trying to steady the load.

With the sinking sun touching the Pacific and the waves touching the wall of sand we, at last, came to a scaleable slope where I attempted to drive Bonny up to safety. It wasn't easy. He was exhausted. I had to shout and hit him a few times to get him to the top of what turned out to be a long line of dunes.

The dunes were covered with desert burgrass – an endemic grass common throughout the dry, sandy hills and flats of the peninsula, but especially common on the Pacific coast south of Laguna San Ignacio. The grass gets its name from the terminal, half-inch wide, bright green burs it produces. These burs, which are covered in long, sharp spines, readily fall from the stems and are easily picked up by animals, birds, and passing gringos; but not so easily removed.

To my amazement Bon was happy to eat the grass, spines and all. It was a blessing because there was nothing else. I tied him to a small lomboy and gave him a gallon of water while I cleared a patch of sand and put up the tent.

The view was marvellous. I sat out late staring at a brightly lit cruise-ship on the moon-sparkling ocean. The black outline of the coast must have been visible to the passengers gazing from the lounges and the decks. Listening to the noises of the night, I was tense and alert. The gentle caressing breeze momentarily brought back a feeling I had almost forgotten – loneliness.

Next morning, as I stuck my head from the tent, I was greeted by an effusive heart-warming hee-haw. Bon looked dramatically pink in the early morning light. I took a picture. The camera shutter sounded different. I finished the film and before slipping in a new one, checked that the shutter was operating properly. To my horror I discovered that it wasn't operating at all. Suspecting the insiduous incursion of a grain of sand, I tried blowing, sucking and banging, but to no avail. The camera had finally succumbed to the conditions. I was amazed it had lasted so long. What to do? I couldn't carry on without a camera. I either had to get it repaired, and that could only mean hitching down to La Paz, or I must return to the States yet again. It was a decision I wanted to put off as long as possible.

At least Bon was behaving while I packed. I threw on the water bottles and made the final adjustments to the ropes before picking up my own pack. Swinging it up, I noticed something shiny and black just where it would be resting on my shoulder blade. A black widow! The biggest I had ever seen. The dunes seemed to be a favourite haunt of the deadly spider. Thank heavens I'd learned to keep my eyes open.

I led my amigo back down the dunes. The final descent was too steep. Bon refused to go down. I hesitated to pull or push him. For several minutes we stood sinking on the brink of the ten-foot drop looking at one another. Finally the dune lost patience and collapsed beneath us. We both slid down in an avalanche of yellow. After dusting ourselves off, we continued on south.

A strange new cactus was now in evidence, the fascinating and aptly named 'creeping devil'. It is related to the pitahaya, but instead of forming impenetrable, sprawling thickets, it grows along the ground, taking root as it goes and dying out behind. Common enough on the fertile Magdalena Plain, it occurs naturally nowhere else in the world. The growing point often rises up as if sniffing the air. The pleated green stems are covered in inch-long spines; and the fruit is pink to scarlet, very similar to, but smaller and not as tasty as the pitahaya.

The creeping devils, the desert, the donkey, I thought everything looked so lovely. Unable to take a picture, I found myself staring, studying and trying to fix every image in my mind.

There on the Pacific coast, nearly all the vegetation is covered with a tattered shroud of Spanish moss, an epiphyte which clings by fine roots to trees, shrubs and cacti, drawing its moisture and nutrients from the dews and fogs of the Pacific air.

Spanish moss, unbelievably a relative of the pineapple, lends its host plants a weirdness that is hard to imagine in a desert that is already incomparably weird. Anyone with a fevered imagination could see ghouls and ghosts all around. There is nothing more eerily beautiful than such a desert seen with the sun burning off the morning mist. A photographer's paradise, and I didn't have a camera.

Apart from its aesthetic qualities, Spanish moss was useful because it burned fiercely. Even after rain or a heavy dew, it dried rapidly and was invaluable in getting the morning fire going.

I had to make a long detour around an estuary-like lagoon that was riotous with life. Butterflies jerked about in dizzying numbers, and the variety of bird life was phenomenal: geese, ducks, herons, egrets, and the usual assortment of long-legged, long-billed wonders filled the air with their honks, squawks and grunts. There was a sound like a passing jet, and I looked up to see a pair of falcons swooping and diving at each other. Judging by all the swirling and splashing, there was no shortage of fish in the 'estero', or crabs. Lizards and snakes were appearing in unprecedented numbers. Rabbits and hares bolted or froze as they saw fit, and more than one confident, curious coyote stood his ground to watch the slow approach of the strange man with his white donkey. The desert was so overgrown that it made for very difficult passage; the thorns and spines noisily scratched the bags and containers protruding from Bonny's back. I had reached the beginning of the vast and fertile Magdalena Plain. Beautiful though it was, I was beginning to think back fondly to the familiar barren stretches of desert I had traversed along the Gulf.

We came to a ranch at the head of the lagoon. While Bon downed several gallons of water and I filled all the bottles, the old couple who lived there tried to explain that there was a strange place up ahead. They spoke about it with awe, but I couldn't quite make out what they were saying. Something about Germans and the sun. I began to wonder if a tribe of primitive, teutonic sun-worshippers had planted their temples down the coast.

Leaving the ranch, we entered a mile-wide canyon and threaded our way between the great cardóns. There was good grazing for Bon, and there were many pitahaya fruits to share. It was hot, the hottest part of the day, the time one least expects to see a rattlesnake. But I was rudely shaken by a sudden fierce hissing and the sight of a rattler wriggling at my ankles. The battle was on – first to control the donkey and then to kill the snake. The end-result – I had something tasty to add to my evening meal of rice.

A more pleasant surprise was to find a small freshwater stream flowing into the side of the lagoon. Bon was able to drink his fill while I borrowed his bowl to wash myself and everything from the snake to my socks.

I had to chuckle at my own absurdity as the rising full moon found me munching on a four-foot, fresh-boiled rattler. Pulling strips of the white meat off the ribs with my teeth and dropping them into my bowl of rice, I thought of how far I'd come from the more dainty eating habits of the West Kent College staff canteen.

Next morning I left all fired up with coffee, determined to solve the riddle of the Teutons. Bonny was less curious. He had found his donkey paradise and he didn't want to go anywhere. Only after I'd dragged him about a mile, did he make any kind of effort to put one hoof in front of another. I had learned how to use his fear of water to hurry him along the beach, but there in the desert we went as frustratingly slow as ever.

Cresting one ridge, I suddenly understood how Cortés must have felt when he looked for the first time on the magnificent capital city of the Aztecs. I was looking down on something that seemed to have been taken from a 'Star Wars' movie set – an incongruous, futuristic, complex of towers, huge shiny dishes, and other high-tech structures.

We wandered down into the fishcamp, village, town – no word seemed appropriate to describe the coastal settlement of Las Barrancas. It didn't belong in Baja. Nor did the primitive fishermen's shacks belong on the same planet as all the impressive technology. I had found the teutonic sunworshippers all right. 'Only the Germans could have thought up this lot,' I said to myself as I led my dumbfounded burro into 'town'.

Passing the school, we picked up an audience of cheering, laughing and waving Mexican children. I waved back and asked one of the bolder youngsters if there was a store. He directed me to a small blue house down the street. The 'store' had the basics but no beer. I was disappointed. I had been dreaming of a cold one all day. Instead, I treated myself to some milk and cookies. A curious but polite crowd gathered around. Thankfully, Bonny remained calm. He was probably exhausted. I still had nightmares about the time he spooked in San Ignacio.

One of the fishermen, who spoke better English than I did Spanish, explained that the plant was a joint German–Mexican project experimenting with wind and solar energy. Wanting to know more, I wandered over to pay my respects to the German engineers. The first person I met had only just arrived from Europe. Clearly, the last thing this jet-lagged, culture-shocked German expected to see was a desert-bedraggled Englishman walking a bewildered little white burro.

I'm not sure who was more curious about whom. But I was invited into their simple quarters, offered a beer (I hadn't wished in vain) and introduced to the other seven Germans. They all worked for the Dornier company (of World War Two bomber fame). One of them was married to a Mexican girl, and he was a more or less permanent resident. The others apparently stayed for just a couple of weeks at a time.

We had much to talk about. I was given a room for the night, so I tied Bonny to a cactus, gave him a cookie and told him to look after himself while I went back to help my fellow Europeans deal with a barrel of beer they had just brought in.

Before anyone got too drunk, I asked if any of them fancied his hand at repairing a camera. One tall, blond chap managed to take the camera apart, but after tinkering around a bit he shook his head and put it back together again.

I drowned my sorrows in the beer and asked about their projects. Apparently the plant was producing twenty tons of fresh water daily by solar evaporation of seawater, and an additional twenty tons by diesel powered osmosis. Solar power was also used to heat water and to make ice, which they were producing at the rate of two tons a day for the local fishermen. They also had in operation a shockfrost room for rapid freezing and a cold storage room. They had just finished boiling and freezing a ton of lobster which had been shipped to La Paz. Wind power was harnessed by an enormous propeller spinning smoothly in the Pacific breeze.

When the room started spinning I decided to hit the sack and leave the die-hard Bierkeller-trained professionals to carry on making merry to the early hours.

Next morning, I was given a huge breakfast and invited on a high-tech tour. I slipped a roll of film into a borrowed camera and snapped my way around the plant. It was a fascinating, futuristic vision of Baja's potential. What a prospect, obtaining ice, fresh water and heat from the wind, the sun and the sea! I should have felt good about this clean and efficient utilization of energy, but I loaded my donkey and walked away a little saddened by what German genius and technical skill might do for the forgotten peninsula.

After a few miles I met some Mexican fishermen who warned me not to continue down the coast as I would soon find myself cut off from the rest of Baja by a lagoon which marked the beginning of the mangrove complex of Magdalena Bay.

Never having visited 'Mag Bay' before, I had little idea what to expect. My initial plan – to walk in the desert just inland from the mangroves – had already been abandoned in the face of the dense profusion of cactus and brush growing there.

I tried walking the very edge of the swamp with my panicky sinking burro. Strange slurps and cracks emanated from the mangroves. Ugly twisted roots clung to the mud like evil talons with their prey. Fiercely spined creeping devils reached for us from the overgrown desert. Repellent devouring mosquitoes filled the dank air. Bon's coat was black and alive. My hands were gory red from swatting our torturers.

I thought, with sudden appreciation, of what Steinbeck had written about these awful swamps:

> We suppose it is the combination of foul odour and the impenetrable quality of the mangrove roots which gives one a feeling of dislike for these salt-water-eating bushes. We sat quietly and watched the moving life in the forests of the roots, and it seemed to us that there was stealthy murder everywhere. On the surf-swept rocks it was a fierce and hungry and joyous killing, committed with energy and ferocity. But here it was like stalking, quiet murder. The roots gave off clicking sounds, and the odour was disgusting. We felt that we were watching something horrible. No one likes the mangroves.

After a couple of days struggling with such conditions, and thinking about the hundred miles of it in front of me, I decided enough was enough. Much as I hated retreating, we retraced our steps back to a desert clearing, made camp and watched a stunningly beautiful, mangrove-wrapped sunset while I considered alternatives.

They weren't marked on my map, but the desert by Mag Bay is criss-crossed by roads cut in by PEMEX, the nationalized Mexican petroleum company, while exploring for oil and gas. Most ran dead straight. Some were used; some not. Some ended against mangrove-lined inlets; some against fences. Several ended in deserted fishcamps. All bore the imprints of countless wriggling snakes. With impenetrable desert all around, I had no option but to follow them to who knows where.

On one trail leading to somewhere, judging by the recent tyre marks, I came across a dead rattlesnake with a mouse half-hanging from its mouth. It had been run over while trying to slip its victim down its throat.

One evening when I was on full rattlesnake alert, Bonny suddenly snorted and I nearly jumped out of my skin. Convinced that he did it deliberately, I waited a minute then shouted to the heavens. Poor Bon! My nerves were fraying and I was increasingly likely to take it out on him.

We were leaving the little town of Santo Domingo heavily laden with food and water. Bon was almost buckling at the knees. I asked a Mexican rancher where I could pick up a trail near the water. He was very helpful, but he was no communicator. I understood most of the words he used, but they made no sense, and neither did the maps he drew in the sand. They seemed upside down and inside out. I gave up, and walked away pretending I understood.

We soon got lost and found ourselves fenced-in in every direction. Several times we had to retrace our painful steps. I became increasingly conscious of Bon's heavy load. The tension and the anger rose; anger at the fences, the directions, the undermined desert into which Bon continually collapsed, but also at the donkey and finally at myself. 'What a time to fuck around with all this weight,' I shouted at the heavens. When Bon naturally pulled back from me, I really went bananas and beat the hell out of him. It was stupid and self-defeating, and I felt terribly guilty that evening as I sat by my fire listening to Bon munching nearby. As I put a log on the flames a scorpion suddenly appeared, running frantically up and down till he finally fell into the fire.

I walked over to Bon and talked to him affectionately. He sniffed a little as if he were reluctantly forgiving me. I felt I hadn't broken his trust entirely. With the lights of Santo Domingo glowing on the horizon, and a pair of owls calling each other across the night, I wrote:

> Why today's tension and anger? We have water and food, and there are lots of pitahaya fruits. What am I afraid of? I'm afraid of my own feelings, the depth of my own anger and frustration.

Instead of easing, the tensions and frustrations multiplied. As well as my fear of snakes, scorpions were turning up in my shoes, on the pack and, once, even in my tent at night. Luckily, I wasn't stung, but I took that invasion of my security badly. My temper grew as short as the day, with all the packing and unpacking, loading and unloading; the constant barrage of mosquitoes and the interminable itching; the bur grass sticking to everything; the ants; the spiders' webs; the countless crawling sounds of the night; I was struggling to keep my cool.

Bon was acting increasingly sullen and hanging back with his 'I hate you, you took me away from my shady palm tree' look. I had to pull him more and more. Something had to give.

'I must break this cycle of frustration, anger and violence,' I wrote, 'I hate hurting him, yet I must pull hard knowing the rope is cutting into his flesh. Of course, he pulls back. He's a dumb animal, doesn't know better. I expect more from myself, there has to be an answer!'

I learned – we learned – burro management the hard way, alone and on the trail. This burro was definitely not going to be led around by the nose. Recalling how he hated someone walking behind, I tried tying two lines to him. Then I stood behind with a line down each side, horse and plough style. At first we were all over the place but then we got the hang of it. Keen to keep away from me his pace quickened markedly; and if he strayed, I only had to pull the appropriate side to get him back in line. Finally, confident that I could control him with just one rope, I had him walking those Baja back roads like an eager puppy straining at the leash. Stalking behind, rope end ready, the constant battle of wits was now heavily loaded in my favour.

I was back to my singing, humming, and feeling very pleased, and all Bon could do was raise his tail and direct the occasional hiss in my direction. 'Cut it out, Bon, you're not a rattlesnake. You can't fool me.'

We were racing along one straight track looking for a place to camp when there was the buzz of a very real rattlesnake. Bon had his customary fit and dragged me fifty yards as I dug my heels in the sand. I tied him to a tree, pulled out my machete and went over to see if the snake was still there. He was. And it was a monster; five foot long, fat, alert and waiting for me. The black and white ringed tail with its long, madly vibrating rattle was sticking out from beneath a bush. I thought of chopping it off, but it was going to be all or nothing. As there were no rocks around, I picked up a stick and tried to drag my dinner into the open. However, the uncooperative serpent kept crawling back, getting increasingly agitated.

He seemed to have wrapped himself around something. I dropped to my hands and knees to get a better look beneath the bush. As I did so, a tail-up, top-heavy scorpion came tottering along the road like an old drunk. That and the sinking sun brought me to my senses; I gave up on the monster snake, returned to Bon and raced ahead.

As we approached the town of Puerto López Mateos, I was surprised to see another large industrial works. This one was more conventional, some kind of mining and dredging operation. It was late. All the workers seemed to have gone home, so I made camp just off the road and helped myself to some water from a conveniently located tap. Bon thought it good enough to drink two whole bowls-full.

Truckloads of workers arrived with the sunrise, and I was bombarded with a dawn-chorus of hoots, horns, waves and greetings. But my main preoccupation that morning was ants. I woke to find a horde of them inside my tent. They had got in through a hole in the floor, ripped by the bur grass. They were two-tone black and red. I killed over a hundred of them.

After chatting with some of the amiable workers, I followed the dusty trail towards town. A pick-up stopped, and I had the pleasure of meeting one of the managers of the Roca Fosforica Company. Speaking perfect English, he explained that the entire Magdalena Plain from Santo Domingo to Puerto San Carlos was composed of low-grade phosphate which they were extracting for fertilizer. They were planning to build a canal inland to flood the extraction sites and thereby minimize the environmental damage. I'm not sure I understood the reasoning, but I told him it sounded very impressive.

He replied tactfully that it wasn't as impressive as what I was doing. He asked me about my journey, then said, 'You have vision, staying power, and you know how to take risks. You have what it takes to succeed.' I felt I was being paid a great compliment.

As I walked into town, a school bus passed by, throwing up a swirling cloud of dust. The dust got under my contacts, leaving my eyes watering and red. Bon was edgy. Puerto López Mateos (population 3,000) was one of the few modern, sizeable settlements along the shores of Magdalena Bay. There was a road out to the main highway. The time had come to get the camera repaired. I found a place to leave Bon and most of my equipment, then hitched down to La Paz.

The tourist office directed me to a small shop on Avenida Reforma where I learned, 'It will cost about twenty dollars and you will have to leave it with me a couple of days.'

I looked in on a young Mexican I'd met while hitching. He invited me to stay with his family till the camera was ready. Then he had a brainwave. He wanted to climb the 7,000-foot peak of La Laguna near the Pacific coast south-west of La Paz. I agreed to go along. We hitched from La Paz to the beautiful, sleepy, tropical town of Todos Santos with its broad, unpaved streets and bougainvillea gardens.

From there we walked and hitched to the base of La Laguna, beginning the long, steep climb in the worst of the afternoon sun. Eighty degrees felt like one hundred. We made camp at about 3,500 feet, finding a perfect patch of green grass on which to pitch our tents. By then most of the cactus and true desert vegetation was behind us. The dense brush off the trail was more chapparal, and there were more and taller trees.

While I cooked a dinner of pasta and chili, Antonio told me how he had last ascended La Laguna on an exercise with the Mexican army. His company had taken two days to get to the top, with mules carrying the baggage and some of the men who dropped out. That was ten years before. Antonio looked a little out of condition now and I wondered if I'd be carrying him before we got to the top. It was a cool night and we were glad to retire to our sleeping bags.

I was in my tent listening to the radio and staring at the stars through the thin tent fabric. Suddenly I noticed a group of strange lights moving among the stars. Quickly I unzipped the tent and stuck my head out into the hushed darkness. The four lights flashed through the trees, travelling in formation north-west to south-east. They looked like the landing lights of an aircraft or distant car headlights, but they couldn't have been either. The night was absolutely still and quiet. There was no noise of a plane and they were obviously not shooting stars. A mystery. I couldn't imagine what they were. My desert journey had made me a believer in many things. That night UFOs joined the list.

Next morning we continued up the trail. Apart from its steepness it was a straightforward climb, in the same way that walking from New York to Los Angeles was an easy walk, or rowing across the Atlantic was an easy row. The problem comes in keeping it up. Antonio was really suffering. I was too, but I kept on going. Is that what fitness is?

Approaching the top of La Laguna, one gets the impression of stumbling upon a lost world. Suddenly there are pine trees and oaks, jays, doves and woodpeckers, and in a basin-like plateau an unexpected grassy meadow through which flows the silver thread of a stream linking up a series of pearl-like pools. In the pools and the stream water-beetles jerkily row beneath the surface, dodging dragonfly nymphs and caddis-fly larvae, while other insects stride across the top.

After so many spines, so much desiccation, and the pungent smells of discouraging saps, I was amazed at the flowers, and the soft, green lushness. La Laguna is 'an Eden' of unnamed plants and insects, a botanist's and entymologist's paradise.

Even in the sun, the air was crisp and cool. Only the bright blue sky and the extruding grey-white granite boulders testified to a kinship with the desert below. The mountains of La Laguna were continually being uplifted, rejuvenating the streams cascading down their steep canyons, and keeping the unique and fragile wildlife safe from the destructive heat below.

Except in the mountains of the far north, there is nothing else in Baja quite like it, an oasis or an island in a desert of sand, rock and cactus. The area has been declared a National Park. The view from on top is breathtaking. One can look down on La Paz and its bay, and on the thirty miles of desert hills and plains that separate it from the golden beaches of the Pacific.

There were a few Mexicans up there. They were the first I had seen walking and backpacking in Baja. La Laguna, apparently, was an increasingly popular destination for La Paz students. If the lakes and pines looked incredible to me after twenty months in the desert, I'm sure it was even more unbelievable to young men who had lived all their lives with cactus and blue water.

We needed a blazing fire that night. I couldn't believe it could get so cold. A freezing mist mingled with the smoke as we discussed the UFOs of the previous night. They had all seen the 'omnis', as they called them, and no one had a plausible explanation except a sullen philosophy student who looked and thought a lot like Trotsky. He made it obvious that he thoroughly disliked Americans. Everything was their fault, including the omnis. Perhaps he was right. Unable to get warm by the fire I crawled into my sleeping bag and shivered the night away. It seemed a long time since I had first struggled with the heat and sun of Baja. Then anything over 20°C. had felt almost unbearably hot. Now anything less than that felt decidedly chilly.

I woke to find frost on the ground, and a frozen water bottle. Someone checked the max-min thermometer at the weather station. The temperature had fallen to −4°C.

Antonio and I tagged on to a jolly bunch from La Paz and, leaving Trotsky with his head in the clouds, we made our way down with the aid of a few swigs of tequila.

Standing in the summery warmth of the mountain foothills, we looked back at the towering granite mass of La Laguna. It gave no hint of the secrets that lay beneath a solitary cloud punctured by a peak that seemed to be forcing its desperate way up, like a drowning man struggling to keep his head above water. It thrilled me to think that although I would never have attempted to climb to the top of Ben Nevis in Scotland, or Snowdon in Wales, I had climbed the 7,000-foot La Laguna.

Back in La Paz, I collected my repaired camera, paid the twenty dollars, and hitched back to Puerto López Mateos where I was greated by a wildly hee-hawing Bonny. He'd actually missed me. After feeding him some goodies, I felt obliged to spend a while on my knees in the church preparing my mind for whatever was ahead.

In La Paz, I'd picked up some more 'special powder' for Bon. He stood quietly and seemed to almost enjoy being washed. I had to laugh, he looked like a soggy, half-drowned rat. I noticed a few dead lice on his coat, but only about six rather than the sixty thousand he shed the previous time.

South of López Mateos, the creeping devils were particularly in evidence, growing as bizarre colonies radiating out from little sandy hillocks rising above the flat, empty desert. They seemed like a caricature of Custer's Last Stand, a final, desperate, last-ditch, backs-to-the-wall, battle on a patch of high ground.

We reached the edge of the mangroves just as the heavens opened and threw down an almighty deluge. I managed to unpack Bon in record time and get the tent up before the worst of the wind came blasting off the bay. Once again poor Bon was a soggy rat. The water flowed sheet-like across the sand. Thank God my new tent had a waterproof outer cover.

The rains turned the trails into a sticky mess, and even the normally solid salt-flats were more like a mush of ice and water. Tinged with pink, they looked unreal but Bon, with his little hooves sinking, was not impressed.

He seemed as glad as I was to be approaching the town of San Carlos, the major port on the shores of Mag Bay. Much of the produce from the prosperous agricultural region skirting Highway One – cotton, alfalfa, etc. – is exported through San Carlos. But many of its 5,000 population make a living from fishing, and an increasing number from tourism.

We left the desert and picked up the road into town. I loved the look of innocent surprise on the faces of the passing Mexicans. When they smiled involuntarily at the sight of a gringo with a white burro, it helped me laugh at myself. Although Bonny was generally good with traffic, I always held him carefully. He was a bit unpredictable. A sudden, surprise crackling of overhead cables had us both leaping in the air trying to avoid an imaginary rattler. And when a huge, friendly pig came rushing up to say hello – grunt, grunt – Bonny took to the hills dragging me behind. By the time he had calmed down, I'd flattened a few cacti and made quite an impression in the local garbage pit.

I wrote in my diary:

> Dug up some chocolate-clams from bay. Walk across the sand and mud of the tide flats and they reveal themselves with little squirts of water – then dig. Morning sun on the mountains of Isla Magdalena. Tide in, sunny, very photogenic, enter town over bridge, Bon very unhappy about the water below. Passed palapas on beach, and beach campsites, San Carlos trying to cream off some of the tourist trade. Why not? Her location on Bahía Magdalena magnificent. Whales still come, bird life incredible, fishing in the protected waters excellent, hardly anyone else there to share miles and miles of mangroves. Only problem – mosquitoes and noseeums. Repellent a must.

I felt a bit conspicuous walking through the town with Bon. Hounded by dogs, suddenly I heard a gringo voice, and met Ed Brennan – half-Irish, and married to a Mexican.

> His 55th birthday. From San Francisco Bay. Retired submariner. Lets Bon graze in his lush, overgrown garden, while I visit post office an_ shop. Townspeople lovely. Letter from home in P.O. Dad still very comehomeish, Mum not too well it seems. Decide to try phoning. I book a transfer-charge call, surprised it goes through immediately. I'm

talking to mum, she's almost in tears, but both mum and dad sound much better than in the letter. They tell me I've had another story published in the *San Diego Union.* The Andersons sent them a copy. A full, front-page story with four colour photos and several black and white ones inside. The article was definitely not meant for 'domestic consumption' with photos of me standing beside the wreck of the pick-up and cutting heads off rattlesnakes, and all the stories about scorpions, rabid donkeys and such like. I tried to reassure them that it all sounded a lot worse than it was, I was nearly finished and I was just idling about on the beach drinking tequila and fishing.

I left the phone building with a rosy glow, feeling like Bon after having his burden removed. The story must have been worth at least $300. The *L.A. Times* hadn't blacked me after all!

Ed Brennan looked after me for a couple of days. I was given a room in his delightful white-walled house. The Mexican plumbing was a bit eccentric, what went down one plug hole came up another, but it was heaven to have a shower, take part in the birthday celebrations, and listen to all his stories about life on the US Navy submarine *Bowfin.*

Bon ate and drank like there was no tomorrow. He just loved all that munchy grass, all free of burs and spines. And a permanent bowl of water! He didn't know when to stop. Like me he was capable of putting on a lot of weight rapido. By the time we came to leave, Bon was so fat that I couldn't tie his harness around his belly.

I owe Ed a lot. I'd arrived like a sub, battered and creaking from a long war patrol. I left rested, refitted, morale sky high, and eager for the fray. To get out of San Carlos, I had to backtrack ten miles north before I could head south again, but it was worth it.

The mangrove swamps of Magdalena Bay weren't going to give up on me without a fight. The 'roads' continued to be both a blessing and a curse. It was always a question of walk and see. The desert remained thick and impenetrable all around. I was trapped on the trails. Once we broke camp, walked all day, reached a dead-end, mangrove inlet, and had to walk all the way back again. We ended up making camp in exactly the same spot as the night before. Bonny was not impressed. He shot me his stupid ass look! But I was quite above petty frustrations. I kept thinking of that *San Diego Union* article. I could almost recall it word for word. I had mentioned the episode with the rabid donkey, and described the scorpions holding claws, and then concluded:

Maybe I had spent too many years and vacations being pampered, entertained and artificially thrilled, a mere spectator on a world looking increasingly unreal. For whatever reason, Baja is a love affair that has come to overshadow every other concern and passion of my life.

If ever I get to heaven, I pray its sky is blue, its slopes are covered with cardón and cirio, the scorpions are dancing and whirling, and from behind the largest cactus of all will emerge a sad-faced black burro ready to carry my pack for all eternity.

Now, of course, it had to be a white burro. But Baja had given me something I'd lacked all my life, a purpose, something to love and believe in. I had an overpowering feeling that I was being led. If it was all meant to be, there was something more for me to do than write a book. I had to find what that something was. I'd been the master cynic all my life. I wasn't going to be cynical now. I was following this road to the end.

Chapter 30
Brotherhood of believers

When we found ourselves on a narrow strip of desert with mangroves on both sides, even Bon realized it had to be a dead-end. He kept looking at me nervously. Neither of us wanted to go all the way back, yet again.

What was left of the trail ended predictably in a deserted fishcamp right on the shores of the bay. The water was flat calm and as blue as the sky. Looking across to the purple-pink mountains of Isla Margarita, one of the long, volcanic islands sheltering Magdalena Bay from the Pacific, I was momentarily reminded of the barren, rocky Gulf with its spectacular off-shore islands. However, the mosquitoes and tiny islets of mangroves served to remind me of the vast body of swamp at my back.

The bay swept invitingly to the south. With the tide out, there was a walkable 'dry' patch along the edge of the mangroves. And a mile ahead there seemed to be a strip of open desert coming down to the water. I decided to gamble and go for it.

All went well until we came to a fifty-yard-wide 'channel' reaching into the mangroves. There was no water, just a bright-green mat of vegetation. I checked it out. It seemed solid enough, so I went back for Bon.

We were almost over when firmness gave way to the springy softness of deep moss. Then suddenly it was like walking on a water bed. I made a quick U-turn and tried to lead Bonny back. Before I could turn him around, I watched in horror as his rear legs slowly disappeared. The poor donkey struggled frantically, but as he did so, his front legs broke the mat of vegetation and they too went down into deep, thick mud. The more he struggled, the deeper he settled. Two gaping holes of brown had opened up threatening to swallow Bon who was braying pitifully.

I backed away on to more solid ground. Bonny hee-hawed so hard he almost turned himself inside out. He was terrified I was going to leave him.

I pulled out my razor-sharp fish knife and ran back onto the treacherous green carpet. Keeping moving to stop myself from breaking through, I frantically cut the lines securing the load, then dragged it from his back.

I picked up the lead rope and tried desperately to get him out. For several heart-racing minutes we struggled, pulled and pushed. But it was hopeless. He was well and truly stuck, right up to his belly, and sinking more with every futile push down on his hooves. In the end he just seemed to give up and lay there with his legs buckled awkwardly beneath him as if he'd dislocated or broken something.

I dashed around like a maniac picking up all the driftwood on the shore and spreading it around the sinking animal. After scraping some of the thick mud away from his rear legs, I jammed in some of the larger logs. Bon called out in pain.

Trying to keep my weight on the pieces of wood, I pulled and shouted and willed him to try again. All I got was a long, loud, pained 'Ugg-gg-gg' which sounded more like a death rattle than a hee-haw. He had just given up, and surrendered to the horror that both of us had dreaded.

I cursed myself and cursed the donkey. 'Get up you bastard. Push. Push. Come on! Heave.' He reacted, perhaps instinctively, to the tone of my voice, pulling desperately on his front legs while I alternately jammed down more driftwood and tugged at his head. The carpet of green was breaking up around him, and my feet were slipping off the wood into the mud.

He was shocked and exhausted, and I knew that, if I didn't get him out soon, I'd never get him out. Grabbing the lead rope and pulling with all my might, I was like a water skier leaning almost horizontally as a plank of driftwood slowly slipped into the mud beneath me.

Bon's neck was stretching grotesquely. The rope was digging into his flesh. I could see blood. Bon looked at me protesting. I couldn't watch. I closed my eyes and pulled and prayed, and pleaded with him to, 'Push, push'.

Something was giving. Either I was doing down, or he was coming out, or his head was coming off. Whatever it was, I kept up the tug-o'-war till . . . I suddenly fell backwards and opened my eyes to see Bonny scrambling from the mud and falling on his side. I picked myself up and quickly led him to firmer ground before his hooves slid down again.

Safe at last, I unashamedly threw my arms around his neck and held him tight, our hearts beating and our bodies trembling in unison.

The rope had badly cut his nose and head. More worrying was the look in his eye. He was lost and distant. When I tied him to a bush, his legs just seemed to buckle under him. He lay awkwardly on the ground and stared at nothing. I left him alone just long enough to make camp on a nearby patch of sand. It was soon dark.

When I returned, he hadn't moved a muscle. By the light of a huge moon, I sat beside him trying in vain to elicit some spark of life. Even when I caressed his big ears, something he normally hated, he didn't seem to care.

I cradled his head, scratched his nose, and blew into his nostrils. His white coat glowed in the moonlight. I was convinced he was half way to becoming a ghost.

'Bonny love, it's Grahamy. Are you O.K.? I'm sorry, Bon, please be O.K.'

Raising my voice, I added, 'We've come a long way together, Bon, don't die on me, you rat!'

I felt awful. I couldn't imagine carrying on without him. Oblivious to scorpions and rattlers, I continued to cradle his head and whisper in his ear, 'Tomorrow, Bon, if you're O.K. It'll be your day. No more short cuts. We'll keep well away from the mangroves and stop lots for you to graze, and I'll carry all the water. I'll make it a real easy day, no rushing and we'll stop early so you can munch all evening and night.'

No response. I returned to the tent for an orange, and peeled it under his nose. He loved orange peel. Once or twice I'd almost been trampled to death when I made the mistake of eating an orange in front of him. Sharks have feeding frenzies when they smell blood. Bonny reacted similarly to oranges. When he got the scent, he went wild, biting my orange-flavoured fingers and trying to rip out teethfuls of my hair. Nothing even vaguely related to the object of his desire was safe.

At first, I thought Bon had sunk even beyond the tangy tug of citrus, but then I held my breath . . . as he wrinkled his nose with interest. His rubbery lips started pouting, then half-heartedly wrapped themselves around a small piece of peel. He chewed slowly, tried another piece then chewed more fervently. He started moving his legs. There was reason to live. He snatched the next piece of peel from my hand. Then as I stood up and backed away with the rest of the orange, his legs straightened, he got up and followed me. He could walk. I was so relieved, I gave him the whole orange.

Slobber, slurp. He was soon back to his old munching, farting self, grazing everything in sight and happily disposing of a gallon of water.

Several times in the night, I emerged from the tent to check on him and convince myself he really was all right. Had I really vowed at the time I bought him that no way was I going to get sentimental about a stupid ass? I hadn't reckoned on the power of shared hardship and danger, and the bond forged by all those long, lonely nights listening to the hair-raising howls of the coyotes.

True to my word, I gave Bon a string of easy days. We started late and finished early. I carried the water. He got most of the pitahayas; and if he wanted to stop and munch, so be it, I even wandered into the desert and hacked down a few yummy mesquite branches for him to chew on. Ironically, it worked out well. Bon was smart enough not to push his luck. We both seemed to sense what was important to the other, and to take the path of reasoned compromise.

The sun was sinking as we walked into one of the larger fishing communities on 'Mag Bay'. Puerto Chale was a ramshackle collection of about thirty or forty huts. As I passed the first one I was offered a seat and a cup of coffee. While I chatted to my host José, a big man in every way, a crowd of laughing children gathered around Bon. He was too busy tidying up all the discarded orange and lemon peel to take much notice.

As Bon seemed so contented, I accepted José's invitation to pitch my tent and swap stories. At one time José had lived in San Ignacio, and he was able to tell me something about Bonny's previous owner. Although he was a man of many qualities, kindness to burros was not one of them. He was well known for breaking logs across their stubborn heads! Considering that most Mexicans are not over-sentimental about animals, it takes a lot to earn such a reputation.

While José's beautiful wife prepared a fish dinner, our conversation turned to 'treasure'. 'I know there is a fortune here,' José said intriguingly. 'After dinner I shall try again to find it. The rest of the fishermen think I'm loco, but I shall have the last laugh.' He finished his meal, grabbed his shovel and invited me to join him on another dig. And so we wandered off to add another hole and pile of dirt to the desert around Puerto Chale. He asked if I had a metal detector in my pack. I apologized for the oversight, promising to bring one on my next trip.

His eyes lit up as they caught the last golden glow of sunset and he drove his shovel deep into the sandy soil. An hour later he gave up and asked if I'd like to join him on a fishing trip next morning.

There was plenty of gold in the morning sun as our panga raced across the flat, calm waters of Mag Bay, twisting and weaving its way through the narrow channels between the mangroves. Squawking birds rose protesting before the lingering full moon. Occasionally we stopped for José's young assistant Adan to try his hand with the throwing net.

He managed to catch a few guitar-fish but nothing suitable for bait. No matter, as the sun chased away the morning chill, we ripped through the silence and made our way out between the barrier islands to the open ocean. Pulling alongside a shrimp boat, José related our predicament. The boats heaved, fell and banged together as several shovel-loads of shrimp heads landed on our bow.

Bait problems solved, we anchored a mile off Punta Tosca and lowered the handlines. Snappers, bass, sheepshead, triggerfish and other rock fish were soon coming aboard. Before long we had something else trying to climb in. A hungry pelican, dragging a shattered wing, lunged at every fish, some almost as big as himself.

He tried it once too often. Adan grabbed his beak and hauled him aboard. Realizing it was probably a hopeless case, I tried to help by chopping away the useless part of the wing. It was a tangle of splintered bone and putrid flesh. Unencumbered he paddled away, then hung back sulking for a while.

In the distance, a group of frigate birds squabbled over a small fish. Performing their aerial acrobatics, they forced each other to drop the prize. The last I saw of that gutsy little pelican, he was paddling furiously in their direction. That never-say-die spirit, so typical of everyone and everything scratching a living from that raw and rugged land was a constant source of inspiration.

We returned to our fishing. Suddenly there was a bump against the boat. A dark shape appeared in the crystal clear, blue-black water beneath. It was a shark. José and Adan got excited. One was leaning over the side pointing, while the other was fumbling around for the harpoon. All they could see was hundreds of pounds of precious shark meat that had conveniently taken up residence in the shade beneath the boat. All I could see was a bloody big, man-eating monster that had taken an inordinate interest in us. I had no wish to antagonize him. Certainly plunging a harpoon into his back did not seem like a good idea. Luckily by the time they'd readied the harpoon, the shark had moved away and was swimming around out of range. Even when he disappeared, I sensed his presence all afternoon and half-expected every fish we hauled up to be suddenly seized by a huge pair of jaws.

The Mexicans started to smoke something that definitely wasn't tobacco. They got increasingly boisterous, laughing at everything. I got the feeling that, if the shark appeared again, they'd jump over the side and try to grab hold of it.

At last, satisfied with the catch, José started the outboard and raced back towards the bay. We passed the wreck of a ship that had gone aground on a sandbar in the channel between the two large islands. When José realized I was curious about it, he sped in close, riding a series of thunderous waves over the dangerous shoal. If we'd capsized, it would have been curtains. I persuaded my laughing amigos that I'd seen enough, and we curved back to the main channel.

There were other shallows. Speeding over one, there was a thud, the boat rose and the motor cut. José almost went over the side. We'd hit the bottom. Adios propellor. Out came the oars. Luckily we were inside the shelter of the bay and able to row back. Yes, for thrills and spills you can't beat a day out with the Mexicans.

It was good to leave behind the problems of Bahía Magdalena and emerge again on to a seemingly endless parade of magnificent Pacific beaches. However, the soft, strength-sapping sands were no easy option; and in most places the beach sloped steeply into the sea with the waves breaking dangerously right on the shore. It was easy to cast into deep water and catch fish, but swimming was extremely risky. If the sea was anything but flat-calm, it was a struggle to get out.

Having failed to pick up water for a few days, we were approaching Todos Santos, and the Christmas season, forced into an ever-tightening round of water rationing. While the western world was beginning its annual over-indulgence, we were visibly losing weight by the hour.

With Bonny vocally expressing his thirst, we cut into the desert. There were no pitahayas to be found. So I sliced away the tough, fish-hook spines of a barrel cactus. Chopping off a section of the white heart for Bon, I put the other 5lbs or 6lbs of water-bearing tissue into a bag for later.

Continuing down the beach I made camp a little early. There was a lot to do. Cautiously shaking off the scorpions, I collected a pile of driftwood, made a small fire, fetched a couple of gallons of seawater, then sat connecting tubes to kettle as I set up my still.

As darkness descended all seemed well. The distant glow of La Paz was comforting. The twinkling lights of Todos Santos beckoned down the coast. 'Soon have a nice gallon of water in your bowl, Bon; first here's some more cactus.' While he slobbered away, I prepared myself for a long night bent over a boiling kettle.

Unfortunately an hour later, the kettle sprang a leak. We had just a few pints of water to fight over. The burro fought dirty with a whole battery of parched, pathetic and heart-rending hee-haws. He was probably chuckling to himself as I gave him most of it. We would just have to get up early and dash to Todos Santos.

I had resigned myself to a lonely Christmas on the beach. But when I finally led an exhausted Bonny into Todos Santos, there were several tourists in town. I was told about a beach to the south where a few of them were gathering for the big day. It sounded perfect.

Christmas shopping was delightfully simple. I bought a bottle of booze, some basics such as flour, milk and cereals, and some of the cheap local fruits and vegetables. My presents list had just two items on it – carrots and oranges. And after loading up with water, we headed for the promised beach.

San Pedrito Beach was even better than I expected. The mile-long, broad band of golden sand was sandwiched between cliffs and cactus-covered, barren, brown hills, and backed by a shallow cut-off lagoon surrounded by coconut palms. We were bang on the Tropic of Cancer; and looking inland from the sea, the scene was about as tropical as you could imagine. The beach itself was one of the few on that stretch of coast perfect for swimming and surfing. Instead of a dangerous shore-break and a drop off into deep water, the waves came rolling in for a hundred yards. There was even a spring of sweet water right on the beach. All I had to do was gouge out a bit of sand and take Bon down to drink from the pool.

There were about ten tourists camped there. I'd met some of them in town, and was quickly introduced to the rest: a family from Canada, two guys and a gal from Switzerland, and a young couple from Montana. All escaping from cold climes, it seemed.

We all felt that we had found a very special spot. The Swiss trio had decorated the bushes near the campsite with cut-out stars and tinsel. I was looking forward to Christmas.

> December 25, 1984. Christmas. I woke just before dawn, listening to Christmas music from KFI Los Angeles and KJJJ Phoenix. I was full of thoughts of home and family and friends. A few sentimental tears rolled down as I watched the light coming into the world.

I lay zipped up in my tent and caught up with my diary while the day got going. The two Canadian kids were opening their presents and shouting: 'I've got a kite.' 'I've got a camera, and a cabbage patch colouring book.' I crawled out to greet the world and wish everyone Merry Christmas. Then I wandered over to see Bon. I got my Christmas hee-haw, and I gave him a hunk of cabbage, a nice orange skin and a handful of carrots. The guy from Montana had already given him an apple and a tomato. Others had brought him all their skins and peelings. Bonny soon caught on that it was a very special day.

It was beautifully warm. After breakfast, we decided to offer the sharks their Christmas presents. We went snorkeling off the rocks at the north end of the bay, staying in the water over an hour and swimming a long way out together. I would never have ventured as far on my own. There were shoals of anchovies, some large bass, surgeon fish, and lots of needle-sharp sea urchins on the rocks. We had to be very careful with the waves throwing us around. Out of the water we soon warmed in the still, dry air.

After a few beers we were back in the surf. The bigger the waves, the more we laughed

Someone had the bright idea of acting out a Christmas nativity scene with Bonny as the leading actor. Before letting the kids try riding Bon I thought it wise to try it myself. He was a pack animal. I wasn't sure how he'd take to being ridden. He didn't! He jumped and kicked till I flew off and landed crumpled on the sand. So much for the nativity, but at least everyone appreciated the rodeo.

Christmas dinner was a lively international affair. We all brought something to the table and left with so much more. The blindfolded children battered a piñata full of sweets and presents. The magic of the season and the magic of Baja had come together to produce the merriest, most memorable Christmas of my life. Even Bon's little hooves seemed to dance as I sang his favourite song, 'Bonny the burro', to the tune of 'Frosty the Snowman'. Recalling the anxieties and hardships of just two days before, we both had good reason to make merry.

I had only intended staying a day or two, but that beautiful beach with its coconut palms and spring of fresh water was hard to leave. Day after day, I fished, snorkeled, kayaked, partied, debated and enjoyed myself.

On New Year's Eve I was so drunk that I found myself making the most inexplicable resolution of my life. I held up my glass of tequila and vowed, 'This will be my first and last drink of 1985.' Midnight came. I emptied my glass. The party continued, I was offered whisky, tequila, beer and wine, but no alcohol passed my lips. The next day it was the same. Having said I was going to give up drinking, it became a matter of personal honour. I was well practised in determination, for it was that kind of thinking that had seen me through all the crises that had gone before.

While watering Bon the next day, I found a large gull washed up on the beach. He was staggering as if drunk, then he collapsed and lay helpless, allowing me to pick him up without a struggle. Always the joker, I saw one of the Swiss chaps with his back to me, sitting reading something. I crept up, gull in hand and tapped him on the head with the long, yellow beak. As he turned around the look on his face was priceless. We did our best to care for the bird, but he showed little sign of life beyond occasionally raising his head as if something was stuck in his throat or he was asking God for help. After one long neck stretch, he keeled over and died. We buried him on the beach.

Early in the new year, feeling the need for new adventures, I loaded up a somewhat plumper Bonny for the final dash down to journey's end – Cabo San Lucas. However, in a way I didn't want to get there. Suddenly I didn't mind how slowly Bon walked. I loved being with him, being in Baja, and just being alive. As long as there was no threat to the latter, 'manaña' seemed as good a time as any.

Those final sober sunrises and sunsets seemed more glorious than ever. I looked at them with the heightened awareness of someone about to say goodbye to life. There was sadness, but also the joy of knowing that it wasn't so much the end, rather a new beginning.

I wasn't 'an adventurer'. I wasn't about to dash off up the Amazon, or trek the Kalahari, or go searching for something one step ahead. I had found what I wanted. I belonged to Baja and to those who felt that they belonged. Again it was the feeling that was the undeniable truth, the absolute certainty that this land was sacred to me.

Warm by my campfire, I tried to put my feelings into words and to face up to the implications of a philosophy I'd been slowly working towards with each new cross marked on my map.

> It has been more than just a physical adventure. Baja gave me an intermittent, fleeting glance into another world; not just a world of columned cacti and strange creatures, but a world of spiritual experience a thousand times more different from my old rational, logical, scientific conception of reality than the desert was from the greens and greys of England. . . .
>
> It should be the duty of every man and woman to take themselves into the empty corners of the world, to be truly alone and receptive, to see who they are and where they're going; and, if they glimpse there a worthy destiny, to espouse it with confidence and faith. . . .
>
> Perhaps when we are alone, we can escape from the fads and fashions of society, find our real selves, have our psychic powers unleashed, and gain an insight into the future. . . .
>
> We can know future generations and we can influence the past through our prayers and adulation. We are all in touch, caught up in an incredible cycle. Maybe every man has the capacity, through the consciousness of future generations, to look back on his own life. Is that the nature of this sense of destiny?
>
> Maybe the greatness of man lies in the fact that not only can he learn from the past but he can also learn from the future. And there lies my feeling of brotherhood with the likes of Ugarte, Salvatierra, Steinbeck, Vizcaíno and Erle Stanley Gardner. We were all drawn to Baja and in touch with each other, sharing a common sense of the sacred. As Steinbeck had said of the Gulf: 'there is some quality that trips a trigger of recognition so that one finds oneself nodding and saying inwardly, "Yes I know" and we know we must go back if we live, and we don't know why.' I belong to them; they belong to me. I lived in them. They live in me. And we all belong to Baja.
>
> But why Baja? God knows! Perhaps the new messiah is destined to appear here in Mexico, in Baja California. Perhaps it's just a personal thing. Nothing would surprise me. That is the beauty of having so much time alone. My mind is as open as the heavens above.

Bonny and I spent our last morning together on the dazzling white sand a few miles north of Cabo San Lucas. I woke early and listened to my radio till dawn. Having put behind me the best part of two years, 3,000 miles and seven pairs of boots, it was sadly ironic to hear a Los Angeles radio station urging its listeners to vacation in Baja – 'daily flights to La Paz, Loreto and Cabo San Lucas . . . or drive from the border to the tip . . . it's never been easier to get to Baja California.'

As recently as 1967, the American essayist and critic Joseph Wood Krutch was able to write, 'Baja has never needed protection because the land protected itself.' A lot has changed in twenty years. The forgotten peninsula has been discovered. I dread to think what changes the next twenty years will bring to one of the most fascinating and stunningly beautiful places on earth.

Bonny seemed to know that the last day had come. We lay together on the beach in the early morning sun, at peace with ourselves, our universe and each other. Handfuls of coarse, white sand slipped through my fingers as I delivered my final pep talk.

I muttered something about him being the best burro in the world, and thanked him for all his help and assistance over the past difficult months. He looked at me as if I was an idiot.

Packed and ready, we dragged our tired and thirsty bodies along the final mile of beach before cutting over the hills and down towards the booming hotels and big cruise ships of Cabo San Lucas.

I thought back to the first mile I walked from San Felipe, and how alone and frightened I felt in the face of a burning vastness that seemed to be mocking each pathetic little step along the sand. I had carried on because I felt that I was answering the call of something much bigger than my fears. And here I was. In an hour or two the end would be in sight. Then I would have the rest of my life to try to figure out what it was all about.

With memories of the two previous years flooding back, I watched the apparently gentle ocean rise and crash in tumultuous fury against Cabo Falso. Having gained our attention, the Pacific proceeded to put on a show breathtaking in its spectacle. Schools of dolphin gracefully leapt and splashed in almost-touching closeness to the beach. Beyond them, manta rays flipped and flopped. Even a whale slid along in the surf.

It was as if Baja was saying goodbye!

Short Bibliography

Johnson, William Weber, and the editors of Time-Life. *Baja California.* Time-Life Books, New York. 1972.

Steinbeck, John. *The Log from the Sea of Cortez.* Pan Books. 1960. First published Viking Press, 1941.

Gardner, Earle Stanley. *Hunting the Desert Whale.* Jarrolds. 1963.

Krutch, Joseph Wood. *The Forgotten Peninsula.* William Morrow. 1961.

Wheelock, Walt, and Gulick, Howard. *Baja California Guidebook.* H. Clark. 1975.

McMahan, Mike. *There it is: Baja!* Brooke House. 1973.

Cannon, Ray. *The Sea of Cortez.* Lane Publishing. 1966.

Miller, Tom, and Baxter, Elmar. *The Baja Book II.* Baja Trail Publications. 1982.

Zwinger, Ann. *A Desert Country near the Sea.* Harper and Row. 1983.

Coyle, Jeanette, and Roberts, Norman C. *A Field Guide To The Common And Interesting Plants Of Baja California.* Natural History Publishing Company, La Jolla, California. 1975.

Wayne, Scott. *Baja California, a travel survival kit.* Lonely Planet Publications. 1988.

Caras, Roger A. *Dangerous to Man.* Barrie and Jenkins. 1976.

Cloudsley-Thompson, J. L. *Tooth and Claw.* Dent. 1980.

Carson, Rachel. *The Sea Around Us.* Hart-Davis, 1978.

Sweeney, James. *Sea Monsters.* Nelson-Crown. 1972.

Bombard, Alain. *The Bombard Story.* Grafton Books, 1986

Robin, Bernard. *Survival at Sea.* Stanley Paul. 1981.

Kraus, Joe. *Alive in the Desert.* Sycamore Island Books. 1978.

Bonington, Chris. *Quest for Adventure.* Hodder and Stoughton. 1981.

Acknowledgements

My thanks go to all those who made it possible, especially: Kestral Leisure Ltd of Tunbridge Wells; Camera Gear of Tunbridge Wells; Breeds the Cutlers of Tunbridge Wells; the Friendly Fisherman of Tunbridge Wells; Natural Life Ltd of Tunbridge Wells; Prides of Tunbridge Wells; Chris Potter Guns of Tunbridge Wells; Colour Processing Laboratories of Edenbridge, Kent; Johnson and Johnson of Slough; Nicholas Kiwi Ltd of Slough; Combined Optical Industries Ltd of Slough; National Panasonic of Slough; Superguard Ltd of Slough; Airborne Industries Ltd of Leigh-on-Sea, Essex; EMTRAD Ltd of Hull; Konica UK Ltd; Endsleigh Insurance Services Ltd of Cheltenham; Pacific Mountain Sports of La Canada, California; The Sport Chalet of La Canada; Wilderness Experience of Chatsworth, California; Mark and Maggie Blaber; Dora Marriott; Robert Dowling; Jennifer Reeves; Judy McAdam; Richard and Carol Anderson; Ralph and Shirley Elmquist; and a very special thank you to Dave and Denise Bowyer for giving me a base in Los Angeles.